The Tragedies of Euripides

Volume I

CW00819184

Euripides

(Translator: Theodore Alois Buckley)

Alpha Editions

This edition published in 2024

ISBN : 9789357966139

Design and Setting By
Alpha Editions
www.alphaedis.com
Email - info@alphaedis.com

VOL. I.

PREFACE.

The translations of the first six plays in the present volume were published at Oxford some years since, and have been frequently reprinted. They are now carefully revised according to Dindorf's text, and are accompanied by a few additional notes adapted to the requirements of the student.

The translations of the Bacchæ, Heraclidæ, and the two Iphigenias, are based upon the same text, with certain exceptions, which are pointed out at the foot of the page. The annotations on the Iphigenias are almost exclusively critical, as it is presumed that a student who proceeds to the reading of these somewhat difficult plays[1], will be sufficiently advanced in his acquaintance with the Greek drama to dispense with more elementary information.

T.A. BUCKLEY,

CHRIST CHURCH, OXFORD.

[1] The reader will obtain some notion of the difficulties alluded to, and the best mode of grappling with them, by consulting the recent Cambridge edition, published with English notes (Iph. in Aulide, 1840, in Tauris, 1846), performances of great critical acumen, attributed to the present Bishop of Gloucester.

INTRODUCTION.

Euripides, son of Mnesarchus, was born in the island of Salamis, on the day of the celebrated victory (B.C. 480). His mother, Clito, had been sent thither in company with the other Athenian women, when Attica was given up, and the ships became at once the refuge of the male population, and the national defense. Mr. Donaldson[1] well remarks, that the patronymic form of his name, derived from the Euripus, which was the scene of the first successful resistance offered to the Persian navy, shows that the attention of his parents was fully excited by the stirring events of the time.

Notwithstanding the fact that his mother had been an herb-seller, it is probable that his father was a man of some family. That he was at least possessed of ample means, is evident from the care and expense bestowed upon our poet's education. Under the tutorship of Anaxagoras, Prodicus, and Protagoras, he had studied both natural philosophy and rhetoric in its sophistical form. In gymnastic exercises he exhibited a successful prowess, being twice victorious in the Eleusinian and Thesean games. Of his skill in painting, some specimens were preserved at Megara.

His appearance as a dramatist was at an earlier age than that of his predecessors, as he was only five and twenty years old when he produced the "Peliades," his first tragedy. On this occasion, he gained the third prize in the tragic contests, but the first, fourteen years after, and subsequently, with the "Hippolytus," in 428 B.C. The peculiar tendency of some of the ideas expressed in his plays, was the probable cause of the retirement of Euripides to Macedonia, where he obtained the friendship of King Archelaus. Perhaps, however, the unhappiness of his connubial state, arising from the infidelity of his two wives, might have rendered Athens a disagreeable place of abode for the woman-hating poet, especially when his "domestic bliss" was continually seasoned by the sarcastic jokes and allusions of his political enemy, Aristophanes. Moreover, his acquaintance with the talking philosopher, Socrates, must have been unfavorable to the continuance of his popularity.

The fate of Pentheus in our author's noble play, the "Bacchæ," appears to have given origin to the tradition that he himself was torn to pieces by dogs. If we reflect that this play was probably the last of his works, the mistake seems a plausible one. The death of Euripides, which probably happened in the ordinary course of nature, has, like that of Æschylus, been associated with the marvelous.

The Athenians vainly craved the honor of giving a resting-place to the ashes of their philosopher-poet. He was buried at Pella, but a cenotaph at Athens showed that his countrymen had not forgotten Euripides. His death took place B.C. 406.

The inferiority of our author to the greater tragedians, prevents our feeling much desire to enter upon the respective merits and demerits of his several plays, especially as we are completely anticipated by Schlegel, with whose masterly analysis every reader ought to be acquainted. Nevertheless, a few general remarks may, perhaps, be not wholly unprofitable.

It has been truly remarked, that tragedy, in no small degree, owed its downfall to Euripides. Poetry was gradually superseded by rhetoric, sublimity by earnestness, pathos by reasoning. Thus, Iphigenia and Macaria give so many good reasons for dying, that the sacrifice appears very small, and a modern wag in the upper regions of the theatre would, at the end of the speech of the latter heroine, almost have exclaimed, "Then why don't you die?"

It has been said, that our poet drew the characters of life as he found them, but bad as his characters are, they exhibit only a vulgar wickedness. Unable to portray a Clytæmnestra, he revels in the continual paltriness of a Menelaus or Ulysses. As if he took a delight in the black side of humanity, he loves to show the strength of false reasoning, of sophistry antagonistic to truth, and of cold expediency in opposition to the natural feelings of humanity. From a similar reason, his occasional attempts at comedy degenerate into mere farce. We question whether the scene between Death and Apollo in the "Alcestis," could be surpassed in vulgarity, even by the modern school of English dramatists, while his exaggerations in the minor characters are scarcely to be surpassed by the lowest writer of any period.

Under Euripides, the stage began gradually to approximate more closely to the ordinary and, at that time, debased character of Athenian society. A contempt for the Lacedæmonians, a passionate taste for the babbling and trickery of the forum, and an attempt to depreciate the social position and influence of the weaker sex, form the most unamiable features of this change. Yet we must allow, that if Euripides has reveled in the amiabilities of a Melanippe or a Phædra, in the gentle revenge of a Medea or Hecuba, he has at the same time given us an Alcestis, the only real example of genuine conjugal affection on the Greek stage.

Nor must we forget that Euripides is a greater admirer of nature, a more complete delineator of her workings, than the two greater tragedians. He has more of illustrative philosophy, more of regard to the objects of the animated creation, the system of the universe, than his greater rivals exhibit. He is, as Vitruvius has justly styled him, a "stage-philosopher." Did we possess a larger acquaintance with the works of Parmenides, Empedocles, and other early cosmogonists, we should perhaps think less of his merits on this head: as it is, the possession of some such fragments of our poet makes us deeply regret the loss of the plays themselves.

But his very love for the contemplation of nature has in no small degree contributed to the mischievous skepticism promulgated by our poet. In early times, when a rural theogony was the standard of belief, when each star had its deity, each deity its undisputed, unquestioned prerogative and worship, there was little inclination, less opportunity, for skepticism. Throughout the poetry of Hesiod, we find this feeling ever predominant, a feeling which Virgil and Tibullus well knew how to appreciate. Even Euripides himself, perhaps taught by some dangerous lessons at home, has expressed his belief that it is best "not to be too clever in matters regarding the Gods."[2] A calm retreat in the wild, picturesque tracts of Macedonia, might have had some share in reforming this spoiled pupil of the sophists. But as we find that the too careful contemplation of nature degenerates into superstition or rationalism in their various forms, so Euripides had imbibed the taste for saying startling things,[3] rather than wise; for reducing the principles of creation to materialism, the doctrines of right and wrong to expediency, and immutable truths to a popular system of question and answer. Like the generality of sophists, he took away a received truth, and left nothing to supply its place; he reasoned falsehood into probability, truth into nonentity.

At a period when the Prodico-Socratic style of disputing was in high fashion, the popularity of Euripides must have been excessive. His familiar appeals to the trifling matters of ordinary life, his characters all philosophizing, from the prince to the dry-nurse, his excellent reasons for doing right or wrong, as the case might be, must have been inestimably delightful to the accommodating morals of the Athenians. The Court of Charles the Second could hardly have derived more pleasure from the writings of a Behn or a Hamilton, than these unworthy descendants of Codrus must have experienced in hearing a bad cause so cleverly defended. Whether the orators and dikasts followed the example of the stage in those days, can scarcely be ascertained, but it is more than certain that they practically illustrated its principles. At least, the Sicilians were so fond of our author, that a few of the unfortunate survivors of the Syracusan disaster, were enabled to pick up a living by quoting such passages of our author as they had learned by heart. A compliment paid to few living dramatists in our days!

In dramatic conduct, Euripides is at an even greater disadvantage with Æschylus and Sophocles. The best characters of the piece are often the least employed, as in the instance of Macaria in the "Heraclidæ," while the play is dwindled away with dull, heavy dirges, and the complaints of senile childishness. The chorus, as Aristotle[4] has remarked, is most unfortunately independent of the plot, although the finest poetry is generally to be found in the lyric portions of our author's plays. In fact, Euripides rather wanted management in employing his resources, than the resources themselves. An ear well attuned to the harmony of verse, a delicate perception of the graceful points of language, and a finished subtilty in touching the more minute feelings and impulses of the mind, were all thrown away either upon bad subjects or worse principles. There is no true tragedy in Euripides, He is a melodramatist, but not according to the modern acceptation. His plays might end either happily or the reverse. A deity conveniently brought in, the arrival of a messenger, however unexpectedly, together with a liberal allowance for a cowardly revenge upon the vanquished—these are the Euripidean elements for giving a tragic end to a play. Nay, so great is the prodigality of slaughter throughout his dramas, that we can but imagine morbid cruelty to have formed a considerable ingredient in the disposition of Euripides. Even his pathos is somewhat tinctured with this taste for painful images. As we have beheld in our own times a barbarian alternately glut his sight with executions, and then shed floods of tears, and sink into idiot despondency; so the poetry of Euripides in turn disgusts us with outrageous cruelty, and depresses us with the most painful demands upon our compassion.

In the lyric portions of his dramas, our poet has been far more successful. The description of the capture of Troy by night,[5] is a splendid specimen of animation blended with true pathos. But taken as a whole. Euripides is a most unequal author. We may commence a play with pleasure (but O for the prologues!), we may proceed with satisfaction, but the feeling rarely lasts to the end. If I may venture an opinion upon so uncertain a subject, I should name the Hippolytus, Ion, Troades, Bacchæ, and Iphigenia in Aulis as his best plays, placing the Phœnissæ, Alcestis, Medea, Hecuba, and Orestes in a lower rank. The Helena is an amusing heap of absurdities, and reads much better in the burlesque of Aristophanes; the Electra is utterly beneath criticism; the Cyclops a weak, but humorous imitation of Homer. The other plays appear to be neither bad nor good.

The style of Euripides is, generally speaking, easy; and I can mention no author from whom a taste for elegant Greek and a facility in composition can more easily be derived. Some of his plays have suffered severely from the ravages of time, the ignorance of copyists, and the more dangerous officiousness of grammarians. Some passages of the Bacchæ, Rhesus, Troades, and the two Iphigenias, despite the ingenuity and erudition of such scholars as Porson, Elmsley, Monk, Burges, and a host of others, must still remain mere matter for guessing. Hermann's Euripides is, as a whole, sadly unworthy the abilities of the Humboldt of Greek literature.

The present volume contains the most popular of our author's works, according to present usage. But the spirit which is gradually infusing itself into the minds of those who are most actively engaged in the educational system of England, fully warrants a hope that Porson's "four plays" will shortly cease to be the boundaries of the student's acquaintance with Euripides.

I need scarcely observe, that the study of Aristophanes is indissolubly connected with that of our author. If the reader discover the painful fact that the burlesque writer is greater than the tragedian, he will perhaps also recollect that such a literary relation is, unfortunately, by no means confined to the days of Aristophanes.

Notes on the Introduction

[1] See Theatre of the Greeks, p. 92. sqq.

[2] Bacch. 200. This play was written during his sojourn with Archelaus.

[3] τοιουτονι τι παρακεκινδευμενον. Aristoph. Ran. 99.

[4] Poet. § xviii.

[5] Hec. 905 sqq.

HECUBA.

PERSONS REPRESENTED.

GHOST OF POLYDORE.

HECUBA.

CHORUS OF FEMALE CAPTIVES.

POLYXENA.

ULYSSES.

TALTHYBIUS.

FEMALE ATTENDANT.

AGAMEMNON.

POLYMESTOR AND HIS CHILDREN.

The Scene lies before the Grecian tents, on the coast of the Thracian Chersonese.

THE ARGUMENT.

After the capture of Troy, the Greeks put into the Chersonese over against Troas, But Achilles, having appeared by night, demanded one of the daughters of Priam to be slain. The Greeks therefore, in honor to their hero, tore Polyxena from Hecuba, and offered her up in sacrifice. Polymestor moreover, the king of the Thracians, murdered Polydore, a son of Priam's. Now Polymestor had received him from the hands of Priam as a charge to take care of, together with some money. But when the city was taken, wishing to seize upon his wealth, he determined to dispatch him, and disregarded the ill-fated friendship that subsisted between them; but his body being cast out into the sea, the wave threw him up on the shore before the tents of the captive women. Hecuba, on seeing the corse, recognized it; and having imparted her design to Agamemnon, sent for Polymestor to come to her with his sons, concealing what had happened, under pretense that she might discover to him some treasures hidden in Ilium. But on his arrival she slew his sons, and put out his eyes; but pleading her cause before the Greeks, she gained it over her accuser (Polymestor). For it was decided that she did not begin the cruelty, but only avenged herself on him who did begin it.

HECUBA.

GHOST OF POLYDORE.

I am present, having left the secret dwellings of the dead and the gates of darkness, where Pluto has his abode apart from the other Gods, Polydore the son of Hecuba the daughter of Cisseus,[1] and Priam my sire, who when the danger of falling by the spear of Greece was threatening the city of the Phrygians, in fear, privately sent me from the Trojan land to the house of Polymestor, his Thracian friend, who cultivates the most fruitful soil of the Chersonese, ruling a warlike people with his spear.[2] But my father sends privately with me a large quantity of gold, in order that, if at any time the walls of Troy should fall, there might not be a lack of sustenance for his surviving children. But I was the youngest of the sons of Priam; on which account also he sent me privately from the land, for I was able neither to bear arms nor the spear with my youthful arm. As long then indeed as the landmarks of the country remained erect, and the towers of Troy were unshaken, and Hector my brother prevailed with his spear, I miserable increased vigorously as some young branch, by the nurture I received at the hands of the Thracian, my father's friend. But after that both Troy and the life of Hector were put an end to, and my father's mansions razed to the ground, and himself falls at the altar built by the God, slain by the blood-polluted son of Achilles, the friend of my father slays me, wretched man, for the sake of my gold, and having slain me threw me into the surf of the sea, that he might possess the gold himself in his palace. But I am exposed on the shore, at another time on the ocean's surge, borne about by many ebbings and flowings of the waves, unwept, unburied; but at present I am hastening on my dear mother's account, having left my body, borne aloft this day already the third,[3] for so long has my wretched mother been present in this territory of the Chersonese from Troy. But all the Grecians, holding their ships at anchor, are sitting quiet on the shores of this land of Thrace. For Achilles the son of Peleus, appearing above his tomb, stayed all the army of the Grecians as they were directing homeward their sea dipped oars; and asks to receive my sister Polyxena as a dear victim, and a tribute of honor to his tomb. And this he will obtain, nor will he be without this gift from his friends; and fate this day leads forth my sister to death. But my mother will see the two corses of her two children, both mine and the unhappy virgin's; for I shall appear on a breaker before the feet of a female slave, that I wretched may obtain sepulture; for I have successfully entreated those who have power beneath to find a tomb, and to fall into my mother's hands. As much then as I wish to have shall be mine; but I will withdraw myself out of the way of the aged Hecuba, for she is advancing her step beyond the tent of Agamemnon, dreading my phantom. Alas! O my mother, who, from kingly palaces, hast beheld the day of slavery, how unfortunate art thou now, in the degree that thou wert once fortunate! but some one of the Gods counterpoising your state, destroys you on account of your ancient prosperity.

HECUBA. CHORUS.

HEC. Lead onward, ye Trojan dames, the old woman before the tent; lead onward, raising up one now your fellow-slave, but once your queen; take me, bear me, conduct me, support my body, holding my aged hand; and I, leaning on the bending staff of my hand,[4] will hasten to put forward the slow motion of my joints. O lightning of Jove! O thou gloomy night! why, I pray, am I thus disquieted in the night with terrors, with phantoms? O thou venerable Earth, the mother of black-winged dreams, I renounce the nightly vision, which regarding my son who is preserved in Thrace, and regarding Polyxena my dear daughter, in my dreams have I beheld, a fearful sight, I have learned, I have understood. Gods of this land, preserve my son, who, my only son, and, [as it were,] the anchor of my house, inhabits the snowy Thrace under the protection of his father's friend. Some strange event will take place, some strain will come mournful to the mournful. Never did my mind so incessantly shudder and tremble. Where, I pray, ye Trojan dames, can I behold the divine spirit of Helenus, or Cassandra, that they may interpret my dreams? For I beheld a dappled hind torn by the blood-stained fang of the wolf, forcibly dragged from my bosom, a miserable sight. And dreadful this vision also; the spectre of Achilles came above the summit of his tomb, and demanded as a tribute of honor one of the wretched Trojan women. From my daughter then, from my daughter avert this fate, ye Gods, I implore you.

CHOR. Hecuba, with haste to thee I flew, leaving the tents of our lords, where I was allotted and ordained a slave, driven from the city of Troy, led captive of the Greeks by the point of the spear, not to alleviate aught of your sufferings, but bringing a heavy weight of tidings, and to thee, O lady, a herald of woe. For it is said that it has been decreed in the full council of the Greeks to make thy daughter a sacrifice to Achilles: for you know how that having ascended o'er his tomb, he appeared in his golden arms and restrained the fleet ships, as they were setting their sails with their halliards, exclaiming in these words; "Where speed ye, Grecians, leaving my tomb unhonored!" Then the waves of great contention clashed together, and a divided opinion went forth through the army of the Greeks; to some it appeared advisable to give a victim to his tomb, and to others it appeared not. But Agamemnon was studious to advance your good, cherishing the love of the infuriated prophetess. But the two sons of Theseus, scions of Athens, were the proposers of different arguments, but in this one opinion they coincided, to crown the tomb of Achilles with fresh blood; and declared they would never prefer the bed of Cassandra before the spear of Achilles. And the strength of the arguments urged on either side was in a manner equal, till that subtle adviser, that babbling knave,[5] honeyed in speech, pleasing to the populace, that son of Laertes, persuades the army, not to reject the suit of the noblest of all the Greeks on account of a captive victim, and not to put it in the power of any of the dead standing near Proserpine to say that the Grecians departed from the plains of Troy ungrateful to the heroes who died for the state of Greece. And Ulysses will come only not now, to tear your child from your bosom, and to take her from your aged arms. But go to the temples, speed to the altars, sit a suppliant at the knees of Agamemnon, invoke the Gods, both those of heaven, and those under the earth; for either thy prayers will prevent thy being deprived of thy wretched daughter, or thou must behold the virgin falling before the tomb, dyed in blood gushing forth in a dark stream from her neck adorned with gold.[6]

HEC. Alas! wretched me! what shall I exclaim? what shriek shall I utter? what lamentation? miserable through miserable age, and slavery not to be endured, insupportable. Alas! who is there to defend me? what offspring, what city! The old man is gone. My children are gone. Whither shall I turn me? and whither shall I go? Where is any god or deity to succor me? O Trojan dames, bearers of evil tidings, bearers of woe, you have destroyed me utterly, you have destroyed me. Life in the light is no more desirable! O wretched foot, lead, lead an aged woman to this tent! O child, daughter of the most afflicted mother, come forth, come forth from the tent, hear thy mother's voice, that thou mayest know what a report I hear that concerns thy life.

HECUBA, POLYXENA, CHORUS.

POLYX. O mother, why dost thou call! proclaiming what new affliction hast thou frighted me from the tent, as some bird from its nest, with this alarm?

HEC. Alas! my child!

POLYX. Why address me in words of ill omen? This is an evil prelude.

HEC. Alas! for thy life.

POLYX. Speak, conceal it no longer from me. I fear, I fear, my mother; why I pray dost thou groan?

HEC. O child, child of an unhappy mother!

POLYX. Why sayest thou this?

HEC. My child, the common decree of the Greeks unites to slay thee at the tomb of the son of Peleus.

POLYX. Alas, my mother! how are you relating unenviable ills? Tell me, tell me, my mother.

HEC. I declare, my child, the ill-omened report, they bring word that a decree has passed by the vote of the Greeks regarding thy life.

POLYX. O thou that hast borne affliction! O thou wretched on every side! O mother unhappy in your life, what most hated and most unutterable calamity has some destiny again sent against thee! This child is no longer thine; no longer indeed shall I miserable share slavery with miserable age. For as a mountain whelp or heifer shalt thou wretched behold me wretched torn from thine arms, and sent down beneath the darkness of the earth a victim to Pluto, where I shall lie bound in misery with the dead. But it is for thee indeed, my afflicted mother, that I lament in these mournful strains, but for my life, my wrongs, my fate, I mourn not; but death, a better lot, has befallen me.

CHOR. But see Ulysses advances with hasty step, to declare to thee, Hecuba, some new determination.

ULYSSES, HECUBA, POLYXENA, CHORUS.

ULYSS. Lady, I imagine that you are acquainted with the decree of the army, and the vote which has prevailed; nevertheless, I will declare it. It has been decreed by the Greeks to offer on the lofty mound of Achilles's tomb thy daughter Polyxena. But they order me to conduct and convey the damsel; but the son of Achilles is appointed to be the priest, and to preside over the rites. Do you know then what to do? Be not dragged away by violence, nor enter into a contest of strength with me, but acknowledge superior force and the presence of thy ills; it is wise to have proper sentiments even in adversity.

HEC. Alas! alas! the great trial is at hand, as it seems, of lamentations full, nor without tears; for I have not died in the state in which I ought to have died, nor hath Jove destroyed me, but preserves me, that I wretched may behold other misfortunes greater than [past] misfortunes. But if it be allowed slaves to put questions to the free, not offensive nor grating to the feelings, it will be your part to be questioned, and ours who are asking to attend.

ULYSS. You have permission, ask freely, I grudge not the time.

HEC. Dost thou remember when thou camest a spy on Troy, disfigured by a vile dress, and from thine eyes drops caused by the fear of death bedewed thy beard?

ULYSS. I remember well; for it made no slight impression on my heart.

HEC. But Helen knew thee, and told me alone.

ULYSS. I remember the great danger I encountered.

HEC. And didst thou embrace my knees in thy humility?

ULYSS. So that my hand was numbered[7] through fear on thy garments.

HEC. What then didst thou say, being then my slave?

ULYSS. Many arguments that I invented to save me from death.

HEC. Did I preserve thee then, and conduct thee safe from the land?

ULYSS. Yes, so that I now behold the light of the sun.

HEC. Art thou not then convicted of baseness by this conduct, who hast received benefits from me such as thou acknowledgest thou hast, and doest us no good in return, but evil, as far as in thee lies? Thankless is your race, as many of you as court honor from oratory before the populace; be ye not known to me, who care not to injure your friends, provided you say what is gratifying to the people. But plotting what dark design have they determined upon a decree of death against my child? Did fate impel them to offer human sacrifices at the tomb, where it were rather right to sacrifice cattle? Or does Achilles, desirous of devoting in his turn to death those that wrought his death, with a color of justice meditate her destruction? But she has done him no ill: he should demand Helen as a sacrifice on his tomb; for she destroyed him, and brought him to Troy. But if some captive selected from the rest, and excelling in beauty, ought to die, this is not ours. For the daughter of Tyndarus is most preeminent in beauty, and has been found to be no less injurious than us. On the score of justice then I urge this argument; but with respect to what you ought to repay at my demand, hear: thou hast touched my hand, as thou ownest, and this aged cheek also, falling at my knees. Thy hand and knees I in return grasp, and re-demand the favor I granted you then, and beseech you, do not tear my child from my arms, nor kill her; enough have died already. In her I rejoice, and forget my misfortunes; she serves as my consolation in the stead of many things, she is my city, my nurse, my staff, the guide of my way. It becomes not those who have power to exercise their power in things wherein they ought not, nor should the fortunate imagine their fortune will last forever. For I too have had my time of prosperity, but now have I ceased to be: one day wrenched from me all my happiness. But by thy beard which I supplicate, reverence me, pity me; go to the Grecian army, and remind them that it is a shameful thing to slay women whom ye have once spared, and that too dragging them from the altar. But show mercy. But the laws of blood among you are laid down alike for the free and the slave. But your worth will carry with it persuasion, although your arguments be bad; for the same words from those of little character, have not the same force as when they proceed from those of high reputation.

CHOR. There is no nature of man so obdurate, which on hearing thy groans, and thy long plaints of misery, would not let fall the tear.

ULYSS. Hecuba, be advised, nor through passion deem him thine enemy who gives thee good advice. I indeed am ready to preserve thy person through the means of which I was fortunate; and I say no other. But what I declared before all I will not deny, that, Troy being captured, we should give thy daughter as a victim to the noblest man of the army, who demands her; for in this many cities fail, when any man who is brave and zealous receives no more honor than those who are less valiant. But Achilles, O lady, is worthy of honor from us, a man who died most gloriously in behalf of the Grecian country. Were not then this disgraceful, if when living we treat him as a friend, but after he is gone we no longer treat him so? Well! what then will any one say, if there again should be an assembling of the army, and a contest with the enemy: "Shall we fight or preserve our lives, seeing that he who falls lies unhonored?" But for me at least, living from day to day, although I have but little, that little is sufficient; but I would wish that my monument should be beheld crowned with honor, for the gratification is for a long time. But if thou sayest thou sufferest affliction, hear this in return from me. There are with us aged matrons, and hoary sires, not less wretched than thou art, and brides bereft of the noblest husbands, whose ashes this land of Troy conceals. Endure this. But we, if we injudiciously determine to honor the brave man, shall incur the charge of folly. But you barbarians neither consider your friends as friends, nor do you hold up to admiration those who have died honorably; thus shall Greece be prosperous, but you shall experience fortune corresponding to your counsels.

CHOR. Alas! alas! how wretched is the state of slavery, and to endure indignities compelled by superior force! (Note [B].)

HEC. O daughter, my words respecting thy death are vanished in the air, set forth in vain; but thou, if thou hast greater powers [of persuasion] than thy mother, use all thy influence, uttering every note as the throat of the nightingale, that thou mayest not be deprived of life. But fall before the knees of Ulysses in all the eloquence of grief, and persuade him; thou hast a pretext, for he also hath children; so that he may be inclined to pity thy fortune.

POLYX. I see, Ulysses, that thou art hiding thy hand beneath thy robe, and turnest thy face away, that I may not touch thy beard. Be not afraid; thou hast avoided my suppliant Jove; for I will follow thee both on account of fate, and even wishing to die; but if I were not willing, I should appear base, and too fond of life. For wherefore should I live, whose father was monarch of all the Trojans; this my dawn of life. Then was I nurtured under fair hope, a bride for princes, having no small competition for my hand, to whose palace and hearth I should come. But I, wretched now, was mistress among the Trojan women, and conspicuous in the train of virgins, equal to goddesses, death only excepted. But now I am a slave; first of all the very name, not being familiar, persuades me to love death. Then perhaps I might meet with masters cruel in disposition, who will buy me for silver, the sister both of Hector and many other [heroes.] And imposing the task of making bread in his palace, will compel me, passing the day in misery, both to sweep the house, and stand at the loom. And some slave somewhere purchased will defile my bed, before wooed by princes. This never shall be. I will quit this light from mine eyes free, offering my body to Pluto. Lead on then, Ulysses, conduct me to death; for I see neither confidence of hope, nor of expectation, present to me that I can ever enjoy good fortune. But do thou, my mother, in no wise hinder me by your words or by your actions; but assent to my death before I meet with indignities unsuited to my rank. For one who has not been accustomed to taste misfortunes bears indeed, but grieves, to put his neck under the yoke. But he would be far more blessed in death than in life; for to live otherwise than honorably is a great burden.

CHOR. It is a great and distinguishing feature among men to be born of generous parents, and the name of nobility of birth among the illustrious, proceeds from great to greater still.

HEC. You have spoken honorably, my daughter, but in that honorable dwells grief. But if the son of Peleus must be gratified, and you must escape blame, Ulysses, kill not her; but leading me to the pyre of Achilles, strike me, spare me not; I brought forth Paris, who destroyed the son of Thetis, having pierced him with his arrows.

ULYSS. The phantom of Achilles did not demand that thou, O aged lady, but that thy daughter here should die.

HEC. Do thou then at least slay me with my daughter, and there will be twice the libation of blood for the earth, and the dead who makes this request.

ULYSS. Thy daughter's death suffices; one must not be heaped on another; would that we required not even this one.

HEC. There is a strong necessity for me to die with my daughter.

ULYSS. How so? for I am not aware of any master that I have.

HEC. As the ivy the oak, so will I clasp her.

ULYSS. Not so; if you will take the advice of your superiors in knowledge.

HEC. Never will I willingly quit my child here.

ULYSS. Nor will I leave this place without the virgin.

POLYX. Mother, be persuaded; and thou, son of Laertes, be gentle to a parent with reason moved to anger. But thou, O wretched mother, contend not with conquerors. Dost thou wish to fall on the earth and to wound thy aged flesh dragged by violence, and to suffer the indignity of being torn by a youthful arm? which things you will suffer. Do not, I pray thee, for it is not seemly. But, my dear mother, give me thy beloved hand, and grant me to join cheek to cheek; since never hereafter, but now for the last time shall I behold the rays of the sun and his bright orb. Receive my last address, O mother! O thou that bearedst me, I am going below.

HEC. And I, O daughter, shall be a slave in the light of day.

POLYX. Without the bridegroom, without the bridal song, which I ought to have obtained.

HEC. Mournful thou, my child; but I am a wretched woman.

POLYX. There shall I lie in darkness far from thee.

HEC. Alas me, what shall I do? where end my life?

POLYX. I shall die a slave, born of a free father.

HEC. But I bereft indeed of fifty children.

POLYX. What message shall I bear to Hector, and to thy aged husband?

HEC. Tell them that I am most miserable of all women.

POLYX. O ye breasts that tenderly nursed me.

HEC. O daughter of an untimely and unhappy fate.

POLYX. Farewell, O mother, farewell Cassandra too.

HEC. Others farewell, but this is not for thy mother.

POLYX. Farewell, my brother Polydore, among the warlike Thracians.

HEC. If he lives at least: but I doubt, so unfortunate am I in every thing.

POLTX. He lives, and shall close thy dying eye.

HEC. I am dead, before my death, beneath my ills.

POLYX. Lead me, Ulysses, having covered my face with a veil, since, before I am sacrificed indeed, I am melted in heart at my mother's plaints, her also I melt by my lamentations. O light, for yet it is allowed me to express thy name, but I have no share in thee, except during the time that I am going between the sword and the pyre of Achilles.

HEC. Ah me! I faint; and my limbs fail me.—O daughter, touch thy mother, stretch forth thy hand—give it me—leave me not childless—I am lost, my friends. Would that I might see the Spartan Helen, the sister of the twin sons of Jove, thus, for through her bright eyes that most vile woman destroyed the happy Troy.

CHOR. Gale, gale of the sea,[8] which waftest the swift barks bounding through the waves through the surge of the ocean, whither wilt thou bear me hapless? To whose mansion shall I come, a purchased slave? Or to the port of the Doric or Phthian shore, where they report that Apidanus, the most beautiful father of floods, enriches the plains? or wilt thou bear me hapless urged by the maritime oar, passing a life of misery in my prison-house, to that island[9] where both the first-born palm tree and the laurel shot forth their hallowed branches to their beloved Latona, emblem of the divine parturition? And with the Delian nymphs shall I celebrate in song the golden chaplet and bow of Diana? Or, in the Athenian city, shall I upon the saffron robe harness the steeds to the car of Minerva splendid in her chariot, representing them in embroidery upon the splendid looms of brilliant threads, or the race of Titans, which Jove the son of Saturn sends to eternal rest with his flaming lightning? Alas, my children! Alas, my ancestors, and my paternal land, which is overthrown, buried in smoke, captured by the Argive sword! but I indeed am[10] a slave in a foreign country, having left Asia the slave of Europe, having changed my bridal chamber for the grave.

TALTHYBIUS, HECUBA, CHORUS.

TAL. Tell me, ye Trojan dames, where can I find Hecuba, late the queen of Troy?

CHOR. Not far from thee, O Talthybius, she is lying stretched on the ground, muffled in her robes.

TAL. O Jupiter, what shall I say? Shall I say that thou beholdest mortals? or that they have to no end or purpose entertained false notions, who suppose the existence of a race of Deities, and that fortune has the sovereign control over men? Was not this the queen of the opulent Phrygians? was not this the wife of the all-blest Priam? And now all her city is overthrown by the spear, but she a captive, aged, childless, lies on the ground defiling her ill-fated head with the dust. Alas! alas! I too am old, but rather may death be my portion before I am involved in any such debasing fortune; stand up, oh unhappy, raise thy side, and lift up thy hoary head.

HEC. Let me alone: who art thou that sufferest not my body to rest? why dost thou, whoever thou art, disturb me from my sadness?

TAL. I am here, Talthybius, the herald of the Greeks, Agamemnon having sent me for thee, O lady.

HEC. Hast thou come then, thou dearest of men, it having been decreed by the Greeks to slay me too upon the tomb? Thou wouldest bring dear news indeed. Then haste we, let us speed with all our might: lead on, old man.

TAL. I am here and come to thee, O lady, that thou mayest entomb thy dead daughter. Both the two sons of Atreus and the Grecian host send me.

HEC. Alas! what wilt thou say? Art thou not come for me as doomed to death, but to bring this cruel message? Thou art dead, my child, torn from thy mother; and I am childless as far as regards thee; oh! wretch that I am. But how did ye slay her? was it with becoming reverence? Or did ye proceed in your butchery as with an enemy, O old man? Tell me, though you will relate no pleasing tale.

TAL. Twice, O lady, thou desirest me to indulge in tears through pity for thy daughter; for both now while relating the mournful circumstance shall I bedew this eye, as did I then at the tomb when she perished. The whole host of the Grecian army was present before the tomb, at the sacrifice of thy daughter. But the son of Achilles taking Polyxena by the hand, placed her on the summit of the mound; but I stood near him: and there followed a chosen band of illustrious youths in readiness to restrain with their hands thy daughter's struggles; then the son of Achilles took a full-crowned goblet of entire gold, and poured forth libations to his deceased father; and makes signal to me to proclaim silence through all the Grecian host. And I standing forth in the midst, thus spoke: "Be silent, O ye Greeks, let all the people remain silent; silence, be still:" and I made the people perfectly still. But he said, "O son of Peleus, O my father, accept these libations which have the power of soothing, and which speed the dead on their way; and come, that thou mayest drink the pure purple blood of this virgin, which both the army and myself offer unto thee; but be propitious to us, and grant us to weigh anchor, and to loose the cables of our ships, and to return each to his country, having met with a prosperous return from Troy." Thus much he said, and all the army joined in the prayer. Then taking by the hilt his sword decked with gold, he drew it from its scabbard, and made signs to the chosen youths of the Greeks to hold the virgin. But she, when she perceived it,[11] uttered this speech: "O Argives, ye that destroyed my city, I die willingly; let none touch my body; for I will offer my neck to the sword with a good heart. But, by the Gods, let me go free while ye kill me, that I may die free, for to be classed as a slave among the dead, when a queen, is what I am ashamed of." But the people murmured assent, and king Agamemnon ordered the young men to quit the virgin; [but they, soon as they heard the last words of him who had the seat of chief authority among them, let go their hold,] and she, on hearing this speech of her lords, took her robe, and rent it, beginning from the top of her shoulder down to her waist: and showed her breasts and bosom beauteous, as a statue's, and bending her knee on the ground, spoke words the most piteous ever heard, "Lo! strike, if this bosom thou desirest, O youth; or wouldest thou rather under the neck, here is this throat prepared." But he at once resolved and unresolved through pity of the virgin, cuts with the sword the passage of her breath; and fountains of blood burst forth. But she, e'en in death, showed much care to fall decently, and to veil from the eyes of men what ought to be concealed. But after that she breathed forth her spirit under the fatal blow, not one of the Greeks exercised the same offices; but some scattered leaves from their hands on the dead; some heap the funeral pile, bringing whole trunks of pines: but he that would not bring, heard rebukes of this sort from him that was thus employed: "Standest thou idle, thou man of most mean spirit? Hast in thy hand no robe, no ornament for the maiden? Hast thou naught to give to her so exceeding brave in heart and most noble in soul?" These things I tell thee of the death of thy daughter, but I behold thee at once the most happy, at once the most unhappy of all women in thine offspring.

CHOR. Dreadful calamities have risen fierce against the house of Priam; such the hard fate of the Gods.

HEC. O daughter! which of my ills I shall first attend to, amidst such a multitude, I know not: for if I touch on any, another does not suffer me; and thence again some fresh grief draws me aside, succeeding miseries upon miseries. And now I can not obliterate from my mind thy sufferings, so as not to bewail them: but excess of grief hast thou taken away, having been reported to me as noble. Is it then no paradox, if land indeed naturally bad, when blest with a favorable season from heaven, bears well the ear; but good land, robbed of the advantages it ought to have, brings forth bad fruit: but ever among men, the bad by nature is nothing else but bad; the good always good, nor under misfortune does he degenerate from his nature, but is the same good man? Is it, that the parents cause this difference, or the education? The being brought up nobly hath indeed in it the knowledge and principles of goodness; but if one is acquainted well with this, he knows what is vicious, having already learned it by the rule of virtue. And this indeed has my mind been ejaculating in vain. But do thou go, and signify these things to the Greeks, that no one be suffered to touch my daughter, but bid them keep off the multitude. In so vast an army the rabble are riotous, and the sailors' uncontrolled insolence is fiercer than fire; and he is evil, who does not evil. But do thou, my old attendant, taking an urn, fill it with sea water, and bring it hither, that I may wash my girl in her last bath, the bride no bride now, and the virgin no longer a virgin, wash her, and lay her out; according to her merits—whence can I? This I can not; but as I can, I will, for what can I do! And collecting ornaments from among the captured women, who dwell beside me in these tents, if any one, unobserved by our new lords, has by her any stolen memorial of her home. O state of my house, O mansions once happy! O Priam, of vast wealth possessed, and supremely blest in thine offspring, and I too, this aged woman, the mother of such children! How have we come to nothing, bereft of our former grandeur! And yet still forsooth we are elated, one of us in his gorgeous palaces; another, when honored among his citizens. These are nothing. In vain the counsels of the mind, and the tongue's boast. He is most blest, to whom from day to day no evil happens.

CHORUS.

Against me was it fated that calamity, against me was it fated that woe should spring, when Paris first hewed the pine in Ida's forest, preparing to cut his way over the ocean surge to the bed of Helen, the fairest that the sun's golden beams shine upon. For toils, and fate more stern than toils, close us round: and from the folly of one came a public calamity fatal to the land of Simois, and woes springing from other woes: and when the dispute was decided, which the shepherd decided between the three daughters of the blessed Gods on Ida's top, for war, and slaughter, and the desolation of my palaces. And many a Spartan virgin at her home on the banks of the fair-flowing Eurotas sighs while bathed in tears: and many an aged matron strikes her hand against her hoary head, for her children who have perished, and tears her cheek making her nails all blood-stained with her wounds.

FEMALE ATTENDANT, CHORUS, HECUBA.

ATT. O attendants, where, I pray, is the all-wretched Hecuba, who surpasses the whole race of man and woman kind in calamities? no one shall wrest from her the crown.

CHOR. But what dost thou want, O wretch, in thy words of ill omen? for thy messages of woe never rest.

ATT. I bring this grief to Hecuba; but in calamity 'tis no easy thing for men to speak words of good import.

CHOR. And see, she is coming out of the house, and appears in the right time for thy words.

ATT. O all-wretched mistress, and yet still more wretched than I can express in words, thou art undone, and no longer beholdest the light, childless, husbandless, cityless, entirely destroyed.

HEC. Thou has said nothing new, but hast reproached me who already know it: but why dost thou bring this corse of my Polyxena, whose sepulture was reported to me as in a state of active progress through the labors of all the Grecians?

ATT. She nothing knows, but, woe's me! laments Polyxena, nor does she apprehend her new misfortunes.

HEC. O wretched me! dost bring hither the body of the frantic and inspired Cassandra?

ATT. She whom thou mentionedst, lives; but thou dost not weep for him who is dead; but behold this corse cast naked [on the shore,] and look if it will appear to thee a wonder, and what thou little expectest.

HEC. Alas me! I do indeed see my son Polydore a corse, whom (*I fondly hoped*) the man of Thrace was preserving in his palace. Now am I lost indeed, I no longer exist. Oh my child, my child! Alas! I begin the Bacchic strain, having lately learned my woes from my evil genius.

ATT. Thou knowest then the calamity of thy son, O most unfortunate.

HEC. I see incredible evils, still fresh, still fresh: and my immeasurable woes follow one upon the other. No longer will a day without a tear, without a groan, have part with me.

CHOR. Dreadful, oh! dreadful are the miseries that we endure!

HEC. O child, child of a wretched mother, by what fate art thou dead, by what hap liest thou here? by the hand of what man?

ATT. I know not: on the wave-washed shore I found him.

HEC. Cast up from the sea, or fallen by the blood-stained spear? (Note [C].)

ATT. The ocean's billow cast him up from the deep on the smooth sand.

HEC. Woe is me! Now understand I the dream, the vision of mine eyes; the black-winged phantom has not flitted by me in vain, which I saw concerning thee, my child, as being no longer in the light of day.

CHOR. But who slew him? canst thou, O skilled in dreams, declare him?

HEC. My friend, my friend, who curbs the steed in Thrace, where his aged father placed him for concealment.

CHOR. Ah me! what wilt thou say? Was it to possess his gold that he slew him!

HEC. Unutterable deeds, unworthy of a name, surpassing miracles, unhallowed, insufferable! Where are the laws of hospitality? O most accurst of men, how didst thou mar that skin, how sever with the cruel sword the poor limbs of this boy, nor didst feel pity?

CHOR. O hapless woman, how has the deity made thee by far the most wretched of mortals, whoever he be that presses heavy on thee! But, my friends, let us henceforward be silent, for I see our lord Agamemnon advancing.

AGAMEMNON, CHORUS, HECUBA.

AGA. Why, Hecuba, delayest thou to come, and bury thy girl in her tomb, agreeably to what Talthybius told me, that no one of the Argives should be suffered to touch thy daughter. For our part we leave her alone, and touch her not; but thou art slow, whereat I am astonished. I am come therefore to fetch thee, for every thing there has been well and duly performed, if aught of well there be in this. Ah! what corse is this I see before the tent? some Trojan's too? for that it is no Grecian's, the robes that vest his limbs inform me.

HEC. (*aside*) Thou ill-starr'd wretch! myself I mean, when I say "thou." O Hecuba, what shall I do? Shall I fall at the knees of Agamemnon here, or bear my ills in silence?

AGA. Why dost lament turning thy back upon me, and sayest not what has happened? Who is this?

HEC. (*aside*) But should he, thinking me a slave, an enemy, spurn me from his knees, I should be adding to my present sufferings.

AGA. No prophet I, so as to trace, unless by hearing, the path of thy counsels.

HEC. (*aside*) Am I not rather then putting an evil construction on this man's thoughts, whereas he has no evil intention toward me?

AGA. If thou art willing that I should nothing of this affair, thou art of a mind with me, for neither do I wish to hear.

HEC. (*aside*) I can not without him take vengeance for my children. Why do I thus hesitate? I must be bold, whether I succeed, or fail. Agamemnon, by these knees, and by thy beard I implore thee, and by thy blessed hand—

AGA. What thy request? Is it to pass thy life in freedom? for this is easy for thee to obtain.

HEC. Not this indeed; but so that I avenge myself on the bad, I am willing to pass my whole life in slavery.

AGA. And for what assistance dost thou call on me?

HEC. In none of those things which thou imaginest, O king. Seest thou this corse, o'er which I drop the tear?

AGA. I see it; thy meaning however I can not learn from this.

HEC. Him did I once bring forth, him bore I in my bosom.

AGA. Is this indeed one of thy children, O unhappy woman?

- 23 -

HEC. It is, but not of the sons of Priam who fell under the walls of Troy.

AGA. Didst thou then bear any other besides those, O lady?

HEC. In vain, as it appears, this whom you see.

AGA. But where did he chance to be, when the city fell?

HEC. His father sent him out of the country, dreading his death.

AGA. Whither, having removed him alone of his children then alive?

HEC. To this country, where he was found a corse.

AGA. To him who is king over this state, to Polymestor?

HEC. Hither was he sent, the guardian of gold, which proved most destructive to him.

AGA. By whose hand then he is dead, and having met with what fate?

HEC. By whom else should he? The Thracian host slew him.

AGA. O wretch! was he so inflamed with the desire of obtaining the gold?

HEC. Even so, after he had heard of Troy's disasters.

AGA. And where didst thou find him, or who brought the body?

HEC. She, meeting with it on the sea-shore.

AGA. In quest of it, or occupied in some other employment?

HEC. She was going to bring from the sea wherewith to bathe Polyxena.

AGA. This friend then, as it seems, murdered him, and after that cast him out.

HEC. To toss upon the waves thus gashing his body.

AGA. O thou unhappy from thy unmeasured ills!

HEC. I perish, no woe is left, O Agamemnon.

AGA. Alas! alas! What woman was ever so unfortunate?

HEC. There is none, except you reckon Misfortune herself. But for what cause I fall at thy knees, now hear: if I appear to you to suffer these ills justly, I would be reconciled to them; but if otherwise, be thou my avenger on this man, this most impious of false friends; who revering neither the Gods beneath[12] the earth, nor the Gods above, hath done this most unholy deed, having often partaken of the same table with me, [and in the list of hospitality the first of my friends; and having met with whatever was due,[13] and having received a full consideration for his services,[14]] slew him, and deigned not to give him a tomb, *which he might have given*, although he purposed to slay him, but cast him forth at the mercy of the waves. We indeed are slaves, and perhaps weak; but the Gods are strong, and strong the law, which governs them; for by the law we judge that there arc Gods, and we live having justice and injustice strictly defined; which if when referred to thee it be disregarded, and they shall suffer no punishment who slay their guests, or dare to pollute the hallowed statutes of the Gods, there is nothing equitable in the dealings of men. Beholding these things then in a base and proper light, reverence me; pity me, and, as the artist stands aside *to view a picture*, do thou view my living portrait, and see what woes I am enduring. Once was I a queen, but now I am thy slave; once was I blest in my children, but now aged, and at the same time childless, cityless, destitute, the most miserable of mortals. Alas me wretched! whither withdrawest from me thy foot? It seems[15] I shall make no impression, wretch that I am. Why then do we mortals toil after all other sciences, as a matter of duty, and dive into them, but least of all strive to learn thoroughly Persuasion, the sole mistress o'er the minds of men, giving a price for her knowledge, that at some time we may have it in our power at once to persuade and obtain what we wish?—How then can any one hereafter hope that he shall be fortunate? So many children that I had, and now not one is left to me. But I am perishing a captive in base servitude, and yet see the smoke there leaping aloft from the city. And however this part of my argument may perchance be vain, the bringing forward love; still nevertheless it shall be urged. My daughter is wont to sleep by thy side, that prophetess, whom the Trojans call Cassandra. Where wilt thou show that thy nights were nights of love, O king, or will my daughter receive any recompense for her most fond embraces, and I through her? [For from the secret shade, and from night's joys, the greatest delight is wont to spring to mortals.] Now then attend. Thou seest this corse? Him assisting, thou wilt assist one joined to thee in affinity. One thing my speech wants yet. I would fain I had a voice in my arms, and hands, and in my hair, and in my footsteps, or by the skill of Dædalus, or some God, that each at once might hold thy knees, weeping, and imploring in all the strains of eloquence. O my lord. O greatest light of the Greeks, be persuaded; lend thy hand to avenge this aged woman, although she is of no consequence, yet avenge her. For it belongs to a good man to minister justice, and always and in every case to punish the bad.

CHOR. It is strange, how every thing happens to mortals, and laws determine even the fates, making the greatest enemies friends, and enemies of those who before were on good terms.

AGA. I, O Hecuba, have pity both on thee and thy son, thy misfortunes, and thy suppliant touch, and I am willing in regard both to the Gods and to justice, that this impious host should give thee full revenge, provided a way could be found, that both you might be gratified, and I might in the eyes of the army not seem to meditate this destruction against the king of Thrace for Cassandra's sake. For there is a point in which apprehension hath reached me. This man the army deems a friend, the dead an enemy; but if he is dear to thee, this is a private feeling and does not affect the army. Wherefore consider, that thou hast me willing to labor with thee, and ready to assist thee, but backward, should I be murmured against among the Greeks.

HEC. Alas! no mortal is there who is free. For either he is the slave of money or of fortune; or the populace of the city or the dictates of the law constrain him to adopt manners not accordant with his natural inclinations. But since thou fearest, and payest too much regard to the multitude, I will liberate thee from this fear. For consent with me, if I meditate vengeance against the murderer of this youth, but do not act with me. But should any tumult or offer of assistance arise from out of the Greeks, when the Thracian feels the punishment he shall feel, suppress it, not appearing to do it for my sake: but of the rest be confident: I will dispose all things well.

AGA. How then? What wilt thou do? Wilt thou grasp the sword in thine aged hand, and strike the barbarian? or with poison wilt thou work, or with what assistance? What hand will conspire with thee? whence wilt thou procure friends?

HEC. These tents inclose a host of Trojan dames.

AGA. Meanest thou the captives, the booty of the Greeks?

HEC. With these will I avenge me of my murderer.

AGA. And how shall the victory over men be to women?

HEC. Numbers are powerful, with stratagem invincible.

AGA. Powerful, I grant; I mistrust however the race of women.

HEC. And why? Did not women slay the sons of Ægyptus,[16] and utterly extirpated the race of men from Lemnos?[17] But thus let it be. Give up this discussion. But grant this woman to pass in safety through the army. And do thou go to the Thracian host and tell him, "Hecuba, once queen of Troy, sends for you on business of no less importance to yourself than to her, and your sons likewise, since it is of consequence that your children also should hear her words."—And do thou, O Agamemnon, as yet forbear to raise the tomb over the newly-sacrificed Polyxena, that these two, the brother and the sister, the divided care of their mother, may, when reduced to ashes by one and the same flame, be interred side by side.

AGA. Thus shall it be. And yet, if the army could sail, I should not have it in my power to grant thy request: but now, for the deity breathes not prosperous gales, we must wait, watching for a calm voyage. But may things turn out well some way or other: for this is a general principle among all, both individuals in private and states, That the wicked man should feel vengeance, but the good man enjoy prosperity.

CHORUS.

O thou, my country of Troy, no longer shall thou be called the city of the invincible, such a cloud of Grecians envelops thee, with the spear, with the spear having destroyed thee. And thou hast been shorn of thy crown of turrets, and thou hast been discolored by the dismal blackness of smoke; hapless city, no longer shall I tread my steps in thee.

In the midnight hour I perished, when after the feast sweet sleep is scattered over the eyes. And my husband, from the song and cheerful sacrifice retired, was sleeping peacefully in my bed, his spear on its peg, no more dreaming to behold the naval host of the Greeks treading the streets of Troy. But I was binding my braided hair with fillets fastened on the top of mine head, looking into the round polished surface of the golden mirror, that I might get into my bed prepared for me. On a sudden a tumultuous cry penetrated the city; and this shout of exhortation was heard in the streets of Troy, "When indeed, ye sons of Grecians, when, *if not now*, will ye return to your homes having overthrown the proud citadel of Ilium!" And having left my dear bed, in a single robe, like a Spartan virgin, flying for aid to the venerable shrine of Diana, I hapless fled in vain. And I am dragged, after having seen my husband slain, to the ocean waves; and casting a distant look back upon my city, after the vessel had begun her way in her return to Greece, and divided me from the land of Troy, I wretched fainted through anguish. And consigning to curses Helen, the sister of the Twin Brothers, and the Idean shepherd, the ruthless Paris, since his marriage, no marriage, but some Fury's hate hath utterly destroyed me far from my native land, and hath driven me from my home. Whom may the ocean refuse ever to bear back again; and may she never reach again her paternal home.

POLYMESTOR, HECUBA, CHORUS.

POLY. O Priam, thou dearest of men, and thou most dear Hecuba, at thy sight I weep for thee, and thy city, and thy daughter who has lately died. Alas! there is nothing secure, neither glory, nor when one is faring well is there a certainty that he will not fare ill. But the Gods mingle these things promiscuously to and fro, making all confusion, so that we through ignorance may worship them. But wherefore should I utter these plaints, which in no way tend to free thee from thy former calamities. But thou, if thou hast aught to blame for my absence, forbear; for I chanced to be afar off in the middle of my Thracian territories, when thou camest hither; but soon as I returned, as I was already setting out from my house, this maid of thine met me for the self-same purpose, and delivered thy message, which when I had heard, I came.

HEC. O Polymestor, I am ashamed to look thee in the face, sunk as I am in such miseries; for before one who has seen me in prosperity, shame overwhelms me, being in the state in which I now am, nor can I look upon thee with unmoved eyes. But impute not this to any enmity I bear thee; but there are other causes, and in some degree this law; "that women ought not to gaze at men."

POLY. And 'tis indeed no wonder; but what need hast thou of me? for what purpose didst thou send for me to come from home?

HEC. I am desirous of communicating a private affair of my own to thee and thy children; but order thy attendants to retire from these tents.

POLY. Depart, for here to be alone is safe. Friendly thou art, this Grecian army too is friendly toward me, but it is for thee to signify, in what manner I, who am in good circumstances, ought to succor my friends in distress; since, on my part, I am ready.

HEC. First then tell me of my son Polydore, whom thou retainest, receiving him from mine, and from his father's hand, if he live; but the rest I shall inquire of thee afterward.

POLY. He lives, and in good health; as far as regards him indeed thou art happy.

HEC. O my best friend, how well thou speakest, and how worthily of thyself!

POLY. What dost thou wish then to inquire of me in the next place?

HEC. Whether he remembers at all me, his mother?

POLY. Yes: and he even sought to come to thee by stealth.

HEC. And is the gold safe, which he brought with him from Troy?

POLY. It is safe, at least it is guarded in my house.

HEC. Preserve it therefore, nor covet the goods of others.

POLY. Certainly not. May I enjoy what is mine own, O lady.

HEC. Knowest thou then, what I wish to say to thee and thy children?

POLY. I do not: this shalt thou signify by thy speech.

HEC. Be my son loved by thee, as thou art now loved of me.

POLY. What is it, that I and my sons must know?

HEC. The ancient buried treasures of the family of Priam.

POLY. Is it this thou wishest me to inform thy son of?

HEC. Yes, certainly; through thee at least, for thou art a pious man.

POLY. What necessity then is there for the presence of these children?

HEC. 'Tis better in case of thy death, that these should know.

POLY. Well hast thou thus said, and 'tis the wiser plan.

HEC. Thou knowest then where the temple of Minerva in Troy is—

POLY. Is the gold there! but what is the mark?

HEC. A black rock rising above the earth.

POLY. Hast any thing further to tell me of what is there?

HEC. No, but I wish thee to take care of some treasures, with which I came out of the city.

POLY. Where are they then? Hast thou them hidden beneath thy robes?

HEC. Amidst a heap of spoils they are preserved in this tent.

POLY. But where? These are the naval encampments of the Grecians.

HEC. The habitations of the captive women are private.

POLY. And is all secure within, and untenanted by men?

HEC. Not one of the Greeks is within, but we women only. But come into the tent, for the Greeks are desirous of loosing the sheets of their vessels homeward from Troy; so that, having done every thing that thou oughtest, thou mayest go with thy children to that place where thou hast given my son to dwell.

CHOR. Not yet hast thou suffered, but peradventure thou wilt suffer vengeance; as a man falling headlong into the gulf where no harbor is, shalt thou be hurled from thy dear heart, having lost thy life;[18] for where the rites of hospitality coincide[19] with justice, and with the Gods, *on the villain who dares to violate these* destructive, destructive indeed impends the evil. But thy hopes will deceive thee, which thou entertainedst from this journey, which has brought thee, thou wretched man, to the deadly mansions of Pluto; but thou shalt quit thy life by no warrior's hand.

POLYMESTOR, HECUBA, SEMICHORUS.

POLY. Oh me! I wretch am deprived of the sight of mine eyes.

SEMI. Heard ye the shriek of the man of Thrace, my friends?

POLY. Oh me; there again—Oh my children, thy miserable butchery!

SEMI. My friends, some strange ills have been perpetrated within the tents.

POLY. But for all your nimble feet, ye never can escape me, for by my blows will I burst open the recesses of these tents.

SEMI. Behold, he uses violently the weapon of his heavy hand. Will ye that we fall on; since the instant calls on us to be present with assistance to Hecuba and the Trojan dames?

HEC. Dash on, spare nothing, break down the gates, for thou never shalt replace the clear sight in those pupils, nor shalt thou behold alive those children which I have slain.

SEMI. What! hast thou vanquished the Thracian? and hast thou got the mastery over this host, my mistress? and hast thou done such deeds, as thou sayest?

HEC. Thou wilt see him quickly before the house, blind, with blind wandering steps approaching, and the bodies of his two children, whom I have slain with these most valiant Trojan women; but he has felt my vengeance; but he is coming as thou seest from the tent. But I will retire out of his way, and make good my retreat from the boiling rage of this most desperate Thracian.

POLY. Alas me! whither can I go? where stand? whither shall I direct my way, advancing my steps like the four-footed mountain beast on my hands and on my feet in pursuit? What new path shall I take in this direction or in that, desirous of seizing these murderous Trojan dames, who have utterly destroyed me; O ye impious, impious Phrygian daughters! Ah the accursed, in what corner do they shrink from me in flight? Would that thou, O sun, could'st heal, could'st heal these bleeding lids of my eyes, and remove this gloomy-darkness. Ah, hush, hush! I hear the carefully-concealed step of these women. Whither shall I direct my course in order that I may glut myself on the flesh and bones of these, making the wild beasts' banquet, inflicting vengeance on them, in return for the injuries done me. Wretch that I am! Whither, whither am I borne, having left my children deserted, for these fiends of hell to tear piecemeal, a mangled, bleeding, savage prey to dogs, and a thing to cast out on the mountains? Where shall I stand? Whither turn? Whither go, as a ship setting her yellow canvas sails with her sea-washed palsers, rushing to this lair of death, the protector of my children?

CHOR. O miserable man, what intolerable evils have been perpetrated by thee! but on thee having done base deeds the God hath sent dreadful punishment, whoever he be that presses heavy on thee.

POLY. Alas! alas! O Thracian nation, brandishing the spear, warlike, bestriding the steed, nation ruled by Mars; O ye Greeks, sons of Atreus; I raise the cry, the cry, the cry; Come, come, hasten, I entreat you by the Gods. Does any hear, or will no one assist me? Why do ye delay? The women have destroyed me, the captive women. Horrible, horrible treatment have I suffered. Alas me for my ruin! Whither can I turn? Whither can I go? Shall I soar through the ethereal skies to the lofty mansions where Orion or Sirius dart from their eyes the flaming rays of fire: or shall I hapless rush to the gloomy shore of Pluto?

CHOR. It is pardonable, when any one suffers greater misfortunes than he can bear, for him to be desirous to quit a miserable life.

AGAMEMNON, POLYMESTOR, HECUBA, CHORUS.

AGA. I came having heard the clamor: for Echo, the mountain's daughter, did not sound in gentle strains through the army, causing a disturbance. But did we not know that the Phrygian towers are fallen beneath the Grecian spear, this tumult might have caused no little terror.

POLY. O my dearest friend (for I know thee, Agamemnon, having heard thy voice), seest thou what I am suffering?

AGA. Ah! wretched Polymestor, who hath destroyed thee? who made thine eyes sightless, having drowned their orbs in blood? And who hath slain these thy children? Sure, whoe'er it was, felt the greatest rage against thee and thy sons.

POLY. Hecuba with the female captives hath destroyed me—nay, not destroyed me, but more than destroyed me.

AGA. What sayest thou? Hast thou done this deed, as he affirms? Hast thou, Hecuba, dared this inconceivable act of boldness?

POLY. Ah me! what wilt thou say? Is she any where near me? Show me, tell me where she is, that I may seize her in my hands, and tear piecemeal and mangle her body.

AGA. What ho! what are you doing?

POLY. By the Gods I entreat thee, suffer me to lay my raging hand upon her.

AGA. Forbear. And having banished this barbarous deed from thy thoughts, speak; that having heard both thee and her in your respective turns, I may decide justly, in return for what thou art suffering these ills.

POLY. I will speak then. There was a certain youth, the youngest of Priam's children, by name Polydore, the son of Hecuba; him his father Priam sent to me from Troy to bring up in my palace, already presaging[20] the capture of Troy. Him I put to death. But for what cause I put him to death, with what policy and prudent forethought, now hear. I feared, lest the boy being left an enemy to thee, should collect the scattered remnants of Troy, and again people the city. And lest the Greeks, having discovered that one of the sons of Priam was alive, should again direct an expedition against the Phrygian land, and after that should harass and lay waste the plains of Thrace; and it might fare ill with the neighbors of the Trojans, under which misfortune, O king, we are now laboring. But Hecuba, when she had discovered her son's death, by such treachery as this lured me hither, as about to tell me of treasure belonging to Priam's family concealed in Troy, and introduces me alone with my sons into the tent, that no one else might know it. And I sat, having reclined on the centre of the couch; but many Trojan damsels, some from the left hand, and others from the right, sat round me, as by an intimate friend, holding in their hands the Edonian looms, and praised these robes, looking at them in the light; but others, beholding with admiration my Thracian spear, deprived me of my double ornament. But as many as were mothers caressed my children in their arms in seeming admiration, that they might be farther removed from their father, successively handing them from one to another: and then, amidst their kind blandishments, what think you? in an instant, snatching from somewhere beneath their garments their daggers, they stab my children. But they having seized me in an hostile manner held my hands and feet; and if, wishing to succor my children, I raised my head, they held me by the hair: but if I attempted to move my hands, I wretched could effect nothing through the host of women. But at last, cruelty and worse than cruelty, they perpetrated dreadful things; for having taken their clasps they pierce and gore the wretched pupils of my eyes, then vanish in flight through the tent. But I, having leaped out, like some exasperated beast, pursue the blood-stained wretches, searching every wall, as the hunter, casting down, rending. This have I suffered, while studious to advance thy interest, Agamemnon, and having killed thine enemy. But that I may not extend my speech to a greater length, if any one of those of ancient times hath reviled women, or if any one doth now, or shall hereafter revile them, I will comprise the whole when I say, that such a race neither doth the sea nor the earth produce, but he who is always with them knows it best.

CHOR. Be not at all insolent, nor, in thy calamities, thus comprehending the female sex, abuse them all. For of us there are many, some indeed are envied *for their virtues*, but some are by nature in the catalogue of bad things.

HEC. Agamemnon, it never were fitting among men that the tongue should have greater force than actions. But if a man has acted well, well should he speak; if on the other hand basely, his words likewise should be unsound, and never ought he to be capable of speaking unjust things well. Perhaps indeed they who have brought these things to a pitch of accuracy are accounted wise, but they can not endure wise unto the end, but perish vilely, nor has any one yet escaped this. And this in my prelude is what I have to say to thee. Now am I going to direct my discourse to this man, and I will answer his arguments. Thou, that assertest, that in order to rid the Greeks of their redoubled toil, and for Agamemnon's sake that thou didst slay my son? But, in the first place, monstrous villain, never can the race of barbarians be friendly to the Grecians, never can this take place. But what favor wert thou so eagerly currying? wert thou about to contract an alliance, or was it that thou wert of kindred birth, or what pretext hadst thou? or were they about to ravage the crops of thy country, having sailed thither again? Whom, thinkest thou, wilt thou persuade of these things? The gold, if thou wert willing to speak truth, the gold destroyed my son, and thy base gains. For come, tell me this; how when Troy was prosperous, and a tower yet girt around the city, and Priam lived, and the spear of Hector was in its glory, why didst thou not then, if thou wert willing to lay him under this obligation, bringing up my child, and retaining him in thy palace, why didst thou not then slay him, or go and take him alive to the Greeks? But when we were no longer in the light of prosperity, and the city by its smoke showed that it was in the power of the enemy, thou slewest thy guest who had come to thy hearth. Now hear besides how thou wilt appear vile: thou oughtest, if thou wert the friend of the Greeks, to have given the gold, which thou confessedst thou hast, not thine, but his, distributing to those who were in need, and had long been strangers to their native land. But thou, even now, hast not courage to part with it from thy hand, but having it, thou still art keeping it close in thine house. And yet, in bringing up my child, as it was thy duty to bring him up, and in preserving him, thou hadst had fair honor. For in adversity friends are most clearly proved good. But good circumstances have in every case their friends. But if thou wert in want of money, and he in a flourishing condition, my son had been to thee a vast treasure; but now, thou neither hast him for thy friend, and the benefit from the gold is gone, and thy sons are gone, and thou art—as thou art. But to thee, Agamemnon, I say; if thou aidest this man, thou wilt appear to be doing wrong. For thou wilt be conferring a benefit on a host, who is neither pious, nor faithful to those to whom he ought, not holy, not just. But we shall say that thou delightest in the bad, if thus thou actest: but I speak no offense to my lords.

CHOR. Ah! Ah! How do good deeds ever supply to men the source of good words!

AGA. Thankless my office to decide on others' grievances; but still I must, for it brings disgrace on a man, having taken a thing in hand, to give it up. But to me, be assured, thou neither appearest for my sake, nor for the sake of the Grecians, to have killed this man thy guest, but that thou mightest possess the gold in thy palace. But thou talkest of thy advantage, when thou art in calamities.[21] Perhaps with you it is a slight thing to kill your guests; but with us Grecians this thing is abhorred. How then, in giving my decision that thou hast not injured, can I escape blame? I can not; but as thou hast dared to do things dishonorable, endure now things unpleasant.

POLY. Alas me! worsted, as it seems, by a woman who is a slave, I shall submit to the vengeance of my inferiors.

AGA. Will it not then be justly, seeing thou hast acted wrong?

POLY. Alas me! wretched on account of these children and on account of my eyes.

HEC. Thou sufferest? but what do I? Thinkest thou I suffer not for my child?

POLY. Thou rejoicest in insulting me, O thou malicious woman.

HEC. For ought not I to rejoice on having avenged myself on thee?

POLY. But thou wilt not soon, when the liquid wave—

HEC. Shall bear me, *dost thou mean*, to the confines of the Grecian land?

POLY. —shall cover thee, having fallen from the shrouds.

HEC. From whom meeting with this violent leap?

POLY. Thyself shalt climb with thy feet up the ship's mast.

HEC. Having wings on my back, or in what way?

POLY. Thou shalt become a dog with a fiery aspect.

HEC. But how dost thou know of this my metamorphose?

POLY. Dionysius the Thracian prophet told it me.

HEC. But did he not declare to thee any of the evils which thou sufferest?

POLY. No: for, *if he had*, thou never wouldst thus treacherously have taken me.

HEC. [22]Thence shall I conclude my life in death, or still live on?

POLY. Thou shalt die. But the name of thy tomb shall be—

HEC. Dost thou speak of it as in any way correspondent to my shape?

POLY. [23]The tomb of the wretched dog, a mark to mariners.

HEC. I heed it not, since thou at least hast felt my vengeance.

POLY. And it is fated too for thy daughter Cassandra to die.

HEC. I renounce these prophecies; I give them for thyself to bear.

POLY. Him shall his wife slay, a cruel guardian of his house.

HEC. Never yet may the daughter of Tyndarus have arrived at such madness.

POLY. Even this man himself, having lifted up the axe.

AGA. What ho! thou art mad, and art desirous of obtaining greater ills.

POLY. Kill me, for the murderous bath at Argos awaits thee.

AGA. Will ye not, slaves, forcibly drag him from my presence?

POLY. Thou art galled at what thou hearest.

AGA. Will ye not stop his mouth?

POLY. Stop it: for the word is spoken.

AGA. Will ye not as quick as possible cast him out on some desert island, since he is thus, and past endurance insolent? But do thou, wretched Hecuba, go and bury thy two dead: and you, O Trojan dames, must approach your masters' tents, for I perceive that the gales are favorable for wafting us to our homes. And may we sail in safety to our native country, and behold our household and families in prosperity, having found rest from these toils.

CHOR. Come, my friends, to the harbor, and the tents, to undergo the tasks imposed by our masters. For necessity is relentless.

NOTES ON HECUBA

[1] Homer makes Dymas, not Cisseus, the father of Hecuba. Virgil however follows Euripides, the rest of the Latin poets Virgil.

[2] In the martial time of antiquity the spear was reverenced as something divine, and signified the chief command in arms, it was also the insigne of the highest civil authority: in this sense Euripides in other places uses the word δορυ. See Hippol. 988.

[3] τριταιος properly signifies *triduanus*; here it is used for τριτος, the cardinal number for the ordinal. So also Hippol. 275.

Πως δ' ου, τριταιαν γ' ουσ' ασιτος 'ημεραν:

[4] Most interpreters render this, *leaning on the crooked staff with my hand.* Nor has Beck altered it in his Latin version, though he transcribed Musgrave's note. "σκολιω, σκιμπωνι (*for which Porson directs* σκιπωνι,) Scipiones in universum recti sunt, non curvi. Loquitur igitur non de vero scipione, sed metaphorice de brachio,

quod ancillis innitens, scipionis usum præstabat; quodque, ob cubiti flexuram, σκολιον σκιμπωμα vocat."

[5] *that babbling knave.*] Tzetzes on Lycophron, line 763. κοπις, 'ο 'ρητωρ, και εμπειρος, 'ο 'υπο πολλων πραγματων κεκομμενος. In the Index to Lycophron κοπις is translated *scurra*.

[6] Among the ancients it was the custom for virgins to have a great quantity of golden ornaments about them, to which Homer alludes, Il. B. 872.

'Ος και χρυσον εχων πολεμον δ' ιεν ηϋτε κουρη. PORSON.

[7] This is the only sense that can be made of ενθανειν, and this sense seems strained: Brunck proposes εντακηναι for ενθανειν γε. See Note [A].

[8] λιμνη is used for the *sea* in Troades 444; as also in Iliad N. 21, and Odyssey Γ. 1. and in many other passages of Homer.

[9] The construction is η πορευσεις με ενθα νασων; for εις εκεινην των νασων, ενθα.

[10] κεκλημαι for ειμι, not an unusual signification. Hippol. 2, θεα κεκλημαι Κυπρις.

[11] *When she perceived it,* εφρασθη, συνηκεν, εγνω, ενοησεν. *Hesych.*

[12] The Gods beneath he despised, by casting him out without a tomb; the Gods above, as the guardians of the rites of hospitality.

[13] *Whatever was due,* either on the score of friendship, or as an equivalent for his care and protection.

[14] Musgrave proposes to read προμισθιαν for προμηθιαν: the version above is in accordance with the scholiast and the paraphrast.

[15] See note on Medea 338.

[16] The story of the daughters of Danaus is well known.

[17] Of this there are two accounts given in the Scholia. The one is, that the women of Lemnos being punished by Venus with an ill savor, and therefore neglected by their husbands, conspired against them and slew them. The other is found in Herodotus, Erato, chap. 138. see also Æsch. Choephoræ, line 627, ed. Schutz.

[18] Polymestor was guilty of two crimes, αδικιας and ασεβειας, for he had both violated the laws of men, and profaned the deity

of Jupiter Hospitalis. Whence Agamemnon, v. 840, hints that he is to suffer on both accounts.

και βουλομαι θεων θ' 'ουνεκ ανοσιον ξενον,

και του δικαιον, τηνδε σοι δουναι δικην.

The Chorus therefore says, *Ubi contingit eundem et Justitiæ et Diis esse addictum, exitiale semper malum esse*; or, as the learned Hemsterheuyse has more fully and more elegantly expressed, it, *Ubi*, id est, *in quo*, vel *in quem cadit et concurrit, ut ob crimen commissum simul et humanæ justitiæ et Deorum vindictæ sit obnoxius, ac velut oppignoratus; illi certissimum exitium imminet.* This sense the words give, if for ου, we read 'ου, i.e. in the sense of 'οπου. MUSGRAVE. Correct Dindorf's text to 'ου.

[19] συμπεσεειν *in unum coire, coincidere.* In this sense it is used also, Herod. Euterpe, chap. 49.

[20] The verbal adjective in τος is almost universally used in a passive sense; 'υποπτος, however, in this place is an exception to the rule, as are also, καλυπτης, Soph. Antig. 1011, μεμπτος, Trachin. 446.

[21] Perhaps the preferable way is to make κακοισιν agree with ανθρωποις understood; that the sense may be, *You are a bad man to talk of your advantage as a plea for having acted thus.*

[22] Θανουσα δ' η ζωσ' ενθαδ' εκπλησω βιον; a similar expression occurs in the Anthologia.

σιγων παρερχου τον ταλαιπωρον βιον,

αυτος σιωπηι τον χρονον μιμουμενος,

λαθων δε και βιωσον. ει δε μη, θανων.

[23] The place of her burial was called Cynosema, a promontory of the Thracian Chersonese. It was here that the Athenians gained a naval victory over the Peloponnesians and Syracusans, in the twenty-first year of the Peloponnesian war. Thucydides, book viii.

ADDITIONAL NOTES.

[A] Vs. 246, ενθανειν γε. "Pravam esse scripturam dici Brunckius et Corayus viderunt; quorum ille legere voluit 'ωστ' εντακηναι, hic vero 'ωστ' εμβαλειν. Sed neuter rem acu tetigit. Euripides scripsit: 'ωστ' εν γε φυναι, uti patet ex Hom. Il. Z. 253, εν τ' αρα 'οι φυ χειρι, Od. Π. 21, παντα κυσεν περιφυς, Theocrit. Id. xiii. 47, ται δ' εν χερι πασαι εφυσαν, et, quod rem conficit, ex Euripidis ipsius Ion. 891, λευκοις δ' εμφυσας καρποις χειρων." G. BURGES, apud *Revue de Philologie*, vol. i. No. 5. p. 457.

[B] We must, I think, read τολμαιν.

[C] Dindorf disposes these lines differently, but I prefer Porson's arrangement, as follows:

ΕΚ. εκβλητον, η πες. φ. δορος;

ΘΕΡ. εν ψαμαθωι λευραι

ποντου νιν, κ.τ.λ.

ORESTES.

PERSONS REPRESENTED.

ELECTRA.

HELEN.

HERMIONE.

CHORUS.

ORESTES.

MENELAUS.

TYNDARUS.

PYLADES.

A PHRYGIAN.

APOLLO.

THE ARGUMENT.

Orestes, in revenge for the murder of his father, took off Ægisthus and Clyætmnestra; having dared to slay his mother, he was instantly punished for it by being afflicted with madness. But on Tyndarus, the father of her who was slain, laying an accusation against him, the Argives were about to give a public decision on this question, "What ought he, who has dared this impious deed, to suffer?" By chance Menelaus, having returned from his wanderings, sent in Helen indeed by night, but himself came by day, and being entreated by Orestes to aid him, he rather feared Tyndarus the accuser: but when the speeches came to be spoken among the populace, the multitude were stirred up to kill Orestes. * * * * But Pylades, his friend, accompanying him, counseled him first to take revenge on Menelaus by killing Helen. As they were going on this project, they were disappointed of their hope by the Gods snatching away Helen from them. But Electra delivered up Hermione, when she made her appearance, into their hands, and they were about to kill her. When Menelaus came, and saw himself bereft by them at once of his wife and child, he endeavored to storm the palace; but they, anticipating his purpose, threatened to set it on fire. Apollo, however, having appeared, said that he had conducted Helen to the Gods, and commanded Orestes to take

Hermione to wife, and Electra to dwell with Pylades, and, after that he was purified of the murder, to reign over Argos.

The scene of the piece is laid at Argos; But the chorus consists of Argive women, intimate associates of Electra, who also come on inquiring about the calamity of Orestes. The play has a catastrophe rather suited to comedy. The opening scene of the play is thus arranged. Orestes is discovered before the palace of Agamemnon, fatigued, and, on account of his madness, lying on a couch on which Electra is sitting by him at his feet. A difficulty has been started, why does not she sit at his head? for thus would she seem to watch more tenderly over her brother, if she sat nearer him. The poet, it is answered, seems to have made this arrangement on account of the Chorus; for Orestes, who had but just then and with difficulty gotten to sleep, would have been awakened, if the women that constituted the Chorus had stood nearer to him. But this we may infer from what Electra says to the Chorus, "Σιγα, σιγα, λεπτον ιχνος αρβυληις." It is probable then that the above is the reason of this arrangement.

The play is among the most celebrated on the stage, but infamous in its morals; for, with the exception of Pylades, all the characters are bad persons.

ORESTES.

ELECTRA.

There is no word so dreadful to relate, nor suffering, nor heaven-inflicted calamity, the burden of which human nature may not be compelled to bear. For Tantalus, the blest, (and I am not reproaching his fortune, *when I say this,*) the son of Jupiter, as they report, trembling at the rock which impends over his head, hangs in the air, and suffers this punishment, as they say indeed, because, although being a man, yet having the honor of a table in common with the Gods upon equal terms, he possessed an ungovernable tongue, a most disgraceful malady. He begat Pelops, and from him sprung Atreus, for whom the Goddess having carded the wool[1] spun the thread of contention, *and doomed him* to make war on Thyestes his relation; (why must I commemorate things unspeakable?) But Atreus then[2] killed his children— and feasted him. But from Atreus, for I pass over in silence the misfortunes which intervened, sprung Agamemnon, the illustrious, (if he was indeed illustrious,) and Menelaus; their mother Aërope of Crete. But Menelaus indeed marries Helen, the hated of the Gods, but King Agamemnon *obtained* Clytæmnestra's bed, memorable throughout the Grecians: from whom we virgins were born, three from one mother; Chrysothemis, and Iphigenia, and myself Electra; and Orestes the male part of the family, from a most unholy mother, who slew her husband, having covered him around with an inextricable robe; the reason however it is not decorous in a virgin to tell; I leave this undeclared for men to consider as they will. But why indeed must I accuse the injustice of Phœbus? Yet persuaded he Orestes to kill that mother that brought him forth, a deed which gained not a good report from all men. But nevertheless he did slay her, as he would not be disobedient to the God. I also took a share in the murder, but such as a woman ought to take. As did Pylades also who perpetrated this deed with us. From that time wasting away, the wretched Orestes is afflicted with a grievous malady, but falling on his couch there lies, but his mother's blood whirls him to frenzy (for I dread to mention those Goddesses, the Eumenides, who persecute him with terror). Moreover this is the sixth day since his slaughtered mother was purified by fire as to her body. During which he has neither taken any food down his throat, he has not bathed his limbs, but covered beneath his cloak, when indeed his body is lightened of its disease, on coming to his right mind he weeps, but at another time starts suddenly from his couch, as a colt from his yoke. But it has been decreed by this city of Argos, that no one shall receive us who have slain a mother under their roof, nor at their fire, and that none shall speak to us; but this is the appointed day, in the which the city of the Argives will pronounce their vote, whether it is fitting that we should die being stoned with stones, or having whet the sword, should plunge it into our necks. But I yet have some hope that we may not die, for Menelaus has arrived at this country from Troy, and filling the Nauplian harbor with his oars is mooring his fleet off the shore, having been lost in wanderings from Troy a long time: but the much-afflicted Helen has he sent before to our palace, having taken advantage of the night, lest any of those, whose children died under Ilium, when they saw her coming, by day, might go so far as to stone her; but she is within bewailing her sister, and the calamity of her family. She has however some consolation in her woes, for the virgin Hermione, whom Menelaus bringing from Sparta, left at our palace, when he sailed to Troy, and gave as a charge to my mother to bring up, in her she rejoices, and forgets her miseries. But I am looking at each avenue when I shall see Menelaus present, since, for the rest, we ride on slender power,[3] if we receive not some succor from him; the house of the unfortunate is an embarrassed state of affairs.

ELECTRA. HELEN.

HEL. O daughter of Clytæmnestra and Agamemnon, O Electra, thou that hast remained a virgin a long time. How are ye, O wretched woman, both you, and your brother, the wretched Orestes (he was the murderer of his mother)? For by thy converse I am not polluted, transferring, as I do, the blame to Phœbus. And yet I groan the death of Clytæmnestra, whom, after that I sailed to Troy, (how did I sail, urged by the maddening fate of the Gods!) I saw not, but of her bereft I lament my fortune.

ELEC. Helen, why should I inform thee of things thou seest thyself here present, the race of Agamemnon in calamities. I indeed sleepless sit companion to the wretched corse, (for he is a corse, in that he breathes so little,) but at his fortune I murmur not. But thou a happy woman, and thy husband a happy man, have come to us, who fare most wretchedly.

HEL. But what length of time has he been lying on his couch?

ELEC. Ever since he shed his parent's blood.

HEL. Oh wretched, and his mother too, that thus she perished!

ELEC. These things are thus, so that he is unable to speak for misery.

HEL. By the Gods wilt thou oblige me in a thing, O virgin?

ELEC. As far as I am permitted by the little leisure I have from watching by my brother.

HEL. Wilt thou go to the tomb of my sister?

ELEC. My mother's tomb dost thou desire? wherefore?

HEL. Bearing the first offerings of my hair, and my libations.

ELEC. But is it not lawful for thee to go to the tomb of thy friends?

HEL. No, for I am ashamed to show myself among the Argives.

ELEC. Late art thou discreet, then formerly leaving thine home disgracefully.

HEL. True hast thou spoken, but thou speakest not pleasantly to me.

ELEC. But what shame possesses thee among the Mycenæans?

HEL. I fear the fathers of those who are dead under Ilium.

ELEC. For this is a dreadful thing; and at Argos thou art declaimed against by every one's mouth.

HEL. Do thou then grant me this favor, and free me from this fear.

ELEC. I can not look upon the tomb of my mother.

HEL. And yet it is disgraceful for servants to bear these.

ELEC. But why not send thy daughter Hermione?

HEL. It is not well for virgins to go among the crowd.

ELEC. And yet she might repay the dead the care of her education.

HEL. Right hast thou spoken, and I obey thee, O virgin, and I will send my daughter, for thou sayest well. Come forth, my child Hermione, before the house, and take these libations in thine hand, and my hair, and, going to the tomb of Clytæmnestra, leave there this mixture of milk and honey, and the froth of wine, and standing on the summit of the mound, say thus: "Helen, thy sister, presents thee with these libations, in fear herself to approach thy tomb, and afraid of the populace of Argos:" and bid her hold kind intentions toward me, and thyself, and my husband, and toward these two miserable persons whom the God has destroyed. But promise all the offerings to the manes, whatever it is fitting that I should perform for a sister. Go, my child, hasten, and when thou hast offered the libations at the tomb, remember to return back as speedily as possible.

ELEC. [alone] O Nature, what a great evil art thou among men, and the safeguard of those who possess thee, with virtue! For see, how she has shorn off the extremities of her hair, in order to preserve her beauty; but she is the same woman she always was. May the Gods detest thee, for that thou hast destroyed me, and this man, and the whole state of Greece: oh wretch that I am! But my dear friends that accompany me in my lamentations are again present; perhaps they will disturb the sleeper from his slumber, and will melt my eyes in tears when I behold my brother raving.

ELECTRA, CHORUS.

ELEC. O most dear woman, proceed with a gentle foot, make no noise, let there be heard no sound. For your friendliness is very kind, but to awake him will be a calamity to me. Hush, hush—gently advance the tread of thy sandal, make no noise, let there be heard no sound. Move onward from that place—onward from before the couch.

CHOR. Behold, I obey.

ELEC. St! st! Speak to me, my friend, as the breathing of the soft reed pipe.

CHOR. See, I utter a voice low as an under note.

ELEC. Ay, thus come hither, come hither, approach quietly—go quietly: tell me, for what purpose, I pray, are ye come? For he has fallen on his couch, and been sleeping some time.

CHOR. How is he? Give us an account of him, my friend.

ELEC. What fortune can I say of him? and what his calamities? still indeed he breathes, but sighs at short intervals.

CHOR. What sayest thou? Oh, the unhappy man!

ELEC. You will kill him if you move his eyelids, now that he is taking the sweetest enjoyment of sleep.

CHOR. Unfortunate on account of these most angry deeds from heaven! oh! wretched on account of thy sufferings!

ELEC. Alas! alas! Apollo himself unjust, then spoke unjust things, when at the tripod of Themis he commanded the unhallowed, inauspicious murder of my mother.

CHOR. Dost thou see? he moves his body in the robes that cover him.

ELEC. You by your cries, O wretch, have disturbed him from his sleep.

CHOR. I indeed think he is sleeping yet.

ELEC. Will you not depart from us? will you not bend your footsteps back from the house, ceasing this noise?

CHOR. He sleeps.

ELEC. Thou sayest well.

CHOR. Venerable, venerable Night, thou that dispensest sleep to languid mortals, come from Erebus; come, come, borne on thy wings to the house of Agamemnon; for by our griefs and by our sufferings we are quite undone, undone.

ELEC. Ye were making a noise.

CHOR. No. (Note [A].)

ELEC. Silently, silently repressing the high notes of your voice, apart from his couch, you will enable him to have the tranquil enjoyment of sleep.

CHOR. Tell us; what end to his miseries awaits him?

ELEC. Death, death; what else can? for he has no appetite for food.

CHOR. Death then is manifestly before him.

ELEC. Phœbus offered us as victims, when he commanded[4] the dreadful, abhorred murder of our mother, that slew our father.

CHOR. With justice indeed, but not well.

ELEC. Thou hast died, thou hast died, O mother, O thou that didst bring me forth, but hast killed the father, and the children of thy blood. We perish, we perish, even as two corses. For thou art among the dead, and the greatest part of my life is passed in groans, and wailings, and nightly tears; marriageless, childless, behold, how like a miserable wretch do I drag out my existence forever!

CHOR. O virgin Electra, approach near, and look that thy brother has not died unobserved by thee; for by this excessive quiet he doth not please me.

ORESTES, ELECTRA, CHORUS.

ORES. O precious balm of sleep, thou that relievest my malady, how pleasant didst thou come to me in the time of need! O divine oblivion of my sufferings, how wise thou art, and the goddess to be supplicated by all in distress!—whence, in heaven's name, came I hither? and how brought? for I remember not things past, bereaved, as I am, of my senses.

ELEC. My dearest brother, how didst thou delight me when thou didst fall asleep! wilt thou I touch thee, and raise thy body up?

ORES. Raise me then, raise me, and wipe the clotted foam from off my wretched mouth, and from my eyes.

ELEC. Behold, the task is sweet, and I refuse not to administer to a brother's limbs with a sister's hand.

ORES. Lay thy side by my side, and remove the squalid hair from my face, for I see but imperfectly with my eyes.

ELEC. O wretched head, sordid with ringlets, how art thou disordered from long want of the bath!

ORES. Lay me on the couch again; when my fit of madness gives me a respite, I am feeble and weak in my limbs.

ELEC. Behold, the couch is pleasant to the sick man, an irksome thing to keep, but still a necessary one.

ORES. Again raise me upright—turn my body.

CHOR. Sick persons are hard to be pleased from their feebleness.

ELEC. Wilt thou set thy feet on the ground, putting forward thy long-discontinued[5] step? In all things change is sweet.

ORES. Yes, by all means; for this has a semblance of health, but the semblance is good, though it be distant from the truth.

ELEC. Hear now therefore, O my brother, while yet the Furies suffer thee to have thy right faculties.

ORES. Wilt thou tell any news? and if good indeed, thou art conferring pleasure; but if it pertain at all to mischief—I have enough distress.

ELEC. Menelaus has arrived, the brother of thy father, but his ships are moored in the Nauplian bay.

ORES. How sayest? Is he come, a light in mine and thy sufferings, a man of kindred blood, and that hath received benefits from our father?

ELEC. He is come; take this a sure proof of my words, bringing with him Helen from the walls of Troy.

ORES. Had he been saved alone, he had been more blest. But if he brings his wife, he has arrived with a mighty evil.

ELEC. Tyndarus begat an offspring of daughters, a conspicuous mark for blame, and infamous throughout Greece.

ORES. Do thou then be unlike the bad, for it is in thy power. And not only say, but also hold these sentiments.

ELEC. Alas! my brother, thine eye rolls wildly; quick art thou changed to madness, so late in thy senses.

ORES. O mother, I implore thee, urge not on me those Furies gazing blood, horrid with snakes, for these, these are leaping around me.

ELEC. Remain, O wretched man, calmly on thy couch, for thou seest none of those things, which thou fanciest thou seest plainly.

ORES. O Phœbus, these dire Goddesses in the shape of dogs will kill me, these gorgon-visaged ministers of hell.

ELEC. I will not let thee go, but, putting my arm around thee, will stop thy starting into those unfortunate convulsions.

ORES. Loose me. Thou art one of my Furies, and seizest me by the middle, that thou mayest hurl me into Tartarus.

ELEC. Oh! wretched me! what assistance can I obtain, since we have on us the vengeful wrath of heaven!

ORES. Give me my bow of horn, the gift of Phœbus, with which Apollo said I should repel the Fiends, if they appalled me by their maddened raging.

ELEC. Shall any God be wounded by mortal hand? (Note [B].)

ORES. *Yes. She shall*, if she will not depart from my sight... Hear ye not—see ye not the winged shafts impelled from the distant-wounding bow? Ha! ha! Why tarry ye yet? Skim the high air with your wings, and impeach the oracles of Phœbus.—Ah! why am I thus disquieted, heaving my panting breath from my lungs? Whither, whither have I wandered from my couch? For from the waves again I see a calm.—Sister, why weepest, hiding thine eyes beneath thy vests, I am ashamed to have thee a partner in my sufferings, and to give a virgin trouble through my malady. Pine not away on account of my miseries: for thou indeed didst assent to this, but the shedding of my mother's blood was accomplished by me: but I blame Apollo, who, after having instigated me to a most unholy act, with words indeed consoled me, but not with deeds. But I think that my father, had I, beholding him, asked him if it were right for me to slay my mother, would have put forth many supplications, beseeching me by this beard not to impel my sword to the slaughter of her who bore me, if neither he thereby could be restored to life, and I thus wretched must go through such miseries. And now then unveil thyself, my sister, and cease from tears, even though we be very miserable: but when thou seest me desponding, do thou restrain my distraction, and that which preys upon my mind, and console me; but when thou groanest, it becomes my duty to come to thee, and suggest words of comfort. For these are the good offices friends ought to render each other. But go thou into the house, O unfortunate sister, and, stretched at full length, compose thy sleepless eyelids to sleep, and take refreshment, and pour the bath upon thy fair skin. For if thou forsakest me, or gettest any illness by continually sitting by me, we perish; for thee I have my only succor, by the rest, as thou seest, abandoned.

ELEC. This can not be: with thee will I choose to die, with thee to live; for it is the same: for if then shouldst die, what can I do, a woman? how shall I be preserved, alone and destitute? without a brother, without a father, without a friend: but if it seemeth good to thee, these things it is my duty to do: but recline thy body on the bed, and do not to such a degree conceive to be real whatever frightens and startles thee from the couch, but keep quiet on the bed strewn for thee. For though thou be not ill, but only seem to be ill, still this even is an evil and a distress to mortals. (Note [C].)

CHORUS. Alas! alas! O swift-winged, raving[6] Goddesses, who keep up the dance, not that of Bacchus, with tears and groans. You, dark Eumenides, you, that fly through the wide extended air, executing vengeance, executing slaughter, you do I supplicate, I supplicate: suffer the offspring of Agamemnon to forget his furious madness; alas! for his sufferings. What were they that eagerly grasping at, thou unhappy perishest, having received from the tripod the oracle which Phœbus spake, on that pavement, where are said to be the recesses in the midst of the globe! O Jupiter, what pity is there? what is this contention of slaughter that comes persecuting thee wretched, to whom some evil genius casts tear upon tear, transporting to thy house the blood of thy mother which drives thee frenzied! Thus I bewail, I bewail. Great prosperity is not lasting among mortals; but, as the sail of the swift bark, some deity having shaken him, hath sunk him in the voracious and destructive waves of tremendous evils, as in the waves of the ocean. For what other[6a] family ought I to reverence yet before that sprung from divine nuptials, sprung from Tantalus?—But lo! the king! the prince Menelaus, is coming! but he is very easily discernible from the elegance of his person, as king of the house of the Tantalidæ.

O thou that didst direct the army of a thousand vessels to Asia's land, hail! but thou comest hither with good fortune, having obtained the object of thy wishes from the Gods.

MENELAUS, ORESTES, CHORUS.

MEN. O palace, in some respect indeed I behold thee with pleasure, coming from Troy, but in other respect I groan when I see thee. For never yet saw I any other house more completely encircled round with lamentable woes. For I was made acquainted with the misfortune that befell Agamemnon, [and his death, by what death he perished at the hands of his wife,][6b] when I was landing my ships at Malea; but from the waves the prophet of the mariners declared unto me, the foreboding Glaucus the son of Nereus, an unerring God, who told me thus in evident form standing by me. "Menelaus, thy brother lieth dead, having fallen in his last bath, which his wife prepared." But he filled both me and my sailors with many tears; but when I come to the Nauplian shore, my wife having already landed there, expecting to clasp in my friendly embraces Orestes the son of Agamemnon, and his mother, as being in prosperity, I heard from some fisherman[7] the unhallowed murder of the daughter of Tyndarus. And now tell me, maidens, where is the son of Agamemnon, who dared these terrible deeds of evil? for he was an infant in

Clytæmnestra's arms at that time when I left the palace on my way to Troy, so that I should not know him, were I to see him.

ORES. I, Menelaus, am Orestes, whom thou seekest, I of my own accord will declare my evils. But first I touch thy knees in supplication, putting up prayers from my mouth, not using the sacred branch:[8] save me. But thou art come in the very season of my sufferings.

MEN. O ye Gods, what do I behold! whom of the dead do I see!

ORES. Ay! well thou sayest the dead; for in my state of suffering I live not; but see the light.

MEN. Thou wretched man, how disordered thou art in thy squalid hair!

ORES. Not the appearance, but the deeds torment me.

MEN. But thou glarest dreadfully with thy shriveled eyeballs.

ORES. My body is vanished, but my name has not left me.

MEN. Alas, thy uncomeliness of form which has appeared to me beyond conception!

ORES. I am he, the murderer of my wretched mother.

MEN. I have heard; but spare a little the recital of thy woes.

ORES. I spare it; but in woes the deity is rich to me.

MEN. What dost thou suffer? What malady destroys thee?

ORES. The conviction that I am conscious of having perpetrated dreadful deeds.

MEN. How sayest thou? Plainness, and not obscurity, is wisdom.

ORES. Sorrow is chiefly what destroys me,—

MEN. She is a dreadful goddess, but sorrow admits of cure.

ORES. And fits of madness in revenge for my mother's blood.

MEN. But when didst first have the raging? what day was it then?

ORES. That day in which I heaped the tomb on my mother.

MEN. What? in the house, or sitting at the pyre?

ORES. As I was guarding by night lest any one should bear off her bones.[9]

MEN. Was any one else present, who supported thy body?

ORES. Pylades, who perpetrated with me the vengeance and death of my mother.

MEN. But by what visions art thou thus afflicted?

ORES. I appear to behold three virgins like the night.

MEN. I know whom thou meanest, but am unwilling to name them.

ORES. Yes: for they are awful; but forbear from speaking such high polished words.[10]

MEN. Do these drive thee to distraction on account of this kindred murder?

ORES. Alas me for the persecutions, with which wretched I am driven!

MEN. It is not strange that those who do strange deeds should suffer them.

ORES. But we have whereto we may transfer the criminality[11] of the mischance.

MEN. Say not the death *of thy father;* for this is not wise.

ORES. Phœbus who commanded us to perpetrate the slaying of our mother.

MEN. Being more ignorant than to know equity, and justice.

ORES. We are servants of the Gods, whatever those Gods be.

MEN. And then does not Apollo assist thee in thy miseries?

ORES. He is always about to do it, but such are the Gods by nature.

MEN. But how long a time has thy mother's breath gone from her?

ORES. This is the sixth day since; the funeral pyre is yet warm.

MEN. How quickly have the Goddesses come to demand of thee thy mother's blood!

ORES. I am not wise, but a true friend to my friends.

MEN. But what then doth the revenge of thy father profit thee?

ORES. Nothing yet; but I consider what is in prospect in the same light as a thing not done.

MEN. But regarding the city how standest thou, having done these things?

ORES. We are hated to that degree, that no one speaks to us.

MEN. Nor hast thou washed thy blood from thy hands according to the laws?

ORES. *How can I?* for I am shut out from the houses, whithersoever I go.

MEN. Who of the citizens thus contend to drive thee from the land?

ORES. Œax,[12] imputing to my father the hatred which arose on account of Troy.

MEN. I understand. The death of Palamede takes its vengeance on thee.

ORES. In which at least I had no share—but I perish by the three.

MEN. But who else? Is it perchance one of the friends of Ægisthus?

ORES. They persecute me, whom now the city obeys.

MEN. But does the city suffer thee to wield Agamemnon's sceptre?

ORES. How should they? who no longer suffer us to live.

MEN. Doing what, which thou canst tell me as a clear fact?

ORES. This very day sentence will be passed upon us.

MEN. To be exiled from this city? or to die? or not to die?

ORES. To die, by being stoned with stones by the citizens.

MEN. And dost thou not fly then, escaping beyond the boundaries of the country?

ORES. *How can we?* for we are surrounded on every side by brazen arms.

MEN. By private enemies, or by the hand of Argos?

ORES. By all the citizens, that I may die—the word is brief.

MEN. O unhappy man! thou art come to the extreme of misfortune.

ORES. On thee my hope builds her escape from evils, but, thyself happy, coming among the distressed, impart thy good fortune to thy friends, and be not the only man to retain a benefit thou hast received, but undertake also services in thy turn, paying their father's kindness to those to whom thou oughtest. For those friends have the name, not the reality, who are not friends in adversity.

CHOR. And see the Spartan Tyndarus is toiling hither with his aged foot, in a black vest, and shorn, his locks cut off in mourning for his daughter.

ORES. I am undone, O Menelaus! Lo! Tyndarus is coming toward us, to come before whose presence, most of all men's, shame covereth me, on account of what has been done. For he used to nurture me when I was little, and satiated me with many kisses, dandling in his arms Agamemnon's boy, and Leda with him, honoring me no less than the twin-born of Jove. For which, O my wretched heart and soul, I have given no good return: what dark veil can I take for my countenance? what cloud can I place before me, that I may avoid the glances of the old man's eyes?

TYNDARUS, MENELAUS, ORESTES, CHORUS.

TYND. Where, where can I see my daughter's husband Menelaus? For as I was pouring my libations on the tomb of Clytæmnestra, I heard that he was come to Nauplia with his wife, safe through a length of years. Conduct me, for I long to stand by his hand and salute him, seeing my friend after a long lapse of time.

MEN. O hail! old man, who sharest thy bed with Jove.

TYND. O hail! thou also, Menelaus my dear relation,—ah! what an evil is it not to know the future! This dragon here, the murderer of his mother, glares before the house his pestilential gleams—the object of my detestation—Menelaus, dost thou speak to this unholy wretch?

MEN. Why not? he is the son of a father who was dear to me.

TYND. What! was he sprung from him, being such as he is?

MEN. He was; but, though he be unfortunate, he should be respected.

TYND. Having been a long time with barbarians, thou art thyself turned barbarian.

MEN. Nay! it is the Grecian fashion always to honor one of kindred blood.

TYND. *Yes*, and also not to wish to be above the laws.

MEN. Every thing proceeding from necessity is considered as subservient to her[13] among the wise.

TYND. Do thou then keep to this, but I'll have none of it.

MEN. *No*, for anger joined with thine age, is not wisdom.

TYND. With this man what controversy can there be regarding wisdom? If what things are virtuous, and what are not virtuous, are plain to all, what man was ever more unwise that this man? who did not indeed consider justice, nor applied to the common existing law of the Grecians. For after that Agamemnon breathed forth his last, struck by my daughter on the head, a most foul deed (for never will I approve of this), it behooved him indeed to lay against her a sacred charge of bloodshed, following up the accusation, and to cast his mother from out of the house; and he would have taken the wise side in the calamity, and would have kept to law, and would have been pious. But now has he come to the same fate with his mother. For with justice thinking her wicked, himself has become more wicked in slaying his mother.

But thus much, Menelaus, will I ask thee; If the wife that shared his bed were to kill him, and his son again kills his mother in return, and he that is born of him shall expiate the murder with murder, whither then will the extremes of these evils proceed? Well did our fathers of old lay down these things; they suffered not him to come into the sight of their eyes, not to their converse, who was under an attainder[14] of blood; but they made him atone by banishment; they suffered however none to kill him in return. For always were one about to be attainted of murder, taking the pollution last into his hands. But I hate indeed impious women, but first among them my daughter, who slew her husband. But never will I approve of Helen thy wife, nor would I speak to her, neither do I commend[15] thee for going to the plain of Troy on account of a perfidious woman. But I will defend the law, as far at least as I am able, putting a stop to this brutish and murderous practice, which is ever destructive both of the country and the state.—For what feelings of humanity hadst thou, thou wretched man, when she bared her breast in supplication, thy mother? I indeed, though I witnessed not that scene of misery, melt in my aged eyes with tears through wretchedness. One thing however goes to the scale of my arguments; thou art both hated by the Gods, and sufferest vengeance of thy mother, wandering about with madness and terrors; why must I hear by the testimony of others, what it is in my power to see? That thou mayest know then *once for all*, Menelaus, do not things contrary to the Gods, through thy wishes to assist this man. But suffer him to be slain by the citizens with stones, or set not thy foot on Spartan ground. But my daughter in dying met with justice, but it was not fitting that she should die by him.[16] In other respects indeed have I been a happy man, except in my daughters, but in this I am not happy.

CHOR. He is enviable, who is fortunate in his children, and has not on him some notorious calamities.

ORES. O old man, I tremble to speak to thee, wherein I am about to grieve thee and thy mind. But I am unholy in that I slew my mother; but holy at least in another point of view, having avenged my father. Let then thine age, which hinders me through fear from speaking, be removed out of the way of my words, and I will go on in a direct path; but now do I fear thy gray hairs. What could I do? for oppose the facts, two against two. My father indeed begat me, but thy daughter brought me forth, a field receiving the seed from another; but without a father there never could be a child. I reasoned therefore with myself, that I should assist the prime author of my birth rather than the aliment which under him produced me. But thy daughter (I am ashamed to call her mother), in secret and unchaste nuptials, had approached the bed of another man; of myself, if I speak ill of her, shall I be speaking, but yet will I tell it. Ægisthus was her secret husband in her palace. Him I slew, and after him I sacrificed my mother, doing indeed unholy things, but avenging my father. But as touching those things for which thou threatenest that I must be stoned, hear, how I shall assist all Greece. For if the women shall arrive at such a pitch of boldness as to murder the men, making good their escape with regard to their children, seeking to captivate their pity by their breasts, it would be as nothing with them to slay their husbands, having any pretext that might chance; but I having done dreadful things (as thou sayest), have put a stop to this law, but hating my mother deservedly I slew her, who betrayed her husband absent from home in arms, the generalissimo of the whole land of Greece, and kept not her bed undefiled. But when she perceived that she had done amiss, she inflicted not vengeance on herself, but, that she might not suffer vengeance from her husband, punished and slew my father. By the Gods, (in no good cause have I named the Gods, pleading against a charge of murder,) had I by my silence praised my mother's actions, what then would the deceased have done to me? To my mother indeed the Furies are present as allies, but would they not be present to him, who has received the greater injury? Would he not, detesting me, have haunted me with the Furies? Thou then, O old man, by begetting a bad daughter, hast destroyed me; for through her boldness deprived of my father, I became a matricide. Dost see? Telemachus slew not the wife of Ulysses, for she married not a husband on a husband, but her marriage-bed remains unpolluted in the palace. Dost see? Apollo, who, dwelling in his habitation in the midst of the earth, gives the most clear oracles to mortals, by whom we are entirely guided, whatever he may say, on him relying slew I my mother. 'Twas he who erred, not I: what could I do? Is not the God sufficient for me, who transfer *the deed* to him, to do away with the pollution? Whither then can any fly for succor, unless he that commanded me shall deliver me from death? But say not these things have been done "not well;" but *say* "not fortunately" for us who did them. But to whatsoever men their marriages are well established, there is a happy life, but to those to whom they fall not out well, with regard to their affairs both at home and abroad they are unfortunate.

CHOR. Women were born always to be in the way of what may happen to men, to the making of things unfortunate.

TYND. Since thou art bold, and yieldest not to my speech, but thus answerest me so as to grieve my mind, thou wilt rather inflame me to urge thy death. But this I shall consider a handsome addition to those labors for which I came, *namely*, to deck my daughter's tomb. For going to the multitude of the Argives assembled, I will rouse the state willing and not unwilling, to pass the sentence[16a] of being stoned on thee and on thy sister; but she is worthy of death rather than thee, who irritated thee against her mother, always pealing in thine ear words to increase thy hatred, relating dreams she had of Agamemnon, and this also, that the infernal Gods detested the bed of Ægisthus; for even here *on earth* it were hard *to be endured*; until she set the house in flames with fire more strong than Vulcan's.—Menelaus, but to thee I speak this, and will moreover perform it. If thou regard my hate, and my alliance, ward not off death from this man in opposition to the Gods; but suffer him to be slain by the citizens with stones, or set not thy foot on Spartan ground. Thus much having heard, depart, nor choose the impious for thy friends, passing over the pious.—But O attendants, conduct us from this house.

ORES. Depart, that the remainder of my speech may reach this man uninterrupted by the clamors of thy age: Menelaus, whither dost thou roam in thought, entering on a double path of double care?

MEN. Suffer me; having some thoughts with myself, I am perplexed to which side of fortune to turn me.

ORES. Do not make up thy opinion, but having first heard my words, then deliberate.

MEN. Say on; for thou hast spoken rightly; but there are seasons where silence may be better than talking, and there are seasons where talking may be better than silence.

ORES. I will speak then forthwith: Long speeches have the preference before short ones, and are more plain to hear. Give thou to me nothing of what thou hast, O Menelaus, but what thou hast received from my father, return; I mean not riches—yet riches, which are the most dear of what I possess, if thou wilt preserve my life. Say I am unjust, I ought to receive from thee, instead of this evil, something contrary to what justice demands; for Agamemnon my father having collected Greece in arms, in a way justice did not demand, went to Troy, not having erred himself, but in order to set right the error, and injustice of thy wife. This one thing indeed thou oughtest to give me for one thing, but he, as friends should for friends, of a truth exposed his person for thee toiling at the shield, that thou mightest receive back thy wife. Repay me then this kindness for that which thou receivedst there, toiling for one day in standing as my succor, not completing ten years. But the sacrifice of my sister, which Aulis received, this I suffer thee to have; do not kill Hermione, *I ask it not.* For, I being in the state in which I now am, thou must of necessity have the advantage, and I must suffer it to be so. But grant my life to my wretched father, and my sister's, who has been a virgin a long time. For dying I shall leave my father's house destitute. Thou wilt say "impossible:" this is the very thing *I have been urging*, it behooves friends to help their friends in misfortunes. But when the God gives prosperity, what need is there of friends? For the God himself sufficeth, being willing to assist. Thou appearest to all the Greeks to be fond of thy wife; (and this I say, not stealing under thee imperceptibly with flattery;) by her I implore thee; O wretched me for my woes, to what have I come? but why must I suffer thus? For in behalf of the whole house I make this supplication. O divine brother of my father, conceive that the dead man beneath the earth hears these things, and that his spirit is hovering over thee, and speaks what I speak. These things have I said, with tears, and groans, and miseries,[17] and have prayed earnestly, looking for preservation, which all, and not I only, seek.

CHOR. I too implore thee, although a woman, yet still I implore thee to succor those in need, but thou art able.

MEN. Orestes, I indeed reverence thy person, and I am willing to labor with thee in thy misfortunes. For thus it is right to endure together the misfortunes of one's relations, if the God gives the ability, even so far as to die, and to kill the adversary; but this ability again I want from the Gods. For I am come having my single spear unaided by allies, having wandered with infinite labors with small assistance of friends left me. In battle therefore we can not come off superior to Pelasgian Argos; but if we can by soft speeches, to that hope are we equal. For how can any one achieve great actions with small means? For when the rabble is in full force falling into a rage, it is equally difficult to extinguish as a fierce fire. But if one quietly yields to it as it is spreading, and gives in to it, watching well his opportunity, perhaps it may spend its rage, but when it has remitted from its blast, you may without difficulty have it your own way, as much as you please. For there is inherent in them pity, but there is inherent also vehement passion, to one who carefully watches his opportunity a most excellent advantage. But I will go and endeavor to persuade Tyndarus, and the city, to use their great power in a becoming manner. For a ship, the main sheet stretched out to a violent degree, is wont to pitch, but stands upright again, if you slacken the main sheet. For the God hates too great vehemence, and the citizens hate it; but I must (I speak as I mean) save thee by wisdom, not by opposing my superiors. But I can not by force, as perchance thou thinkest, preserve thee; for it is no easy matter to erect from one single spear trophies from the evils, which are about thee. For never have we approached the land of Argos by way of supplication; but now there is necessity for the wise to become the slaves of fortune.

ORESTES, CHORUS.

ORES. O thou, a mere cipher in other things except in warring for the sake of a woman; O thou most base in avenging thy friends, dost thou fly, turning away from me? But all Agamemnon's services are gone: thou wert then without friends, O my father, in thy affliction. Alas me! I am betrayed, and there no longer are any hopes, whither turning I may escape death from the Argives. For he was the refuge of my safety. But I see this most dear of men, Pylades, coming with hasty step from the Phocians, a pleasing sight, a man faithful in adversity, more grateful to behold than the calm to the mariners.

PYLADES, ORESTES, CHORUS.

PYL. I came through the city with a quicker step than I ought, having heard of the council of state assembled, and seeing it plainly myself, against thee and thy sister, as about to kill you instantly.—What is this? how art thou? in what state, O most dear to me of my companions and kindred? for all these things art thou to me.

ORES. We are gone—briefly to show thee my calamities.

PYL. Thou wilt have ruined me too; for the things of friends are common.

ORES. Menelaus has behaved most basely toward me and my sister.

PYL. It is to be expected that the husband of a bad wife be bad.

ORES. He is come, and has done just as much for me as if he had not come.

PYL. What! is he in truth come to this land?

ORES. After a long season; but nevertheless he was very soon discovered to be too base to his friends.

PYL. And has he brought in his ship with him his most infamous wife?

ORES. Not he her, but she brought him hither.

PYL. Where is she, who, beyond any woman,[18] destroyed most of the Grecians?

ORES. In my palace, if I may indeed be allowed to call this mine.

PYL. But what words didst thou say to thy father's brother?

ORES. *I requested him* not to suffer me and my sister to be slain by the citizens.

PYL. By the Gods, what said he to this request; this I wish to know.

ORES. He declined, from motives of prudence, as bad friends act toward their friends.

PYL. Going on what ground of excuse? This having learned, I am in possession of every thing.

ORES. The father himself came, he that begat such excellent daughters.

PYL. Tyndarus you mean; perhaps enraged with thee on account of his daughter.

ORES. You are right: he paid more attention to his ties with him, than to his ties with my father.

PYL. And dared he not, being present, to take arms against thy troubles?

ORES. *No*: for he was not born a warrior, but brave among women.

PYL. Thou art then in the greatest miseries, and it is necessary for thee to die.

ORES. The citizens must pass their vote on us for the murder *we have committed.*[19]

PYL. Which vote what will it decide? tell me, for I am in fear.

ORES. Either to die or live; not many words on matters of great import.

PYL. Come fly, and quit the palace with thy sister.

ORES. Seest thou not? we are watched by guards on every side,

PYL. I saw the streets of the city lined with arms.

ORES. We are invested as to our persons, as a city by the enemy.

PYL. Now ask me also, what I suffer; for I too am undone.

ORES. By whom? This would be an evil added to my evils.

PYL. Strophius, my father, being enraged, hath driven me an exile from his house.

ORES. Bringing against thee some private charge, or one in common with the citizens?

PYL. Because I perpetrated with thee the murder of thy mother, he banished me, calling me unholy.

ORES. O thou unfortunate! it seems that thou also sufferest for my evils.

PYL. We have not Menelaus's manners—this must be borne.

ORES. Dost thou not fear lest Argos should wish to kill thee, as it does also me?

PYL. We do not belong to these to punish, but to the land of the Phocians.

ORES. The populace is a terrible thing, when they have evil leaders.

PYL. But when they have good ones, they always deliberate good things.

ORES. Be it so: we must speak on our common business.

PYL. On what affair of necessity?

ORES. Supposing I should go to the citizens, and say—

PYL. —that thou hast acted justly?

ORES. Ay, avenging my father:

PYL. I fear they might not receive thee gladly.

ORES. But shall I die then shuddering in silence!

PYL. This were cowardly.

ORES. How then can I do?

PYL. Hast thou any chance of safety, if thou remainest?

ORES. I have none.

PYL. But going, is there any hope of thy being preserved from thy miseries?

ORES. Should it chance well, there might be.

PYL. Is not this then better than remaining?

ORES. Shall I go then?

PYL. Dying thus, at least thou wilt die more honorably.

ORES. And I have a just cause.

PYL. Only pray for its appearing so.

ORES. Thou sayest well: this way I avoid the imputation of cowardice.

PYL. More than by tarrying here.

ORES. And some one perchance may pity me—

PYL. Yes; for thy nobleness of birth is a great thing.

ORES. —indignant at my father's death.

PYL. All this in prospect.

ORES. Go I must, for it is not manly to die ingloriously.

PYL. These sentiments I praise.

ORES. Shall we then tell these things to my sister?

PYL. No, by the Gods.

ORES. Why, there might be tears.

PYL. This then is a great omen.

ORES. Clearly it is better to be silent.

PYL. Thou art a gainer by delay.

ORES. This one thing only opposes me.

PYL. What new thing again is this thou sayest?

ORES. I fear lest the goddesses should stop me with their torments.

PYL. But I will take care of thee.

ORES. It is a difficult and dangerous task to touch a man thus disordered.

PYL. Not for me to touch thee.

ORES. Take care how thou art partner of my madness.

PYL. Let not this be thought of.

ORES. Wilt thou not then be timid to assist me?

PYL. No, for timidity is a great evil to friends.

ORES. Go on now, the helm of my foot.

PYL. Having a charge worthy of a friend.

ORES. And guide me to my father's tomb.

PYL. To what end is this?

ORES. That I may supplicate him to save me.

PYL. This at least is just.

ORES. But let me not see my mother's monument.

PYL. For she was an enemy. But hasten, that the decree of the Argives condemn thee not before thou goest; leaning thy side, weary with disease, on mine: since I will conduct thee through the city, little caring for the multitude, nothing ashamed; for where shall I show myself thy friend, if I assist thee not when them art in perilous condition?

ORES. This it is to have companions, not relationship alone; so that a man who is congenial in manners, though a stranger in blood, is a better friend for a man to have, than ten thousand relatives.

CHORUS.

The great happiness, and the valor high sounding throughout Greece, and by the channels of the Simois, has again withdrawn from the fortune of the Atridæ, as of old, from the ancient calamity of the house, when the strife of the golden lamb[20] arose among the descendants of Tantalus; most shocking feasts, and the slaughter of noble children; from whence murder responsive to murder fails not to attend on the two sons of Atreus. What seems good is not good, to gash the parents' skin with a fierce hand, and brandish the sword black-stained with blood in the sunbeams. But, on the other hand, to act wickedly[21] is mad impiety, and the folly of evil-minded men.

But the wretched daughter of Tyndarus in the fear of death shrieked out, "My son, thou darest impious deeds, killing thy mother; do not, attending to the gratification of thy father, kindle an everlasting disgrace."

What malady, or what tears, or what pity on earth is greater, than to imbrue one's hand in a mother's blood? What a deed, what a deed having performed, does the son of Agamemnon rave with madness, a prey to the Eumenides, marked for death, giddy with his rolling eyes! O wretched on account of his mother, when though seeing the breast bared from the robe of golden texture, he stabbed the mother in retaliation for the father's sufferings.

ELECTRA, CHORUS.

ELEC. Ye virgins, has the wretched Orestes, overcome with heaven-inflicted madness, rushed any where from this house?

CHOR. By no means; but he is gone to the Argive people, to undergo the trial proposed regarding life, by which you must either live or die.

ELEC. Alas me! what thing has he done? but who persuaded him?

CHOR. Pylades.—But this messenger seems soon about to inform us of what has passed there concerning thy brother.

MESSENGER, ELECTRA, CHORUS.

MESS. O wretched hapless daughter of the chief Agamemnon, revered Electra, hear the unfortunate words which I am come to bring.

ELEC. Alas! alas! we are undone; this thou signifiest by thy speech. For thou comest, as it seems, a messenger of woes.

MESS. It has been carried by the vote of the Pelasgians, that thy brother and thou must die this day.

ELEC. Ah me! the expected event has come, which long since fearing, I pined away with lamentations on account of what was in prospect.—But what was the debate? What arguments among the Argives condemned us, and confirmed our sentence of death? Tell me, old man, whether by the hand raised to stone me, or by the sword must I breathe out my soul, having this calamity in common with my brother?

MESS. I chanced indeed to be entering the gates from the country, anxious to hear both what regarded thee, and what regarded Orestes; for at all times I had a favorable inclination toward thy father: and thy house fed me, poor indeed, but noble in my conduct toward friends. But I see the crowd going and sitting down on an eminence; where they say Danaus first collected the people to a common council, when he suffered punishment at the hands of Ægyptus. But seeing this concourse, I asked one of the citizens, "What new thing is stirring in Argos? Has any message from hostile powers roused the city of the Danaids?" But he said, "Seest thou not this Orestes walking near us, who is about to run in the contest of life and death?" But I see an unexpected sight, which oh that I had never seen! Pylades and thy brother walking together, the one indeed broken with sickness, but the other, like a brother, sympathizing with his friend, tending his weakened state with fostering care. But when the assembly of the Argives was full, a herald stood forth and said, "Who wishes to speak *on the question*, whether it is right that Orestes, who has killed his mother, should die, or not?" And on this Talthybius rises, who, in conjunction with thy father, laid waste the Phrygians. But he spoke words of divided import, being the constant slave of those in power; struck with admiration indeed at thy father, but not commending thy brother (speciously mixing up words of bad import), because he laid down no good laws toward his parents: but he was continually casting a smiling glance on Ægisthus's friends. For such is this kind; heralds always dance attendance on the prosperous; but that man is their friend, whoever may chance to have power in the state, and to be in office. But next to him prince Diomed harangued; he indeed was for suffering them to kill neither thee nor thy brother, but *bid them* observe piety by punishing you with banishment. But some indeed murmured their assent, that he spoke well, but others praised him not.[22] And after him rises up some man, intemperate in speech, powerful in boldness, an Argive, yet not an Argive,[23] forced upon us, relying both on the tumult, and on ignorant boldness, prompt by persuasion to involve them in some mischief. (For when a man, sweet in words, holding bad sentiments, persuades the multitude, it is a great evil to the city. But as many as always advise good things with understanding, although not at the present moment, eventually are of service to the state: but the intelligent leader ought to look to this, for the case is the same with the man who speaks words, and the man who approves them.) Who said, that they ought to kill Orestes and thee by stoning. But Tyndarus was privily making up such sort of speeches for him who wished your death to speak. But another man stood up, and spoke in opposition to him, in form indeed not made to catch the eye; but a man endued with the qualities of a man, rarely polluting the city, and the circle of the forum; one who farmed his own land,[24] which class of persons[25] alone preserve the country, but prudent, and wishing the tenor of his conduct to be in unison with his words, uncorrupted, one that had conformed to a blameless mode of living; he proposed to crown Orestes the son of Agamemnon,[25a] who was willing to avenge his father by slaying a wicked and unholy woman, who took this out of the power of men, and would no one have been the cause of arming the hand for war, nor undertaking an expedition, leaving his home, if those who are left destroy what is intrusted to their charge in the house, disgracing their husbands' beds. And to right-minded men at least he appeared to speak well:

and none spoke besides, but thy brother advanced and said, "O inhabitants of the land of Inachus, avenging you no less than my father, I slew my mother, for if the murder of men shall become licensed to women, ye no longer can escape dying, or ye must be slaves to your wives. But ye do the contrary to what ye ought to do. For now she that was false to the bed of my father is dead; but if ye do indeed slay me, the law has lost its force, and no man can escape dying, forasmuch as there will be no lack of this audacity."

But he persuaded not the people, though appearing to speak well. But that villain, who spoke among the multitude, overcomes him, he that harangued for the killing of thy brother and thee. But scarcely did the wretched Orestes persuade them that he might not die by stoning; but he promised that this day he would quit his life by self-slaughter together with thee:—but Pylades is conducting him from the council, weeping: but his friends accompany him bewailing him, pitying him; but he is coming a sad spectacle to thee, and a wretched sight. But prepare the sword, or the noose for thy neck, for thou must die, but thy nobleness of birth hath profited thee nothing, nor the Pythian Phœbus who sits on the tripod, but hath destroyed thee.

CHOR. O unhappy virgin! how art thou dumb, casting thy muffled countenance toward the ground, as though about to run into a strain of groans and lamentations!

ELEC. I begin the lament, O land of Greece, digging my white nail into my cheek, sad bleeding woe, and dashing my head, which[26] the lovely[27] goddess of the manes beneath the earth has to her share. And let the Cyclopian land[28] howl, applying the steel to their head cropped of hair over the calamity of our house. This pity, this pity, proceeds for those who are about to die, who once were the princes of Greece. For it is gone, it is gone, the entire race of the children of Pelops has perished, and the happiness which once resided in these blest abodes. Envy from heaven has now seized it, and the harsh decree of blood in the state. Alas! alas! O race of mortals that endure for a day, full of tears, full of troubles, behold how contrary to expectation fate comes. But in the long lapse of time each different man receives by turns his different sufferings.[29] But the whole race of mortals is unstable and uncertain.

Oh! could I go to that rock stretched from Olympus in its loftiness midst heaven and earth by golden chains, that mass of clay borne round with rapid revolutions, that in my plaints I might cry out to my ancient father Tantalus; who begat the progenitors of my family, who saw calamities, what time in the pursuing of steeds, Pelops in his car drawn by four horses perpetrated, as he drove, the murder of Myrtilus, *by casting him* into the sea, hurling him down to the surge of the ocean, as he guided his car on the shore of the briny sea by Geræstus foaming with its white billows. Whence the baleful curse came on my house since, by the agency of Maia's son,[30] there appeared the pernicious, pernicious prodigy of the golden-fleeced lamb, a birth which took place among the flocks of the warlike Atreus. On which both Discord drove back the winged chariot of the sun, directing it from the path of heaven leading to the west toward Aurora borne on her single horse.[31] And Jupiter drove back the course of the seven moving Pleiads another way: and from that period[32] he sends deaths in succession to deaths, and "the feast of Thyestes," so named from Thyestes. And the bed of the Cretan Ærope deceitful in a deceitful marriage has come as a finishing stroke on me and my father, to the miserable destruction of our family.

CHOR. But see, thy brother is advancing, condemned by the vote of death, and Pylades the most faithful of all, a man like a brother, supporting the enfeebled limbs of Orestes, walking by his side[33] with the foot of tender solicitude.

ELECTRA, ORESTES, PYLADES, CHORUS.

ELEC. Alas me! for I bewail thee, my brother, seeing thee before the tomb, and before the pyre of thy departed shade: alas me! again and again, how am I bereft of my senses, seeing with my eyes the very last sight of thee.

ORES. Wilt thou not in silence, ceasing from womanish groans, make up thy mind to what is decreed? These things indeed are lamentable, but yet we must bear our present fate.

ELEC. And how can I be silent? We wretched no longer are permitted to view this light of the God.

ORES. Do not thou kill me; I, the unhappy, have died enough already under the hands of the Argives; but pass over our present ills.

ELEC. O Orestes! oh wretched in thy youth, and thy fate, and thy untimely death, then oughtest thou to live, when thou art no more.

ORES. Do not by the Gods throw cowardice around me, bringing the remembrance of my woes so as to cause tears.

ELEC. We shall die; it is not possible not to groan our misfortunes; for the dear life is a cause of pity to all mortals.

ORES. This is the day appointed for us! but we must either fit the suspended noose, or whet the sword with our hand.

ELEC. Do thou then kill me, my brother; let none of the Argives kill me, putting a contumely on the offspring of Agamemnon.

ORES. I have enough of thy mother's blood, but thee I will not slay; but die by thine own hand in whatever manner thou wilt.

ELEC. These things shall be; I will not be deserted by thy sword;[34] but I wish to clasp my hands around thy neck.

ORES. Thou enjoyest a vain gratification, if this be an enjoyment, to throw thy hands around those who are hard at death's door.

ELEC. Oh thou most dear! oh thou that hast the desirable and most sweet name, and one soul with thy sister!

ORES. Thou wilt melt me; and still I wish to answer thee in the endearment of encircling arms, for why am I any longer ashamed? O bosom of my sister, O dear object of my caresses, these embraces are allowed to us miserable beings instead of children and the bridal bed.

ELEC. Alas! How can the same sword (if this request be lawful) kill us, and one tomb wrought of cedar receive us?

ORES. This would be most sweet; but thou seest how destitute we are, in respect to being able to share our sepulture.

ELEC. Did not Menelaus speak in behalf of thee, taking a decided part against thy death, the base man, the deserter of my father? [Note [G].]

ORES. He showed it not even in his countenance, but keeping his hopes on the sceptre, he was cautious how he saved his friends. But let be, he will die acting in a manner nobly, and most worthily of Agamemnon. And I indeed will show my high descent to the city, striking home to my heart with the sword; but thee, on the other hand, it behooveth to act in concert with my bold attempts. But do thou, Pylades, be the umpire of our death, and well compose the bodies of us when dead, and bury us together, bearing us to our father's tomb. And farewell—but I am going to the deed, as thou seest.

PYL. Hold. This one thing indeed first I bring in charge against thee—Dost thou think that I can wish to live when thou diest?[35]

ORES. For how does it concern thee to die with me?

PYL. Dost ask? But how does it to live without thy company?

ORES. Thou didst not slay my mother, as I did, a wretch.

PYL. With thee I did at least; I ought also to suffer these things in common with thee.

ORES. Take thyself back to thy father, do not die with me. For thou indeed hast a city (but I no longer have), and the mansion of thy father, and a great harbor of wealth. But thou art frustrated in thy marriage with this unhappy virgin, whom I betrothed to thee, revering thy friendship. Nevertheless do thou, contracting other nuptials, be a blest father, but the connection between me and thee no longer subsists, But thou, O darling name of my converse, farewell, be happy, for this is not allowed me, but it is to thee; for we, the dead, are deprived of happiness.

PYL. Surely thou art wide astray from my purposes. Nor may the fruitful plain receive my blood, nor the bright air, if ever I betraying thee, having freed myself, forsake thee; for I committed the slaughter with thee (I will not deny it), and I planned all things, for which now thou sufferest vengeance. Die then I must with thee and her together, for her, whose marriage I have courted, I consider as my wife; for what good excuse ever shall I give, going to the Delphian land to the citadel of the Phocians, I, who was present with you, your friend, before indeed you were unfortunate, but now, when you are unfortunate, am no longer thy friend? It is not possible —but these things are my care also. But since we are about to die, let us come to a common conference, how Menelaus may be involved in our calamity.

ORES. O thou dearest man: for would I see this and die.

PYL. Be persuaded then, but defer the slaughtering sword.

ORES. I will defer, if any how I can avenge myself on my enemy.

PYL. Be silent then, for I have but small confidence in women.

ORES. Do not at all fear these, for they are friends that are present.

PYL. Let us kill Helen, which will cause great grief to Menelaus.

ORES. How? for the will is here, if it can be done with glory.

PYL. Stabbing her; but she is lurking in thy house.

ORES. Yes indeed, and is putting her seal on all my effects.

PYL. But she shall seal no more, having Pluto for her bridegroom.

ORES. And how can this be? for she has a train of barbarian attendants.

PYL. Whom? for I would be afraid of no Phrygian.

ORES. Such men as should preside over mirrors and scents.

PYL. For has she brought hither her Trojan fineries?

ORES. *Oh yes!* so that Greece is but a cottage for her.

PYL. A race of slaves is a mere nothing against a race that will not be slaves.

ORES. In good truth, this if I could achieve, I shrink not from two deaths.

PYL. But neither do I indeed, if I could revenge thee at least.

ORES. Disclose thy purpose, and go through it as thou sayest.

PYL. We will enter then the house, as men about to die.

ORES. Thus far I comprehend, but the rest I do not comprehend.

PYL. We will make our lamentation to her of the things we suffer.

ORES. So that she shall weep, though joyed within her heart.

PYL. And the same things will be for us to do afterward, which she does then.

ORES. Then how shall we finish the contest?

PYL. We will wear our swords concealed beneath our robes.

ORES. But what slaughter can there be before her attendants?

PYL. We will bolt them out, scattered in different parts of the house.

ORES. And him that is not silent we must kill.

PYL. Then the circumstances of the moment will point out what steps to take.

ORES. To kill Helen, I understand the sign.

PYL. Thou seest: but hear on what honorable principles I meditate it. For, if we draw our sword on a more modest woman, the murder will blot our names with infamy. But in the present instance, she shall suffer vengeance for the whole of Greece, whose fathers she slew, and made the brides bereaved of their spouses; there shall be a shout, and they will kindle up fire to the Gods, praying for many blessings to fall to thee and me, inasmuch as we shed the blood of a wicked woman. But thou shalt not be called the matricide, when thou hast slain her, but dropping this name thou shalt arrive at better things, being styled the slayer of the havoc-dealing Helen. It never, never were right that Menelaus should be prosperous, and that thy father, and thou, and thy sister should die, and thy mother; (this I forbear, for it is not decorous to mention;) and that he should seize thy house, having recovered his bride by the means of Agamemnon's valor. For may I live no longer, if I draw not my black sword upon her. But if then we do not compass the murder of Helen, having fired the palace we will die, for we shall have glory, succeeding in one of these two things, nobly dying, or nobly rescued.

CHOR. The daughter of Tyndarus is an object of detestation to all women, being one that has given rise to scandal against the sex.

ORES. Alas! There is no better thing than a real friend, not riches, not kingdoms; but the popular applause becomes a thing of no account to receive in exchange for a generous friend. For thou contrivedst the destruction that befell Ægisthus, and wast close to me in my dangers. But now again thou givest me to revenge me on mine enemies, and art not out of the way—but I will leave off praising thee, since there is some burden even in this "to be praised to excess." But I altogether in a state of death, wish to do something to my foes and die, that I may in turn destroy those who betrayed me, and those may groan who also made me unhappy. I am the son of Agamemnon, who ruled over Greece by general consent; no tyrant, but yet he had the power as it were of a God, whom I will not disgrace, suffering a slavish death, but breathe out my soul in freedom, but on Menelaus will I revenge me. For if we could gain this one thing, we should be prosperous, if from any chance safety should come unhoped for on the slayers *then*, not the slain: this I pray for. For what I wish is sweet to delight the mind without fear of cost, though with but fleeting words uttered through the mouth.

ELEC. I, O brother, think that this very thing brings safety to thee, and thy friend, and in the third place to me.

ORES. Thou meanest the providence of the Gods: but where is this? for I know that there is understanding in thy mind.

ELEC. Hear me then, and thou too give thy attention.

ORES. Speak, since the existing prospect of good affords some pleasure.

ELEC. Art thou acquainted with the daughter of Helen? Thou knowest her of whom I ask.

ORES. I know her, Hermione, whom my mother brought up.

ELEC. She is gone to Clytæmnestra's tomb.

ORES. For what purpose? what hope dost thou suggest?

ELEC. To pour libations on the tomb in behalf of her mother.

ORES. And what is this, thou hast told me of, that regards our safety?

ELEC. Seize her as a pledge as she is coming back.

ORES. What remedy for the three friends is this thou sayest?

ELEC. When Helen is dead, if Menelaus does any harm to thee or Pylades, or me (for this firm of friendship is all one), say that thou wilt kill Hermione; but thou oughtest to draw thy sword, and hold it to the neck of the virgin. And if indeed Menelaus save thee, anxious that the virgin may not die; when he sees Helen's corse weltering in blood, give back the virgin for her father to enjoy; but should he, not governing his angry temper, slay thee, do thou also plunge the sword into the virgin's neck, and I think that he, though at first he come to us very big, will after a season soften his heart; for neither is he brave nor valiant: this is the fortress of our safety that I have; my arguments on the subject have been spoken.

ORES. O thou that hast indeed the mind of a man, but a form among women beautiful, to what a degree art thou more worthy of life than death! Pylades, wilt thou miserably be disappointed of such a woman, or dwelling with her obtain this happy marriage?

PYL. For would it could be so! and she could come to the city of the Phocians meeting with her deserts in splendid nuptials!

ORES. But when will Hermione come to the house? Since for the rest thou saidst most admirably, if we could succeed in taking the whelp of the impious father.

ELEC. Even now I guess that she must be near the house, for *with this supposition* the space itself of the time coincides.

ORES. It is well; do thou therefore, my sister Electra, waiting before the house, meet the arrival of the virgin. And watch, lest any one, either some ally, or the brother of my father, should be beforehand with us coming to the palace: and make some noise toward the house, either knocking at the doors, or sending thy voice within. But let us, O Pylades (for thou undertakest this labor with me), entering in, arm our hands with the sword to one last attempt. O my father, that inhabitest the realms of gloomy night, Orestes thy son invokes thee to come a succor to thy suppliants; for on thy account I wretched suffer unjustly, and am betrayed by thy brother, myself having acted justly: whose wife I wish to take and destroy; but be thou our accomplice in this affair.

ELEC. O father, come then, if beneath the earth thou hearest thy children calling, who die for thee.

PYL. O thou relation[36] of my father, give ear, O Agamemnon, to my prayers also, preserve thy children.

ORES. I slew my mother.

PYL. But I directed the sword.

ELEC. But I at least incited you, and freed you from delay.

ORES. Succoring thee, my father.

ELEC. Neither did I forsake thee.

PYL. Wilt thou not therefore, hearing these things that are brought against thee,[37] defend thy children?

ORES. I pour libations on thee with my tears.

ELEC. And I with lamentations.

PYL. Cease, and let us haste forth to the work, for if prayers penetrate under the earth, he hears; but, O Jove our ancestor, and thou revered deity of justice, grant us to succeed, him, and myself, and this virgin, for over us three friends one hazard, one cause impends, either for all to live, or all to die!

ELECTRA, CHORUS.

ELEC. O dear Mycenian virgins, who have the first place at the Pelasgian seat of the Argives;—

CHOR. What voice art thou uttering, my respected mistress? for this appellation awaits thee in the city of the Danaids.

ELEC. Arrange yourselves, some of you in this beaten way, and some there, in that other path, to guard the house.

CHOR. But on what account dost thou command this, tell me, my friend.

ELEC. Fear possesses me, lest any one being in the palace, on account of this murderous deed, should contrive evils on evils.

SEMICHOR. Go, let us hasten, I indeed will guard this path, that tends toward where the sun flings his first rays.

SEMICHOR. And I indeed this, which leads toward the west.

ELEC. Now turn the glances of your eyes around in every position, now here, now there, then take some other view.

CHOR. We are, as thou commandest.

ELEC. Now roll your eyelids over your pupils, glance them every way through your ringlets.

SEMICHOR. Is this any one here appearing in the path?—Who is this rustic that is standing about thy palace?

ELEC. We are undone then, my friends; he will immediately show to the enemy the lurking beasts of prey armed with their swords.

SEMICHOR. Be not afraid, the path is clear, which thou thinkest not.

ELEC. But what?—does all with you remain secure? Give me some good report, whether the space before the hall be empty?

SEMICHOR. All here at least is well, but look to thy province, for no one of the Danaids is approaching toward us.

SEMICHOR. Thy report agrees with mine, for neither is there a disturbance here.

ELEC. Come now,—I will listen at the door: why do ye delay, ye that are within, to sacrifice the victim, now that ye are in quiet?—They hear not: Alas me! wretched in misery! Are the swords then struck dumb at her beauty? Perhaps some Argive in arms rushing in with the foot of succor will approach the palace.—Now watch more carefully; it is no contest that admits delay; but turn *your eyes* some this way, and some that.

CHOR. I turn each different way, looking about on all sides.

HELEN. (*within*) Oh! Pelasgian Argos! I am miserably slain!

ELEC. Heard ye? The men are employing their head in the murder.—It is the shriek of Helen, as I may conjecture.

SEMICHOR. O eternal might of Jove, come to assist my friends in every way.

HEL. Menelaus, I die! But thou art at hand, and dost not help me!

ELEC. Kill, strike, slay, plunging with your hands the two double-edged swords into the deserter of her father, the deserter of her husband, who destroyed numbers of the Grecians perishing by the spear at the river, whence tears fell into conjunction with tears, fell on account of the iron weapons around the whirlpools of Scamander.

CHOR. Be still, be still: I heard the sound of some one coming along the path around the palace.

ELEC. O most dear women, in the midst of the slaughter behold Hermione is present; let us cease from our clamor, for she comes about to fall into the meshes of our toils. A goodly prey will she be, if she be taken. Again to your stations with a calm countenance, and with a color that shall not give evidence of what has been done. I too will preserve a pensive cast of countenance, as though perfectly unacquainted with what has happened.

HERMIONE, ELECTRA, CHORUS.

ELEC. O virgin, art thou come from crowning Clytæmnestra's tomb, and pouring libations to her manes?

HERM. I am come, having obtained her good services; but some terror has come upon me, on account of the noise in the palace, which I hear being a far distance off the house.

ELEC. But why? There have happened to us things worthy of groans.

HERM. Speak good words; but what news dost thou tell me?

ELEC. It has been decreed by this land, that Orestes and I die.

HERM. No, I hope not so; you, who are my relations.

ELEC. It is fixed; but we stand under the yoke of necessity.

HERM. Was the noise then in the house on this account?

ELEC. For falling down a suppliant at the knees of Helen, he cries out—

HERM. Who? for I know no more, except thou tellest me.

ELEC. The wretched Orestes, that he may not die, and in behalf of me.

HERM. For a just reason then the house lamented.

ELEC. For on what other account should one rather cry out? But come, and join in supplication with thy friends, falling down before thy mother, the supremely blest, that Menelaus will not see us perish. But, O thou, that receivedst thy education at the hands of my mother, pity us, and alleviate our sufferings. Come hither to the trial; but I will lead the way, for thou alone hast the ends of our preservation.

HERM. Behold I direct my footstep toward the house. Be preserved, as far as lies in me.

ELEC. O ye in the house, my dear warriors, will ye not take your prey?

HERM. Alas me! who are these I see?

ORES. (*advancing*) Thou must be silent; for thou art come to preserve us, not thyself.

ELEC. Hold her, hold her; and pointing a sword to her neck be silent, that Menelaus may know, that having found men, not Phrygian cowards, he has treated them in a manner he should treat cowards. What ho! what ho! my friends, make a noise, a noise, and shout before the palace, that the murder that is perpetrated spread not a dread alarm among the Argives, so that they run to assist to the king's palace, before I plainly see the slaughtered Helen lying weltering in her blood within the house, or else we hear the report from some of her attendants. For part of the havoc I know, and part not accurately.

CHOR. With justice came the vengeance of the Gods on Helen. For she filled the whole of Greece with tears on account of the ruthless, ruthless Idean Paris, who brought the Grecian state to Ilium. But be silent, for the bolts of the royal mansion resound, for some one of the Phrygians comes forth, from whom we shall hear of the affairs within the house, in what state they are.

PHRYGIAN, CHORUS.

PHRY. I have escaped from death by the Argive sword in these barbaric slippers, *climbing* over the cedar beams of the bed and the Doric triglyphs, by the flight of a barbarian.[38] Thou art gone, thou art gone, O my country, my country! Alas me! whither can I escape, O strangers, flying through the hoary air, or the sea, which the Ocean, with head in shape like a bull's, rolling with his arms encircles the earth?

CHOR. But what is the matter, O attendant of Helen, thou man of Ida?

PHRY. O Ilion, Ilion! alas me! O thou fertile Phrygian city, thou sacred mount of Ida, how do I lament for thee destroyed, a sad,[39] sad strain for my barbaric voice, on account of that form of the hapless, hapless Helen, born from a bird, the offspring of the beauteous Leda in shape of a swan, the fiend of the splendid Apollonian Pergamus! Alas! Oh! lamentations! lamentations! O wretched Dardania, warlike school[40] of Ganymede, the companion of Jove!

CHOR. Relate to us clearly each circumstance that happened in the house, for I do not understand your former account, but merely conjecture.

PHRY. Αιλινον, αιλινον, the Barbarians begin the song of death in the language of Asia, Alas! alas! when the blood of kings has been poured on the earth by the ruthless swords of death. There came to the palace (that I may relate each circumstance) two Grecians, lions, of the one the leader of the Grecian host was said to be the father, the other the son of Strophius, a man of dark design; such was Ulysses, secretly treacherous, but faithful to his friends, bold in battle, skilled in war, cruel as the dragon. May he perish for his deep concealed design, the worker of evil! But they having advanced within her chamber, whom the archer Paris had as his wife, their eyes bathed with tears, they sat down in humble mien, one on each side of her, on the right and on the left, armed with swords. And around her knees did they both fling their suppliant hands, around the knees of Helen did they fling them. But the Phrygian attendants sprung up, and fled in amazement: and one called out to another in terror, *See*, lest there be treachery. To some indeed there appeared no danger; but to others the dragon stained with his mother's blood appeared bent to infold in his closest toils the daughter of Tyndarus.

CHOR. But where wert thou then, or hadst thou long before fled through fear?

PHRY. After the Phrygian fashion I chanced with the close circle of feathers to be fanning the gale, *that sported* in the ringlets of Helen, before her cheek, after the barbaric fashion. But she was winding with her fingers the flax round the distaff, but what she had spun she let fall on the ground, desirous of making from the Phrygian spoils a robe of purple as an ornament for the tomb, a gift to Clytæmnestra. But Orestes entreated the Spartan girl; "O daughter of Jove, here, place thy footstep on the ground, rising from thy seat, come to the place of our ancestor Pelops, the ancient altar, that thou mayest hear my words." And he leads her, but she followed, not dreaming of what was about to happen. But his accomplice, the wicked Phocian, attended to other points. "Will ye not depart from out of the way, but are the Phrygians always vile?" and he bolted us out scattered in different parts of the house, some in the stables of the horses, and some in the outhouses, and some here and there, dispersing them some one way, some another, afar from their mistress.

CHOR. What calamity took place after this?

PHRY. O powerful, powerful Idean mother, alas! alas! the murderous sufferings, and the lawless evils, which I saw, I saw in the royal palace! From beneath their purple robes concealed having their drawn swords in their hands, they turned each his eye on either side, lest any one might chance to be present. But like mountain boars standing over against the lady, they say, "Thou shalt die, thou shalt die! thy vile husband kills thee, having given up the offspring of his brother to die at Argos." But she shrieked out, Ah me! ah me! and throwing her white arm on her breast inflicted on her head miserable blows, and, her feet turned to flight, she stepped, she stepped with her golden sandals; but Orestes thrusting his fingers into her hair, outstripping her flight,[41] bending back her neck over his left shoulder, was about to plunge the black sword into her throat.

CHOR. Where then were the Phrygians, who dwell under the same roof, to assist her?

PHRY. With a clamor having burst by means of bars the doors and cells where we were waiting, we run to her assistance, each to different parts of the house, one bringing stones, another spears, another having a long-handled sword in his hand. But Pylades came against us, impetuous, like as the Phrygian Hector or Ajax in his triple-crested helmet, whom I saw, I saw at the gates of Priam: but we clashed together the points of our swords: then indeed, then did the Phrygians give clear proof how inferior we were in the force of Mars to the spear of Greece. One indeed turning away, a fugitive, but another wounded, and another deprecating the death that threatened him: but under favor of the darkness we fled: and the corses fell, but some staggered, and some lay prostrate. But the wretched Hermione came to the house at the time when her murdered mother fell to the ground, that unhappy woman that gave her birth. And running upon her as Bacchanals without their thyrsus, as a heifer in the mountains they bore her away in their hands, and again eagerly rushed upon the daughter of Jove to slay her. But she vanished altogether from the chamber through the palace. O Jupiter and O earth, and light, and darkness! or by her enchantments, or by the art of magic, or by the stealth of the Gods. But of what followed I know no farther, for I sped in stealth my foot from the palace. But Menelaus having endured many, many severe toils, has received back from Troy the violated rites of Helen to no purpose.

CHOR. And see something strange succeeds to these strange things, for I see Orestes with his sword drawn walking before the palace with agitated step,

ORESTES, PHRYGIAN, CHORUS.

ORES. Where is he that fled from my sword out of the palace?

PHRY. I supplicate thee, O king, falling prostrate before thee after the barbaric fashion.

ORES. The case before us is not in Ilium, but the Argive land.

PHRY. In every region to live is sweeter than to die, in the opinion of the wise.

ORES. Didst thou not raise a cry for Menelaus to come with succor?

PHRY. I indeed am present on purpose to assist thee; for thou art the more worthy.

ORES. Perished then the daughter of Tyndarus justly?

PHRY. Most justly, even had she three lives for vengeance.

ORES. With thy tongue dost thou flatter, not having these sentiments within?

PHRY. For ought she not? She who utterly destroyed Greece as well as the Phrygians themselves?

ORES. Swear, I will kill thee else, that thou art not speaking to curry favor with me.

PHRY. By my life have I sworn, which I should wish to hold a sacred oath.

ORES. Was the steel thus dreadful to all the Phrygians at Troy also?

PHRY. Remove thy sword, for being so near me it gleams horrid slaughter.

ORES. Art thou afraid, lest thou shouldest become a rock, as though looking on the Gorgon?

PHRY. Lest I should become a corse, but I know not of the Gorgon's head.

ORES. Slave as thou art, dost thou fear death, which will rid thee from thy woes?

PHRY. Every one, although a man be a slave, rejoices to behold the light.

ORES. Thou sayest well; thy understanding; saves thee, but go into the house.

PHRY. Thou wilt not kill me then?

ORES. Thou art pardoned.

PHRY. This is good word thou hast spoken.

ORES. Yet we may change our measures.

PHRY. But this thou sayest not well.

ORES. Thou art a fool, if thou thinkest I could endure to defile me by smiting thy neck, for neither art thou a woman, nor oughtest thou to be ranked among men. But that thou mightest not raise a clamor came I forth out of the house: for Argos, when it has heard a noise, is soon roused, but we have no dread in meeting Menelaus, as far as swords go; but let him come exulting with his golden ringlets flowing over his shoulders, for if he collects the Argives, and brings them against the palace seeking revenge for the death of Helen, and is not willing to let me be in safety, and my sister, and Pylades my accomplice in this affair, he shall see two corses, both the virgin and his wife.

CHORUS.

Alas! alas! O fate, the house of the Atridæ again falls into another, another fearful struggle.

SEMICHOR. What shall we do? shall we carry these tidings to the city, or shall we keep in silence?

SEMICHOR. This is the safer plan, my friends.

SEMICHOR. Behold before the house, behold this smoke leaping aloft in the air portends *something*.

SEMICHOR. They are lighting the torches, as about to burn down the mansion of Tantalus, nor do they forbear from murder.

CHOR. The God rules the events that happen to mortals, whichsoever way he wills. But some vast power by the instigation of the Furies has struck, has struck these palaces to the shedding of blood on account of the fall of Myrtilus from the chariot.

But lo! I see Menelaus also here approaching the house with a quick step, having by some means or other perceived the calamity which now is present. Will ye not anticipate him by closing the gates with bolts, O ye children of Atreus, who are in the palace? A man in prosperity is a terrible thing to those in adversity, as now them art in misery, Orestes.

MENELAUS *below*, ORESTES, PYLADES, ELECTRA, HERMIONE *above*, CHORUS.

MEN. I am present, having heard the horrid and atrocious deeds of the two lions, for I call them not men. For I have now heard of my wife, that she died not, but vanished away, this that I heard was empty report, which one deceived by fright related; but these are the artifices of the matricide, and much derision. Open some one the door, my attendants I command to burst open these gates here, that my child at least we may deliver from the hand of these blood-polluted men, and may receive my unhappy, my miserable lady, with whom those murderers of my wife must die by my hand.

ORES. What ho there! Touch not these gates with thine hands: to Menelaus I speak, that thou towerest in thy boldness, or with this pinnacle will I crush thy head, having rent down the ancient battlement, the labor of the builders. But the gates are made fast with bolts, which will hinder thee from thy purpose of bringing aid, so that thou canst not pass within the palace.

MEN. Ha! what is this? I see the blaze of torches, and these stationed on the battlements, on the height of the palace, and the sword placed over the neck of my daughter to guard her.

ORES. Whether is it thy will to question, or to hear me?

MEN. I wish neither, but it is necessary, as it seems, to hear thee.

ORES. I am about to slay thy daughter if thou wish to know.

MEN. Having slain Helen, dost thou perpetrate murder on murder?

ORES. For would I had gained my purpose not being deluded, as I was, by the Gods.

MEN. Thou hast slain her, and deniest it, and speakest these things to insult me.

ORES. It is a denial that gives me pain, for would that—

MEN. Thou had done what deed? for thou callest forth alarm.

ORES. I had hurled to hell the fury of Greece.

MEN. Give back the body of my wife, that I may bury her in a tomb.

ORES. Ask her of the Gods; but I will slay thy daughter.

MEN. The matricide contrives murder on murder.

ORES. The avenger of his father, whom thou gavest up to die.

MEN. Was not the blood of thy mother formerly shed sufficient for thee?

ORES. I should not be weary of slaying wicked women, were I to slay them forever.

MEN. Art thou also, Pylades, a partaker in this murder?

ORES. By his silence he assents, but if I speak, it will be sufficient.

MEN. But not with impunity, unless indeed thou fliest on wings.

ORES. We will not fly, but will set fire to the palace?

MEN. What! wilt thou destroy thy father's mansion?

ORES. Yes, that thou mayest not possess it, will I, having stabbed this virgin here over the flames.

MEN. Slay her; since having slain thou shalt at least give me satisfaction for these deeds.

ORES. It shall be so then.

MEN. Alas! on no account do this!

ORES. Be silent then; but bear to suffer evil justly.

MEN. What! is it just for thee to live?

ORES. Yes, and to rule over the land.

MEN. What land!

ORES. Here, in Pelasgian Argos.

MEN. Well wouldst thou touch the sacred lavers!

ORES. And pray why not?

MEN. And wouldst slaughter the victim before the battle!

ORES. And thou wouldst most righteously.

MEN. Yes, for I am pure as to my hands.

ORES. But not thy heart.

MEN. Who would speak to thee?

ORES. Whoever loves his father.

MEN. And whoever reveres his mother.

ORES. —Is happy.

MEN. Not thou at least.

ORES. For wicked women please me not.

MEN. Take away the sword from my daughter.

ORES. Thou art false in thy expectations.

MEN. But wilt thou kill my daughter?

ORES. Thou art no longer false.

MEN. Alas me! what shall I do?

ORES. Go to the Argives, and persuade them.

MEN. With what persuasion?

ORES. Beseech the city that we may not die.[41a]

MEN. Otherwise ye will slay my daughter?

ORES. The thing is so.

MEN. O wretched Helen!—

ORES. And am I not wretched?

MEN. I brought thee hither from the Trojans to be a victim.

ORES. For would this were so!

MEN. Having endured ten thousand toils.

ORES. Except on my account.

MEN. I have met with dreadful treatment.

ORES. For then, *when thou oughtest*, thou wert of no assistance.

MEN. Thou hast me.

ORES. Thou at least hast caught thyself. But, ho there! set fire to the palace, Electra, from beneath: and thou, Pylades, the most true of my friends, light up these battlements of the walls.

MEN. O land of the Danai, and inhabitants of warlike Argos, will ye not, ho there! come in arms to my succor? For this man here, having perpetrated the shocking murder of his mother, brings destruction on your whole city, that he may live.

APOLLO.

Menelaus, cease from thy irritated state of mind; I Phœbus the son of Latona, in thy presence, am addressing thee. Thou too, Orestes, who standest over that damsel with thy sword drawn, that thou mayest know what commands I bring with me. Helen indeed, whom thou minded to destroy, working Menelaus to anger, didst fail of thy purpose, she is here, whom ye see wrapt

- 79 -

in the bosom of the sky, preserved, and not slain by thy hands. Her I preserved, and snatched from thy sword, commanded by my father Jove. For being the daughter of Jove, it is right that she should live immortal. And she shall have her seat by Castor and Pollux in the bosom of the sky, the guardian of mariners. But take to thyself another bride, and lead her home, since for the beauty of this woman the Gods brought together the Greeks and Trojans, and caused deaths, that they might draw from off the earth the pride of mortals, who had become an infinite multitude. Thus is it with regard to Helen; but thee, on the other hand, Orestes, it behooveth, having passed beyond the boundaries of this land, to inhabit the Parrhasian plain during the revolution of a year, and it shall be called by a name after thy flight, so that the Azanes and Arcadians shall call it Oresteum: and thence having departed to the city of the Athenians, undergo the charge of shedding thy mother's blood laid by the three Furies. But the Gods the arbiters of the cause shall pass on thee most sacredly their decree on the hill of Mars, in which it behooveth thee to be victorious. But Hermione, to whose neck thou art holding the sword, it is destined for thee, Orestes, to wed, but Neoptolemus, who thinks to marry her, shall never marry her. For it is fated to him to die by the Delphic sword, as he is demanding of me satisfaction for his father Achilles. But to Pylades give thy sister's hand, as thou didst formerly agree, but a happy life now coming on awaits him. But, O Menelaus, suffer Orestes to reign over Argos. But depart and rule over the Spartan land, having it as thy wife's dowry, who exposing thee to numberless evils always was bringing thee to this. But what regards the city I will make all right for him, I, who compelled him to slay his mother.

ORES. O Loxian prophet, thou wert not then a false prophet in thine oracles, but a true one. And yet a fear comes upon me, that having heard one of the Furies, I might think that I have been hearing thy voice. But it is well fulfilled, and I will obey thy words. Behold I let go Hermione from slaughter, and approve her alliance, whenever her father shall give her.

MEN. O Helen, daughter of Jove, hail! but I bless thee inhabiting the happy mansions of the Gods. But to thee, Orestes, do I betroth my daughter at Phœbus's commands, but illustrious thyself marrying from an illustrious family, be happy, both thou and I who give her.

APOL. Now depart each of you whither we have appointed, and dissolve your quarrels.

MEN. It is our duty to obey.

ORES. I too entertain the same sentiments, and I receive with friendship thee in thy sufferings, O Menelaus, and thy oracles, O Apollo.

APOL. Go now, each his own way, honoring the most excellent goddess Peace; but I will convey Helen to the mansions of Jove, passing through the pole of the shining stars, where sitting by Juno, and Hercules's Hebe, a goddess, she shall ever be honored by mortals with libations, in conjunction with the Tyndaridæ, the sons of Jove, presiding over the sea to the benefit of mariners.

CHOR. O greatly glorious Victory, mayest thou uphold my life, and cease not from crowning me!

NOTES ON ORESTES

[1] στεμματα, ερια, *Schol.* "eo quod colum cingant seu coronant," Scapula explains it.

[2] "*Then*" is not to be considered as signifying point of time, but it is meant to express ουν, *continuativam.* See Hoogeveen de Particula ουν, Sect. ii. § 6.

[3] The original Greek phrase was ελπιδος λεπτης, which Euripides has changed to ασθενους 'ρωμης, though the other had equally suited the metre. But Euripides is fond of slight alterations in proverbs. PORSON.

[4] δους—δυναται δε και αποδους. SCHOL.

[5] Perhaps this interpretation of χρονιον is better than "slow," for the considerate Electra would hardly go to remind her brother of his infirmities.

[6] Ποτνιαδες. The Furies have this epithet from Potnia, a town in Bœotia, where Glaucus's horses, having eaten of a certain herb and becoming mad, tore their own master in pieces. SCHOL.

[6a] Note [D].

[6b] Dindorf would omit this verse.

[7] 'αλιτυπων, 'αλιεων, 'οι ταις κωπαις τυπτουσι την θαλασσαν. SCHOL.

[8] αφυλλου. Alluding to the branch, which the ancients used to hold in token of supplication.

[9] "κατα την νυκτα πεπονθα τηρων την αναιρεσιν, και την αναληψιν των οστεων, τουτεστιν, 'ινα μη τις αφεληται ταυτα." PARAPH. Heath translates it, *watchfully observing, till her bones were collected.*

[10] The old reading was απαιδευτα. The meaning of the present reading seems to be, "Yes, they are awful 'tis true, but still however you need not be so very scrupulous about naming them."

[11] αναφορα was a legal term, and signified the line of defense adopted by the accused, when he transferred the charge brought against himself to some other person.—See Demosthenes in Timocr.

[12] Œax was Palamede's brother.

[13] And therefore we are not to impeach the *man*. Some would have δουλον to bear the sense of δουλοποιον, enslaves, and therefore can not be avoided.

[14] εχω for ενοχος ειμι.

[15] Ζηλω, το μακαριζω. ενταυθα δε αντι του επαινω. SCHOL.

[16] Conf. Ter. Eun. Act. v. Sc. 2.

Non dedignum, Chærea,

Fecisti; nam si ego digna hac contumelia

Sum maxume, at tu indignus, qui faceres, tamen.

[16a] Note [E].

[17] Of this passage the Scholiast gives two interpretations; either it may mean μετα δακρυων και γοων ειπον: or, ειπον ταυτα εις δακρυα και γοους, και ξυμφορας, ηγουν 'ινα μη τυχω, τουτων: τευξομαι δε, ει πετρωθηναι με εασηις.

[18] *"Beyond any woman,"* γυνη μια, this is a mode of expression frequently met with in the Attic writers, especially in Xenophon.

[19] επι τωι φονωι, τουτεστι δια τον φονον, 'ον ειργασαμεθα. PARAPH.

[20] Thyestes and Atreus, having a dispute about their father Pelops's kingdom, agreed, that whichever should discover the first prodigy should have possession of the throne. There appeared in Atreus's flock a golden lamb, which, however, Ærope his wife secretly had conveyed to Thyestes to show before the judges. Atreus afterward invited Thyestes to a feast, and served up before him Aglaiis, Orchomenus, and Caleus, three sons he had by his intrigues with Ærope.

[21] Alluding to the murder of Agamemnon by Clytæmnestra. This is the interpretation and explanation of the Scholiast; but it is perhaps better translated, "*but on the other hand to play the coward is great impiety, and the error of cowardly-minded men;*" the chorus meaning, that this might have been said of Orestes, had he not avenged his father.

[22] That is, *blamed him*. So St. Paul, 1 Cor. xi. 21, επαινεσω 'υμας εν τουτοι; ουκ επαινω. Ter. And. Act. II. Sc. 6. "Et, quod dicendum hic siet, Tu quoque perparce nimium, non laudo."

[23] An Argive as far as he was born there, and therefore ηναγκασμενος; not an Argive, inasmuch as his parents were not of that state. This is supposed to allude to Cleophon. SCHOL. See Dindorf.

[24] This is the interpretation of one Scholiast; another explains it οικειαις χερσιν εργαζομενος. Grotius translates it *agricola*.

[25] The same construction occurs in the Supplicants, 870. φιλοις δ' αληθης ην φιλος, παρουσι τε και μη παρουσιν: 'ων (of which sort of men) αριθμος ου πολυς. PORSON.

[25a] See Note [F].

[26] Which, κτυπον namely: ονυχα and κτυπον are each governed by τιθεισα; but it is not easy to find a single verb in English that should be transitive to both these substantives.

[27] καλλιπαις, *lovely*, not lovely in her children: so in Phœn. 1634. ευτεκνος ξυνωρις.

[28] Argos, so called from the Cyclopes, a nation of Thrace, who, being called in as allies, afterward settled here.

[29] 'ετεροις may perhaps seem to make the construction plainer than 'ετερος; but Porson has received the latter into his text on account of the metre.

[30] Myrtilus was the son of Mercury, who therefore sowed this dissension between the two brothers in revenge for his death by Pelops. See note at line 802.

[31] Some would understand by μονοπωλον not that Aurora was borne on one horse, but that this alteration in the course of nature took place for one day. SCHOL.

[32] και απο τωνδε, ητοι μετα ταυτα. PARAPH.

[33] παρασειρος is used to signify a loose horse tied abreast of another in the shaft, and is technically termed "the outrigger." The metaphorical application of it to Pylades, who voluntarily attached himself to the misfortunes of his friend, is extremely beautiful.

[34] Or, *"I will not be at all behind thy slaughter."*

[35] ευ in this passage *interrogat oblique,* see Hoogeveen, xvi. § 1. 15.

[36] Strophius, the father of Pylades, married Anaxibia, Agamemnon's sister.

[37] ονειδη, των ευεργεσιων τας 'υπομνησεις. SCHOL. Ter. And. i. 1. "isthæc commemoratio quasi exprobratio est immemoris benefici."

[38] i.e. being a barbarian, and therefore not knowing whither to go.

[39] 'αρματειον, such a strain as that raised over Hector, 'ελκομενω, δια του 'αρματος. See two other explanations in the Scholia.

[40] 'ιπποσυνα, 'ητις 'υπηρχες 'ιππηλασια του Γ. BRUNCK.

[41] Literally, *her Mycenian slipper.*

[41a] Read θανειν with Pors. Dind.

ADDITIONAL NOTES.

[A] But Dindorf reads κτυπου η ηγαγετ'. ουχι; interrogatively, thus: "Ye were making a noise. Will ye not ... enable him," etc.?

[B] Dindorf would continue this verse to Orestes.

[C] Dindorf supposes something to be wanting after vs. 314.

[D] The use of αλλος 'ετερος is learnedly illustrated by Dindorf.

[E] Elmsley, on Heracl. 852, more simply regards the datives σοι σηι τ' αδελφη as dependent upon επισεισω, understanding 'ωστε δουναι δικην. This is better than to suppose (with Porson) that δουναι δικην can mean to *inflict* punishment.

[F] Dindorf (in his notes) agrees with Porson in omitting the following verse.

[G] Dindorf's text and punctuation must be altered.

THE PHŒNICIAN VIRGINS.

PERSONS REPRESENTED.

JOCASTA.

TUTOR.

ANTIGONE.

CHORUS OF PHŒNICIAN VIRGINS.

POLYNICES.

ETEOCLES.

CREON.

MENŒCEUS.

TIRECIAS.

MESSENGERS.

ŒDIPUS.

The Scene is in the Court before the royal palace at Thebes.

THE ARGUMENT.

Eteocles having gotten possession of the throne of Thebes, deprived his brother Polynices of his share; but he having come as an exile to Argos, married the daughter of the king Adrastus; but ambitious of returning to his country, and having persuaded his father-in-law, he assembled a great army for Thebes against his brother. His mother Jocasta made him come into the city, under sanction of a truce, and first confer with his brother respecting the empire. But Eteocles being violent and fierce from having possessed the empire, Jocasta could not reconcile her children.—Polynices, prepared as against an enemy, rushed out of the city. Now Tiresias prophesied that victory should be on the side of the Thebans, if Menœceus the son of Creon would give himself up to be sacrificed to Mars. Creon refused to give his son to the city, but the youth was willing, and, his father pointing out to him the means of flight and giving him money, he put himself to death.—The Thebans slew the leaders of the Argives. Eteocles and Polynices in a single combat slew each other, and their mother having found the corses of her sons laid violent hands on herself; and Creon her brother received the kingdom. The Argives defeated in battle retired. But Creon, being morose, would not give up those of the enemy who had fallen at Thebes, for sepulture, and exposed the body of Polynices without burial, and banished Œdipus from his country; in the one instance disregarding the laws of humanity, in the other giving way to passion, nor feeling pity for him after his calamity.

THE PHŒNICIAN VIRGINS.

JOCASTA.

O thou that cuttest thy path through the constellations[1] of heaven, and art mounted on thy golden-joined seats, thou sun, whirling thy flame with[2] thy swift steeds, how inauspicious didst thou dart thy ray on that day when Cadmus came to this land having left the sea-washed coast of Phœnicia; who in former time having married Harmonia, daughter of Venus, begat Polydorus; from him they say sprung Labdacus, and from him Laius. But I am[3] the daughter of Menœceus, and Creon my brother was born of the same mother; me they call Jocasta (for this name[4] my father gave me), and Laius takes me for his wife; but after that he was childless, for a long time sharing my bed in the palace, he went and inquired of Apollo, and at the same time demands the mutual offspring of male children in his family; but the God said, "O king of Thebes renowned for its chariots, sow not for such a harvest of children against the will of the Gods, for if thou shalt beget a son, he that is born shall slay thee, and the whole of thy house shall wade through blood." But having yielded to pleasure, and having fallen into inebriety, he begot to us a son, and having begot him, feeling conscious of his error and the command of the God, gives the babe to some herdsmen to expose at the meads of Juno and the rock of Cithæron, having bored sharp-pointed iron through the middle of his ankles, from which circumstance Greece gave him the name of Œdipus. But him the grooms who attend the steeds of Polybus find and carry home, and placed him in the arms of their mistress. But she rested beneath her bosom him that gave me a mother's pangs, and persuades her husband that she had brought forth. But now my son showing signs of manhood in his darkening cheek, either having suspected it by instinct, or having learned it from some one, went to the temple of Apollo, desirous of discovering his parents; at the same time went Laius my husband, seeking to gain intelligence of his son who had been exposed, if he were no longer living; and both met at the same point of the road at Phocis where it divides itself; and the charioteer of Laius commands him, "Stranger, withdraw out of the way of princes;" but he moved slowly, in silence, with haughty spirit; but the steeds with their hoof dyed with blood the tendons of his feet. At this (but why need I relate each horrid circumstance besides the deed itself?) the son kills his father, and having taken the chariot, sends it as a present to his foster-father Polybus. Now at this time the sphinx preyed vulture-like[5] upon the city with rapacity, my husband now no more, Creon my brother proclaims that he will give my bed as a reward to him who would solve the enigma of the crafty virgin. But by some chance or other Œdipus my son happens to discover the riddle of the sphinx, [and he receives as a prize the sceptre of this land,][5a] and marries me, his mother, wretched he not knowing it, nor knew his mother that she was lying down with her son. And I bear children to my child, two sons, Eteocles and the illustrious Polynices, and two daughters, one her father named Ismene, the elder I called Antigone. But Œdipus, after having gone through all sufferings, having discovered in my bed the marriage with his mother, he perpetrated a deed of horror on his own eyes, having drenched in blood their pupils with his golden buckles. But after that the cheek of my children grows dark with manly down, they hid their father confined with bolts that his sad fortune might be forgotten, which indeed required the greatest policy. He is still living in the palace, but sick in mind through his misfortunes he imprecates the most unhallowed curses on his children, that they may share this house with the sharpened sword. But these two, dreading lest the Gods should bring to completion these curses,[6] should they dwell together, in friendly compact determined that Polynices the younger son should first go a willing exile from this land, but that Eteocles remaining here should hold the sceptre for a year, changing in his turn; but after that he sat on the throne of power, he moves not from his seat, but drives Polynices an exile from this land. But he having fled to Argos, and having contracted an alliance with Adrastus, assembles together and leads a vast army of Argives; and having marched to these very walls with seven gates he demands his father's sceptre and his share of the land. But I to quell this strife persuaded my son to come to his brother, confiding in a truce before he grasped the spear. And the messenger who was sent declares that he will come. But, O thou that inhabitest the shining clouds of heaven, Jove, preserve us, give reconciliation to my children; it becomes thee, if thou art wise, not to suffer the same man always to be unfortunate.

TUTOR, ANTIGONE.

TUT. O thou fair bud in thy father's house, Antigone, since thy mother has permitted thee to leave the virgin's apartments for the extreme chamber[7] of the mansion, in order to view the Argive army in compliance with thy entreaties, yet stay, until I shall first investigate the path, lest any citizen should appear in the pass, and to me taunts should come as a slave, and to thee as a princess: and I who well know each circumstance will tell you all that I saw or heard from the Argives, when I went bearing the offer of a truce to thy brother, from this place thither, and again to this place from him. But no citizen approaches this house; come, ascend with thy steps these ancient stairs of cedar, and survey the plains, and by the streams of Ismenus and Dirce's fount how great is the host of the enemy.

ANT. Stretch forth now, stretch forth thine aged hand from the stairs to my youth, raising up the steps of my feet.

TUT. Behold, join thy hand, virgin, thou hast come in lucky hour, for the Pelasgian host is now in motion, and they are separating the bands from one another.

ANT. O awful daughter of Latona, Hecate, the field all brass[8] gleaming like lightning.

TUT. For Polynices hath not come tamely to this land, raging with host of horsemen, and ten thousand shields.

ANT. Are the gates fastened with bars, and is the brazen bolt fitted to the stone-work of Amphion's wall?

TUT. Take courage; as to the interior the city is safe, But view the first chief, if thou desirest to know.

ANT. Who is he with the white-plumed helmet, who commands in the van of the army, moving lightly round on his arm his brazen shield?

TUT. He is a leader, lady.

ANT. Who is he? From whom sprung? Speak, aged man, what is he called by name?

TUT. He indeed is called by birth a Mycenæan, and he dwells at the streams of Lerna,[9] the king Hippomedon.

ANT. Ah! how haughty, how terrible to behold! like to an earth-born giant, starlike in countenance amidst his painted devices,[10] he corresponds not with the race of mortals.

TUT. Dost thou not see him now passing the stream of Dirce, a general?

ANT. Here is another, another fashion of arms. But who is he?

TUT. He is the son of Œneus, Tydeus, and bears on his breast the Ætolian Mars.

ANT. Is this the prince, O aged man, who is husband to the sister of my brother's wife?[11] In his arms how different of color, of barbaric mixture!

TUT. For all the Ætolians, my child, bear the target, and hurl with the lance, most certain in their aim.

ANT. But how, O aged man, dost thou know these things so perfectly?

TUT. Having seen the devices of the shields, then I remarked them, when I went to bear the offer of a truce to thy brother, beholding which, I recognize the warriors.

ANT. But who is this, who is passing round the tomb of Zethus, with clustering locks, in his eyes a Gorgon to behold, in appearance a youth?

TUT. A general he is. [See Note [A].]

ANT. How a crowd in complete armor attends him behind![12]

TUT. This is Parthenopæus, son of Atalanta.

ANT. But, may Diana who rushes over the mountains with his mother destroy him, having subdued him with her arrows, who has come against my city to destroy it.

TUT. May it be so, my child, nevertheless they are come with justice to this land; wherefore also I fear lest the Gods should judge rightly.

ANT. Where, but where is he who was born of one mother with me in hard fate, O dearest old man; tell me, where is Polynices?

TUT. He is standing near the tomb of the seven virgin daughters of Niobe, close by Adrastus. Seest thou him?

ANT. I see indeed, but not distinctly; but somehow I see the resemblance of his form, and his shape shadowed out. Would that with my feet I could perform the journey of the winged cloud through the air to my brother, then would I fling my arms round his dearest neck, after so long a time a wretched exile. How splendid is he, O old man, in his golden armor, glittering like the morning rays of the sun.

TUT. He will come to this house confiding in the truce, so as to fill thee with joy.

ANT. But who, O aged man, is this, who guides his milk-white steeds seated in his chariot?

TUT. The prophet Amphiaraus this, O my mistress, and with him the victims, the libations of the earth delighting in blood.

AST. O thou daughter of the brightly girded sun, thou moon, golden-circled light, applying what quiet and temperate blows to his steeds does he direct his chariot! But where is he who utters such dreadful insults against this city, Capaneus?

TUT. He is scanning the approach to the towers, measuring the walls both from their foundation to the top.

ANT. O vengeance, and ye loud-roaring thunders of Jove, and thou blasting fire of the lightning, do thou quell this more-than-mortal arrogance. This is he who will with his spear give to Mycenæ, and to the streams of Lernæan Triæna,[13] and to the Amymonian[14] waters of Neptune, the Theban women, having invested them with slavery. Sever, O awful Goddess, never, O daughter of Jove, with golden clusters of ringlets, Diana, may I endure servitude.

TUT. My child, enter the palace, and at home remain in thy virgin chambers, since thou hast arrived at the indulgement of thy desire, as to what you were anxious to behold. For, since confusion has entered the city, a crowd of women is advancing to the royal palace. The race of women is prone to complaint, and if they find but small occasion for words, they add more, and it is a sort of pleasure to women, to speak nothing well-advised one of another.[15]

CHORUS.

I have come, having left the Tyrian wave, the first-fruits of Loxias, from the sea-washed Phœnicia, a slave for the shrine of Apollo, that I might dwell under the snowy brows of Parnassus, having sped my way over the Ionian flood by the oar, the west wind with its blasts riding over the barren plains of waters[16] which flow round Sicily, the sweetest murmur in the heavens. Chosen out from my city the fairest present to Apollo, I came to the land of the Cadmeans, the illustrious descendants of Agenor, sent hither to these kindred towers of Laius. And I am made the slave of Apollo in like manner with the golden-framed images. Moreover the water of Castalia awaits me, to lave the virgin pride of my tresses, in the ministry of Apollo. O blazing rock, the flame of fire that seems[17] double above the Dionysian heights of Bacchus, and thou vine, who distillest the daily nectar, producing the fruitful cluster from the tender shoot; and ye divine caves of the dragon,[18] and ye mountain watch-towers of the Gods, and thou hallowed snowy mountain, would that I were the chorus of the immortal God free from alarms encompassing thee around, by the caves of Apollo in the centre of the earth, having left Dirce. But now impetuous Mars having advanced before the walls lights up against this city, which may the Gods avert, hostile war; for common are the misfortunes of friends, and common is it, if this land defended by its seven turrets should suffer any calamity, to the Phœnician country, alas! alas! common is the affinity,[19] common are the descendants of Io bearing horns; of which woes I have a share. But a thick cloud of shields glares around the city, the likeness of gory battle, bearing which destruction from the Furies to the children of Œdipus Mars shall quickly advance. O Pelasgian Argos, I dread thy power, and vengeance from the Gods, for he rushes not his arms to this war unjustly, who seeks to recover his home.

POLYNICES, CHORUS.

POL. The bolts indeed of the gate-keepers have with ease admitted me, that I might come within the walls; wherefore also I fear, lest, having caught me within their nets, they let[19a] not my body go without bloodshed. On which account my eye must be turned about on every side, both that way and this, lest there be treachery. But armed in my hand with this sword, I will give myself confidence of daring. Ha! Who is this; or do we fear a noise? Every thing appears terrible even to the bold, when his foot shall pass across a hostile country. I trust however in my mother, at the same time I scarce trust, who persuaded me to come hither confiding in a truce. But protection is nigh; for the hearths of the altars are at hand, and houses not deserted. Come. I will let go my sword into its dark scabbard, and will question these who they are, that are standing at the palace. Ye female strangers, tell me, from what country do ye approach Grecian habitations?

CHOR. The Phœnician is my paternal country, she that nurtured me: and the descendants of Agenor sent me hither from the spoils, the first-fruits to Apollo. And while the renowned son of Œdipus was preparing to send me to the revered shrine, and to the altars of Phœbus, in the mean time the Argives marched against the city. But do thou in turn answer me, who thou art, who hast come to this bulwark of the Theban land with its seven gates?

POL. My father is Œdipus the son of Laius; Jocasta daughter of Menœceus brought me forth; the Theban people call me Polynices.

CHOR. O thou allied to the sons of Agenor, my lords, by whom I was sent, I fall at thy knees in lowly posture, O king, preserving my country's custom. Thou hast come, thou hast come, after a length of time, to thy paternal land. O venerable matron, come forth quickly, open the doors; dost thou hear, O mother, that producedst this hero? why dost thou delay to leave thy lofty mansion, and to embrace thy child with thine arms?

JOCASTA, POLYNICES, CHORUS.

JOC. Hearing the Phœnician tongue, ye virgins, within this mansion, I drag my steps trembling with age. Ah! my son, after length of time, after numberless days, I behold thy countenance; clasp thy mother's bosom in thine arms, throw around her[20] thy kisses, and the dark ringlets of thy clustering hair, shading my neck. Ah! scarce possible is it that thou appearest in thy mother's arms so unhoped for, and so unexpected. How shall I address thee? how shall I perform all? how shall I, walking in rapture around thee on that side and this, both with my hands and words, reap the varied pleasure, the delight of my former joys? O my son, thou hast left thy father's house deserted, sent away an exile by wrongful treatment from thy brother. How longed for by thy friends! how longed for by Thebes! From which time I am both shorn of my hoary locks, letting them fall with tears, with wailing;[21] deprived, my child, of the white robes, I receive in exchange around me these dark and dismal weeds. But the old man in the palace deprived of sight, always preserving with tears regret for the unanimity of the brothers which is separated from the family, has madly rushed on self-destruction with the sword and with the noose above the beams of the house, bewailing the curse imprecated on his children; and with cries of woe he is always hidden in darkness. But thou, my child, I hear, art both joined in marriage, and hast the joys of love in a foreign family, and cherishest a foreign alliance; intolerable to this thy mother and to the aged Laius, the woe of a foreign marriage brought upon us. But neither did I light the torch of fire for you, as is customary in the marriage rites, as befits the happy mother; nor was Ismenus careful of the bridal rites in the luxury of the bath: and the entrance of thy bride was made in silence through the Theban city. May these ills perish, whether the sword, or discord, or thy father is the cause, or whether fate has rushed with violence upon the house of Œdipus; for the weight of these sorrows has fallen upon me.

CHOR. Parturition with the attendant throes has a wonderful effect on women;[22] and somehow the whole race of women have strong affection toward their children.

POL. My mother, determining wisely, and yet not determining wisely, have I come to men my foes; but it is necessary that all must be enamored of their country; but whoever says otherwise, pleases himself with vain words, but has his heart there. But so far have I come to trouble and terror, lest any treachery from my brother should slay me, so that having my hand on my sword I proceeded through the city rolling round my eye; but one thing is on my side, the truce and thy faith, which has brought me within my paternal walls: but I have come with many tears, after a length of time beholding the courts and the altars of the Gods, and the schools wherein I was brought up, and the fount of Dirce, from which banished by injustice, I inhabit a foreign city, having a stream of tears flowing through my eyes. But, for from one woe springs a second, I behold thee having thy head shorn of its locks, and these sable garments; alas me! on account of my misfortunes. How dreadful a thing, mother, is the enmity of relations, having means of reconciliation seldom to be brought about! For how fares the old man my father in the palace, vainly looking upon darkness; and how fare my two sisters? Are they indeed bewailing my wretched banishment?

JOC. Some God miserably destroys the race of Œdipus; for thus began it, when I brought forth children in that unhallowed manner, and thy father married me in evil hour, and thou didst spring forth. But why relate these things? What is sent by the Gods we must bear. But how I may ask the questions I wish, I know not, for I fear lest I wound at all thy feelings; but I have a great desire.

POL. But inquire freely, leave nothing out. For what you wish, my mother, this is dear to me.

JOC. I ask thee therefore, first, for the information that I wish to obtain. What is the being deprived of one's country, is it a great ill?

POL. The greatest: and greater is it in deed than in word.

JOC. What is the reason of that? What is that so harsh to exiles?

POL. One thing, and that the greatest, not to have the liberty of speaking.

JOC. This that you have mentioned belongs to a slave, not to give utterance to what one thinks.

POL. It is necessary to bear with the follies of those in power.

JOC. And this is painful, to be unwise with the unwise.

POL. But for interest we must bend to slavery contrary to our nature.

JOC. But hopes support exiles, as report goes.

POL. They look upon them with favorable eyes, at least, but are slow of foot.

JOC. Hath not time shown them to be vain?

POL. They have a certain sweet delight to set against misfortunes.

JOC. But whence wert thou supported, before thou foundest means of sustenance by thy marriage?

POL. At one time I had food for the day, at another I had not.

JOC. And did the friends and hosts of your father not assist you?

POL. Be prosperous, *and thou shalt have friends*.[23] but friends are none, should one be in adversity.

JOC. Did not thy noble birth raise thee to great distinction?

POL. To want is wretched; high birth fed me not.

JOC. Their own country, it appears, is the dearest thing to men.

POL. You can not express by words how dear it is.

JOC. But how camest thou to Argos? What intention hadst thou?

POL. Apollo gave a certain oracle to Adrastus.

JOC. What is this thou hast mentioned? I am unable to discover.

POL. To unite his daughters in marriage with a boar and lion.

JOC. And what part of the name of beasts belongs to you, my son.

POL. I know not. The God called me to this fortune.

JOC. For the God is wise. But in what manner didst thou obtain her bed?

POL. It was night; but I came to the portals of Adrastus.

JOC. In search of a couch to rest on, as a wandering exile?

POL. This was the case, and then indeed there came a second exile.

JOC. Who was this? how unfortunate then was he also!

POL. Tydeus, who they say sprung from Œneus his sire.

JOC. In what then did Adrastus liken you to beasts?

POL. Because we came to blows for lodging.

JOC. In this the son of Talaus understood the oracle.

POL. And gave in marriage to us two his two virgin daughters.

JOC. Art thou fortunate then in thy marriage alliance, or unfortunate?

POL. My marriage can not be found fault with up to this day.

JOC. But how didst thou persuade an army to follow you hither?

POL. Adrastus swore this oath to his two sons-in-law, that he would replace both in their own country, but me first. And many princes of the Argives and Mycenæans are at hand, rendering to me a sad, but necessary favor; for I am leading an army against this my own city; but I have called the Gods to witness how unwillingly I have raised the spear against my dearest parents. But the dissolution of these ills extends to thee, my mother, that having reconciled the friendly brothers, you may free from toil me and thyself, and the whole city. It is a proverb long ago chanted, but nevertheless I will repeat it; wealth is honored most of all things by men, and has the greatest influence of any thing among men. In pursuit of which I am come, leading hither ten thousand spears: for a nobly-born man in poverty is nothing.

CHOR. And see Eteocles here comes to this mediation; thy business it is, O Jocasta, being their mother, to speak words, with which thou shalt reconcile thy children.

ETEOCLES, POLYNICES, JOCASTA, CHORUS.

ETEO. Mother, I am present; giving this grace to thee, I have come; what must I do? Let some one begin the conference. Since arranging also around the walls the chariots of the bands, I restrained the city, that I may hear from thee the common terms[24] of reconciliation, for which thou hast permitted this man to come within the walls under sanction of a truce, having persuaded me.

JOC. Stay; precipitate haste has not justice; but slow counsels perform most deeds in wisdom. But repress that fierce eye and those blasts of rage; for thou art not looking on the Gorgon's head cut off at the neck, but thou art looking on thy brother who is come to thee. And do thou again, Polynices, turn thy face toward thy brother; for looking at the same point with thine eyes, thou wilt both speak better, and receive his words better. But I wish to give you a wise piece of advice. When a friend is enraged with a man his friend, having met him face to face, let him fix his eyes on his friend's eyes, this only ought he to consider, the end for which he is come, but to have no recollection of former grievances. Thy words then first, my son, Polynices; for thou art come leading an army of Argives, having suffered injustice, as thou sayest; and may some God be umpire and the reconciler of your strife.

POL. The speech of truth is simple, and those things which are just need not wily interpretations; for they have energy themselves; but the unjust speech, unsound in itself, requires cunning preparations to gloze it. But I have previously considered for my father's house, and my own advantage and that of this man; desiring to escape the curses, which Œdipus denounced formerly against us, I myself of my own accord departed from this land, having given him to rule over his own country for the space of a year, so that I myself should have the government again, having received it in turn, and not having come into enmity and bloodshed with this man to perform some evil deed, and to suffer what is now taking place. But he having assented to this, and having brought the Gods to witness his oaths, has performed nothing of what he promised, but himself holds the regal power and my share of the palace. And now I am ready, having received my own right, to send the army away from out of this land, and to regulate my house, having received it in my turn, and to give it up again to this man for the same space of time, and neither to lay my country waste, nor to apply to its towers the means of ascent by the firmly-fixed ladders. Which, should I not meet with justice, will I endeavor to put in execution: and I call the Gods as witnesses of this, that acting in every thing with justice, I am without justice deprived of my country in the most unrighteous manner. These individual circumstances, mother, not having collected together intricacies of argument, have I declared, but both to the wise and to the illiterate just, as appears to me.

CHOR. To me indeed, although we have not been brought up according to the Grecian land, nevertheless to me thou appearest to speak with judgment.

ETEO. If the same thing were judged honorable alike by all, and at the same time wise, there would not be doubtful strife among men. But now nothing is similar, nothing the same among mortals, except in names; but the sense is not the same, for I, my mother, will speak having kept nothing back; I would mount to the rising of the stars, and sink beneath the earth, were I able to perform this, so that I might possess the greatest of the Goddesses, kingly power.[25] This prize then, my mother, I am not willing rather to give up to another, than to preserve for myself. For it implies cowardice in him, whoever having lost the greater share, hath received the less; but in addition to this I feel ashamed, that this man having come with arms, and laying the country waste, should obtain what he wishes; for to Thebes this would be a reproach, if through fear of the Mycenæan spear I should give up my sceptre for this man to hold. But he ought, my mother, to effect a reconciliation, not by arms: for speech does every thing which even the sword of the enemy could do. But if he is desirous of inhabiting this land in any other way, it is in his power; but the other point I will never give up willingly. When it is in my power to rule, ever to be a slave to him? Wherefore come fire, come sword, yoke thy steeds, fill the plains with chariots, since I will not give up my kingly power to this man. For if one must be unjust, it is most glorious to be unjust concerning empire, but in every thing else one should be just.

CHOR. It is not right to speak well, where the deeds are not glorious; for this is not honorable, but galling to justice.

JOC. My son, Eteocles, not every ill is added to age, but experience has it in its power to evince more wisdom than youth.[26] Why, my child, dost thou so desirously court ambition, the most baneful of the deities? do not thou; the Goddess is unjust. But she hath entered into many families and happy states and hath come forth again, to the destruction of those who have to do with her. Of whom thou art madly enamored. This is more noble, my son, to honor equality, which ever links friends with friends, and states with states, and allies with allies: for equality is sanctioned by law among men. But the lesser share is ever at enmity with the greater, and straight begins the day of hatred. For equality arranged also among mortals measures, and the divisions of weights, and defined numbers. And the dark eye of night, and the light of the sun, equally walk their annual round, and neither of them being overcome hath envy of the other. Thus the sun and the night are subservient to men, but wilt not thou brook having an equal share of government, and give his share to him? Then where is justice? Why dost thou honor so unboundedly that prosperous injustice, royalty, and think so highly of her? Is the being conspicuous honorable? At least, it is empty honor. Or dost thou desire to labor much, possessing much in thy house? but what is superfluity? It possesses but a name; since a sufficiency indeed to the temperate is abundance. Neither do men enjoy riches as their own, but having the property of the Gods do we cherish them. And when they list, again do they take them away. Come, if I ask thee, having proposed together two measures, whether it is thy wish to reign, or save the city? Wilt thou say, to reign? But should he conquer thee, and the Argive spears overcome the Cadmæanforces, thou wilt behold this city of the Thebans vanquished, thou wilt behold many captive maidens with violence ravished by men your foes. Bitter then to Thebes will be the power which thou seekest to hold; but yet thou art ambitious of it. To thee I say this: but to thee, Polynices, say I, that Adrastus hath conferred an unwise favor on thee; and foolishly hast thou also come to destroy this city. Come, if thou wilt subdue this land (may which never happen), by the Gods, how wilt thou erect trophies of thy spear? And how again wilt thou sacrifice the first-fruits, having conquered thy country? and how wilt thou engrave upon the spoils by the waters of Inachus, "Having laid Thebes in ashes, Polynices consecrated these shields to the Gods?" Never, my son, may it come to thee to receive such glory from the Greeks. But again, shouldest thou be conquered, and should the arms of the other prevail, how wilt thou return to Argos having left behind ten thousand dead? Surely some one will say, O! unfortunate marriage alliance! O Adrastus, who placed them on us, through the nuptials of one bride we are lost! Thou art hastening two ills, my son, to be deprived of those, and to fail in this. Give up your too great ardor, give it up; the follies of two when they clash together in the same point, are the most hateful ill.

CHOR. O ye Gods, may ye be averters of these ills, and grant to the children of Œdipus some means of agreement.

ETEO. My mother, this is not a contest of words, but intervening time is fruitlessly wasted; and thy earnestness avails nothing; for we shall not agree in any other way, than on the terms proposed, that I holding the sceptre be monarch of this land. Forbearing then tedious admonitions, let me have my way; and do thou begone from out these walls, or thou shalt die.

POL. By whose hand? Who is there so invulnerable, who having pointed the murderous sword against me, shall not bear the same fate?

ETEO. He is near, not far removed from thee: dost thou look on these my hands?

POL. I see them. But wealth is cowardly, and feeble, loving life.

ETEO. And therefore hast thou come, with such a host against one who is nothing in arms?

POL. For a cautious general is better than one daring.

ETEO. Thou art insolent, having trusted in the truce, which preserves you from death.

POL. A second time again I demand of you the sceptre and my share of the land.

ETEO. I will admit no demand, for I will regulate my own family.

POL. Holding more than your share?

ETEO. I own it; but quit this land.

POL. O ye altars of my paternal Gods.

ETEO. Which thou art come to destroy?

POL. Do ye hear me?

ETEO. Who will hear thee, who art marching against thy country?

POL. And ye shrines of the Gods[27] delighting in the milk-white steeds;

ETEO. Who hate thee.

POL. I am driven out of my own country.

ETEO. For thou hast come to destroy it.

POL. With injustice indeed, O ye Gods!

ETEO. At Mycenæ call upon the Gods, not here.

POL. Thou art impious.

ETEO. But not my country's enemy, as thou art.

POL. Who drives me out without my share.

ETEO. And I will put thee to death in addition.

POL. My father, hearest thou what I suffer?

ETEO. For he hears what wrongs thou doest.

POL. And thou, my mother?

ETEO. It is not lawful for thee to mention thy mother.

POL. O my city!

ETEO. To Argos go, and call on Lerna's stream.

POL. I will go, do not distress thyself; but thee, my mother, I mention with honor.

ETEO. Depart from out of the country.

POL. I will go out; but grant me to see my father.

ETEO. You will not obtain your request.

POL. But my virgin sisters then.

ETEO. Never shalt thou behold these.

POL. O my sisters!

ETEO. Why callest thou on these—being their greatest enemy?

POL. My mother, but thou farewell.

JOC. Do I experience any thing that is well, my son?

POL. I am no longer thy child.

JOC. To many troubles was I born.

POL. For he throws insults on us.

ETEO. For I am insulted in turn.

POL. Where wilt thou stand before the towers?

ETEO. Why dost thou ask me this question?

POL. I will oppose myself to thee, to slay thee.

ETEO. Desire of this seizes me also.

JOC. Wretched me! what will ye do, my children?

POL. The deed itself will show.

JOC. Will ye not escape your father's curses?

ETEO. Let the whole house perish!

POL. Since soon my blood-stained sword will not remain any longer in inactivity. But I call to witness the land that nurtured me, and the Gods, how dishonored I am driven from this land, suffering such foul treatment, as a slave and not born of the same father Œdipus. And if any thing befalls thee, my city, blame not me, but him; for against my will have I come, and against my will am I driven from this land. And thou, king Apollo, God of our streets, and ye shrines, farewell, and ye my equals, and ye altars of the Gods receiving the victims; for I know not if it is allowed me ever again to address you. But hope does not yet slumber, in which I have trusted with the favor of the Gods, that having slain this man, I shall be master of this Theban land.

ETEO. Depart from out of the country; with truth indeed did your father give you the name of Polynices by some divine foreknowledge, a name corresponding with strife.

CHORUS.

Cadmus came from Tyre to this land, before whom the quadrupede heifer bent with willing fall,[28] showing the accomplishment of the oracle, where the divine word ordered him to colonize the plains of the Aonians productive of wheat, where indeed the fair-flowing stream of the water of Dirce passes over the verdant and deep-furrowed fields, where the * * * * mother produced Bacchus, by her marriage with Jove, whom the wreathed ivy twining around him instantly, while yet a babe, blest and covered with its verdant shady branches, an event to be celebrated with Bacchic revel by the Theban virgins and inspired women. There was the bloodstained dragon of Mars, the savage guard, watching with far-rolling eyeballs over the flowing fountains and grassy streams; whom Cadmus, having come for water for purification, slew with a fragment of rock, the destroyer of the monster having thrown his arms with blows on his blood-stained head, by the counsel of the divine Pallas born without mother, having thrown the teeth fallen to the earth upon the deep-furrowed plains. Whence the earth sent forth a spectacle, an armed [host] above the extreme limits of the ground; but iron-hearted slaughter again united them with their beloved earth; and sprinkled with blood the ground which showed them to the serene gales of the air. And thee, sprung of old from our ancestor Io, Epaphus, O progeny of Jove, on thee I called, have I called in a foreign tongue, with prayers in foreign accent, come, come to this land (thy descendants have founded it), where the two Goddesses Proserpine and the dear Goddess Ceres, queen of all (since earth nurtures all things), have held their possessions, send the fire-bearing Goddesses to defend this land: since every thing is easy to the Gods.

ETEOCLES, CHORUS, MESSENGER.

ETEO. Go thou, and bring hither Creon son of Menœceus, the brother of my mother Jocasta, saying this, that I wish to communicate with him counsels of a private nature and those which concern the common welfare of the country, before we go into battle and the ranks of war. And see, he spares the trouble of your steps, by his presence; for I see him coming toward my palace.

CREON, ETEOCLES, CHORUS.

CRE. Surely have I visited many places, desiring to see you, O king Eteocles! and I have gone round to the gates and the guards of the Thebans, seeking you.

ETEO. And indeed I have wished to see you, Creon, for I found attempts at reconciliation altogether fail when I came and entered into conference with Polynices.

CRE. I have heard that he aspires to higher thoughts than Thebes, having trusted in his alliance with Adrastus and his army. But it becomes us to hold these things in dependence on the Gods. But what is most immediately before us, this am I come to acquaint you with.

ETEO. What is this? for I understand not your speech.

CRE. A prisoner is arrived from the Argives.

ETEO. Does he bring us any news of those stationed there?

CRE. The Argive army is preparing quickly to surround the city of the Thebans with thickly-ranged arms.(Note [B].)

ETEO. Therefore must we draw our forces out of the Theban city.

CRE. Whither? Dost thou not in the impetuosity of youth see what it behooves thee to see?

ETEO. Without these trenches, as we are quickly about to fight.

CRE. Small are the forces of this land; but theirs innumerable.

ETEO. I know that they are bold in words.

CRE. Argos of the Greeks has some renown.

ETEO. Be confident; quickly will I fill the plain with their slaughter.

CRE. I would it were so: but this I see is a work of much labor.

ETEO. Know that I will not restrain my forces within the walls.

CRE. And yet the whole of victory is prudence.

ETEO. Dost thou wish then that I have recourse to other measures?

CRE. To every measure indeed, rather than hazard all on one battle.

ETEO. What if we were to attack them by night from ambush?

CRE. If, having failed, at least you can have a safe retreat hither.

ETEO. Night brings the same advantage to all, but more to the daring.

CRE. Dreadful is it to fail in the darkness of night.

ETEO. But shall I lead my force against them while at their meal?

CRE. That would cause terror; but we must conquer.

ETEO. The ford of Dirce is indeed deep to pass.

CRE. Every thing is inferior to a good guard.

ETEO. What then, shall I charge the Argive army with my cavalry?

CRE. And there the army is fenced round with chariots.

ETEO. What then shall I do? give up the city to the enemy?

CRE. By no means; but deliberate if thou art wise.

ETEO. What more prudent forethought is there?

CRE. They say that they have seven men, as I have heard.

ETEO. What have they been commanded to do? for their strength is small.

CRE. To head their bands, to besiege the seven gates.

ETEO. What then shall we do? I will not wait this indecision.

CRE. Do thou thyself also choose seven men for the gates.

ETEO. To head divisions, or for single combat?

CRE. To head divisions, having selected the bravest.

ETEO. I understand you; to guard the approach to the walls.

CRE. And with them other generals; one man sees not every thing?

ETEO. Having chosen them for boldness, or prudence in judgment?

CRE. For both; for one without the other availeth nothing.

ETEO. It shall be so: and having gone to the city of the seven towers, I will appoint chiefs at the gates, as you advise, having opposed equal champions against equal foes. But to mention the name of each would be a great delay, the enemy encamped under our very walls. But I will go, that I may not be idle with my hand. And may it befall me to find my brother opposed to me, and being joined with me in battle, to take him with my spear, [and to slay him, who came to desolate my country.] But it is thy duty to attend to the marriage of my sister Antigone and thy son Hæmon, if I fail aught of success; but the firm vow made before I now confirm at my going out. Thou art my mother's brother, why need I use more words? Treat her worthily, both for thine own and my sake. But my father incurs the punishment of the rashness he brought upon himself, having quenched his sight; I praise him not; even us will he put to death with his execrations, should he gain his point. But one thing is left undone by us, if the soothsayer Tiresias have any oracle to deliver, to enquire this of him; but I will send thy son, Creon, Menœceus, of the same name with thy father, to bring Tiresias hither. With pleasure will he enter into conversation with you; but I lately reviled him with his divining art, so that he is offended with me. But this charge I give the city with thee, Creon; if my arms should conquer, that the body of Polynices be never buried in this Theban land; but that the man who buries him shall die, although he be a friend. This I have told you: but my attendants I tell, bring out my arms, and my panoply which covers me, that we may go this appointed contest of the spear with victorious justice. But to Caution, the most valued of the Goddesses, will we address our prayers to preserve this city.

CHORUS.

O Mars, cause of infinite woe, why, I pray, art thou so possessed with blood and death, so discordant with the revels of Bacchus? Thou dost not in the circle of beautiful dancers in the bloom of youth, having let flow thy hair,[29] on the breath of the flute modulate strains, in which there is a lovely power to renew the dance. But with thy armed men, having excited the army of Argives against Thebes with blood, thou dancest before the city in a most inharmonious revel, thou movest not thy foot maddened by the thyrsus clad in fawn-skins, but thy solid-hoofed steed with thy chariot and horses' bits; and bounding at the streams of Ismenus, thou art borne rapidly in the chariot-course, having excited against the race of those sown [by Cadmus,] a raging host that grasp the shield, well armed, adverse to us at the walls of stone: surely Discord is some dreadful Goddess, who devised all these calamities against the princes of this land, the Labdacidæ involved in woe. O thou forest of heavenly foliage, most productive of beasts, thou snowy eye of Diana, Cithæron, never oughtest thou to have nourished him doomed to death, the son of Jocasta, Œdipus, the babe who was cast out from his home, marked by the golden clasps. Neither ought that winged virgin the Sphinx, thou mountain monster, that grief to this land, to have come, with her most inharmonious lays; who formerly approaching our walls, bore in her four talons the descendants of Cadmus to the inaccessible light of heaven, whom the infernal Pluto sends against the Thebans; but other ill-fated discord among the children of Œdipus springs up in the palace and in the city. For that which is not honorable, never can be honorable, as neither can children the unhallowed offspring of the mother, the pollution of the father. But she came to a kindred bed. Thou didst produce, O [Theban] land! thou didst produce formerly (as I heard the foreign report,[30] I heard it formerly at home), the race sprung from teeth from the fiery-crested dragon fed on beasts, the proudest honor of Thebes. But to the nuptials of Harmonia the Gods came of old, and by the harp and by the lyre of Amphion uprose the walls of Thebes the tower of the double streams,[31] at the midst of the pass of Dirce, which waters the verdant plain before Ismenus. And Io, our ancient mother, doomed to bear horns, brought forth a line of Theban kings. But this city receiving ten thousand goods one in change for another, hath stood in the highest chaplets of war.

TIRESIAS (*led by his daughter*), MENŒCEUS, CREON, CHORUS.

TIR. Lead onward, my daughter, since thou art an eye to my blind steps, as the star to the mariners. Placing my steps hither on this level plain, proceed lest we stumble; thy father is feeble; and preserve carefully in thy virgin hand my calculations which I took, having learned the auguries of the birds, sitting in the sacred seats where I fortell the future. My child, Menœceus, son of Creon, tell me, how far is the remainder of the journey through the city to thy father? Since my knees are weary, and with difficulty I accomplish such a long journey.

CRE. Be of good cheer; for thou hast steered thy foot, Tiresias, near to thy friends; but take hold of him, my son. Since every chariot,[32] and the foot of the aged man is used to expect the assistance of another's hand.

TIR. Well: I am present; but why didst thou call me with such haste, Creon?

CRE. We have not as yet forgotten: but recover thy strength, and collect thy breath, having thrown aside the fatigue occasioned by the journey.

TIR. I am relaxed indeed[32a] with toil, brought hither from the Athenians the day before this. For there also was a contest of the spear with Eumolpus, where I made the descendants of Cecrops splendid conquerors. And I wear this golden chaplet, as thou seest, having received the first-fruits of the spoil of the enemy.

CRE. Thy victorious garlands I make a happy omen. For we, as thou well knowest, are tossing in a storm of war with the Greeks, and great is the hazard of Thebes. The king Eteocles has therefore gone forth adorned with his armor already to battle with the Argives. But to me has he sent that I might learn from you, by doing what we should be most likely to preserve the city.

TRE. For Eteocles' sake indeed I would have stopped my mouth, and repressed the oracles, but to thee, since thou desirest to know them, will I declare them: for this land labors under the malady of old, O Creon, from the time when Laïus became the father of children in spite of the Gods, and begat the wretched Œdipus, a husband for his mother. But the cruel lacerations of his eyes were in the wisdom of the Gods, and a warning to Greece. Which things the sons of Œdipus seeking to conceal among themselves by the lapse of time, as about forsooth to escape from the Gods, erred through their ignorance, for they neither giving the honor due to their father, nor allowing him a free liberty, infuriated the unfortunate man: and he breathed out against them dreadful threats, being both in affliction, and moreover dishonored. And I, what things omitting to do, and what words omitting to speak on the subject, have nevertheless fallen into the hatred of the sons of Œdipus? But death from their mutual hands is near them, O Creon. And many corses fallen around corses, having mingled the weapons of Argos and Thebes, shall cause bitter lamentations to the Theban land. And thou, O wretched city, art sapped from thy foundations, unless men will obey my words. For this were the first thing, that not any of the family of Œdipus should be citizens, nor king of the territory, inasmuch as they are possessed by demons, and are they that will overthrow the city. And since the evil triumphs over the good, there is one other thing requisite to insure preservation. But, as this is neither safe for me to say, and distressing to those on whom the lot has fallen, to give to the city the balm of preservation, I will depart: farewell; for being an individual with many shall I suffer what is about to happen if it must be so; for what can I do![33]

CRE. Stay here, old man.

TIR. Lay not hold upon me.

CRE. Remain; why dost thou fly me?

TIR. Thy fortune flies thee, but not I.

CRE. Tell me the means of preserving the citizens and their city.

TRE. Thou wishest now indeed, and soon thou wilt not wish.

CRE. And how am I not willing to preserve my country?

TIR. Art thou willing then to hear, and art thou eager?

CRE. For toward what ought I to have a greater eagerness?

TIR. Hear now then my prophecies.—But this first I wish to ascertain clearly, where is Menœceus who brought me hither.

CRE. He is not far off, but close to thee.

TIR. Let him depart then afar from my oracles.

CRE. He that is my son will keep secret what ought to be kept secret.

TIR. Art thou willing then that I speak in his presence?

CRE. *Yes*: for he would be delighted to hear of the means of preservation.

TIR. Hear now then the tenor of my oracles; what things doing ye may preserve the city of the Cadmeans. It is necessary for thee to sacrifice this thy son Menœceus for the country, since thou thyself callest for this fortune.

CRE. What sayest thou, what word is this thou hast spoken, old man?

TIR. As circumstances are, thus also oughtest thou to act.

CRE. O thou, that hast said many evils in a short time!

TIR. To thee at least; but to thy country great and salutary.

CRE. I heard not, I attended not; let the city go where it will.

TIR. This is no longer the same man; he retracts again what he said.

CRE. Farewell! depart; for I have no need of thy prophecies.

TIR. Has truth perished, because thou art unfortunate?

CRE. By thy knees I implore thee, and by thy reverend locks.

TIR. Why kneel to me? the evils thou askest are hard to be controlled. (Note [E].)

CRE. Keep it secret; and speak not these words to the city.

TIR. Dost thou command me to be unjust? I can not be silent.

CRE. What then wilt thou do to me? Wilt thou slay my son?

TIR. These things will be a care to others; but by me will it be spoken.

CRE. But from whence has this evil come to me, and to my child?

TIR. Well dost thou ask me, and comest to the drift of my discourse. It is necessary that he, stabbed in that cave where the earth-born dragon lay, the guardian of Dirce's fountain, give his gory blood a libation to the earth on account of the ancient wrath of Mars against Cadmus, who avenges the slaughter of the earth-born dragon; and these things done, ye shall obtain Mars as your ally. But if the earth receive fruit in return for fruit, and mortal blood in return for blood, ye shall have that land propitious, which formerly sent forth a crop of men from seed armed with golden helmets; but there must of this race die one, who is the son of the dragon's jaw. But thou art left among us of the race of those sown men, pure in thy descent, both by thy mother's side and in the male line; and thy children too: Hæmon's marriage however precludes his being slain, for he is not a youth, [for, although he has not approached her bed, he has yet contracted the marriage.] But this youth, devoted to this city, by dying may preserve his native country. And he will cause a bitter return to Adrastus and the Argives, casting back death over their eyes, and Thebes will he make illustrious: of these two fates choose the one; either preserve thy child or the state. Every information from me thou hast:—lead me, my child, toward home;—but whoever exercises the art of divination, is a fool; if indeed he chance to show disagreeable things, he is rendered hateful to those to whom he may prophesy; but speaking falsely to his employers from motives of pity, he is unjust as touching the Gods.—Phœbus alone should speak in oracles to men, who fears nobody.

CREON, MENŒCEUS, CHORUS.

CHOR. Creon, why art thou mute compressing thy voice in silence, for to me also there is no less consternation.

CRE. But what can one say?—It is clear however what my answer will be. For never will I go to this degree of calamity, to expose my son a victim for the state. For all men live with an affection toward their children, nor would any give up his own child to die. Let no one praise me for the deed, and slay my children. But I myself, for I am arrived at a mature period of life, am ready to die to liberate my country. But haste, my son, before the whole city hears it, disregarding the intemperate oracles of prophets, fly as quickly as possible, having quitted this land. For he will tell these things to the authorities and chiefs, going to the seven gates, and to the officers: and if indeed we get before him, there is safety for thee, but if thou art too late, we are undone, thou diest.

MEN. Whither then fly? To what city? what friends?

CRE. Wheresoever thou wilt be farthest removed from this country.

MEN. Therefore it is fitting for thee to speak, and for me to do.

CRE. Having passed through Delphi—

MEN. Whither is it right for me to go, my father?

CRE. To the land of Ætolia.

MEN. And from this whither shall I proceed?

CRE. To Thesprotia's soil.

MEN. To the sacred seat of Dodona?

CRE. Thou understandest.

MEN. What then will there be to protect me?

CRE. The conducting deity.

MEN. But what means of procuring money?

CRE. I will supply gold.

MEN. Thou sayest well, my father. Go then, for having proceeded to salute[34] thy sister, whose breast I first sucked, Jocasta I mean, deprived of my mother, and reft from her, an orphan, I will depart and save my life. But haste, go, let not thy purpose be hindered.

MENŒCEUS, CHORUS.

MEN. Ye females, how well removed I my father's fears, having deceived him with words, in order to gain my wishes; who sends me out of the way, depriving the city of its good fortune, and gives me up to cowardice. And these things are pardonable indeed in an old man, but in my case it deserves no pardon to become the deserter of that country which gave me birth. That ye may know then, I will go, and preserve the city, and will give up my life for this land. For it is a disgraceful thing, that those indeed who are free from the oracle, and are not concerned with any compulsion of the Gods, standing at their shields in battle, shall not be slow to die fighting before the towers for their country; and I, having betrayed my father, and my brother, and my own city, shall depart coward-like from out of the land; but wherever I live, I shall appear vile. No: by that Jove that dwelleth amidst the constellations, and sanguinary Mars, who set up those sown men, who erst sprung from the earth, to be kings of this country. But I will depart, and standing on the summit of the battlements, stabbing myself over the dark deep lair of the dragon, where the prophet appointed, will give liberty to the country—the word has been spoken. But I go, by my death about to give no mean gift to the state, and will rid this land of its affliction. For if every one, seizing what opportunity he had in his power of doing good, would persist in it, and bring it forward for his country's weal, states, experiencing fewer calamities, henceforward might be prosperous.

CHOR. Thou camest forth, thou camest forth, O winged monster, production of the earth, and the viper of hell, the ravager of the Cadmeans, big with destruction, big with woes, in form half-virgin, a hostile prodigy, with thy ravening wings, and thy talons that preyed on raw flesh, who erst from Dirce's spot bearing aloft the youths, accompanied by an inharmonious lay, thou broughtest, thou broughtest cruel woes to our country; cruel was he of the Gods, whoever was the author of these things. And the moans of the matrons, and the moans of the virgins, resounded in the house, in a voice, in a strain of misery, they lamented some one thing, some another, in succession through the city. And the groaning and the noise was like to thunder, when the winged virgin bore out of sight any man from the city. But at length came by the mission of the Pythian oracle Œdipus the unhappy to this land of Thebes, to us then indeed delighted, but again came woes. For he, wretched man, having gained the glorious victory over the enigmas, contracts a marriage, an unfortunate marriage with his mother, and pollutes the city. And fresh woes does the unfortunate man cause to succeed with slaughter, devoting by curses his sons to the unhallowed contest.—With admiration, with admiration we look on him, who is gone to kill himself for the sake of his country's land; to Creon indeed having left lamentations, but about to make the seven-towered gates of the land greatly victorious. Thus may we be mothers, thus may we be blest in our children, O dear Pallas, who destroyedst the blood of the dragon by the hurled stone, driving the attention of Cadmus to the action, whence with rapine some fiend of the Gods rushed on this land.

MESSENGER, JOCASTA, CHORUS.

MESS. Ho there! who is at the gate of the palace? Open, conduct Jocasta from out of the house.—What ho! again—after a long time indeed, but yet come forth, hear, O renowned wife of Œdipus, ceasing from thy lamentations, and thy tears of grief.

JOC. O most dear man, surely thou comest bearing the news of some calamity, of the death of Eteocles, by whose shield thou always didst go, warding off the weapons of the enemy. What new message, I pray, dost thou come to deliver? Is my son dead or alive? Tell me.

MESS. He lives, be not alarmed for this, for I will rid thee of this fear.

JOC. But what? In what state are our seven-towered ramparts?

MESS. They stand unshaken, nor is the city destroyed.

JOC. Come they in danger from the spear of Argos?

MESS. To the very extreme of danger; but the arms of Thebes came off superior to the Mycenæan spear.

JOC. Tell me one thing, by the Gods, whether thou knowest any thing of Polynices (since this is a concern to me also) whether he sees the light.

MESS. Thus far in the day thy pair of children lives.

JOC. Be thou blest. But how did ye stationed on the towers drive off the spear of Argos from the gates? Tell me, that I may go and delight the old blind man in the house with the news of his country's being preserved.

MESS. After that the son of Creon, he that died for the land, standing on the summit of the towers, plunged the black-handled sword into his throat, the salvation of this land, thy son placed seven cohorts, and their leaders with them, at the seven gates, guards against the Argive spear; and he drew up the horse ready to support the horse, and the heavy-armed men to reinforce the shield-bearers, so that to the part of the wall which was in danger there might be succor at hand. But from the lofty citadel we view the army of the Argives with their white shields, having quitted Tumessus and now come near the trench, at full speed they reached the city of the land of Cadmus. And the pæan and the trumpets at the same time from them resounded, and off the walls from us. And first indeed Parthenopæus the son of the huntress (*Atalanta*) led his division horrent with their thick shields against the Neïtan[35] gate, having a family device in the middle of his shield, Atalanta destroying the Ætolian boar with her distant-wounding bow. And against the Prætan gate marched the prophet Amphiaraüs, having victims in his car, not bearing an insolent emblem, but modestly having his arms without a device. But against the Ogygian gate stood Prince Hippomedon, bearing an emblem in the middle of his shield, the Argus gazing with his spangled[36] eyes, [some eyes indeed with the rising of the stars awake,[37] and some with the setting closed, as we had the opportunity of seeing afterward when he was dead.] But Tydeus was drawn up at the Homoloïan gate, having on his shield a lion's skin rough with his mane, but in his right hand he bore a torch, as the Titan Prometheus,[38] intent on firing the city. But thy son Polynices drew up his array at the Crenean gate; but the swift Potnian mares, the emblem on his shield, were starting through fright, well circularly[39] grouped within *the orb* at the handle of the shield, so that they seemed infuriated. But Capaneus, not holding less notions than Mars on the approaching battle, drew up his division against the Electran gate. Upon the iron embossments of his shield was an earth-born giant bearing upon his shoulders a whole city, which he had torn up from the foundations with bars, an intimation to us what our city should suffer. But at the seventh gate was Adrastus, having his shield filled with a hundred vipers, bearing on his left arm a representation of the hydra, the boast of Argos, and from the midst of the walls the dragons were bearing the children of the Thebans in their jaws. But I had the opportunity of seeing each of these, as I took the word of battle to the leaders of the divisions. And first indeed we fought with bows, and javelins, and distant-wounding slings, and fragments of rocks; but when we were conquering in the fight, Tydeus shouted out, and thy son on a sudden, "O sons of the Danaï, why delay we, ere we are galled with their missile weapons, to make a rush at the gates all in a body, light-armed men, horsemen, and those who drive the chariots?" And when they heard the cry, no one was backward; but many fell, their heads besmeared with blood; of us also you might have seen before the walls frequent divers toppling to the ground; and they moistened the parched earth with streams of blood. But the Arcadian, no Argive, the son of Atalanta, as some whirlwind falling on the gates, calls out for fire and a spade, as though he would dig up the city. But Periclymenus the son of the God of the Ocean stopped him in his raging, hurling at his head a stone, a wagon-load, a pinnacle[40] *rent* from the battlement; and dashed in pieces his head with its auburn hair, and crushed the suture of the bones, and besmeared with blood his lately blooming cheeks; nor shall he carry back his living form to his mother, glorious in her bow, the daughter of Mænalus. But when thy son saw this gate was in a state of safety, he went to another, and I followed. But I see Tydeus, and many armed with shields around him, darting with their Ætolian lances at the highest battlements of the towers, so that our men put to flight quitted the heights of the ramparts; but thy son, as a hunter, collects them together again; and posted them a second time on the towers; and we hasten on to another gate, having relieved the distress in this quarter. But Capaneus, how can I express the measure of his rage! For he came bearing the ranges of a long-reaching ladder, and made this high boast, "That not even the hallowed fire of Jove should hinder him from taking the city from its highest turrets." And these things soon as he had proclaimed, though assailed with stones, he clambered up, having contracted his body under his shield, climbing the slippery footing of the bars[41] of the ladder: but when he was now mounting the battlements of the walls Jupiter strikes him with his thunder; and the earth resounded, insomuch that all trembled; and his limbs were hurled, as it were by a sling, from the ladder separately from one another, his hair to heaven, and his blood to the ground, and his limbs, like the whirling of Ixion on his wheel, were carried round; and his scorched body falls to the earth. But when Adrastus saw that Jove was hostile to his army, he stationed the host of the Argives without the trench. But ours on the contrary, when they saw the auspicious sign from Jove, drove out their chariots, horsemen and heavy-armed, and rushing into the midst of the Argive arms engaged in fight: and there were all the sorts of misery together: they died, they fell from their chariots, and the wheels leaped up and axles upon axles: and corses were heaped together with corses.—We have preserved then our towers from being overthrown to this present day; but whether for the future this land will be prosperous, rests with the Gods.

CHOR. To conquer is glorious; but if the Gods have the better intent, may I be fortunate!

JOC. Well are the ways of the Gods, and of fortune; for my children live, and my country has escaped; but the unhappy Creon seems to feel the effects of my marriage, and of Œdipus's misfortunes, being deprived of his child; for the state indeed, happily, but individually, to his misery: but recount to me again, what after this did my two sons purpose to do?

MESS. Forbear the rest; for in every circumstance hitherto thou art fortunate.

JOC. This hast thou said so as to raise suspicion; I must not forbear.

MESS. Dost thou want any thing more than that thy sons are safe?

JOC. In what follows also I would hear if I am fortunate.

MESS. Let me go: thy son is deprived of his armor-bearer.

JOC. Thou concealest some ill and coverest it in obscurity.

MESS. I can not speak thy ills after thy happiness.

JOC. *But thou shalt*, unless fleeing from me thou fleest through the air.

MESS. Alas! alas! Why dost thou not suffer me to depart after a message of glad tidings, but forcest me to tell calamities?—Thy sons are intent on most shameful deeds of boldness—to engage in single combat apart from the whole army, having addressed to the Argives and Thebans in common a speech, such as they never ought to have spoken. But Eteocles began, standing on the lofty turret, having commanded to proclaim silence to the army. And he said, "O generals of the Grecian land, and chieftains of the Danaï, who have come hither, and O people of Cadmus, neither for the sake of Polynices barter your lives, nor for my cause. For I myself, taking this danger on myself, alone will enter the lists with my brother; and if indeed I slay him, I will dwell in the palace alone; but should I be subdued, I will give it up to him alone. But you, ceasing from the combat, O Argives, shall return to your land, not leaving your lives here; [of the Theban people also there is enough that lieth dead,"] Thus much he spake; but thy son Polynices rushed from the ranks, and approved his words. But all the Argives murmured their applause, and the people of Cadmus, as thinking this plan just. And after this the generals made a truce, and in the space between the two armies pledged an oath to abide by it. And now the two sons of the aged Œdipus clad their bodies in an entire suit of brazen armor. And their friends adorned them, the champion of this land indeed the chieftains of the Thebans; and him the principal men of the Danaï. And they stood resplendent, and they changed not their color, raging to let forth their spears at each other. But their friends on either side as they passed by encouraging them with words, thus spoke. "Polynices, it rests with thee to erect the statue of Jove, emblem of victory, and to confer a glorious fame on Argos." But to Eteocles on the other hand;

"Now thou fightest for the state, now if thou come off victorious, thou art in possession of the sceptre." These things they said exhorting them to the combat. But the seers sacrificed the sheep, and scrutinized the shooting of the flames, and the bursting *of the gall*, the moisture adverse[42] *to the fire*, and the extremity of the flame, which bears a two-fold import, both the sign of victory,[43] and the sign of being defeated.[44] But if thou hast any power, or words of wisdom, or the soothing charms of incantation, go, stay thy children from the fearful combat, since great the danger, [and dreadful will be the sequel of the contest, *namely*, tears for thee, deprived this day of thy two children.]

JOC. O my child, Antigone, come forth from before the palace; the state of thy fortune suits not now the dance, nor the virgin's chamber, but it is thy duty, in conjunction with thy mother, to hinder two excellent men, and thy brothers verging toward death from falling by each other's hands.

ANTIGONE, JOCASTA, CHORUS.

ANT. With what new horrors, O mother of my being, dost thou call out to thy friends before the house?

JOC. O my daughter, the life of thy brothers is gone from them.

ANT. How sayest thou?

JOC. They are drawn out in single combat.

ANT. Alas me! what wilt thou say, my mother?

JOC. Nothing of pleasant import; but follow.

ANT. Whither? leaving my virgin chamber.

JOC. To the army.

ANT. I am ashamed to go among the crowd.

JOC. Thy present state admits not bashfulness.

ANT. But what shall I do then?

JOC. Thou shalt quell the strife of the brothers.

ANT. Doing what, my mother.

JOC. Falling before them with me.

ANT. Lead to the space between the armies; we must not delay.

JOC. Haste, daughter, haste, since, if indeed I reach my sons before they engage, I still exist in heaven's fair light, but if they die, I shall lie dead with them.

CHORUS.

Alas! alas! shuddering with horror, shuddering is my breast; and through my flesh came pity, pity for the unhappy mother, on account of her two children, whether of them then will distain with blood the other (alas me for my sufferings, O Jove, O earth), the own brother's neck, the own brother's life, in arms, in slaughter? Wretched, wretched I, over which corse then shall I raise the lamentation for the dead? O earth, earth, the two beasts of prey, blood-thirsty souls, brandishing the spear, will quickly distain with blood the fallen, fallen enemy. Wretches, that they ever came to the thought of a single combat! In a foreign strain will I mourn with tears my elegy of groans due to the dead. Destiny is at hand—death is near; this day will decide the event. Ill-fated, ill-fated murder because of the Furies! But I see Creon here with clouded brow advancing toward the house, I will cease therefore from the groans I am uttering.

CREON, CHORUS.

CRE. Ah me! what shall I do? whether am I to groan in weeping myself, or the city, which a cloud of such magnitude encircles as to cast us amidst the gloom of Acheron? For my son has perished having died for the city, having achieved a glorious name, but to me a name of sorrow. Him having taken just now from the dragon's den, stabbed by his own hand, I wretched bore in my arms; and the whole house resounds with shrieks; but I, myself aged, am come after my aged sister Jocasta, that she may wash and lay out my son now no more. For it behooves the living well to revere the God below by paying honors to the dead.

CHOR. Thy sister is gone out of the house, O Creon, and the girl Antigone attending the steps of her mother.

CRE. Whither? and for what hap? tell me.

CHOR. She heard that her sons were about to come to a contest in single battle for the royal palace.

CRE. How sayest thou? whilst I was fondly attending to my son's corse, I arrived not so far *in knowledge*, as to be acquainted with this also.

CHOR. But thy sister has indeed been gone some time; but I think, O Creon, that the contest, in which their lives are at stake, has already been concluded by the sons of Œdipus.

CRE. Ah me! I see indeed this signal, the downcast eye and countenance of the approaching messenger, who will relate every thing that has taken place.

MESSENGER, CREON, CHORUS.

MESS. O wretched me! what language or what words can I utter? we are undone—

CRE. Thou beginnest thy speech with no promising prelude.

MESS. Oh wretched me! doubly do I lament, for I hear great calamities.

CRE. In addition to the calamities that have happened dost thou still speak of others?

MESS. Thy sister's sons, O Creon, no longer behold the light.

CRE. Ah! alas! thou utterest great ills to me and to the state.

MESS. O mansions of Œdipus, do ye hear these things of thy children who have perished by similar fates?

CHOR. Ay, so that, had they but sense, they would weep.

CRE. O most heavy misery! Oh me wretched with woes! alas! unhappy me!

MESS. If that thou knewest the evils yet in addition to these.

CRE. And how can there be more fatal ills than these?

MESS. Thy sister is dead with her two children.

CHOR. Raise, raise the cry of woe, and smite your heads with the blows of your white hands.

CRE. Oh unhappy Jocasta, what an end of thy life and of thy marriage hast thou endured in the riddles of the Sphinx![45] But how took place the slaughter of her two sons, and the combat arising from the curse of Œdipus? tell me.

MESS. The success of the country before the towers indeed thou knowest; for the circuit of the wall is not of such vast extent, but that thou must know all that has taken place. But after that the sons of the aged Œdipus had clad their limbs in brazen armor, they came and stood in the midst of the plain between the two armies, ready for the contest, and the fierceness of the single battle. And having cast a look toward Argos, Polynices uttered his prayer; "O venerable Juno (for I am thine, since in marriage I joined myself with the daughter of Adrastus, and dwell in that land), grant me to slay my brother, and to cover with blood my hostile hand bearing the victory." And Eteocles looking at the temple of Pallas, glorious in her golden shield, prayed; "O Daughter of Jove, grant me with my hand to hurl my victorious spear from this arm home to the breast of my brother, [and slay him who came to lay waste my country."] And when the sound of the Tuscan trumpet was raised, as the torch, the signal for the fierce battle, they sped with dreadful rush toward each other; and like wild boars whetting their savage tusks, they met, their cheeks all moist with foam; and they rushed forward with their lances; but they couched beneath the orbs of their shields, in order that the steel might fall harmless. But if either perceived the other's eye raised above the verge, he drove the lance at his face, intent to be beforehand with him: but dexterously they shifted their eyes to the open ornaments of their shields, so that the spear was made of none effect. And more sweat trickled down the spectators than the combatants, through the fear of their friends. But Eteocles, stumbling with his foot against a stone, which rolled under his tread,[46] places his limb without the shield. But Polynices ran up with his spear, when he saw a stroke open to his steel, and the Argive spear passed through the shank. And all the host of the Danaï shouted for joy. And the hero who first was wounded, when he perceived his shoulder exposed in this effort, pierced the breast of Polynices with his lance, and gave joy to the citizens of Cadmus, but he broke the point of his spear. But being come to a strait for a spear, he retreated backward on his leg, and taking a stone of marble, he hurled it and crashed *his antagonist's* spear in the middle: and the battle was on equal terms, both being deprived of the spear in their hands. Then seizing the handles of their swords they met at close quarters, and, as they clashed their shields together, raised a great tumult of battle around them. And Eteocles having a sort of idea of its success, made use of a Thessalian stratagem, *which he had learned* from his connection with that country. For giving up his present mode of attack, he brings his left foot behind, protecting well the pit of his own stomach; and stepping forward his right leg, he plunged the sword through the navel, and drove it to the vertebræ. But the unhappy Polynices bending together his side and his bowels falls weltering in blood. But the other, as he were now the victor, and had subdued him in the fight, casting his sword on the ground, went to spoil him, not fixing his attention on himself, but on that his purpose. Which thing also deceived him; for Polynices, he that fell first, still breathing a little, preserving his sword e'en in his deathly fall, with difficulty indeed, but he did stretch his sword to the heart of Eteocles. And holding the dust in their gripe they both fall near one another, and determined not the victory.

CHOR. Alas! alas! to what degree, O Œdipus, do I groan for thy misfortunes! but the God seems to have fulfilled thy imprecations.

MESS. Hear now then woes even in addition to these—For when her sons having fallen were breathing their last, at this moment the wretched mother rushes before them, and when she perceived them stricken with mortal wounds she shrieked out, "Oh my sons, I am come too late a succor:" and throwing herself by the side of her children in turn, she wept, she lamented with moans her long anxiety in suckling them *now lost*: and their sister, who accompanied to stand by her in her misery, at the same time *broke forth*; "O supporters of my mother's age! Oh ye that have betrayed my hopes of marriage, my dearest brothers!"—But king Eteocles heaving from his breast his gasping breath, heard his mother, and putting out his cold clammy hand, sent not forth indeed a voice; but from his eyes spoke her in tears to signify affection. But Polynices, who yet breathed, looking at his sister and his aged mother, thus spoke: "We perish, O my mother; but I grieve for thee, and for this my sister, and my brother who lies dead, for being my friend, he became my enemy, but still my friend.—But bury me, O mother of my being, and thou my sister, in my native land, and pacify the exasperated city, that I may obtain thus much at least of my country's land, although I have lost the palace. And close my eyelids with thy hand, my mother" (and he places it himself upon his eyes), "and fare ye well! for now darkness surroundeth me." And both breathed out their lives together. And the mother, when she saw what had taken place, beyond endurance grieving, snatched the sword from the dead body, and perpetrated a deed of horror; for she drove the steel through the middle of her throat, and lies dead on those most dear to her, having each in her arms embraced. But the people rose up hastily to a strife of opinions; we indeed, as holding, that my master was victorious; but they, that the other was; and there was also a contention between the generals, those on the other side *contended*, that Polynices first struck with the spear, but those on ours that there was no victory where the combatants died. [And in the mean time Antigone withdrew from the army;] but they rushed to arms; but fortunately by a sort of foresight the people of Cadmus had sat upon their shields: and we gained the advantage of falling on the Argives not yet accoutred in their arms. And no one made a stand, but flying they covered the plain; and immense quantities of blood were spilt of the corses that fell, but when we were victorious in the fight, some indeed raised the image of Jove emblem of victory, but some of us stripping the shields from the Argive corses sent the spoils within the city. But others with Antigone are bearing hither the dead for their friends to lament over. But these contests have in some respect turned out most happy for this state, but in other respect most unhappy.

CHOR. No longer the misfortunes of the house come to our ears, we may also see before the palace these three fallen corses, who have shared the dark realms by a united death.

[*The dead bodies borne.*]

ANTIGONE, CREON, CHORUS.

ANT. Not veiling the softness of my cheek on which my ringlets fall, nor caring for the purple glow of virginity under my lids, the blush of my countenance, I am borne along the bacchanal of the dead, rending the fillet from my hair, rejecting the saffron robe of delicateness, having the mournful

- 118 -

office of conducting the dead. Alas! alas! woe is me! Oh Polynices, thou well answeredst to thy name! Alas me! Oh Thebes! but thy strife, no strife, but murder consummated with murder,[47] hath destroyed the house of Œdipus with dreadful, with mournful blood. But what groan responsive to my sufferings, or what lament of music shall I invoke to my tears, to my tears, O house, O house, bearing these three kindred bodies, my mother, and her children, the joy of the fury? who destroyed the entire house of Œdipus, what time intelligently[48] he unfolded the difficult song of the fierce monster, having thereby slain the body of the fierce musical Sphinx. Alas me! my father; what Grecian, or what Barbarian, or what other of the noble in birth, of mortal blood, in time of old ever bore such manifest sufferings of so many ills? Wretched I, how do I lament! What bird, sitting on the highest boughs of the oak or pine, will sing responsive to my lamentations, who have lost my mother? who weep the strain of grief in addition to these moans *for my brothers*, about to pass my long life in floods of tears.—Which shall I bewail? On which first shall I scatter the first offerings rent from my hair? On my mother's two breasts of milk, or upon the death-wounds of my two brothers? Alas! alas! Leave thine house, bringing thy sightless eye, O aged father, Œdipus, show thy wretched age, who within thy palace having poured the gloomy darkness over thine eyes, draggest on a long[49] life. Dost thou hear wandering in the hall,—resting thy aged foot upon the couch in a state of misery?

ŒDIPUS, CREON, ANTIGONE, CHORUS.

ŒD. Why, O virgin, hast thou with the most doleful tears called me forth leaning on the support of a blind foot[50] to the light, a bed-ridden man from his darksome chamber, gray-headed, an obscure phantom of air—a dead body beneath the earth—a flitting dream?

ANT. O father, thou shalt receive words of unhappy tidings; no longer do thy children behold the light, nor thy wife, who ever was employed in attending as a staff on thy blind foot, my father: alas me!

ŒD. Alas me, for my sufferings! for well may I groan and vociferate these things. The three souls, tell me, my child, by what fate, how quitted they this light?

ANT. Not for the sake of reproaching thee, nor exulting over thee, but for grief I speak: thy evil genius, heavy with swords, and fire, and wretched combats, has rushed down upon thy children, O my father.

ŒD. Alas me! ah! ah!

ANT. Why dost thou thus groan?

ŒD. Alas me! my children!

ANT. Thou wouldest grieve indeed, if looking on the chariot of the sun drawn by its four steeds, thou couldest direct the sight of thine eyes to these bodies of the dead.

ŒD. The evil of my sons indeed is manifest; but my wretched wife, by what fate, O my child, did she perish?

ANT. Causing to all tears of grief they could not contain, to her children she bared her breast, a suppliant she bared it, holding it up in supplication. But the mother found her children at the Electran gate, in the meàd where the lotus abounds, contending with their lances in the common war, as lions bred in the same cave, with the blood-wounds now a cold, a gory libation, which Plato received, and Mars gave. And having seized the brazen-wrought sword from the dead she plunged it into her flesh, but with grief for her children she fell amidst her children. But all these sufferings, O my father, has the God heaped this day upon our house, whoever he be, that adds this consummation.

CHOR. This day hath been the beginning of many woes to the house of Œdipus; but may life be more fortunate!

CRE. Now indeed cease from your grief, for it is time to think of the sepulture. But hear these words, O Œdipus; Eteocles, thy son, hath given to me the dominion of this land, giving them as a marriage portion to Hæmon, and *with them* the bed of thy daughter Antigone. I therefore will not suffer thee any longer to dwell in this land. For clearly did Tiresias say, that never, whilst thou dost inhabit this land, will the state be prosperous. But depart; and this I say not from insolence, nor being thine enemy, but on account of thy evil genius, fearing lest the country suffer any harm.

ŒD. O Fate, from the beginning how wretched [and unhappy] didst thou form me, [if ever other man was formed!] whom, even before I came into the light from my mother's womb, when yet unborn Apollo foretold that I should be the murderer of my father Laïus, alas! wretch that I am! And when I was born, again my father who gave me life, seeks to take my life, considering that I was born his enemy: for it was fated that he should die by my hands, and he sends me, poor wretch, as I craved the breast, a prey for the wild beasts: where I was preserved—for would that Cithæron, it ought, had sunk to the bottomless chasms of Tartarus, for that it did not destroy me; but the God fixed it my lot to serve under Polybus my master: but I unhappy man, having slain my own father, ascended the bed of my wretched mother, and begat children, my brothers, whom I destroyed, having received down the curse from Laïus, and given it to my sons. For I was not by nature so utterly devoid of understanding, as to have devised such things against my eyes, and against the life of my children, without the interference of some of the Gods. Well!—what then shall I ill-fated do? who will accompany me the guide of my dark steps? She that lies here dead! living, well know I, she would. But my noble pair of sons? I have no sons.—But still in my vigor can I myself procure my sustenance? Whence?—Why, O Creon, dost thou thus utterly kill me? for kill me thou wilt, if thou shalt cast me out of the land. Yet will I not appear base, stretching my hands around thy knees, for I can not belie my former nobleness, not even though my plight is miserable.

CRE. Well has it been spoken by thee, that thou wilt not touch my knees, but I can not permit thee to dwell in the land. But of these corses, the one we must even now bear to the house; but the body of Polynices cast out unburied beyond the borders of this land. And these things shall be proclaimed to all the Thebans: "whoever shall be found either crowning the corse, or covering it with earth, shall receive death for his offense." But thou, ceasing from the groans for the three dead, retire, Antigone, within the house, and behave as beseems a virgin, expecting the approaching day in which the bed of Hæmon awaits thee.

ANT. Oh father, in what a state of woes do we miserable beings lie! How do I lament for thee! more than for the dead! For it is not that one of thy ills is heavy, and the other not heavy, but thou art in all things unhappy, my father.—But thee I ask, our new lord, [wherefore dost thou insult my father here, banishing him from his country?] Why make thy laws against an unhappy corse?

CRE. The determination of Eteocles this, not mine.

ANT. It is absurd, and thou a fool to enforce it.

CRE. How so? Is it not just to execute injunctions?

ANT. No, if they are base, at least, and spoken with ill intent.

CRE. What! will he not with justice be given to the dogs?

ANT. *No*, for thus do ye not demand of him lawful justice.

CRE. *We do*; since he was the enemy of the state, who least ought to be an enemy.

ANT. Hath he not paid then his life to fortune?

CRE. And in his burial too let him now satisfy vengeance.

ANT. What outrage having committed, if he came after his share of the kingdom?

CRE. This man, that you may know once for all, shall be unburied.

ANT. I will bury him; even though the city forbid it.

CRE. Thyself then wilt thou at the same time bury near the corse.

ANT. But that is a glorious thing, for two friends to lie near.

CRE. Lay hold of her, and bear her to the house.

ANT. By no means—for I will not let go this body.

CRE. The God has decreed it, O virgin, not as thou wilt.

ANT. And this too is decreed—that the dead be not insulted.

CRE. Around him none shall place the moist dust.

ANT. Nay, by his mother here Jocasta, I entreat thee, Creon.

CRE. Thou laborest in vain, for thou canst not obtain this.

ANT. But suffer thou me at any rate to bathe the body.

CRE. This would be one of the things forbidden by the state.

ANT. But let me put bandages round his cruel wounds.

CRE. In no way shalt thou show respect to this corse.

ANT. Oh most dear, but I will at least kiss thy lips.

CRE. Thou shalt not prepare calamity against thy wedding by thy lamentations.

ANT. What! while I live shall I ever marry thy son?

CRE. There is strong necessity for thee, for by what means wilt thou escape the marriage?

ANT. That night then shall find me one of the Danaïdæ.

CRE. Dost mark with what audacity she hath insulted us?

ANT. The steel be witness, and the sword, by which I swear.

CRE. But why art thou so eager to get rid of this marriage?

ANT. I will take my flight with my most wretched father here.

CRE. There is nobleness in thee; but there is some degree of folly.

ANT. And I will die with him too, that thou mayest farther know.

CRE. Go—thou shalt not slay my son—quit the land.

CEDIPUS, ANTIGONE, CHORUS.

ŒD. O daughter, I praise thee indeed for thy zealous intentions.

ANT. But if I were to marry, and thou suffer banishment alone, my father?

ŒD. Stay and be happy; I will bear with content mine own ills.

ANT. And who will minister to thee, blind as thou art, my father?

ŒD. Falling wherever it shall be my fate, I will lie on the ground.

ANT. But Œdipus, where is he? and the renowned Enigmas?

ŒD. Perished! one day blest me, and one day destroyed.

ANT. Ought not I then to have a share in thy woes?

ŒD. To a daughter exile with a blind father is shameful.

ANT. Not to a right-minded one however, but honorable, my father.

ŒD. Lead me now onward, that I may touch thy mother.

ANT. There: touch the aged woman with thy most dear hand.

ŒD. O mother! Oh most hapless wife!

ANT. She doth lie miserable, having all ills at once on her.

ŒD. But where is the fallen body of Eteocles, and of Polynices?

ANT. They lie extended before thee near one another.

ŒD. Place my blind hand upon their unhappy faces.

ANT. There: touch thy dead children with thy hand.

ŒD. O ye dear wrecks, unhappy, of an unhappy father.

ANT. O name of Polynices, most dear indeed to me.

ŒD. Now, my child, is the oracle of Apollo come to pass.

ANT. What? but dost thou mention evils in addition to these evils?

ŒD. That I must die an exile at Athens.

ANT. Where? what citadel of Attica will receive thee?

ŒD. The sacred Colonus, and the temple of the Equestrian God. But stay—minister to thy blind father here, since thou art desirous of sharing his exile.

ANT. Go to thy wretched banishment: stretch forth thy dear hand, O aged father, having me as thy guide, as the gale that wafts the ship.

ŒD. Behold, I go, my child, be thou my unhappy conductor.

ANT. We are, we are indeed unhappy above all Theban virgins.

ŒD. Where shall I place my aged footstep? Bring my staff, my child.

ANT. This way, this way come; here, here place thy foot, thou that hast the strength of a dream.

ŒD. Alas! alas! for my most wretched flight!—To drive me, old as I am, from my country—Alas! alas! the dreadful, dreadful things that I have suffered!

ANT. What suffered! what suffered![51] Vengeance sees not the wicked, nor repays the foolishness of mortals.

ŒD. That man am I, who mounted aloft to the victorious heavenly song, having solved the dark enigma of the virgin Sphinx.

ANT. Dost thou bring up again the glory of the Sphinx? Forbear from speaking of thy former successes. These wretched sufferings awaited thee, O father, being an exile from thy country to die any where. Leaving with my dear virgins tears for my loss, I depart far from my country, wandering in state not like a virgin's.

ŒD. Oh! the excellency of thy mind!

ANT. In the calamities of a father at least it will make me glorious. Wretched am I, on account of the insults offered to thee and to my brother, who has perished from the family, a corse denied sepulture, unhappy, whom, even if I must die, my father, I will cover with secret earth.

ŒD. Go, show thyself to thy companions.

ANT. They have enough of my lamentations.

ŒD. But make thy supplications at the altars.

ANT. They have a satiety of my woes.

ŒD. Go then, where stands the fane of Bacchus unapproached, on the mountains of the Mænades.

ANT. To whom I formerly, clad in the skin of the Theban fawn, danced the sacred step of Semele on the mountains, conferring a thankless favor on the Gods?

ŒD. O ye inhabitants of my illustrious country, behold, I, this Œdipus, who alone stayed the violence of the bloodthirsty Sphinx, now, dishonored, forsaken, miserable, am banished from the land. Yet why do I bewail these things, and lament in vain? For the necessity of fate proceeding from the Gods a mortal must endure.

CRE. [O greatly glorious Victory, mayest thou uphold my life, and cease not from crowning me!] (See note [H].)

NOTES ON THE PHŒNICIAN VIRGINS

[1] That is, through the signs of the zodiac: αστηρ differs from αστρον, the former signifying a single star, the latter many.

[2] The preposition συν is omitted, as in Homer,

Αυτηι κεν γαιηι ερυσαιμι.

The same omission occurs in the Bacchæ, αυτηισιν ελαταις, and again in the Hippolytus. It is an Atticism.

[3] See note on Hecuba, 478.

[4] The word τουνομα must be supplied after τουτο, which is implied in the verb καλουσιν.

[5] The ζαρος is a bird of prey of the vulture species. The sphinx was represented as having the face of a woman, the breast and feet of a lion, and the wings of a bird.

[5a] Dindorf would omit this verse.

[6] αραι and αρασθαι are often used by the poets in a good sense for prayers, ευχαι and ευχεσθαι for curses and imprecations.

[7] διηρες 'υπερωον, η κλιμαξ. HESYCHIUS.

[8] Milton, Par. Regained, b. iii. l. 326.

The field, all iron, cast a gleaming brown.

[9] Lerna, a country of Argolis celebrated for a grove and a lake where the Danaides threw the heads of their murdered husbands. It was there also that Hercules killed the famous Hydra.

[10] This alludes to the figure of Argus engraved on his shield. See verse 1130.

[11] Tydeus married Deipyle, Polynices Argia, both daughters of Adrastus, king of Argos.

[12] Some suppose 'υστερωι ποδι to mean with their last steps, that is, with steps which are doomed never to return again to their own country.

[13] Triæna was a place in Argolis, where Neptune stuck his trident in the ground, and immediately water sprung up. SCHOL.

[14] Amymone was daughter of Danaus and Europa; she was employed, by order of her father, in supplying the city of Argos with water, in a great drought. Neptune saw her in this employment, and was enamored of her. He carried her away, and in the place where she stood he raised a fountain, which has been called Amymone. See Propert. ii. El. 20. v. 47.

[15] αλληλας λεγουσιν is, *they say one of another*; αλληλαις λεγουσιν, *they say among themselves.*

[16] By πεδιων ακαρπιστων is to be understood the sea. The construction πεδιων περιρρυτον Σικελιας, that is, 'α Σικελιαν περιρρει. The same construction is found in Sophocles, Œd. Tyr. l. 885. δικας αφοβητος. L. 969. αφαυστος εγχους. See also Horace, Lib. iv. Od. 4. 43.

Ceu flamma per tædas, vel Eurus

Per Siculas equitavit undas.

[17] The fire was on that head of Parnassus which was sacred to Apollo and Diana; to those below it appeared double, being divided to the eye by a pointed rock which rose before it. SCHOL.

[18] The Python which Apollo slew.

[19] Libya the daughter of Epaphus bore to Neptune Agenor and Belus. Cadmus was the son of Agenor, and Antiope the daughter of Belus.

[19a] But Dind. εκφρωσ'. See his note.

[20] The construction is, αμφιβαλλε μοι το των παρηϊδων σου ορεγμα: that is, *genarum ad oscula porrectionem.* It can not be translated literally. The verb αμφιβαλλε is to be supplied before ορεγμα, and before πλοκαμον. See Orestes, 950.

[21] Locus videtur corruptus. PORSON. Valckenaer proposes to read δακρυοεσσ' ανιεισα κ.τ.λ. Markland would supply φωνην after 'ιεισα. Another reading proposed is, δακρυοεσσ' ενιεισα πενθηρη κονιν. *Lacrymabunda, lugubrem cinerem injiciens.* Followed by Dindorf.

[22] Cf. Æsch. Prom. 39. το συγγενες τοι δεινον 'η θ' 'ομιλια, where consult Schutz.

[23] See Porson's note. A similar ellipse is to be found in Luke xiii. 9. Καιν μεν ποιησηι καρπον: ει δε μηγε, εις το μελλον εκκοψεις

αυτην: which is thus translated in our version; "And if it bear fruit, *well*: and if not, *then* after that thou shalt cut it down." See also Iliad, A. 135. Aristoph. Plut. 468. ed. Kuster.

[24] Βραβευς, properly, is the judge in a contest, who confers the prizes, and on whose decision the awarding of the prizes depends: βραβευτης is the same. Βραβειον is the prize. Βραβεια, and in the plural βραβειαι, the very act of deciding the contest.

[25] So Hotspur, of honor:

By heaven, methinks, it were an easy leap,

To pluck bright honor from the pale-faced moon:

Or dive into the bottom of the deep,

Where fathom-line could never touch the ground,

And pluck up drowned honor by the locks;

So he, that doth redeem her thence, might wear,

Without corrival, all her dignities.

Hen. IV. P. i. A. i. Sc. 3.

[26] See Ovid. Met. vi. 28. Non omnia grandior ætas, Quæ fugiamus, habet; seris venit usus ab annis.

[27] The Scholiast doubts whether these Gods were Castor and Pollux, or Zethus and Amphion, but inclines to the latter. See Herc. Fur. v. 29, 30.

[28] Or, *fell with limbs that had never known yoke.*—V. Ovid: Met. iii. 10.

Bos tibi, Phœbus ait, solis occurret in arvis,

Nullum passa jugum.

[29] Valckenaer proposes reading instead of 'οραις or 'ορας, αυραις, writing the passage αυραις βοστρυχον αμπετασας, "per auras leves crine jactato:" which seems peculiarly adapted to this place, where the poet places the tumultuous rage of Mars in contrast with the sweet enthusiasm of the Bacchanalians, who are represented as flying over the plains with their hair streaming in the wind. But see Note [C].

[30] ακοη is here to be understood in the sense of ακουομενον as we find αισθησις for αισθητον, νους for το νοουμενον.

[31] The words διδυμων ποταμων do not refer to Dirce, but to Thebes, Thebes being called πολις διποταμος. The construction is πυργος διδυμων ποταμων. Thus in Pindar οικημα ποταμου means οικημα παρα ποταμωι. Olymp. 2. Antistr. 1.

[32] See note [D].

[32a] γουν. See Dind.

[33] τι γαρ παθω; *Quid enim agam?* est formula eorum, quos invitos natura vel fatum, vel quæcumque alia cogit necessitas. VALCKEN.

[34] Προσηγορησων is to be joined with μολων, not with ειμι. In confirmation of this see line 1011.

[35] So called after Neïs the son of Amphion and Niobe, or from νεαται, "*Newgate.*" SCHOL.

[36] Argus himself might be called στικτος, but not his eyes, hence πυκνοις is proposed by Heinsius. Abreschius receives στικτοις in the sense of ʿοις στικτος εστι.

[37] The Scholiast makes βλεποντα the accusative singular to agree with πανοπτην. Musgrave takes it as agreeing with ομματα; in this latter case κρυπτοντα is used in a neuter signification. Note [F].

[38] This is Musgrave's interpretation, by putting the stop after ʿως, which also Porson adopts; others would join ʿως with πρησων. It seems however more natural that the torch should be referred to Tydeus's emblem, than to himself.

[39] Commentators and interpreters are much at variance concerning the word στροφιγξιν. For his better satisfaction on this passage the reader is referred to the Scholia.

[40] γεισσα is in apposition to λααν in the preceding line. Cf. Orestes, 1585.

[41] Commentators are divided on the meaning of ενηλατα. One Scholiast understands it to mean the uprights of the ladder in which the bars are fixed. Eustathias considers ενηλατων βαθρα a periphrasis for βαθρα, ενηλατα being the βαθρα or βαθμιδες, which ενεληλανται τοις ορθοϊς ξυλοις.

[42] Musgrave would render ‘υγροτητ’ εναντιαν by "mobilitatem male coalescentem;" in this case it would indicate the bad omen, and be opposed to ακραν λαμπαδα, which then should be translated "the pointed flame." Valckenaer considers the passage as desperately corrupt. See Musgrave's note. Cf. Note [G].

[43] If the flame was clear and vivid.

[44] If it terminated in smoke and blackness.

[45] The construction of this passage is the same as that of Il. Δ 155. θανατον νυ τοι ‘ορκι’ εταμνον. "Fœdus, quod pepigi, tibi mortis causa est." PORSON.

[46] Beck, by putting the stop after πετρον, makes ‘υποδρομον to agree with κολον, "*his limb diverted from its tread.*"

[47] The construction is φονος κρανθεις φονωι: αιματι depends on εν understood.

[48] Most MSS. have ξυνετος. Here then is a remarkable instance of the same word having both an active and a passive signification in the same sentence.

[49] μακροπνουν, not μακροπουν, is Porson's reading, μακροπνους ζωη is explained "vita in qua longo tempore spiratur; ergo longa."

[50] See note at Hecuba 65.

[51] The old reading was τι τλας; τι τλας; making it the present tense. Brunck first edited it as it stands in Porson. Antigone repeats the last word of her father.

ADDITIONAL NOTES.

[A] "Signum interrogandi non post νεανιας, sed post λοχαγος ponendum. λοχαγος in libris pedagogo tribuitur: quod correxit Hermannus." DINDORF.

[B] Porson and Dindorf (in his notes) favor Reiske's conjecture, πυκνοισι for πυργοισι.

[C] Dindorf rightly approves the explanation of Musgrave, who takes στεφανοισι, like the Latin *corona*, to mean the *assemblies*. He translates: "*nec in pulchros choros ducentibus circulis juventutis.*"

[D] The full sense, as laid down by Schœfer and Dindorf, is, "for ever when an old man travels, whether in a carriage, or on foot, he requires help from others." πασα απηνη πους τε is rather boldly used, but is not without example.

[E] i.e. "*you ask a thing* (i.e. your son's safety) *dangerous to the city, which you can not preserve.*" SCHŒFER.

[F] These three lines are condemned by Valck. and Dind.

[G] Matthiæ attempts to explain these words as follows: "εμπυροι ακμαι may be put for τα εμπυρα, in which the seers observed (ενωμων) two things, viz. the divisions ('ρηξεις) of the flame, which, if it slid round the altars, was of ill omen (hence 'υγραι, i.e. gliding gently around the altars with many curves, for which is put 'υγροτης εναντια); and 2dly, *the upright shooting of the flame*, ακραν λαμπαδα."

[H] See Dindorf on Orest. 1691. He fully condemns these lines as the work of an interpolator. They are, however, as old as the days of Lucian.

MEDEA.

PERSONS REPRESENTED.

NURSE.

TUTOR.

MEDEA.

CHORUS OF CORINTHIAN WOMEN.

CREON.

JASON.

ÆGEUS

MESSENGER.

SONS OF MEDEA.

The Scene lies in the vestibule of the palace of Jason at Corinth.

THE ARGUMENT.

JASON, having come to Corinth, and bringing with him Medea, espouses Glauce, the daughter of Creon, king of Corinth. But Medea, on the point of being banished from Corinth by Creon, having asked to remain one day, and having obtained her wish, sends to Glauce, by the hands of her sons, presents, as an acknowledgment for the favor, a robe and a golden chaplet, which she puts on and perishes; Creon also having embraced his daughter is destroyed. But Medea, when she had slain her children, escapes to Athens, in a chariot drawn by winged dragons, which she received from the Sun, and there marries Ægeus son of Pandion.

MEDEA.

NURSE OF MEDEA.

Would that the hull of Argo had not winged her way to the Colchian land through the Cyanean Symplegades,[1] and that the pine felled in the forests of Pelion had never fallen, nor had caused the hands of the chiefs to row,[2] who went in search of the golden fleece for Pelias; for neither then would my mistress Medea have sailed to the towers of the Iolcian land, deeply smitten in her mind with the love of Jason; nor having persuaded the daughters of Pelias to slay their father would she have inhabited this country of Corinth with her husband and her children, pleasing indeed by her flight[3] the citizens to whose land she came, and herself concurring in every respect with Jason; which is the surest support of conjugal happiness, when the wife is not estranged from the husband. But now every thing is at variance, and the dearest ties are weakened. For having betrayed his own children, and my mistress, Jason reposes in royal wedlock, having married the daughter of Creon, who is prince of this land. But Medea the unhappy, dishonored, calls on his oaths, and recalls the hands they plighted, the greatest pledge of fidelity, and invokes the gods to witness what return she meets with from Jason. And she lies without tasting food, having sunk her body in grief, dissolving all her tedious time in tears, after she had once known that she had been injured by her husband, neither raising her eye, nor lifting her countenance from the ground; but as the rock, or the wave of the sea, does she listen to her friends when advised. Save that sometimes having turned her snow-white neck she to herself bewails her dear father, and her country, and her house, having betrayed which she hath come hither with a man who has now dishonored her. And she wretched hath discovered from affliction what it is not to forsake one's paternal country. But she hates her children, nor is she delighted at beholding them: but I fear her, lest she form some new design: for violent is her mind, nor will it endure to suffer ills. I know her, and I fear her, lest she should force the sharpened sword through her heart, or even should murder the princess and him who married her, and after that receive some greater ill. For she is violent; he who engages with her in enmity will not with ease at least sing the song of victory. But these her children are coming hither having ceased from their exercises, nothing mindful of their mother's ills, for the mind of youth is not wont to grieve.

TUTOR, WITH THE SONS OF MEDEA, NURSE.

TUT. O thou ancient possession of my mistress's house, why dost thou stand at the gates preserving thus thy solitude, bewailing to thyself our misfortunes? How doth Medea wish to be left alone without thee?

NUR. O aged man, attendant on the children of Jason, to faithful servants the affairs of their masters turning out ill are a calamity, and lay hold upon their feelings. For I have arrived at such a height of grief that desire hath stolen on me to come forth hence and tell the misfortunes of Medea to the earth and heaven.

TUT. Does not she wretched yet receive any respite from her grief?

NUR. I envy thy ignorance; her woe is at its rise, and not even yet at its height.

TUT. O unwise woman, if it is allowable to say this of one's lords, since she knows nothing of later ills.

NUR. But what is this, O aged man? grudge not to tell me.

TUT. Nothing: I have repented even of what was said before.

NUR. Do not, I beseech you by your beard, conceal it from your fellow-servant; for I will preserve silence, if it be necessary, on these subjects.

TUT. I heard from some one who was saying, not appearing to listen, having approached the places where dice is played, where the elders sit, around the hallowed font of Pirene, that the king of this land, Creon, intends to banish from the Corinthian country these children, together with their mother; whether this report be true, however, I know not; but I wish this may not be the case.

NUR. And will Jason endure to see his children suffer this, even although he is at enmity with their mother?

TUT. Ancient alliances are deserted for new, and he is no friend to this family.

NUR. We perish then, if to the old we shall add a new ill, before the former be exhausted.[4]

TUT. But do thou, for it is not seasonable that my mistress should know this, restrain your tongue, and be silent on this report.

NUR. O my children, do you hear what your father is toward you? Yet may he not perish, for he is my master, yet he is found to be treacherous toward his friends.

TUT. And what man is not? dost thou only now know this, that every one loves himself dearer than his neighbor,[5] some indeed with justice, but others even for the sake of gain, unless it be that[6] their father loves not these at least on account of new nuptials.

NUR. Go within the house, my children, for all will be well. But do thou keep these as much as possible out of the way, and let them not approach their mother, deranged through grief. For but now I saw her looking with wildness in her eyes on these, as about to execute some design, nor will she cease from her fury, I well know, before she overwhelm some one with it; upon her enemies however, and not her friends, may she do some [ill.]

MEDEA. (*within*) Wretch that I am, and miserable on account of my misfortunes, alas me! would I might perish!

NUR. Thus it is, my children; your mother excites her heart, excites her fury. Hasten as quick as possible within the house, and come not near her sight, nor approach her, but guard against the fierce temper and violent nature of her self-willed mind. Go now, go as quick as possible within. But it is evident that the cloud of grief raised up from the beginning will quickly burst forth with greater fury; what I pray will her soul, great in rage, implacable, irritated by ills, perform!

MED. Alas! alas! I wretched have suffered, have suffered treatment worthy of great lamentation. O ye accursed children of a hated mother, may ye perish with your father, and may the whole house fall.

NUR. Alas! alas! me miserable! but why should your children share their father's error? Why dost thou hate these! Alas me, my children, how beyond measure do I grieve lest ye suffer any evil! Dreadful are the dispositions of tyrants, and somehow in few things controlled, in most absolute, they with difficulty lay aside their passion. The being accustomed then[7] to live in mediocrity of life is the better: may it be my lot then to grow old if not in splendor, at least in security. For, in the first place, even to mention the name of moderation carries with it superiority, but to use it is by far the best conduct for men; but excess of fortune brings more power to men than is convenient;[8] and has brought greater woes upon families, when the Deity be enraged.

NURSE, CHORUS.

CHOR. I heard the voice, I heard the cry of the unhappy Colchian; is not she yet appeased? but, O aged matron, tell me; for within the apartment with double doors, I heard her cry; nor am I delighted, O woman, with the griefs of the family, since it is friendly to me.

NUR. The family is not; these things are gone already: for he possesses the bed of royalty; but she, my mistress, is melting away her life in her chamber, in no way soothing her mind by the advice of any one of her friends.

MED. Alas! alas! may the flame of heaven rush through my head, what profit for me to live any longer. Alas! alas! may I rest myself in death, having left a hated life.

CHOR. Dost thou hear, O Jove, and earth, and light, the cry which the wretched bride utters? why I pray should this insatiable love of the marriage-bed hasten thee, O vain woman, to death? Pray not for this. But if thy husband courts a new bed, be not thus[9] enraged with him. Jove will avenge these wrongs for thee: waste not thyself so, bewailing thy husband.

MED. O great Themis and revered Diana, do ye behold what I suffer, having bound my accursed husband by powerful oaths? Whom may I at some time see and his bride torn piecemeal with their very houses, who dare to injure me first. O my father, O my city, whom I basely abandoned, having slain my brother.

NUR. Do ye hear what she says, and how she invokes Themis hearing the vow, and Jove who is considered the dispenser of oaths to mortals? It is not possible that my mistress will lull her rage to rest on any trivial circumstance.

CHOR. By what means could she come into our sight, and hear the voice of our discourse, if she would by any means remit her fierce anger and her fury of mind. Let not my zeal however be wanting ever to my friends. But go and conduct her hither from without the house, my friend, and tell her this, hasten, before she injure in any way those within, for this grief of hers is increased to a great height.

NUR. I will do it, but I fear that I shall not persuade my mistress; nevertheless I will give you this favor of my labor. And yet with the aspect of a lioness that has just brought forth does she look sternly on her attendants when any one approaches near attempting to address her. But thou wouldest not err in calling men of old foolish and nothing wise, who invented songs, for festivals, for banquets, and for suppers, the delights of life that charm the ear; but no mortal has discovered how to soothe with music and with varied strains those bitter pangs, from which death and dreadful misfortunes overthrow families. And yet for men to assuage these griefs with music were gain; but where the plenteous banquet is furnished, why raise they the song in vain? for the present bounty of the feast brings pleasure of itself to men.

CHOR. I heard the dismal sound of groans, and in a shrill voice she vents her bitter[10] anguish on the traitor to her bed, her faithless husband—and suffering wrongs she calls upon the Goddess Themis, arbitress of oaths, daughter of Jove, who conducted her to the opposite coast of Greece, across the sea by night, over the salt straits of the boundless ocean.

MEDEA, CHORUS.

MED. Ye Corinthian dames, I have come from out my palace; do not in any wise blame me; for I have known many men who have been[11] renowned, some who have lived far from public notice, and others in the world; but those of a retired turn have gained for themselves a character of infamy and indolence. For justice dwells not in the eyes of man,[12] whoever, before he can well discover the disposition of a man, hates him at sight, in no way wronged by him. But it is necessary for a stranger exactly to conform himself to the state, nor would I praise the native, whoever becoming self-willed is insolent to his fellow-citizens through ignorance. But this unexpected event that hath fallen upon me hath destroyed my spirit: I am going, and having given up the pleasure of life I am desirous to meet death, my friends. For he on whom my all rested, as you well know, my husband, has turned out the basest of men. But of all things as many as have life and intellect, we women are the most wretched race. Who indeed first must purchase a husband with excess of money, and receive him a lord of our persons; for this is a still greater ill than the former. And in this is the greatest risk, whether we receive a bad one or a good one; for divorces bring not good fame to women, nor is it possible to repudiate one's husband. But on passing to new tempers and new laws, one need be a prophetess, as one can not learn of one's self, what sort of consort one shall most likely experience. And if with us carefully performing these things a husband shall dwell not imposing on us a yoke with severity, enviable is our life; if not, to die is better. But a man, when he is displeased living with those at home, having gone abroad is wont to relieve his heart of uneasiness, having recourse either to some friend or compeer. But we must look but to one person. But they say of us that we live a life of ease at home, but they are fighting with the spear; judging ill, since I would rather thrice stand in arms, than once suffer the pangs of child-birth. But, for the same argument comes not home to you and me, this is thy city, and thy father's house, thine are both the luxuries of life, and the society of friends; but I being destitute, cityless, am wronged by my husband, brought as a prize from a foreign land, having neither mother, nor brother, nor relation to afford me shelter from this calamity. So much then I wish to obtain from you, if any plan or contrivance be devised by me to repay with justice these injuries on my husband, and on him who gave his daughter, and on her to whom he was married,[13] that you would be silent; for a woman in other respects is full of fear, and timid to look upon deeds of courage and the sword; but when she is injured in her bed, no other disposition is more blood-thirsty.

CHOR. I will do this; for with justice, Medea, wilt thou avenge thyself on thy husband, and I do not wonder that you lament your misfortunes. But I see Creon monarch of this land advancing, the messenger of new counsels.

CREON, MEDEA, CHORUS.

CRE. Thee of gloomy countenance, and enraged with thy husband, Medea, I command to depart in exile from out of this land, taking with thee thy two children, and not to delay in any way, since I am the arbiter of this edict, and I will not return back to my palace, until I shall drive thee beyond the boundaries of this realm.

MED. Alas! alas! I wretched am utterly destroyed, for my enemies stretch out every cable against me; nor is there any easy escape from this evil, but I will speak, although suffering injurious treatment; for what, Creon, dost thou drive me from this land?

CRE. I fear thee (there is no need for me to wrap my words in obscurity,) lest thou do my child some irremediable mischief, And many circumstances are in unison with this dread. Thou art wise, and skilled in many evil sciences, and thou art exasperated, deprived of thy husband's bed. And I hear that thou threatenest, as they tell me, to wreak some deed of vengeance on the betrother, and the espouser and the espoused; against this then, before I suffer, will I guard. Better is it for me now to incur enmity from you, than softened by your words afterward greatly to lament it.

MED. Alas! alas! not now for the first time, but often, Creon, hath this opinion injured me, and worked me much woe. But whatever man is prudent, let him never educate his children too deep in wisdom. For, independent of the other charges of idleness which they meet with, they find hostile envy from their fellow-citizens. For holding out to fools some new-discovered wisdom, thou wilt seem to be useless and not wise. And being judged superior to others who seem to have some varied knowledge, thou wilt appear offensive in the city. But even I myself share this fortune; for being wise, to some I am an object of envy, but to others, unsuited; but I am not very wise. Thou then fearest me, lest thou suffer some grievous mischief.[14] My affairs are not in a state, fear me not, Creon, so as to offend against princes. For in what hast thou injured me? Thou hast given thy daughter to whom thy mind led thee; but I hate my husband: but thou, I think, didst these things in prudence. And now I envy not that thy affairs are prospering; make your alliances, be successful; but suffer me to dwell in this land, for although injured will I keep silence, overcome by my superiors.

CRE. Thou speakest soft words to the ear, but within my mind I have my fears, lest thou meditate some evil intent. And so much the less do I trust thee than before. For a woman that is quick to anger, and a man likewise, is easier to guard against, than one that is crafty and keeps silence. But begone as quick as possible, make no more words; since this is decreed, and thou hast no art, by which thou wilt stay with us, being hostile to me.

MED. No I beseech you by your knees, and your newly-married daughter.

CRE. Thou wastest words; for thou wilt never persuade me.

MED. Wilt thou then banish me, nor reverence my prayers?

CRE. For I do not love thee better than my own family.

MED. O my country, how I remember thee now!

CRE. For next to my children it is much the dearest thing to me.

MED. Alas! alas! how great an ill is love to man!

CRE. That is, I think, as fortune also shall attend it.

MED. Jove, let it not escape thine eye, who is the cause of these misfortunes.

CRE. Begone, fond woman, and free me from these cares.

MED. Care indeed;[15] and do not I experience cares?

CRE. Quickly shalt thou be driven hence by force by the hands of my domestics.

MED. No, I pray not this at least; but I implore thee, Creon.

CRE. Thou wilt give trouble, woman, it seems.[16]

MED. I will go; I dare not ask to obtain this of you.

CRE. Why then dost thou resist, and wilt not depart from these realms?

MED. Permit me to remain here this one day, and to bring my purpose to a conclusion, in what way we shall fly, and to make provision for my sons, since their father in no way regards providing for his children; but pity them, for thou also art the father of children; and it is probable that thou hast tenderness: for of myself I have no care whether I may suffer banishment, but I weep for them experiencing this calamity.

CRE. My disposition is least of all imperious, and through feeling pity in many cases have I injured myself. And now I see that I am doing wrong, O lady, but nevertheless thou shalt obtain thy request; but this I warn thee, if to-morrow's light of the God of day shall behold thee and thy children within the confines of these realms, thou shalt die: this word is spoken in truth. But now if thou must stay, remain here yet one day, for thou wilt not do any horrid deed of which I have dread.

MEDEA, CHORUS.

CHOR. Unhappy woman! alas wretched on account of thy griefs! whither wilt thou turn? what hospitality, or house, or country wilt thou find a refuge for these ills? how the Deity hath led thee, Medea, into a pathless tide of woes!

MED. Ill hath it been done on every side. Who will gainsay it? but these things are not in this way, do not yet think it. Still is there a contest for those lately married, and to those allied to them no small affliction. For dost thou think I ever would have fawned upon this man, if I were not to gain something, or form some plan? I would not even have addressed him. I would not even have touched him with my hands. But he hath arrived at such a height of folly, as that, when it was in his power to have crushed my plans, by banishing me from this land, he hath granted me to stay this day in which three of mine enemies will I put to death, the father, the bride, and my husband. But having in my power many resources of destruction against them, I know not, my friends, which I shall first attempt. Whether shall I consume the bridal house with fire, or force the sharpened sword through her heart having entered the chamber by stealth where the couch is spread? But one thing is against me; if I should be caught entering the house and prosecuting my plans, by my death I shall afford laughter for my foes. Best then is it to pursue the straight path, in which I am most skilled, to take them off by poison. Let it be so. And suppose them dead: what city will receive me? What hospitable stranger affording a land of safety and a faithful home will protect my person? There is none. Waiting then yet a little time, if any tower of safety shall appear to us, I will proceed to this murder in treachery and silence. But if ill fortune that leaves me without resource force me, I myself having grasped the sword, although I should die, will kill them, and will rush to the extreme height of daring. For never, I swear by my mistress whom I revere most of all, and have chosen for my assistant, Hecate, who dwells in the inmost recesses of my house, shall any one of them wring my heart with grief with impunity. Bitter and mournful to them will I make these nuptials, and bitter this alliance, and my flight from this land. But come, spare none of these sciences in which thou art skilled, Medea, deliberating and plotting. Proceed to the deed of terror: now is the time of resolution: seest thou what thou art suffering? Ill doth it become thee to incur ridicule from the race of Sisyphus, and from the nuptials of Jason, who art sprung from a noble father, and from the sun. And thou art skilled. Besides also we women are, by nature, to good actions of the least capacity, but the most cunning inventors of every ill.

CHOR. The waters of the hallowed streams flow upward to their sources, and justice and every thing is reversed. The counsels of men are treacherous, and no longer is the faith of heaven firm. But fame changes, so that my sex may have the glory.[17] Honor cometh to the female race; no longer shall opprobrious fame oppress the women. But the Muses shall cease from their ancient strains, from celebrating our perfidy. For Phœbus, leader of the choir, gave not to our minds the heavenly music of the lyre, since they would in turn have raised a strain against the race of men. But time of old hath much to say both of our life and the life of men. But thou hast sailed from thy father's house with maddened heart, having passed through the double rocks of the ocean, and thou dwellest in a foreign land, having lost the shelter of thy widowed bed, wretched woman, and art driven dishonored an exile from this land. The reverence of oaths is gone, nor does shame any longer dwell in mighty Greece, but hath fled away through the air. But thou helpless woman hast neither father's house to afford you haven from your woes, and another more powerful queen of the nuptial bed rules over the house.

JASON, MEDEA, CHORUS.

JAS. Not now for the first time, but often have I perceived that fierce anger is an irremediable ill. For though it was in your power to inhabit this land and this house, bearing with gentleness the determination of thy superiors, by thy rash words thou shalt be banished from this land. And to me indeed it is of no importance; never cease from saying that Jason is the worst of men. But for what has been said by thee against the royal family, think it the greatest good fortune that thou art punished by banishment only. I indeed was always employed in diminishing the anger of the enraged princes, and was willing that thou shouldest remain. But thou remittest not of thy folly, always reviling the ruling powers; wherefore thou shalt be banished from the land. But nevertheless even after this am I come, not wearied with my friends, providing for thee, O woman, that thou mightest not be banished with thy children, either without money, or in want of any thing. Banishment draws many misfortunes with it. For although thou hatest me, I never could wish thee evil.

MED. O thou vilest of men (for this is the greatest reproach I have in my power with my tongue to tell thee, for thy unmanly cowardice), hast thou come to us, hast thou come, who art most hateful? This is not fortitude, or confidence, to look in the face of friends whom thou hast injured, but the worst of all diseases among men, impudence. But thou hast done well in coming. For both I shall be lightened in my heart while reviling thee, and thou wilt be pained at hearing me. But I will first begin to speak from the first circumstances. I preserved thee (as those Greeks well know as many as embarked with thee on board the same ship Argo) when sent to master the fire-breathing bulls with the yoke, and to sow the fatal seed: and having slain the dragon who watching around the golden fleece guarded it with spiry folds, a sleepless guard, I raised up to thee a light of safety. But I myself having betrayed my father, and my house, came to the Peliotic Iolcos[18] with thee, with more readiness than prudence. And I slew Pelias by a death which it is most miserable to die, by the hands of his own children, and I freed thee from every fear. And having experienced these services from me, thou vilest of men, thou hast betrayed me and hast procured for thyself a new bed, children being born to thee, for if thou wert still childless it would be pardonable in thee to be enamored of this alliance. But the faith of oaths is vanished: nor can I discover whether thou thinkest that the former Gods are not still in power, or whether new laws are now laid down for men, since thou art at least conscious of being perjured toward me. Alas! this right hand which thou hast often touched, and these knees, since in vain have I been polluted by a wicked husband, and have failed in my hopes. Come (for I will converse with thee as with a friend, not expecting to receive any benefit from thee at least, but nevertheless I will; for when questioned thou wilt appear more base), now whither shall I turn? Whether to my father's house, which I betrayed for thee, and my country, and came hither? or to the miserable daughters of Pelias? friendly would they indeed receive me in their house, whose father I slew. For thus it is: I am in enmity with my friends at home; but those whom I ought not to injure, by obliging thee, I make my enemies. On which account in return for this thou hast made me to be called happy by many dames through Greece, and in thee I, wretch that I am, have an admirable and faithful husband, if cast out at least I shall fly this land, deserted by my friends, lonely with thy lonely children. Fair renown indeed to the new married bridegroom, that his children are wandering in poverty, and I also who preserved thee. O Jove, why I pray hast thou given to men certain proofs of the gold which is adulterate, but no mark is set by nature on the person of men by which one may distinguish the bad man.

CHOR. Dreadful is that anger and irremediable, when friends with friends kindle strife.

JAS. It befits me, it seems, not to be weak in argument, but as the prudent pilot of a vessel, with all the sail that can be hoisted, to run from out of thy violent abuse, O woman. But I, since thou thus much vauntest thy favors, think that Venus alone both of Gods and men was the protectress of my voyage. But thou hast a fickle mind, but it is an invidious account to go through, how love compelled thee with his inevitable arrows to preserve my life. But I will not follow up arguments with too great accuracy, for where thou hast assisted me it is well. Moreover thou hast received more at least from my safety than thou gavest, as I will explain to thee. First of all thou dwellest in Greece instead of a foreign land, and thou learnest what justice is, and to enjoy laws, not to be directed by mere force. And all the Grecians have seen that thou art wise, and thou hast renown; but if thou wert dwelling in the extreme confines of that land, there would not have been fame of thee. But may neither gold in my house be be my lot, nor to attune the strain more sweet than Orpheus, if my fortune be not conspicuous. So much then have I said of my toils; for thou first broughtest forward this contest of words. But with regard to those reproaches which thou heapest on me for my royal marriage, in this will I show first that I have been wise, in the next place moderate, thirdly a great friend to thee, and my children: but be silent. After I had come hither from the Iolcian land bringing with me many grievous calamities, what measure more fortunate than this could I have invented, than, an exile as I was, to marry the daughter of the monarch? not, by which thou art grated, loathing thy bed, nor smitten with desire of a new bride, nor having emulation of a numerous offspring, for those born to me are sufficient, nor do I find fault with that; but that (which is of the greatest consequence) we might live honorably, and might not be in want, knowing well that every friend flies out of the way of a poor man; and that I might bring up my children worthy of my house, and that having begotten brothers to those children sprung from thee, I might place them on the same footing, and having united the family, I might flourish; for both thou hast some need of children, and to me it were advantageous to advance my present progeny by means of the children which might arise; have I determined ill? not even thou couldest say so, if thy bed did not gall thee. But thus far have you come, that your bed being safe, you women think that you have every thing. But if any misfortune befall that, the most excellent and fairest objects you make the most hateful. It were well then that men should generate children from some other source, and that the female race should not exist, and thus there would not have been any evil among men.[19]

CHOR. Jason, thou hast well adorned these arguments of thine, but nevertheless to me, although I speak reluctantly, thou appearest, in betraying thy wife, to act unjustly.

MED. Surely I am in many things different from many mortals, for in my judgment, whatever man being unjust, is deeply skilled in argument, merits the severest punishment. For vaunting that with his tongue he can well gloze over injustice, he dares to work deceit, but he is not over-wise. Thus do not thou also be now plausible to me, nor skilled in speaking, for one word will overthrow thee: it behooved thee, if thou wert not a bad man, to have contracted this marriage having persuaded me, and not without the knowledge of thy friends.

JAS. Well wouldest thou have lent assistance to this report, if I had mentioned the marriage to thee, who not even now endurest to lay aside this unabated rage of heart.

MED. This did not move thee, but a foreign bed would lead in its result to an old age without honor.

JAS. Be well assured of this, that I did not form this alliance with the princess, which I now hold, for the sake of the woman, but, as I said before also, wishing to preserve thee, and to beget royal children brothers to my sons, a support to our house.

MED. Let not a splendid life of bitterness be my lot, nor wealth, which rends my heart.

JAS. Dost thou know how to alter thy prayers, and appear wiser? Let not good things ever seem to you bitter, nor when in prosperity seem to be in adversity.

MED. Insult me, since thou hast refuge, but I destitute shall fly this land.

JAS. Thou chosest this thyself, blame no one else.

MED. By doing what? by marrying and betraying thee?

JAS. By imprecating unhallowed curses on the royal family.

MED. From thy house at least am I laden with curses.

JAS. I will not dispute more of this with thee. But if thou wishest to receive either for thyself or children any part of my wealth as an assistant on thy flight, speak, since I am ready to give with an unsparing hand, and to send tokens of hospitality to my friends, who will treat you well; and refusing these thou wilt be foolish, woman, but ceasing from thine anger, thou wilt gain better treatment.

MED. I will neither use thy friends, nor will I receive aught; do not give to me, for the gifts of a bad man bring no assistance.

JAS. Then I call the Gods to witness, that I wish to assist thee and thy children in every thing; but good things please thee not, but thou rejectest thy friends with audacity, wherefore shalt thou grieve the more.

MED. Begone, for thou art captured by desire of thy new bride, tarrying so long without the palace; wed her, for perhaps, but with the assistance of the God shall it be said, thou wilt make such a marriage alliance, as thou wilt hereafter wish to renounce.

CHOR. The loves, when they come too impetuously, have given neither good report nor virtue among men, but if Venus come with moderation, no other Goddess is so benign. Never, O my mistress, mayest thou send forth against me from thy golden bow thy inevitable shaft, having steeped it in desire. But may temperance preserve me, the noblest gift of heaven; never may dreaded Venus, having smitten my mind for another's bed, heap upon me jealous passions and unabated quarrels, but approving the peaceful union, may she quick of perception sit in judgment on the bed of women. O my country, and my house, never may I be an outcast of my city, having a life scarce to be endured through poverty, the most lamentable of all woes. By death, by death, may I before that be subdued, having lived to accomplish that day; but no greater misfortune is there than to be deprived of one's paternal country. We have seen it, nor have we to speak from others' accounts; for thee, neither city nor friend hath pitied, though suffering the most dreadful anguish. Thankless may he perish who desires not to assist his friends, having unlocked the pure treasures of his mind; never shall he be friend to me.

ÆGEUS, MEDEA, CHORUS.

ÆG. Medea, hail! for no one hath known a more honorable salutation to address to friends than this.

MED. Hail thou also, son of the wise Pandion, Ægeus, coming from what quarter dost thou tread the plain of this land?

ÆG. Having left the ancient oracle of Phœbus.

MED. But wherefore wert thou sent to the prophetic centre of the earth?

ÆG. Inquiring of the God how offspring may arise to me?

MED. By the Gods, tell me, dost thou live this life hitherto childless?

ÆG. Childless I am, by the disposal of some deity.

MED. Hast thou a wife, or knowest thou not the marriage-bed!

ÆG. I am not destitute of the connubial bed.

MED. What then did Apollo tell thee respecting thy offspring?

ÆG. Words deeper than a man can form opinion of.

MED. Is it allowable for me to know the oracle of the God?

ÆG. Certainly, inasmuch as it needs also a deep-skilled mind.

MED. What then did he say? Speak, if I may hear.

ÆG. That I was not to loose the projecting foot of the vessel—

MED. Before thou didst what, or came to what land?

ÆG. Before I revisit my paternal hearth.

MED. Then as desiring what dost thou direct thy voyage to this land?

ÆG. There is one Pittheus, king of the country of Trazene.

MED. The most pious son, as report says, of Pelops.

ÆG. To him I wish to communicate the oracle of the God.

MED. For he is a wise man, and versed in such matters.

ÆG. And to me at least the dearest of all my friends in war.

MED. Mayest thou prosper, and obtain what thou desirest.

ÆG. But why is thine eye and thy color thus faded?

MED. Ægeus, my husband is the worst of all men.

ÆG. What sayest thou? tell me all thy troubles.

MED. Jason wrongs me, having never suffered wrong from me.

ÆG. Having done what? tell me more clearly.

MED. He hath here a wife besides me, mistress of the house.

ÆG. Hath he dared to commit this disgraceful action?

MED. Be assured he has; but we his former friends are dishonored.

ÆG. Enamored of her, or hating thy bed?

MED. [Smitten with] violent love indeed, he was faithless to his friends.

ÆG. Let him perish then, since, as you say, he is a bad man.

MED. He was charmed to receive an alliance with princes.

ÆG. And who gives the bride to him? finish the account, I beg.

MED. Creon, who is monarch of this Corinthian land.

ÆG. Pardonable was it then that thou art grieved, O lady.

MED. I perish, and in addition to this am I banished from this land.

ÆG. By whom? thou art mentioning another fresh misfortune.

MED. Creon drives me an exile out of this land of Corinth.

ÆG. And does Jason suffer it? I praise not this.

MED. By his words he does not, but at heart he wishes [to endure my banishment:] but by this thy beard I entreat thee, and by these thy knees, and I become thy suppliant, pity me, pity this unfortunate woman, nor behold me going forth in exile abandoned, but receive me at thy hearth in thy country and thy house. Thus by the Gods shall thy desire of children be accomplished to thee, and thou thyself shalt die in happiness. But thou knowest not what this fortune is that thou hast found; but I will free thee from being childless, and I will cause thee to raise up offspring, such charms I know.

ÆG. On many accounts, O lady, am I willing to confer this favor on thee, first on account of the Gods, then of the children, whose birth thou holdest forth; for on this point else I am totally sunk in despair. But thus am I determined: if thou comest to my country, I will endeavor to receive thee with hospitality, being a just man; so much however I beforehand apprise thee of, O lady, I shall not be willing to lead thee with me from this land; but if thou comest thyself to my house, thou shalt stay there in safety, and to no one will I give thee up. But do thou of thyself withdraw thy foot from this country, for I wish to be without blame even among strangers.

MED. It shall be so, but if there was a pledge of this given to me, I should have all things from thee in a noble manner.

ÆG. Dost thou not trust me? what is thy difficulty?

MED. I trust thee; but the house of Pelias is mine enemy, and Creon too; to these then, wert thou bound by oaths, thou wouldest not give me up from the country, should they attempt to drag me thence. But having agreed by words alone, and without calling the Gods to witness, thou mightest be their friend, and perhaps[20] be persuaded by an embassy; for weak is my state, but theirs are riches, and a royal house.

ÆG. Thou hast spoken much prudence, O lady. But if it seems fit to thee that I should do this, I refuse not. For to me also this seems the safest plan, that I should have some pretext to show to your enemies, and thy safety is better secured; propose the Gods that I am to invoke.

MED. Swear by the earth, and by the sun the father of my father, and join the whole race of Gods.

ÆG. That I will do what thing, or what not do? speak.

MED. That thou wilt neither thyself ever cast me forth from out of thy country, nor, if any one of my enemies desire to drag me thence, that thou wilt, while living, give me up willingly.

ÆG. I swear by the earth, and the hallowed majesty of the sun, and by all the Gods, to abide by what I hear from thee.

MED. It is sufficient: but what wilt thou endure shouldest thou not abide by this oath?

ÆG. That which befalls impious men.

MED. Go with blessings; for every thing is well. And I will come as quick as possible to thy city, having performed what I intend, and having obtained what I desire.

CHOR. But may the son of Maia the king, the guide, conduct thee safely to thy house, and the plans of those things, which thou anxiously keepest in thy mind, mayest thou bring to completion, since, Ægeus, thou hast appeared to us to be a noble man.

MEDEA, CHORUS.

MED. O Jove, and thou vengeance of Jove, and thou light of the sun, now, my friends, shall I obtain a splendid victory over my enemies, and I have struck into the path. Now is there hope that my enemies will suffer punishment. For this man, where I was most at a loss, hath appeared a harbor to my plans. From him will I make fast my cable from the stern, having come to the town and citadel of Pallas. But now will I communicate all my plans to thee; but receive my words not as attuned to pleasure. Having sent one of my domestics, I will ask Jason to come into my presence; and when he is come, I will address gentle words to him, as that it appears to me that these his actions are both honorable, and are advantageous and well determined on.[21] And I will entreat him that my sons may stay; not that I would leave my children in a hostile country for my enemies to insult, but that by deceit I may slay the king's daughter. For I will send them bearing presents in their hands, both a fine-wrought robe, and a golden-twined wreath.[22] And if she take the ornaments and place them round her person, she shall perish miserably, and every one who shall touch the damsel; with such charms will I anoint the presents. Here however I finish this account; but I bewail the deed such as must next be done by me; for I shall slay my children; there is no one who shall rescue them from me; and having heaped in ruins the whole house of Jason, I will go from out this land, flying the murder of my dearest children, and having dared a deed most unhallowed. For it is not to be borne, my friends, to be derided by one's enemies. Let things take their course; what gain is it to me to live longer? I have neither country, nor house, nor refuge from my ills. Then erred I, when I left my father's house, persuaded by the words of a Grecian man, who with the will of the Gods shall suffer punishment from me. For neither shall he ever hereafter behold the children he had by me alive, nor shall he raise a child by his new wedded wife, since it is fated that the wretch should wretchedly perish by my spells. Let no one think me mean-spirited and weak, nor of a gentle temper, but of a contrary disposition to my foes relentless, and to my friends kind: for the lives of such sort are most glorious.

CHOR. Since thou hast communicated this plan to me, desirous both of doing good to thee, and assisting the laws of mortals, I dissuade thee from doing this.

MED. It can not be otherwise, but it is pardonable in thee to say this, not suffering the cruel treatment that I do.

CHOR. But wilt thou dare to slay thy two sons, O lady?

MED. For in this way will my husband be most afflicted.

CHOR. But thou at least wilt be the most wretched woman.

MED. Be that as it may: all intervening words are superfluous; but go, hasten, and bring Jason hither; for I make use of thee in all matters of trust. And thou wilt mention nothing of the plans determined on by me, if at least thou meanest well to thy mistress, and art a woman.

CHOR. The Athenians happy of old, and the descendants of the blessed Gods, feeding on the most exalted wisdom of a country sacred and unconquered, always tripping elegantly through the purest atmosphere, where they say that of old the golden-haired Harmonia gave birth to the chaste nine Pierian Muses.[23] And they report also that Venus drawing in her breath from the stream of the fair-flowing Cephisus, breathed over their country gentle sweetly-breathing gales of air; and always entwining in her hair the fragrant wreath of roses, sends the loves as assessors to wisdom; the assistants of every virtue. How then will the city of hallowed rivers,[24] or the country which conducts thee to friends, receive the murderer of her children, the unholy one? Consider in conjunction with others of the slaughter of thy children, consider what a murder thou wilt undertake. Do not by thy knees, by every plea,[25] by every prayer, we entreat you, do not murder your children; but how wilt thou acquire confidence either of mind or hand or in heart against thy children, attempting a dreadful deed of boldness? But how, having darted thine eyes upon thy children, wilt thou endure the perpetration of the murder without tears? Thou wilt not[26] be able, when thy children fall suppliant at thy feet, to imbrue thy savage hand in their wretched life-blood.

JASON, MEDEA, CHORUS.

JAS. I am come, by thee requested; for although thou art enraged, thou shalt not be deprived of this at least; but I will hear what new service thou dost desire of me, lady.

MED. Jason, I entreat you to be forgiving of what has been said, but right is it that you should bear with my anger, since many friendly acts have been done by us two. But I reasoned with myself and rebuked myself; wayward woman, why am I maddened and am enraged with those who consult well for me? and why am I in enmity with the princes of the land and with my husband, who is acting in the most advantageous manner for us, having married a princess, and begetting brothers to my children? Shall I not cease from my rage? What injury do I suffer, the Gods providing well for me? Have I not children? And I know that I am flying the country, and am in want of friends. Revolving this in my mind I perceive that I had much imprudence, and was enraged without reason. Now then I approve of this, and thou appearest to me to be prudent, having added this alliance to us; but I was foolish, who ought to share in these plans, and to join in adorning and to stand by the bed, and to delight with thee that thy bride was enamored of thee; but we women are as we are, I will not speak evil of the sex; wherefore it is not right that you should put yourself on an equality with the evil, nor repay folly for folly. I give up, and say that then I erred in judgment, but now I have determined on these things better. O my children, my children, come forth, leave the house, come forth, salute, and address your father with me, and be reconciled to your friends from your former hatred together with your mother. For there is amity between us, and my rage hath ceased. Take his right hand. Alas! my misfortunes; how I feel some hidden ill in my mind! Will ye, my children, in this manner, and for a long time enjoying life, stretch out your dear hands? Wretch that I am! how near am I to weeping and full of fear!—But at last canceling this dispute with your father, I have filled thus my tender sight with tears.

CHOR. In my eyes also the moist tear is arisen; and may not the evil advance to a greater height than it is at present.

JAS. I approve of this, lady, nor do I blame the past; for it is reasonable that the female sex be enraged with a husband who barters them for another union.—But thy heart has changed to the more proper side, and thou hast discovered, but after some time, the better counsel: these are the actions of a wise woman. But for you, my sons, your father not without thought hath formed many provident plans, with the assistance of the Gods. For I think that you will be yet the first in this Corinthian country, together with your brothers. But advance and prosper: and the rest your father, and whatever God is propitious, will effect. And may I behold you blooming arrive at the prime of youth, superior to my enemies. And thou, why dost thou bedew thine eyes with the moist tear, having turned aside thy white cheek, and why dost thou not receive these words from me with pleasure?

MED. It is nothing. I was thinking of my sons.

JAS. Be of good courage; for I will arange well for them.

MED. I will be so, I will not mistrust thy words; but a woman is of soft mould, and was born to tears.

JAS. Why, I pray, dost thou so grieve for thy children?

MED. I brought them into the world, and when thou wert praying that thy children might live, a feeling of pity came upon me if that would be. But for what cause thou hast come to a conference with me, partly hath been explained, but the other reasons I will mention. Since it appeareth fit to the royal family to send me from this country, for me also this appears best, I know it well, that I might not dwell here, a check either to thee or to the princes of the land; for I seem to be an object of enmity to the house; I indeed will set out from this land in flight; but to the end that the children may be brought up by thy hand, entreat Creon that they may not leave this land.

JAS. I know not whether I shall persuade him; but it is right to try.

MED. But do thou then exhort thy bride to ask her father, that my children may not leave this country.

JAS. Certainly I will, and I think at least that she will persuade him, if indeed she be one of the female sex.

MED. I also will assist you in this task, for I will send to her presents which (I well know) far surpass in beauty any now among men, both a fine-wrought robe, and a golden-twined chaplet, my sons carrying them. But as quick as possible let one of my attendants bring hither these ornaments. Thy bride shall be blessed not in one instance, but in many, having met with you at least the best of husbands, and possessing ornaments which the sun my father's father once gave to his descendants. Take these nuptial presents, my sons, in your hands, and bear and present them to the blessed royal bride; she shall receive gifts not indeed to be despised.

JAS. Why, O fond woman, dost thou rob thy hands of these; thinkest thou that the royal palace is in want of vests? in want of gold? keep these presents, give them not away; for if the lady esteems me of any value, she will prefer pleasing me to riches, I know full well.

MED. But do not oppose me; gifts, they say, persuade even the Gods,[27] and gold is more powerful than a thousand arguments to men. Hers is fortune, her substance the God now increases, she in youth governs all. But the sentence of banishment on my children I would buy off with my life, not with gold alone. But my children, enter you the wealthy palace, to the new bride of your father, and my mistress, entreat her, beseech her, that you may not leave the land, presenting these ornaments; but this is of the greatest consequence, that, she receive these gifts in her own hand. Go as quick as possible, and may you be bearers of good tidings to your mother in what she desires to obtain, having succeeded favorably.

CHOR. Now no longer have I any hope of life for the children, no longer [is there hope]; for already are they going to death. The bride shall receive the destructive present of the golden chaplet, she wretched shall receive them, and around her golden tresses shall she place the attire of death, having received the presents in her hands. The beauty and the divine glitter of the robe will persuade her to place around her head the golden-wrought chaplet. Already with the dead shall the bride be adorned; into such a net will she fall, and such a destiny will she, hapless woman, meet with; nor will she escape her fate. But thou, oh unhappy man! oh wretched bridegroom! son-in-law of princes, unknowingly thou bringest on thy children destruction, and on thy wife a bitter death; hapless man, how much art thou fallen from thy state![28] But I lament for thy grief, O wretch, mother of these children, who wilt murder thy sons on account of a bridal-bed; deserting which, in defiance of thee, thy husband dwells with another wife.

TUTOR, MEDEA, CHORUS.

TUT. Thy sons, my mistress, are reprieved from banishment, and the royal bride received thy presents in her hands with pleasure, and hence is peace to thy children.

MED. Ah!

TUT. Why dost thou stand in confusion, when thou art fortunate?

MED. Alas! alas!

TUT. This behavior is not consonant with the message I have brought thee.

MED. Alas! again.

TUT. Have I reported any ill fortune unknowingly, and have I failed in my hope of being the messenger of good?

MED. Thou hast said what thou hast said, I blame not thee.

TUT. Why then dost thou bend down thine eye, and shed tears?

MED. Strong necessity compels me, O aged man, for this the Gods and I deliberating ill have contrived.

TUT. Be of good courage; thou also wilt return home yet through thy children.

MED. Others first will I send to their home,[29] O wretched me!

TUT. Thou art not the only one who art separated from thy children; it behooves a mortal to bear calamities with meekness.

MED. I will do so; but go within the house, and prepare for the children what is needful for the day. O my sons, my sons, you have indeed a city, and a house, in which having forsaken me miserable, you shall dwell, ever deprived of a mother. But I am now going an exile into a foreign land, before I could have delight in you, and see you flourishing, before I could adorn your marriage, and wife, and nuptial-bed, and hold up the torch.[30] O unfortunate woman that I am, on account of my wayward temper. In vain then, my children, have I brought you up, in vain have I toiled, and been consumed with cares, suffering the strong agonies of child-bearing. Surely once there was a time when I hapless woman had many hopes in you, that you would both tend me in my age, and when dead would with your hands decently compose my limbs, a thing desired by men. But now this pleasing thought hath indeed perished; for deprived of you I shall pass a life of misery, and bitter to myself. But you will no longer behold your mother with your dear eyes, having passed into another state of life. Alas! alas! why do you look upon me with your eyes, my children? Why do ye smile that last smile? Alas! alas! what shall I do? for my heart is sinking. Ye females, when I behold the cheerful look of my children, I have no power. Farewell my counsels: I will take my children with me from this land. What does it avail me grieving their father with the ills of these, to acquire twice as much pain for myself? never will I at least do this. Farewell my counsels. And yet what do I suffer? do I wish to incur ridicule, having left my foes unpunished? This must be dared. But the bringing forward words of tenderness in my mind arises also from my cowardice. Go, my children, into the house; and he for whom it is not lawful to be present at my sacrifice, let him take care himself to keep away.[31] But I will not stain my hand. Alas! alas! do not thou then, my soul, do not thou at least perpetrate this. Let them escape, thou wretch, spare thy sons. There shall they live with us and delight thee. No, I swear by the infernal deities who dwell with Pluto, never shall this be, that I will give up my children to be insulted by my enemies. [At all events they must die, and since they must, I who brought them into the world will perpetrate the deed.] This is fully determined by fate, and shall not pass away. And now the chaplet is on her head, and the bride is perishing in the robes; of this I am well assured. But, since I am now going a most dismal path, and these will I send by one still more dismal, I desire to address my children: give, my sons, give thy right hand for thy mother to kiss. O most dear hand, and those lips dearest to me, and that form and noble countenance of my children, be ye blessed, but there;[32] for every thing here your father hath taken away. O the sweet embrace, and that soft skin, and that most fragrant breath of my children. Go, go; no longer am I able to look upon you, but am overcome by my ills. I know indeed the ills that I am about to dare, but my rage is master of my counsels,[33] which is indeed the cause of the greatest calamities to men.

CHOR. Already have I often gone through more refined reasonings, and have come to greater arguments than suits the female mind to investigate; for we also have a muse, which dwelleth with us, for the sake of teaching wisdom; but not with all, for haply thou wilt find but a small number of the race of women out of many not ungifted with the muse.[34]

And I say that those men who are entirely free from wedlock, and have not begotten children, surpass in happiness those who have families; those indeed who are childless, through inexperience whether children are born a joy or anguish to men, not having them themselves, are exempt from much misery. But those who have a sweet blooming offspring of children in their house, I behold worn with care the whole time; first of all how they shall bring them up honorably, and how they shall leave means of sustenance for their children. And still after this, whether they are toiling for bad or good sons, this is still in darkness. But one ill to mortals, the last of all, I now will mention. For suppose they have both found sufficient store, and the bodies of their children have arrived at manhood, and that they are good; but if this fortune shall happen to them, death, bearing away their sons, vanishes with them to the shades of darkness. How then does it profit that the Gods heap on mortals yet this grief in addition to others, the most bitter of all, for the sake of children?

MEDEA, MESSENGER, CHORUS.

MED. For a long time waiting for the event, my friends, I am anxiously expecting what will be the result thence. And I see indeed one of the domestics of Jason coming hither, and his quickened breath shows that he will be the messenger of some new ill.

MESS. O thou, that hast impiously perpetrated a deed of terror, Medea, fly, fly, leaving neither the ocean chariot,[35] nor the car whirling o'er the plain.

MED. But what is done that requires this flight?

MESS. The princess is just dead, and Creon her father destroyed by thy charms.

MED. Thou hast spoken most glad tidings: and hereafter from this time shalt thou be among my benefactors and friends.

MESS. What sayest thou? Art thou in thy senses, and not mad, lady? who having destroyed the king and family, rejoicest at hearing it, and fearest not such things?

MED. I also have something to say to these words of thine at least; but be not hasty, my friend; but tell me how they perished, for twice as much delight wilt thou give me if they died miserably.

MESS. As soon as thy two sons were come with their father, and had entered the bridal house, we servants, who were grieved at thy misfortunes, were delighted; and immediately there was much conversation in our ears, that thy husband and thou had brought the former quarrel to a friendly termination. One kissed the hand, another the auburn head of thy sons, and I also myself followed with them to the women's apartments through joy. But my mistress, whom we now reverence instead of thee, before she saw thy two sons enter, held her cheerful eyes fixed on Jason; afterward however she covered her eyes, and turned aside her white cheek, disgusted at the entrance of thy sons; but thy husband quelled the anger and rage of the young bride, saying this; Be not angry with thy friends, but cease from thy rage, and turn again thy face, esteeming those as friends, whom thy husband does. But receive the gifts, and ask thy father to give up the sentence of banishment against these children for my sake. But when she saw the ornaments, she refused not, but promised her husband every thing; and before thy sons and their father were gone far from the house, she took and put on the variegated robes, and having placed the golden chaplet around her tresses she arranges her hair in the radiant mirror, smiling at the lifeless image of her person. And after, having risen from her seat, she goes across the chamber, elegantly tripping with snow-white foot; rejoicing greatly in the presents, looking much and oftentimes with her eyes on her outstretched neck.[36] After that however there was a sight of horror to behold. For having changed color, she goes staggering back trembling in her limbs, and is scarce in time to prevent herself from falling on the ground, by sinking into a chair. And some aged female attendant, when she thought that the wrath either of Pan or some other Deity[37] had visited her, offered up the invocation, before at least she sees the white foam bursting from her mouth, and her mistress rolling her eyeballs from their sockets, and the blood no longer in the flesh; then she sent forth a loud shriek of far different sound from the strain of supplication; and straightway one rushed to the apartments of her father, but another to her newly-married husband, to tell the calamity befallen the bride, and all the house was filled with frequent hurryings to and fro. And by this time a swift runner, exerting his limbs, might have reached[38] the goal of the course of six plethra;[39] but she, wretched woman, from being speechless, and from a closed eye having groaned deeply writhed in agony; for a double pest was warring against her. The golden chaplet indeed placed on her head was sending forth a stream of all-devouring fire wonderful to behold, but the fine-wrought robes, the presents of thy sons, were devouring the white flesh of the hapless woman. But she having started from her seat flies, all on fire, tossing her hair and head on this side and that side, desirous of shaking off the chaplet; but the golden wreath firmly kept its hold; but the fire, when she shook her hair, blazed out with double fury, and she sinks upon the ground overcome by her sufferings, difficult for any one except her father to recognize. For neither was the expression of her eyes clear, nor her noble countenance; but the blood was dropping from the top of her head mixed with fire. But her flesh was dropping off her bones, as the tear from the pine-tree, by the hidden fangs of the poison; a sight of horror. But all feared to touch the body, for we had her fate to warn us. But the hapless father, through ignorance of her suffering, having come with haste into the apartment, falls on the corpse, and groans immediately; and having folded his arms round her, kisses her, saying these words; O miserable child, what Deity hath thus cruelly destroyed thee? who makes an aged father bowing to the tomb[40] bereaved of thee? Alas me! let me die with thee, my child. But after he had ceased from his lamentations and cries, desiring to raise his aged body, he was held, as the ivy by the boughs of the laurel, by the fine-wrought robes; and dreadful was the struggle, for he wished to raise his knee, but she held him back; but if he drew himself away by force he tore the aged flesh from his bones. But at length the wretched man swooned away, and gave up his life; for no longer was he able to endure the agony. But they lie corses, the daughter and aged father near one another; a calamity that demands tears. And let thy affairs indeed be not matter for my words; for thou thyself wilt know a refuge from punishment. But the affairs of mortals not now for the first time I deem a shadow, and I would venture to say that those persons who seem to be wise and are researchers of arguments, these I say, run into the greatest folly. For no mortal man is happy; but wealth pouring in, one man may be more fortunate than another, but happy he can not be.

CHOR. The Deity, it seems, will in this day justly heap on Jason a variety of ills. O hapless lady, how we pity thy sufferings, daughter of Creon, who art gone to the house of darkness, through thy marriage with Jason.

MED. The deed is determined on by me, my friends, to slay my children as soon as possible, and to hasten from this land; and not by delaying to give my sons for another hand more hostile to murder. But come, be armed, my heart; why do we delay to do dreadful but necessary deeds? Come, O wretched hand of mine, grasp the sword, grasp it, advance to the bitter goal of life, and be not cowardly, nor remember thy children how dear they are, how thou broughtest them into the world; but for this short day at least forget thy children; hereafter lament. For although thou slayest them, nevertheless they at least were dear, but I a wretched woman.

CHOR. O thou earth, and thou all-illuming beam of the sun, look down upon, behold this abandoned woman, before she move her blood-stained hand itself about to inflict the blow against her children; for from thy golden race they sprung; but fearful is it for the blood of Gods to fall by the hand of man. But do thou, O heaven-born light, restrain her, stop her, remove from this house this blood-stained and miserable Erinnys agitated by the Furies. The care of thy children perishes in vain, and in vain hast thou produced a dear race, O thou who didst leave the most inhospitable entrance of the Cyanean rocks, the Symplegades. Hapless woman, why does such grievous rage settle on thy mind; and hostile slaughter ensue? For kindred pollutions are difficult of purification to mortals; correspondent calamities falling from the Gods to the earth upon the houses of the murderers.[41]

FIRST SON. (*within*) Alas! what shall I do? whither shall I fly from my mother's hand?

SECOND SON. I know not, dearest brother, for we perish.

CHOR. Hearest thou the cry? hearest thou the children? O wretch, O ill-fated woman! Shall I enter the house? It seems right to me to ward off the murderous blow from the children.

SONS. Nay, by the Gods assist us, for it is in needful time; since now at least are we near the destruction of the sword.

CHOR. Miserable woman, art thou then a rock, or iron, who cuttest down with death by thine own hand the fair crop of children which thou producedst thyself? one indeed I hear of, one woman of those of old, who laid violent hands on her children, Ino, maddened by the Gods when the wife of Jove sent her in banishment from her home; and she miserable woman falls into the sea through the impious murder of her children, directing her foot over the sea-shore, and dying with her two sons, there she perished! what then I pray can be more dreadful than this? O thou bed of woman, fruitful in ills, how many evils hast thou already brought to men!

JASON, CHORUS.

JAS. Ye females, who stand near this mansion, is she who hath done these deeds of horror, Medea, in this house; or hath she withdrawn herself in flight? For now it is necessary for her either to be hidden beneath the earth, or to raise her winged body into the vast expanse of air, if she would not suffer vengeance from the king's house. Does she trust that after having slain the princes of this land, she shall herself escape from this house with impunity?—But I have not such care for her as for my children; for they whom she has injured will punish her. But I came to preserve my children's life, lest [Creon's] relations by birth do any injury,[42] avenging the impious murder perpetrated by their mother.

CHOR. Unhappy man! thou knowest not at what misery thou hast arrived, Jason, or else thou wouldest not have uttered these words.

JAS. What is this, did she wish to slay me also?

CHOR. Thy children are dead by their mother's hand.

JAS. Alas me! What wilt thou say? how hast thou killed me, woman!

CHOR. Think now of thy sons as no longer living.

JAS. Where did she slay them, within or without the house?

CHOR. Open those doors, and thou wilt see the slaughter of thy sons.

JAS. Undo the bars, as quick as possible, attendants; unloose the hinges, that I may see this double evil, my sons slain, and may punish her.

MED. Why dost thou shake and unbolt these gates, seeking the dead and me who did the deed. Cease from this labor; but if thou wantest aught with me, speak if thou wishest any thing; but never shall thou touch me with thy hands; such a chariot the sun my father's father gives me, a defense from the hostile hand.[43]

JAS. O thou abomination! thou most detested woman, both by the Gods and by me, and by all the race of man; who hast dared to plunge the sword in thine own children, thou who bore them, and hast destroyed me childless. And having done this thou beholdest both the sun and the earth, having dared a most impious deed. Mayest thou perish! but I am now wise, not being so then when I brought thee from thy house and from a foreign land to a Grecian habitation, a great pest, traitress to thy father and the land that nurtured thee. But the Gods have sent thy evil genius on me. For having slain thy brother at the altar, thou embarkedst on board the gallant vessel Argo. Thou begannest indeed with such deeds as these; and being wedded to me, and bearing me children, thou hast destroyed them on account of another bed and marriage. There is not one Grecian woman who would have dared a deed like this, in preference to whom at least, I thought worthy to wed thee, an alliance hateful and destructive to me, a lioness, no woman, having a nature more savage than the Tuscan Scylla. But I can not gall thy heart with ten thousand reproaches, such shameless confidence is implanted in thee. Go, thou worker of ill, and stained with the blood of thy children. But for me it remains to bewail my fate, who shall neither enjoy my new nuptials, nor shall I have it in my power to address while alive my sons whom I begot and educated, but I have lost them.

MED. Surely I could make long reply to these words, if the Sire Jupiter did not know what treatment thou receivedst from me, and what thou didst in return; but you were mistaken, when you expected, having dishonored my bed, to lead a life of pleasure, mocking me, and so was the princess, and so was Creon, who proposed the match to thee, when he expected to drive me from this land with impunity. Wherefore, if thou wilt, call me lioness, and Scylla who dwelt in the Tuscan plain. For thy heart, as is right, I have wounded.

JAS. And thou thyself grievest at least, and art a sharer in these ills.

MED. Be assured of that; but this lessens[44] the grief, that thou canst not mock me.

JAS. My children, what a wicked mother have ye found!

MED. My sons, how did ye perish by your father's fault!

JAS. Nevertheless my hand slew them not.

MED. But injury, and thy new nuptials.

JAS. And on account of thy bed didst thou think fit to slay them?

MED. Dost thou deem this a slight evil to a woman?

JAS. Whoever at least is modest; but in thee is every ill.

MED. These are no longer living, for this will gall thee.

JAS. These are living, alas me! avenging furies on thy head.

MED. The Gods know who began the injury.

JAS. They know indeed thy execrable mind.

Meo. Thou art hateful to me, and I detest thy bitter speech.

JAS. And I in sooth thine; the separation at least is without pain.

MED. How then? what shall I do? for I also am very desirous.

JAS. Suffer me, I beg, to bury and mourn over these dead bodies.

MED. Never indeed; since I will bury them with this hand bearing them to the shrine of Juno, the Goddess guardian of the citadel, that no one of my enemies may insult them, tearing up their graves. But in this land of Sisyphus will I institute in addition to this a solemn festival and sacrifices hereafter to expiate this unhallowed murder. But I myself will go to the land of Erectheus, to dwell with Ægeus son of Pandion. But thou, wretch, as is fit, shalt die wretchedly, struck on thy head with a relic of thy ship Argo, having seen the bitter end of my marriage.

JAS. But may the Fury of the children, and Justice the avenger of murder, destroy thee.

MED. But what God or Deity hears thee, thou perjured man, and traitor to the rights of hospitality?

JAS. Ah! thou abominable woman, and murderer of thy children.

MED. Go to thy home, and bury thy wife.

JAS. I go, even deprived of both my children.

MED. Thou dost not yet mourn enough: stay and grow old.[45]

JAS. Oh my dearest sons!

MED. To their mother at least, but not to thee.

JAS. And yet thou slewest them.

MED. To grieve thee.

JAS. Alas, alas! I hapless man long to kiss the dear mouths of my children.

MED. Now them addressest, now salutest them, formerly rejecting them with scorn.

JAS. Grant me, by the Gods, to touch the soft skin of my sons.

MED. It is not possible. Thy words are thrown away in vain.

JAS. Dost thou hear this, O Jove, how I am rejected, and what I suffer from this accursed and child-destroying lioness? But as much indeed as is in my power and I am able, I lament and mourn over these; calling the Gods to witness, that having slain my children, thou preventest me from touching them with my hands, and from burying the bodies, whom, oh that I had never begotten, and seen them thus destroyed by thee.

CHOR. Jove is the dispenser of various fates in heaven, and the Gods perform many things contrary to our expectations, and those things which we looked for are not accomplished; but the God hath brought to pass things unthought of. In such manner hath this affair ended.

NOTES ON MEDEA

[1] The Cyaneæ Petræ, or Symplegades, were two rocks in the mouth of the Euxine Sea, said to meet together with prodigious violence, and crush the passing ships. See Pindar. Pyth. iv. 386.

[2] ερετμωσαι signifies to make to row; ερετμησαι, to row. In the same sense the two verbs derived from πολεμος are used, πολεμοω signifying ad bellum excito; πολεμεω, bellum gero.

[3] Elmsley reads φυγη in the nominative case, "*a flight indeed pleasing*," etc.

[4] Literally, *Before we have drained this to the very dregs.* So Virgil, Æn. iv. 14. *Quæ bella exhausta canebat!*

[5] Ter. And. Act. ii. Sc. 5. *Omnes sibi malle melius esse quam alteri.* Ac. iv. Sc. 1. *Proximus sum egomet mihi.*

[6] Elmsley reads και for ει, "*And their father,*" etc.

[7] In Elms. Dind. το γαρ ειθισθαι, "*for the being accustomed,*" etc.

[8] δυναται here signifies ισχυει, σθενει; and in this sense it is repeatedly used: ουδενα καιρον, in this place, is not to be interpreted "intempestive", but "immoderate, supra modum." For this signification consult Stephen's Thesaurus, word καιρος. EMSLEY.

[9] 'οδε is used in this sense v. 49, 687, 901, of this Play.

[10] μογερα is best taken with Reiske as the accusative plural, though the Scholiast considers it the nominative singular. ELMSLEY.

[11] γεγωτας need not be translated as νομιζομενους, the sense is [Greek; ontas]: so αυθαδης γεγως, line 225.

[12] That is, the character of man can not be discovered by the countenance: so Juvenal,

Fronti nulla fides.

'οστις, though in the singular number, refers to βροτων in the plural: a similar construction is met with in Homer, Il. Γ. 279.

ανθρωπους τιννυσθον, 'ο τις κ' επιορκον 'ομοσσηι.

[13] Grammarians teach us that γαμειν is applied to the husband, γαμεισθαι to the wife; and this rule will generally be found to hold good. We must either then read 'η τ' εγηματο, which Porson does not object to, and Elmsley adopts; or understand εγηματο in an ironical sense, in the spirit of Martial's *Uxori nubere nolo meæ*: in the latter case 'ηι τ' εγηματο should be read (not 'ην τ'), as being the proper syntax.

[14] The primary signification of πλημμελης is *absonus, out of tune*: hence is easily deduced the signification in which it is often found in Euripides. The word πλημμελησας occurs in the Phœnissæ, l. 1669.

[15] Elmsley approves of the reading adopted by Porson, though he has given in his text

πονουμεν 'ημεις, κ' ον πονων κεχρημεθα.

"*We are oppressed with cares, and want not other cares,*" as being more likely to have come from Euripides. So also Dindorf.

[16] 'ως εοικας; is here used for the more common expression 'ως εοικεν. So Herodotus, Clio, clv. ου παυσονται 'οι Λυδοι, 'ως οικασι, πραγματα παρεχοντες, και αυτοι εχοντες. See also Hecuba, 801.

[17] Beck interprets this passage, "Mea quidem vita ut non habeat laudem, fama obstat." Heath translates it, "Jam in contrariam partem tendens fama efficit, ut mea quoque vita laudem habeat." We are told by the Scholiast, that by βιοταν is to be understood φυσιν.

[18] Iolcos was a city of Thessaly, distant about seven stadii from the sea, where the parents of Jason lived: Pelion was both a mountain and city of Thessaly, close to Iolcos; whence Iolcos is called Peliotic.

[19] For the same sentiment more fully expressed, see Hippolytus, 616-625. See also Paradise Lost, x. 890.

Oh, why did God,

Creator wise, that peopled highest heaven

With spirits masculine, create at last

This novelty on earth, this fair defect

Of nature, and not fill the world at once

With men, as angels, without feminine?

[20] Porson rightly reads ταχ' αν πιθοιο with Wyttenbach.

[21] Elmsley has

"'ως και δοκει μοι ταυτα, και καλως εχειν

γαμους τυραννων, 'ους προδους 'ημας εχει,

και ξυμφορ' ειναι, και καλως εγνωσμενα."

"that these things appear good to me, and that the alliance with the princes, which he, having forsaken me, has contracted, are both advantageous and well determined on." So also Dind. but καλως εχει. Porson omits the line.

[22] In Elmsley this line is omitted, and instead of it is inserted

"νυμφηι φεροντας, τηνδε μη φευγειν χθονα."

"offering them to the bride, that they may not be banished from this country," which Dindorf retains, and brackets the other.

[23] Although the Scholiast reprobates this interpretation, it seems to be the best, nor is it any objection, that Μνημοσυνη is elsewhere represented as the Mother of the Muses; so much at variance is the poetry of Euripides with the received mythology of the ancients. ELMSLEY.

[24] The construction is πολις 'ιερων ποταμων; thus Thebes, Phœnis. l. 831, is called πυργος διδυμων ποταμων. A like expression occurs in 2 Sam. xii. 27. I have fought against Rabbah,

and have taken *the city of waters*, πολιν των ‘υδατων in the Septuagint version.

[25] Elmsley reads παντες, "*we all entreat thee.*" So Dindorf.

[26] Elmsley reads ‘η δυνασει with the note of interrogation after θυμωι; "*or how wilt thou be able,*" etc.

[27] An allusion to that well-known saying in Plato, de Repub. 1. 3. Δωρα θεους πειθει, δωρ' αιδοιους βασιληας. Ovid. de Arte Am. iii. 635.

Munera, crede mini, capiunt hominesque deosque.

[28] Vertit Portus, *O infelix quantam calamitatem ignoras.* Mihi sensus videtur esse, *quantum a pristina fortuna excidisti.* ELMSLEY.

[29] Medea here makes use of the ambiguous word καταξω, which may be understood by the Tutor in the sense of "bringing back to their country," but implies also the horrid purpose of destroying her children: τοδε 'καταξω' αντι του πεμψω εις τον Αιδην, as the Scholiast explains it.

[30] It was the custom for mothers to bear lighted torches at their children's nuptials. See Iphig. Aul. l. 372.

[31] ‘οτωι δε φησιν ουκ ευσεβες φαινεται παρειναι τωι φονωι, και δεχεσθαι τοιαυτας θυσιας, ‘ουτος αποτω.—τωι δε αυτωι μελησει συναπτεον το μη παρειναι. SCHOL.

[32] *But there*; that is, in the regions below.

[33] Ovid. Metamorph. vii. 20.

Video meliora proboque,

Deteriora sequor.

[34] Elmsley reads

παυρον δε γενος (μιαν εν πολλαις

‘ευροις αν ισως)

ουκ, κ.τ.λ.

"*But a small number of the race of women (you may perchance find one among many) not ungifted with the muse.*"

[35] A similar expression is found in Iphig. Taur, v. 410. ναϊον οχημα. A ship is frequently called Ἑρμα θαλασσης: so Virgil, Æn. vi. Classique immittit habenas.

[36] Elmsley is of opinion that *the instep* and not *the neck* is meant by τενων.

[37] The ancients attributed all sudden terrors, and sudden sicknesses, such as epilepsies, for which no cause appeared, to Pan, or to some other Deity. The anger of the God they endeavored to avert by a hymn, which had the nature of a charm.

[38] Elmsley has ανθηπτετο, which is the old reading: this makes no difference in the construing or the construction, as, in the line before, he reads αν ἑλκων, where Porson has ανελκων.

[39] The space of time elapsed is meant to be marked by this circumstance. MUSGRAVE. PORSON. Thus we find in M of the Odyssey, l. 439, the time of day expressed by the rising of the judges; in Δ of the Iliad, l. 86, by the dining of the woodman. When we recollect that the ancients had not the inventions that we have whereby to measure their time, we shall cease to consider the circumlocution as absurd or out of place.

[40] The same expression occurs in the Heraclidæ, l. 168. The Scholiast explains it thus; τυμβογεροντα, τον πλησιον θανατου ῾οντα: τυμβους δε καλουσι τους γεροντας, παροσον πλησιον εισι του θανατου και του ταφου.

[41] αυτοφονταις may be taken as an adjective to agree with δομοις, or the construction may be αχη πιτνοντα αυτοφονταις επι δομοις, in the same manner as λιθος επεσε μοι επι κεφαληι. ELMSLEY.

[42] μη με τι δρασωσι' had been "lest they do *me* any injury." Elmsley conceives that νιν is the true reading, which might easily have been corrupted into μοι.

[43] Here Medea appears above in a chariot drawn by dragons, bearing with her the bodies of her slaughtered sons. SCHOL. See Horace, Epod. 3.

Hoc delibutis ulta donis pellicem,

Serpente fugit alite.

[44] λυει may also be interpreted, with the Scholiast, in the sense of λυσιτελει, "the grief delights me." The translation given in the text is proposed by Porson, and approved of by Elmsley.

[45] Elmsley has

μενε και γηρας.

"*Stay yet for old age.*" So also Dindorf.

HIPPOLYTUS.

PERSONS REPRESENTED.

VENUS.

HIPPOLYTUS.

ATTENDANTS.

PHÆDRA.

NURSE.

THESEUS.

MESSENGER.

DIANA.

CHORUS OF TRŒZENIAN DAMES.

THE ARGUMENT.

Theseus was the son of Othra and Neptune, and king of the Athenians; and having married Hippolyta, one of the Amazons, he begat Hippolytus, who excelled in beauty and chastity. When his wife died, he married, for his second wife, Phædra, a Cretan, daughter of Minos, king of Crete, and Pasiphaë. Theseus, in consequence of having slain Pallas, one of his kinsmen, goes into banishment, with his wife, to Trœzene, where it happened that Hippolytus was being brought up by Pittheus: but Phædra having seen the youth was desperately enamored, not that she was incontinent, but in order to fulfill the anger of Venus, who, having determined to destroy Hippolytus on account of his chastity, brought her plans to a conclusion. She, concealing her disease, at length was compelled to declare it to her nurse, who had promised to relieve her, and who, though against her inclination, carried her words to the youth. Phædra, having learned that he was exasperated, eluded the nurse, and hung herself. At which time Theseus having arrived, and wishing to take her down that was strangled, found a letter attached to her, throughout which she accused Hippolytus of a design on her virtue. And he, believing what was written, ordered Hippolytus to go into banishment, and put up a prayer to Neptune, in compliance with which the god destroyed Hippolytus. But Diana declared to Theseus every thing that had happened, and blamed not Phædra, but comforted him, bereaved of his child and wife, and promised to institute honors in the place to Hippolytus.

The scene of the play is laid in Trœzene. It was acted in the archonship of Ameinon, in the fourth year of the 87th Olympiad. Euripides first, Jophon second, Jon third. This Hippolytus is the second of that name, and is called ΣΤΕΦΑΝΙΑΣ: but it appears to have been written the latest, for what was unseemly and deserved blame is corrected in this play. The play is ranked among the first.

HIPPOLYTUS.

VENUS.

Great in the sight of mortals, and not without a name am I the Goddess Venus, and in heaven: and of as many as dwell within the ocean and the boundaries of Atlas, beholding the light of the sun, those indeed, who reverence my authority, I advance to honor; but overthrow as many as hold themselves high toward me. For this is in sooth a property inherent even in the race of the Gods, that "they rejoice when honored by men." But quickly will I show the truth of these words: for the son of Theseus, born of the Amazon, Hippolytus, pupil of the chaste Pittheus, alone of the inhabitants of this land of Trœzene, says that I am of deities the vilest, and rejects the bridal bed, and will have nothing to do with marriage. But Dian, the sister of Phœbus, daughter of Jove, he honors, esteeming her the greatest of deities. And through the green wood ever accompanying the virgin, with his swift dogs he clears the beasts from off the earth, having formed a fellowship greater than mortal ought. This indeed I grudge him not; for wherefore should I? but wherein he has erred toward me, I will avenge me on Hippolytus this very day: and having cleared most of the difficulties beforehand,[1] I need not much labor. For Phædra, his father's noble wife, having seen him, (as he was going once from the house of Pittheus to the land of Pandion, in order to see and afterward be fully admitted to the hallowed mysteries,) was smitten in her heart with fierce love by my design. And even before she came to this land of Trœzene, at the very rock of Pallas that overlooks this land, she raised a temple to Venus, loving an absent love; and gave out afterward,[2] that the Goddess was honored with her temple for Hippolytus's sake. But now since Theseus has left the land of Cecrops, in order to avoid the pollution of the murder of the sons of Pallas, and is sailing to this land with his wife, having submitted to a year's banishment from his people; there indeed groaning and stricken with the stings of love, the wretched woman perishes in secret; and not one of her domestics is conscious of her malady. But this love must by no means fall to the ground in this way: but I will open the matter to Theseus, and it shall become manifest. And him that is our enemy shall the father kill with imprecations, which Neptune, king of the ocean, granted as a privilege to Theseus, that he should make no prayer thrice to the God in vain. But Phædra dies, an illustrious woman indeed, yet still [she must die]; for I will not make her ills of that high consequence, that will hinder my enemies from giving me such full vengeance as may content me. But, as I see the son of Theseus coming, having left the toil of the chase, I will depart from this spot. But with him a numerous train of attendants following behind raise a clamor, praising the

Goddess Dian with hymns, for he knows not that the gates of hell are opened, and that this day is the last he beholds.

HIPPOLYTUS, ATTENDANTS.

HIPP. Follow, follow, singing the heavenly Dian, daughter of Jove; Dian, under whose protection we are.

ATT. Holy, holy, most hallowed offspring of Jove, hail! hail! O Dian, daughter of Latona and of Jove, most beauteous by far of virgins, who, born of an illustrious sire, in the vast heaven dwellest in the palace of Jove, that mansion rich in gold.

HIPP. Hail, O most beauteous, most beauteous of virgins in Olympus, Dian! For thee, my mistress, bear I this wreathed garland from the pure mead, where neither does the shepherd think fit to feed his flocks, nor yet came iron there, but the bee ranges over the pure and vernal mead, and Reverence waters it with river dews. Whosoever has chastity, not that which is taught in schools, but that which is by nature, for this description of persons it is lawful thence to pluck, but for the evil it is not lawful.[3] But, O my dear mistress, receive this wreath to bind your golden tresses from a pious hand. For to me alone of mortals is allowed this privilege. With thee I am both present, and exchange words with thee, hearing thy voice, but not seeing thy countenance. But may I finish the last turn of my course of life, even as I began.

ATT. O king, (for the Gods alone ought we to call Lords,) will you hear somewhat from me, who advise you well?

HIPP. Most certainly, or else I should not seem wise.

ATT. Knowest thou then the law, which is established among men?

HIPP. I know not; but what is the one, about which thou askest me?

ATT. To hate haughtiness, and that which is disagreeable to all.

HIPP. And rightly; for what haughty mortal is not odious?

ATT. And in the affable is there any charm?

HIPP. A very great one indeed, and gain with little toil.

ATT. Dost thou suppose that the same thing holds also among the Gods?

HIPP. Certainly, forasmuch as we mortals use the laws of the Gods.

ATT. How is it then that thou addressest not a venerable Goddess?

HIPP. Whom? but take heed that thy mouth err not.[4]

ATT. Venus, who hath her station at thy gates.

HIPP. I, who am chaste, salute her at a distance.

ATT. Venerable is she, however, and of note among mortals.

HIPP. Different Gods and men are objects of regard to different persons.

ATT. May you be blest, having as much sense as you require.[5]

HIPP. No one of the Gods, that is worshiped by night, delights me.

ATT. My son, we must conform to the honors of the Gods.

HIPP. Depart, my companions, and having entered the house, prepare the viands: delightful after the chase is the full table.—And I must rub down my horses, that having yoked them to the car, when I am satiated with the repast, I may give them their proper exercise. But to your Venus I bid a long farewell.

ATT. But we, for one must not imitate the young, having our thoughts such, as it becomes slaves to give utterance to, will adore thy image, O Venus, our mistress; but thou shouldest pardon, if any one having intense feelings of mind by reason of his youth, speak foolishly: seem not to hear these things, for Gods must needs be wiser than men.

CHOR. There is a rock near the ocean,[6] distilling water, which sends forth from its precipices a flowing fountain, wherein they dip their urns; where was a friend of mine wetting the purple vests in the dew of the stream, and she laid them down on the back of the warm sunny cliff: from hence first came to me the report concerning my mistress, that she, worn with the bed of sickness, keeps her person within the house, and that fine vests veil her auburn head. And I hear that she this day for the third keeps her body untouched by the fruit of Ceres, [which she receives not] into her ambrosial mouth, wishing in secret suffering to hasten to the unhappy goal of death. For heaven-possessed, O lady, or whether by Pan, or by Hecate, or by the venerable Corybantes, or by the mother who haunts the mountains, thou art raving. But thou art thus tormented on account of some fault committed against the Cretan huntress, profane because of unoffered sacred cakes. For she goes through the sea and beyond the land on the eddies of the watery brine. Or some one in the palace misguides thy noble husband, the chief of the Athenians, by secret concubinage in thy bed. Or some sailor who put from port at Crete, hath sailed to the harbor most friendly to mariners, bringing some message to the queen; and, confined to her couch, she is bound in soul by sorrow for its sufferings. But wretched helplessness is wont to dwell with the wayward constitution of women, both on account of their throes and their loss of reason. Once through my womb shot this thrill, but I invoked the heavenly Dian, who gives easy throes, who presides over the bow, and to me she came ever much to be blessed, as well as the other Gods. But lo! the old nurse is bringing her out of the palace before the gates; and the sad cloud upon her brows is increased. What it can possibly be, my soul desires to know, with what can be afflicted the person of the queen, of color so changed.[7]

PHÆDRA, NURSE, CHORUS.

Alas! the evils of men, and their odious diseases! what shall I do for thee? and what not do? lo! here is the clear light for thee, here the air: and now is thy couch whereon thou liest sick removed from out of the house: for every word you spoke was to come hither; but soon you will be in a hurry to go to your chamber back again: for you are soon changed, and are pleased with nothing. Nor does what is present delight you, but what is not present you think more agreeable. It is a better thing to be sick, than to tend the sick: the one is a simple ill, but with the other is joined both pain of mind and toil of hands. But the whole life of men is full of grief, nor is there rest from toils. But whatever else there be more dear than life, darkness enveloping hides it in clouds. Hence we appear to dote on this present state, because it gleams on earth, through inexperience of another life, and the non-appearance of the things beneath the earth. But we are blindly carried away by fables.

PHÆ. Raise my body, place my head upright—I am faint in the joints of my limbs, my friends, lay hold of my fair-formed hands, O attendants—The dressing on my head is heavy for me to support—take it off, let flow my ringlets on my shoulders.

NUR. Be of good courage, my child, and do not thus painfully shift [the posture of] your body. But you will bear your sickness more easily both with quiet, and with a noble temper, for it is necessary for mortals to suffer misery.

PHÆ. Alas! alas! would I could draw from the dewy fountain the drink of pure waters, and that under the alders, and in the leafy mead reclining I might rest!

NUR. O my child, what sayest thou? Wilt thou not desist from uttering these things before the multitude, blurting forth a speech of madness?[8]

PHÆ. Bear me to the mountain—I will go to the wood, and by the pine-trees, where tread the dogs the slayers of beasts, pursuing the dappled hinds—By the Gods I long to cheer on the hounds, and by the side of my auburn hair to hurl the Thessalian javelin bearing the lanced weapon in my hand.

NUR. Wherefore in the name of heaven, my child, do you hanker after these things? wherefore have you any anxiety for hunting? and wherefore do you long for the fountain streams? for by the towers there is a perpetual flow of water, whence may be your draught.

PHÆ. O Dian, mistress of Limna near the sea, and of the exercises of the rattling steeds, would that I were on thy plains, breaking the Henetian colts.

NUR. Wherefore again have you madly uttered this word? at one time having ascended the mountain you set forth with the desire of hunting; but now again you long for the colts on the wave-beaten sands. These things demand much skill in prophecy [to find out], who it is of the Gods that torments thee, O lady, and strikes mad thy senses.

PHÆ. Wretch that I am, what then have I committed? whither have I wandered from my sound mind? I have gone mad; I have fallen by the evil influence of some God. Alas! alas! unhappy that I am—Nurse, cover my head again, for I am ashamed of the things I have spoken: cover me; a tear trickles down my eyes, and my sight is turned to my disgrace. For to be in one's right mind causes grief: but madness is an ill; yet it is better to perish, nothing knowing of one's ills.

NUR. I cover thee—but when in sooth will death cover my body? Length of life teaches me many things. For it behooves mortals to form moderate friendships with each other, and not to the very marrow of the soul: and the affections of the mind should be dissoluble, and so that we can slacken them, or tighten.[9] But that one soul should feel pangs for two, as I now grieve for her, is a heavy burden. The concerns of life carried to too great an extent, they say, bring rather destruction than delight, and are rather at enmity with health. Thus I praise what is in extreme less than *the sentiment of* "Nothing in excess;" and the wise will agree with me.

CHOR. O aged woman, faithful nurse of the queen Phædra, we see indeed the wretched state of this lady, but it is not clear what her disease is: but we would wish to inquire and hear from you.

NUR. I know not by my inquiries; for she is not willing to speak.

CHOR. Nor what is the origin of these pangs?

NUR. You come to the same result; for she is silent with regard to all these things.

CHOR. How feeble she is, and wasted away as to her body!

NUR. How could it be otherwise, seeing that she has abstained from food these three days?

CHOR. From the violence of her calamity is it, or does she endeavor to die?

NUR. To die; but she fasts to the dissolution of her life.

CHOR. An extraordinary thing you have been telling me, if this conduct meets the approbation of her husband.

NUR. [He nothing knows,] for she conceals this calamity, and denies that she is ill.

CHOR. But does he not guess it, looking into her face?

NUR. [How should he?] for he is out of this country.

CHOR. But do you not urge it as a matter of necessity, when you endeavor to ascertain her disease and the wandering of her senses?

NUR. I have tried every thing, and have made no further advances. I will not however abate even now from my zeal, so that you being present may bear witness with me, how I behave to my mistress when in calamity—Come, dear child, let us both forget our former conversations; and be both thou more mild, having smoothed that contracted brow, and altered the bent of your design; and I giving up that wherein I did not do right to follow thee, will have recourse to other better words. And if indeed you are ill with any of those maladies that are not to be mentioned, these women here can allay the disease: but if it may be related to men, tell it, that the thing may be mentioned to physicians.—Well! why art thou silent? It doth not behoove thee to be silent, my child, but either shouldst thou convict me, if aught I say amiss, or yield to words well spoken.—Say something—look hither—O wretch that I am! Ladies, in vain do we undergo these toils, while we are as far off from our purpose as before: for neither then was she softened by our words, nor now does she give heed to us. Still however know (now then be more obstinate than the sea) that, if thou shalt die, thou wilt betray thy children, who will have no share in their paternal mansion. I swear by the warlike queen the Amazon, who brought forth a lord over thy children, base-born yet of noble sentiments, thou knowest him well, Hippolytus.

PHÆ. Ah me!

NUR. This touches thee.

PHÆ. You have destroyed me, nurse, and by the Gods I entreat thee henceforth to be silent with respect to this man.

NUR. Do you see? you judge well indeed, but judging well you are not willing both to assist your children and to save your own life.

PHÆ. I love my children; but I am wintering in the storm of another misfortune.

NUR. You have your hands, my child, pure from blood.

PHÆ. My hands are pure, but my mind has some pollution.

NUR. What! from some calamity brought on you by any of your enemies?

PHÆ. A friend destroys me against my will, himself unwilling.

NUR. Has Theseus sinned any sin against thee?

PHÆ. Would that I never be discovered to have injured him.

NUR. What then this dreadful thing that impels thee to die?

PHÆ. Suffer me to err, for against thee I err not.

NUR. Not willingly [dost thou do so,] but 'tis through thee that I shall perish.[10]

PHÆ. What are you doing? you oppress me, hanging on me with your hand.

NUR. And never will I let go these knees.

PHÆ. Ills to thyself wilt thou hear, O wretched woman, if thou shalt hear these ills.

NUR. [Still will I cling:] for what greater evil can befall me than to lose thee?

PHÆ. You will be undone.[11] The thing however brings honor to me.

NUR. And dost thou then hide what is useful, when I beseech thee?

PHÆ. *Yes*, for from base things we devise things noble.

NUR. Wilt not thou, then, appear more noble by telling it?

PHÆ. Depart, by the Gods, and let go my hand!

NUR. No in sooth, since thou givest me not the boon that were right.

PHÆ. I will give it; for I have respect unto the reverence of thy hand.

NUR. Now will I be silent: for hence is it yours to speak.

PHÆ. O wretched mother, what a love didst thou love!

NUR. That which she had for the bull, my child, or what is this thou meanest?

PHÆ. Thou, too, O wretched sister, wife of Bacchus!

NUR. Child, what ails thee? thou speakest ill against thy relations.

PHÆ. And I the third, how unhappily I perish!

NUR. I am struck dumb with amazement. Whither will thy speech tend?

PHÆ. *To that point*, whence we have not now lately become unfortunate.

NUR. I know not a whit further of the things I wish to hear.

PHÆ. Alas! would thou couldst speak the things which I must speak.

NUR. I am no prophetess so as to know clearly things hidden.

PHÆ. What is that thing, which they do call men's loving![12]

NUR. The same, my child, a most delightful thing, and painful withal.

PHÆ. One of the two feelings I must perceive.

NUR. What say'st? Thou lovest, my child? What man!

PHÆ. Him whoever he is,[13] that is born of the Amazon.

NUR. Hippolytus dost thou say?

PHÆ. From thyself, not me, you hear—this name.

NUR. Ah me! what wilt thou go on to say? my child, how hast thou destroyed me! Ladies, this is not to be borne; I will not endure to live, hateful is the day, hateful the light I behold. I will hurl myself down, I will rid me of this body: I will remove from life to death—farewell—I no longer am. For the chaste are in love with what is evil, not willingly indeed, yet still [they love.] Venus then is no deity, but if there be aught mightier than deity, that is she, who hath destroyed both this my mistress, and me, and the whole house.

CHOR. Thou didst hear, O thou didst hear the queen lamenting her wretched sufferings that should not be heard. Dear lady, may I perish before I come to thy state of mind! Alas me! alas! alas! O hapless for these pangs! O the woes that attend on mortals! Thou art undone, thou hast disclosed thy evils to the light. What time is this that has eternally[14] awaited thee? Some new misfortune will happen to the house. And no longer is it obscure where the fortune of Venus sets, O wretched Cretan daughter.

PHÆ. Women of Trœzene, who inhabit this extreme frontier of the land of Pelops. Often at other times in the long season of night have I thought in what manner the life of mortals is depraved.[15] And to me they seem to do ill, not from the nature of their minds, for many have good thoughts, but thus must we view these things. What things are good we understand and know, but practice not; some from idleness, and others preferring some other pleasures to what is right: for there are many pleasures in life-long prates, and indolence, a pleasing ill, and shame; but there are two, the one indeed not base, but the other the weight that overthrows houses, but if the occasion on which each is used, were clear, the two things would not have the same letters. Knowing them as I did these things beforehand, by no drug did I think I should so far destroy these *sentiments*, as to fall into an opposite way of thinking. But I will also tell you the course of my determinations. After that love had wounded me, I considered how best I might endure it. I began therefore from this time to be silent, and to conceal this disease. For no confidence can be placed in the tongue, which knows to advise the thoughts of other men, but itself from itself has very many evils. But in the second place, I meditated to bear well my madness conquering it by my chastity. But in the third place, since by these means I was not able to subdue Venus, it appeared to me best to die: no one will gainsay this resolution. For may it be my lot, neither to be concealed where I do noble deeds, nor to have many witnesses, where I act basely. Besides this I knew I was a woman—a thing hated by all. O may she most miserably perish who first began to pollute the marriage-bed with other men! From noble families first arose this evil among women: for when base things appear right to those who are accounted good, surely they will appear so to the bad. I hate moreover those women who are chaste in their language indeed, but secretly have in them no good deeds of boldness: who, how, I pray, O Venus my revered mistress, look they on the faces of their husbands, nor dread the darkness that aided their deeds, and the ceilings of the house, lest they should some time or other utter a voice? For this bare idea kills me, friends, lest I should ever be discovered to have disgraced my husband, or my children, whom I brought forth; but free, happy in liberty of speech may they inhabit the city of illustrious Athens, in their mother glorious! For it enslaves a man, though he be valiant-hearted, when he is conscious of his mother's or his father's misdeeds. But this alone they say in endurance compeers with life, an honest and good mind, to whomsoever it belong. But Time, when it so chance, holding up the mirror as to a young virgin, shows forth the bad, among whom may I be never seen!

CHOR. Alas! alas! In every way how fair is chastity, and how goodly a report has it among men!

NUR. My mistress, just now indeed thy calamity coming upon me unawares, gave me a dreadful alarm. But now I perceive I was weak; and somehow or other among mortals second thoughts are the wisest. For thou hast not suffered any thing excessive nor extraordinary, but the anger of the Goddess hath fallen upon thee. Thou lovest—what wonder this? with many mortals.—And then will you lose your life for love? There is then no advantage for those who love others, nor to those who may hereafter, if they must needs die. For Venus is a thing not to be borne, if she rush on vehement. Who comes quietly indeed on the person who yields; but whom she finds haughty and of lofty notions, him taking (how thinkest thou?) she chastises. But Venus goes through air, and is on the ocean wave; and all things from her have their birth. She it is that sows and gives forth love, from whence all we on earth are engendered. As many indeed as ken the writings of the ancients, or are themselves ever among the muses, they know indeed, how that Jove was formerly inflamed with the love of Semele; they know too, how that formerly the lovely bright Aurora bore away Cephalus up to the Gods, for love, but still they live in heaven, and fly not from the presence of the Gods: but they acquiesce yielding, I ween, to what has befallen them. And wilt thou not bear it? Thy father then ought to have begotten thee on stipulated terms, or else under the dominion of other Gods, unless thou wilt be content with these laws. How many, thinkest thou, are in full and complete possession of their senses, who, when they see their bridal bed diseased, seem not to see it! And how many fathers, thinkest thou, have aided their erring sons in matters of love, for this is a maxim among the wise part of mankind, "that things that show not fair should be concealed." Nor should men labor too exactly their conduct in life, for neither would they do well to employ much accuracy in the roof wherewith their houses are covered; but having fallen into fortune so deep as thou hast, how dost thou imagine thou canst swim out? But if thou hast more things good than bad, mortal as thou art, thou surely must be well off. But cease, my dear child, from these evil thoughts, cease too from being haughty, for nothing else save haughtiness is this, to wish to be superior to the Gods. But, as thou art in love, endure it; a God hath willed it so: and, being ill, by some good means or other try to get rid of thy illness. But there are charms and soothing spells: there will appear some medicine for this sickness. Else surely men would be slow indeed in discoveries, if we women should not find contrivances.

CHOR. Phædra, she speaks indeed most useful advice in thy present state: but thee I praise. Yet is this praise less welcome than her words, and to thee more painful to hear.

PHÆ. This is it that destroys cities of men and families well governed— words too fair. For it is not at all requisite to speak words pleasant to the ear, but that whereby one may become of fair report.

NUR. Why dost thou talk in this grand strain? thou needest not gay decorated words, but a man: as soon as possible must those be found, who will speak out the plain straightforward word concerning thee. For if thy life were not in calamities of such a cast, I never would have brought thee thus far for the sake of lust, and for thy pleasure: but now the great point is to save thy life; and this is not a thing deserving of blame.

PHÆ. O thou that hast spoken dreadful things, wilt thou not shut thy mouth? and wilt not cease from uttering again those words most vile?

NUR. Vile they are, but better these for thee than fair; but better will the deed be (if at least it will save thee), than the name, in the which while thou boastest, thou wilt die.

PHÆ. Nay do not, I entreat thee by the Gods (for thou speakest well, but base are [the things thou speakest]) go beyond this, since rightly have I surrendered my life to love; but if thou speak base things in fair phrase, I shall be consumed, [being cast] into that [evil] which I am now avoiding.

NUR. If in truth this be thy opinion, thou oughtest not to err, but if thou hast erred, be persuaded by me, for this is the next best thing thou canst do.[16] I have in the house soothing philters of love (and they but lately came into my thought); which, by no base deed, nor to the harm of thy senses, will rid you of this disease, unless you are obstinate. But it is requisite to receive from him that is the object of your love, some token, either some word, or some relic of his vest, and to join from two one love.

PHÆ. But is the charm an unguent or a potion?

NUR. I know not: wish to be relieved, not informed, my child.

PHÆ. I fear thee, lest thou should appear too wise to me.

NUR. Know that you would fear every thing, *if you fear this*, but what is it you are afraid of?

PHÆ. Lest you should tell any of these things to the son of Theseus.

NUR. Let be, my child, I will arrange these matters honorably, only be thou my coadjutor, O Venus, my revered mistress; but the other things which I purpose, it will suffice to tell to my friends within.

CHORUS, PHÆDRA.

CHOR. Love, love, O thou that instillest desire through the eyes, inspiring sweet affection in the souls of those against whom thou makest war, mayst thou never appear to me to my injury, nor come unmodulated: for neither is the blast of fire nor the bolt of heaven more vehement, than that of Venus, which Love, the boy of Jove, sends from his hands. In vain, in vain, both by the Alpheus, and at the Pythian temples of Phœbus does Greece then solemnize the slaughter of bulls: but Love, the tyrant of men, porter of the dearest chambers of Venus, we worship not, the destroyer and visitant of men in all shapes of calamity, when he comes. That virgin in Œchalia, yoked to no bridal bed, till then unwedded, and who knew no husband, having taken from her home a wanderer impelled by the oar, her, like some Bacchanal of Pluto, with blood, with smoke, and murderous hymeneals did Venus give to the son of Alcmena. O unhappy woman, because of her nuptials! O sacred wall of Thebes, O mouth of Dirce, you can assist me in telling, in what manner Venus comes: for by the forked lightning, by a cruel fate, did she put to eternal sleep the parent of the Jove-begotten Bacchus, when she was visited as a bride. For dreadful doth she breathe on all things, and like some bee hovers about.

PHÆ. Women, be silent: I am undone.

CHOR. What is there that affrights thee, Phædra, in thine house?

PHÆ. Be silent, that I may make out the voice of those within.

CHOR. I am silent: this however is an evil bodement.

PHÆ. Alas me! O! O! O! oh unhappy me, because of my sufferings!

CHOR. What sound dost thou utter? what word speakest thou? tell me what report frightens thee, lady, rushing upon thy senses!

PHÆ. We are undone. Do you, standing at these gates, hear what the noise is that strikes on the house?

CHOR. Thou art by the gate, the noise that is sent forth from the house is thy care. But tell me, tell me, what evil, I pray thee, came *to thine ears?*

PHÆ. The son of the warlike Amazon, Hippolytus, cries out, abusing in dreadful forms my attendant.

CHOR. I hear indeed a noise, but can not plainly tell how it is. The voice came, it came through to the door.

PHÆ. But hark! he calls her plainly the pander of wickedness, the betrayer of her master's bed.

CHOR. Alas me for thy miseries! Thou art betrayed, dear mistress. What shall I counsel thee? for hidden things are come to light, and thou art utterly destroyed——

PHÆ. O! O!

CHOR. Betrayed by thy friends.

PHÆ. She hath destroyed me by speaking of my unhappy state, kindly but not honorably endeavoring to heal this disease.

CHOR. How then? what wilt thou do, O thou that hast suffered things incurable?

PHÆ. I know not, save one thing; to die as soon as possible is the only cure of my present sufferings.

HIPPOLYTUS, PHÆDRA, NURSE, CHORUS.

HIPP. O mother earth, and ye disclosing rays of the sun, of what words have I heard the dreadful sound!

NUR. Be silent, my son, before any one hears thy voice.

HIPP. It is not possible for me to be silent, when I have heard such dreadful things.

NUR. Nay, I implore thee by thy beauteous hand.

HIPP. Wilt not desist from bringing thy hand near me, and from touching my garments?

NUR. O! by thy knees, I implore thee, do not utterly destroy me.

HIPP. But wherefore this? since, thou sayest, thou hast spoken nothing evil.

NUR. This word, my son, is by no means to be divulged.

HIPP. It is more fair to speak fair things to many.

NUR. O my child, by no means dishonor your oath.

HIPP. My tongue hath sworn—my mind is still unsworn.[17]

NUR. O my son, what wilt thou do? wilt thou destroy thy friends?

HIPP. *Friends!* I reject the word: no unjust person is my friend.

NUR. Pardon, my child: that men should err is but to be expected.

HIPP. O Jove, wherefore in the name of heaven didst thou place in the light of the sun that specious[18] evil to men, women? for if thou didst will to propagate the race of mortals, there was no necessity for this to be done by women, but men might, having placed an equivalent in thy temples, either in brass, or iron, or the weighty gold, buy a race of children, each for the consideration of the value paid, and thus might dwell in unmolested houses, without females. But now, first of all, when we prepare to bring this evil to our homes, we squander away the wealth of our houses. By this too it is evident, that woman is a great evil; for the father, who begat her and brought her up, having given her a dowry sends her away in order to be rid of the evil. But the husband, on the other hand, when he has received the baneful evil[19] into his house, rejoices, having added a beautiful decoration to a most vile image, and tricks her out with robes, unhappy man, while he has been insensibly minishing the wealth of the family. But he is constrained; so that having made alliance with noble kinsmen, he retains with [seeming] joy a marriage bitter to him: or if he has received a good bride, but worthless parents in law, he suppresses the evil that has befallen him by the consideration of the good. But his state is the easiest, whose wife is settled in his house, a cipher, but useless by reason of simplicity. But a wise woman I detest: may there not be in my house at least a woman more highly gifted with mind than woman ought to be. For Venus engenders mischief rather among clever women, but a woman who is not endowed with capacity, by reason of her small understanding, is removed from folly. But it is right that an attendant should have no access to a woman, but with them ought to dwell the speechless brute beasts, in which case they would be able neither to address any one, nor from them to receive a voice in return. But now, they that are evil follow after their evil devices within, and the servants carry it forth abroad. As thou also hast, O evil woman, come to the purpose of admitting me to share a bed which must not be approached—a father's. Which impious things I will wash out with flowing stream, pouring it into my ears: how then could I be the vile one, who do not even deem myself pure, because I have heard such things?—But be well assured, my piety protects thee, woman, for, had I not been taken unawares by the oaths of the

Gods, never would I have refrained from telling these things to my father. But now will I depart from the house, *and stay* during the time that Theseus is absent from the land, and will keep my mouth silent; but I will see, returning with my father's return, how you will look at him, both you and your mistress. But your boldness I shall know, having before had proof of it. May you perish: but never shall I take my fill of hating women, not even if any one assert, that I am always saying this. For in some way or other they surely are always bad. Either then let some one teach them to be modest, or else let him suffer me ever to utter my invectives against them.

CHORUS, PHÆDRA, NURSE.

CHOR. Oh unhappy ill-fated fortune of women! what art now or what words have we, having failed as we have, to extricate the knot caused by [these] words?

PHÆ. We have met a just reward; O earth, and light, in what manner, I pray, can I escape from my fortunes? and how, my friends, can I conceal my calamity? Who of the Gods will appear my succorer, or what mortal my ally, or my fellow-worker in unjust works? for the suffering of my life that is at present on me comes hardly to be escaped.[20] I am the most ill-fated of women.

CHOR. Alas! alas! we are undone, lady, and the arts of thy attendant have not succeeded, and it fares ill with us.

PHÆ. O thou most vile, and the destruction of thy friends, what hast thou done to me! May Jove, my ancestor, tear thee up by the roots, having stricken thee by his fire. Did not I tell thee (did not I foresee thy intention?) to be silent with regard to those things with which I am now tormented? but thou couldst not refrain; wherefore I can no longer die with glory: but I must now in sooth employ new measures. For he, now that his mind is made keen with rage, will tell, to my detriment, thy errors to his father, and will fill the whole earth with the most vile reports. Mayst thou perish, both thou and whoever else is forward to assist friends against their will otherwise than by honorable means.

NUR. Lady, thou canst indeed blame the evil I have wrought; for that which gnaws upon thee masters thy better judgment;—but I too have somewhat to say in answer to these things, if thou wilt admit it: I brought thee up, and have a kind affection toward thee; but, while searching for medicine for thy disease, I found not that I wished for. But if I had succeeded, I had been surely ranked among the wise; for we have the reputation of sense according to our success.

PHÆ. What? is this conduct just, and satisfactory to me, to injure me first, and then to meet me in argument?

NUR. We talk too long—I did not behave wisely. But even from this state of things it is possible that thou mayest be saved, my child.

PHÆ. Desist from speaking; for before also thou didst not well advise for me, and didst attempt evil things. But depart from my sight, and take care about thyself; for I will settle my own affairs in an honorable manner. But you, noble daughters of Trœzene, grant thus much to me requesting it, bury in silence what you here have heard.

CHOR. I swear by hallowed Dian, daughter of Jove, that I will never reveal to the face of day one of thy evils.

PHÆ. Thou hast well spoken: but one kind of resource, while I search around me,[21] do I find for my present calamity, so that I may make the life of my children glorious, and may myself be assisted as things have now fallen out. For never will I disgrace the house of Crete at least, nor will I come before the face of Theseus having acted basely, for one's life's sake.

CHOR. But what irremediable evil art thou then about to perpetrate?

PHÆ. To die: but how, this will I devise.

CHOR. Speak words of better omen.

PHÆ. And do thou at least advise me well. But having quitted life this day, I shall gratify Venus, who destroys me, and shall be conquered by bitter love. But when I am dead, I shall be an evil to another at least,[22] so that he may know not to exult over my misfortunes; but, having shared this malady in common with me, he shall learn to be modest.

CHOR. Would that I were under the rocks' vast retreats,[23] and that there the God would make me a winged bird among the swift flocks, and that I were lifted up above the ocean wave that dashes against the Adriatic shore, and the water of Eridanus, where for grief of Phaethon the thrice wretched virgins let fall into their father's billow the amber-beaming brightness of their tears: and that I could make my way to the shore where the apples grow of the harmonious daughters of Hesperus, where the ruler of the ocean no longer permits the passage of the purple sea to mariners, dwelling in that dread bourn of heaven which Atlas doth sustain, and the ambrosial founts stream forth hard by the couches of Jove's palaces, where the divine and life-bestowing earth increases the bliss of the Gods. O white-winged bark of Crete, who didst bear my queen through the perturbed[24] ocean wave of brine from a happy home, thereby aiding her in a most evil marriage. For surely in both instances, or at any rate from Crete she came ill-omened to renowned Athens, when on the Munychian shore they bound the platted ends of their cables, and disembarked on the continent. Wherefore she was heartbroken with the terrible disease of unhallowed love by the influence of

Venus; and now that she can no longer hold out against the heavy calamity,[25] she will fit around her the noose suspended[26] from the ceiling of her bridal chamber, adjusting it to her white neck, having revered the hateful Goddess, and embracing an honorable name, and ridding from her breast the painful love.

FEMALE SERVANT, CHORUS, THESEUS.

SERV. Alack! alack! run to my succor all that are near the house—My mistress the wife of Theseus is hanging.

CHOR. Alas! alas! the deed is done: the queen is indeed no more—she is suspended in the noose that hangs there.

SERV. Will ye not haste? will not some one bring a two-edged sword, with which we may undo this knot around her neck?

SEMICHOR. My friends, what do we? does it seem good to enter the house and to free the queen from the tight-drawn noose?

SEMICHOR. Why we? Are not the young men-servants at hand? The being over-busy is not a safe plan through life.

SERV. Lay right the wretched corpse, pull her limbs straight. A grievous housekeeping this for my master!

CHOR. The unhappy woman, as I hear, has perished, for already are they laying her out as a corpse.

THES. Know ye, females, what noise this is in my house? a heavy sound of my attendants reached me. For the family does not think fit to open the gates to me and to hail me with joy as having returned from the oracle. Has any ill befallen the aged Pittheus? His life is now indeed far advanced; but still he would be much lamented by us, were he to leave this house.

CHOR. This that has happened, Theseus, extends not to the old; the young are they that by their death will grieve thee.

THES. Alas me! is the life of any of my children stolen from me?

CHOR. They live, but their mother is dead in a way that will grieve thee most.

THES. What sayest? My wife dead? By what fate?

CHOR. She suspended the noose, wherewith she strangled herself.

THES. Wasted with sorrow, or from some sudden calamity?

CHOR. Thus much we know—*nothing further*, for I am but just come to thy house, Theseus, to bewail thy evils.

THES. Alas! alas! why then have I my head crowned with entwined leaves, who am the unhappy inquirer of the oracle? Servants, undo the bars of the gates; unloose the bolts, that I may behold the mournful spectacle of my wife, who by her death hath utterly undone me.

CHOR. Alas! alas! unhappy for thy wretched ills: thou hast been a sufferer; thou hast perpetrated a deed of such extent as to throw this house into utter confusion. Alas! alas! thy boldness, O thou who hast died a violent death, and, by an unhallowed chance, the act committed by thy wretched hand. Who is it then, thou unhappy one, that destroys thy life?

THES. Alas me for my sufferings![27] I have suffered, unhappy wretch, the extreme of my troubles—O fortune, how heavy hast thou come upon me and my house, an imperceptible spot from some evil demon! the wearing out of a life not to be endured;[28] and I, unhappy wretch, perceive a sea of troubles so great, that never again can I emerge from it, nor escape beyond the flood of this calamity. What mention making can I unhappy, what heavy-fated fortune of thine, lady, saying that it was, can I be right? For as some bird thou art vanished from my hand, having leaped me a sudden leap to the realms of Pluto. Alas! alas! wretched, wretched are these sufferings, but from some distant period or other receive I this calamity from the Gods, for the errors of some of those of old.

CHOR. Not to thee alone, O king, have these evils happened; but with many others thou hast lost an excellent wife.[29]

THES. In the shades beneath the earth, I unhappy wish, dying, to dwell in darkness, reft as I am of thy most dear company, for thou hast destroyed rather than perished—What then do I hear? whence came the deadly chance, lady, to thine heart? Will any speak what has happened, or does my royal palace contain to no purpose the crowd of my attendants?—Alas me on thy account! unhappy that I am, what grief in my house have I seen, intolerable, indescribable! but—we are undone! my house left desolate, and my children orphans.

CHOR. Thou hast left us, thou hast left us, O dear among women, and most excellent of those as many as both the light of the sun, and the star-visaged moon of night behold. O unhappy man! how great ill doth the house contain! with tears gushing over, my eyelids are wet at thy calamity. But the woe that will ensue on this I have long since been dreading.

THES. Alas! alas! What I pray is this letter suspended from her dear hand? does it mean to betoken some new calamity?—What, has the unhappy woman written injunctions to me, making some request about[30] my bridal bed and my children? Be of good courage, hapless one; for no woman exists, who shall enter the bed and the house of Theseus. But lo! the impressions of the golden seal[31] of her no more here court my attention.[32] Come, let me unfold the envelopments of the seal, and see what this letter should say to me.

CHOR. Alas! alas! this new evil in succession again doth the God bring on. To me indeed the condition of life will be impossible to bear,[33] from what has happened; for I consider, alas! as ruined and no more the house of my kings. O God, if it be in any way possible, do not overthrow the house; but hear me as I pray, for from some quarter, as though a prophet, I behold an evil omen.

THES. Ah me! what other evil is this in addition to evil, not to be borne, nor spoken! alas wretched me!

CHOR. What is the matter? Tell me if it may be told me.

THES. It cries out—the letter cries out things most dreadful: which way can I fly the weight of my ills; for I perish utterly destroyed. What, what a complaint have I seen speaking in her writing!

CHOR. Alas! thou utterest words foreboding woes.

THES. No longer will I keep within the door of my lips this dreadful, dreadful evil hardly to be uttered. O city, city, Hippolytus has dared by force to approach my bed, having despised the awful eye of Jove. But O father Neptune, by one of these three curses, which thou formerly didst promise me, by one of those destroy my son, and let him not escape beyond this day, if thou hast given me curses that shall be verified.

CHOR. O king, by the Gods recall back this prayer, for hereafter you will know that you have erred; be persuaded by me.

THES. It can not be: and moreover I will drive him from this land. And by one or other of the two fates shall he be assailed: for either Neptune shall send him dead to the mansions of Pluto, having respect unto my wish; or else banished from this country, wandering over a foreign land, he shall drag out a miserable existence.

CHOR. And lo! thy son Hippolytus is present here opportunely, but if thou let go thy evil displeasure, king Theseus, thou wilt advise the best for thine house.

HIPPOLYTUS, THESEUS, CHORUS.

HIPP. I heard thy cry, my father, and came in haste; the thing however, for which you are groaning, I know not; but would fain hear from you. Ha! what is the matter? I behold thy wife, my father, a corpse: this is a thing meet for the greatest wonder.—Her, whom I lately left, her, who beheld the light no great time since. What ails her? In what manner died she, my father, I would fain hear from you. Art silent? But there is no use of silence in misfortunes; for the heart which desires to hear all things, is found eager also in the case of ills. It is not indeed right, my father, to conceal thy misfortunes from friends, and even more than friends.

THES. O men, who vainly go astray in many things, why then do ye teach ten thousand arts, and contrive and invent every thing; but one thing ye do not know, nor yet have investigated, to teach those to be wise who have no intellect!

HIPP. A clever sophist this you speak of, who is able to compel those who have no wisdom to be rightly wise. But (for thou art arguing too refinedly on no suitable occasion) I fear, O father, lest thy tongue be talking at random through thy woes.

THES. Alas! there ought to be established for men some infallible proof of their friends, and some means of knowing their dispositions, both who is true, and who is not a friend, and men ought all to have two voices, the one true, the other as it chanced, that the untrue one might be convicted by the true, and then we should not be deceived.

HIPP. Has some one then falsely accused me in your ear, and am I suffering who am not at all guilty? I am amazed, for your words, wandering beyond the bounds of reason, do amaze me.

THES. Alas! the mind of man, to what lengths will it go? what will be the limit to its boldness and temerity? For if it shall increase with each generation of man, and the successor shall be wicked a degree beyond his predecessor, it will be necessary for the Gods to add to the earth another land, which[34] will contain the unjust and the evil ones.—But look: ye on this man, who being born of me hath defiled my bed, and is manifestly convicted by the deceased of being most base.—But, since thou hast come to this attaint, show thy face here before thy father. Dost thou forsooth associate with the Gods, as being an extraordinary person? art thou chaste and uncontaminated with evil? I will not believe thy boasts, attributing (*as I must, if I do believe*) to the Gods the folly of thinking evil. Now then vaunt, and with thy feeding on inanimate food retail your doctrines upon men, and having Orpheus[35] for your master, revel it, reverencing the emptiness of many letters; *which avail you not*; since you are caught.

But such sort of men I warn all to shun; for they hunt with fair-sounding words, while they devise base things. She is dead: dost thou think this will save thee? By this thou art most detected, O thou most vile one! For what sort of oaths, what arguments can be more strong than what she says, so that thou canst escape the accusation? Wilt thou say that she hated thee, and that the bastard race is hateful forsooth to those of noble birth? A bad housewife then of life you account her, if through hatred of thee she lost what was most dear to her. But wilt thou say that there is not this folly in men, but that there is in women? I myself have known young men who were not a whit more steady than women, when Venus disturbed the youthful mind: but their pretense of manliness protects them. Now however, why do I thus contend against thy words, when the corse, the surest witness, is here? Depart an exile from this land as soon as possible. And neither go to the divine-built Athens, nor to the confines of that land over which my sceptre rules. For if I thus suffering by thee be vanquished, never will the Isthmian Sinis bear witness of me that I killed him, but will say that I vainly boast. Nor will the Scironian rocks, that dwell by the sea, confess that I am formidable to the bad.

CHOR. I know not how I can say that any of mortals is happy; for the things that were most excellent are turned back again.

HIPP. Father, thy rage indeed, and the commotion of thy mind is terrible; this thing, however, though it have fair arguments, if any one unravel it, is not fair. But I am unadorned with phrase to speak to the multitude, but to speak to my equals and to a few, more expert: but this also has consistency in it; for those, who are of no account among the wise, are more fitted to speak before the rabble. But yet it is necessary for me, since this calamity has come, to unloose my tongue. But first will I begin to speak from that point where first you attacked, as though you would destroy, and as though I should not answer again. Dost thou behold this light and this earth? In these there is not a man more chaste than me, not even though thou deny it. For, first indeed, I know to reverence the Gods, and to have such friends as attempt not to be unjust, but those, to whom there is modesty, so that neither they give utterance to evil thoughts, nor minister in return base services to those who use their friendship: nor am I the derider of my associates, O father, but the same man to my friends when they are not present, and when I am with them. But of one thing by which thou thinkest to crush me, I am pure;[36] for to this day my body is undefiled by the couch of love; and I know not the deed except hearing of it by report, and seeing it in a picture, nor even am I forward to look at these things, having a virgin mind. And perhaps my modesty persuades you not. Behooves it thee then to show in what manner I lost it. Did this woman's person excel in beauty all women? Or did I hope to rule over thine house, having thy bridal bed as carrying dowry with it? I must in that case have been a fool, and not at all in my senses. But did I do it as though to reign were pleasant to the modest? By no means indeed is it, except monarchy have destroyed the minds of men who are pleased with her. But I would wish indeed to be first victor in the Grecian games, but second in the state ever to be happy with the most excellent friends. For thus is it possible to be well circumstanced: but the absence of the danger gives greater joy than dominion. One of my arguments has not been spoken, but the rest you are in possession of: for, if I had a witness such as myself am, and were she alive during my contention, you would know the evil ones, searching them by their works. But now I swear by Jove, the guardian of oaths,[37] and by the plain of the earth, that never touched I thy bridal bed, nor ever wished it, nor conceived the thought. Else may I perish inglorious, without a name, and may neither sea nor earth receive the flesh of me when dead, if I be a wicked man. But whether or no she have destroyed her life through fear, I know not: for it is not lawful for me to speak further. Cautious[38] she was, though she could not be chaste; but I, who could be, had the power to no good purpose.

CHOR. Thou hast said sufficient to rebut the charge, in offering the oaths by the Gods, no slight proof.

THES. Is not this man then an enchanter and a juggler, who trusts that he will overcome my mind by his goodness of disposition, after he has dishonored his father?

HIPP. I too very much wonder at this conduct of yours, my father; for if you were my son, and I your father, I should slay you, and not punish you by banishment, if you had dared to defile my wife.

THES. How fitly hast thou said this! yet thou shalt not so die, as thou hast laid down this law for thyself; for a quick grave is easiest to the miserable man; but wandering an exile from thy country's land to foreign realms, thou shalt drag out a life of bitterness; for this is the reward for the impious man.

HIPP. Ah me! what wilt thou do? wilt thou not even await time as evidence against me, but wilt thou banish me from the land?

THES. Ay, beyond the ocean, and the place of Atlas,[39] if any way I could, so much do I hate thee.

HIPP. Without having even examined oath, or proof, or the sayings of the seers, wilt thou cast me uncondemned from out the land?

THES. This letter here, that waiteth no seer's observations,[40] accuses thee faithfully; but to the birds that flit above my head I bid a long farewell.

HIPP. O Gods, wherefore then do I not ope my mouth, who am destroyed by you whom I worship?—And yet not so—for thus I should not altogether persuade those whom I ought, but should be violating to no purpose the oaths which I have sworn.

THES. Alas me! how thy sanctity kills me! Wilt not thou go as quick as possible from thy country's land?

HIPP. Whither then shall I unhappy turn me; what stranger's mansion shall I enter, banished on this charge?

THES. His, who delights to entertain defilers of women, and those who dwell with[41] evil deeds.

HIPP. Alas! alas! this goes to my heart, and almost makes me weep: if indeed I appear vile, and seem so to thee.

THES. Then oughtest thou to have groaned, and owned the guilt before, when thou daredst to wrong thy father's wife.

HIPP. O mansions, would that ye could utter me a voice, and bear witness whether I be a vile man!

THES. Dost fly to dumb witnesses? this deed, though it speak not, clearly proves thee vile.

HIPP. Alas! would that I could look upon myself standing opposite, to that degree do I weep for the evils which I suffer!

THES. Thou hast accustomed thyself much more to regard thyself, than to be a just man, and to do what is righteous to thy parents.

HIPP. O unhappy mother! O wretched natal hour! may none of my friends ever be illegitimate.

THES. Servants, will ye not drag him out? did you not hear me long ago pronounce him banished!

HIPP. Any one of them shall touch me to his cost however; but thou thyself, if it be thy desire, thrust me out from the land.

THES. I will do this, unless thou wilt obey my words, for no pity for thy banishment comes over me.

HIPP. It is fixed, as it seems; alas, wretch that I am! since I know these things indeed, but know not how to say them. O most dear to me of deities, daughter of Latona, thou that assortest with me, huntest with me, we shall then indeed be banished illustrious Athens: but farewell O city, and land of Erectheus. O plain of Trœzene, how many things hast thou to employ the happy youth! Farewell! for I address thee, beholding thee for the last time— Come youths of this land my companions, bid me farewell, and conduct me from the land, for never shall you see a man more chaste, even though I seem not to my father.

CHORUS.

Surely the providence of the Gods, when it comes into my mind, greatly takes away sorrow: but cherishing in my hope some knowledge, I am utterly deficient, when I look on the fortunes and on the deeds of men, for they are changed in different manners, and the life of man varies, ever exceeding vague. Would that in answer to my petitions fate from the Gods would give me this, prosperity with riches, and a mind unsullied by griefs. And be my character neither too high, nor on the other hand infamous. But changing my easy habits with the morrow ever may I lead a happy life; for no longer have I an unperturbed mind, but I see things contrary to my expectations: since we have seen the brightest star of Grecian Minerva sent forth to another land on account of his father's rage. O sands of the neighboring shore, and mountain wood, where with the swift-footed dogs he wont to slay the wild beasts, accompanying the chaste Dian! No more shalt thou mount the car drawn by the team of Henetian steeds, restraining with thy foot the horses in their exercise on the course round Limna.[42] And the sleepless song that used to dwell under the bridge of the chords shall cease in thy father's house. And the haunts of the daughter of Latona in the deep wood shall be without their garlands: and the contest among the damsels for thy bridal bed has died away by reason of thy exile. But I, for thy misfortunes, shall endure with tears a fortuneless fortune.[43] O unhappy mother, thou hast brought forth in vain! Alas! I am enraged with the Gods. Alas! alas! united charms of marriage, wherefore send ye the unhappy one, guilty of no crime, away from his country's land—away from these mansions?

But lo! I perceive a follower of Hippolytus with a sad countenance coming toward the house in haste.

MESSENGER, CHORUS.

MESS. Ye females, whither going can I find Theseus, king of this land? If ye know, tell me: is he within this palace?

CHOR. The [king] himself is coming out of the palace.

MESSENGER, THESEUS, CHORUS.

MESS. I bring a tale that demands concern, of thee and of thy subjects, both those who inhabit the city of the Athenians, and the realms of the Trœzenian land.

THES. What is it? Has any sudden calamity come upon the two neighboring states?

MESS. To speak the word—Hippolytus is no more. He views the light however for a short moment.

THES. *Killed?* By whom? Has any come to enmity with him, whose wife, as his father's, he has forcibly defiled?

MESS. His own chariot slew him, and the imprecations of thy mouth, which thou didst put up to thy father, the ruler of the ocean, concerning thy son.

THES. O ye Gods! and O Neptune! how truly then wert thou my father, when thou didst duly hear my imprecations! Tell me too, how did he perish? in what way did the staff of Justice strike him that disgraced me?

MESS. We indeed near the wave-beaten shore were combing out with combs the horses' hair, weeping, for there had come a messenger saying, that Hippolytus no longer trod on this land, having from thee received the sentence of wretched banishment. But he came bringing to us on the shore the same strain of tears: and an innumerable throng of his friends and companions came following with him. But at length after some time he spake, having ceased from his groans. "Wherefore am I thus disquieted? My father's words must be obeyed. My servants, yoke to my car the harnessed steeds, for this city is for me no more." Then indeed every man hasted, and sooner than one could speak we drew up the horses caparisoned before our master; and he seizes with his hands the reins from off the bow of the chariot, mounting with his foot sandaled as it was.[44] And first indeed he addressed the Gods with outstretched hands: "Jove, may I no longer exist, if I am a base man; but may my father perceive how unworthily he treats me, either when I am dead, or while I view the light." And on this having taken the whip in his hands he struck the horses both at once: and we the attendants followed our master by the chariot close to the reins, along the road that leads straightway to Argos and Epidauria, but when we came into the desert country, there is a certain shore beyond this land which slopes even down to the Saronic Sea, from thence a voice like the subterraneous thunder of Jove sent forth a dreadful groan appalling to hear, and the horses pointed their heads erect and their ears toward the sky, and on us there came a vehement fear, whence possibly the voice could come: but looking toward the sea-beaten shore we beheld a vast wave pillared in heaven, so that the view of the heights of Sciron was taken from mine eye:[45] and it concealed the Isthmus and the rock of Æsculapius. And then swelling up and splashing forth[46] much foam around in the ocean surf, it moves toward the shore, where was the chariot drawn by its four horses. But together with its breaker and its tripled surge,[47] the wave sent forth a bull, a fierce monster; with whose bellowing the whole land filled resounded fearfully: and to the lookers-on a sight appeared more dreadful than the eyes could bear. And straightway a dreadful fear comes over the steeds. But their master, being much conversant with the ways of horses, seized the reins in his hands, and pulls them as a sailor pulls his oar, having fixed his body in an opposite direction to the reins.[48] But they, champing with their jaws the forged bits, bare him on forcibly, heeding neither the hand that steered them, nor the traces, nor the compact chariot: and, if indeed holding the reins he directed their course toward the softer ground, the bull appeared in front, so as to turn them away maddening with fright the four horses that drew the chariot. But if they were borne to the rocks maddened in mettle, silently approaching the chariot he followed so far, until he overthrew it and drove it backward, dashing the felly of the wheel against the rock. And all was in confusion, and the naves of the wheels flew up, and the linch-pins of the axles. But the unhappy man himself entangled in the reins is dragged along, bound in a difficult bond, his head dashed against the rocks, and torn his flesh, and crying out in a voice dreadful to hear, "Stop, O ye that have been trained up in my stalls, do not destroy me. Oh unhappy imprecation of my father! Who will come near and save a most excellent man?" But many of us wishing so to do failed through want of swiftness: and he indeed freed, in what manner I know not, from the entanglements of the reins, falls, having the breath of life in him, but for a very short time. And the horses vanished, and the woeful monster of the bull I know not where in the mountain country. I am indeed the slave of thy house, O king, but thus much never shall I at least be able to be persuaded of thy son, that he is evil, not even if the whole race of women were hung, and though one should fill with writing all the fir of Ida,[49] since I am confident that he is virtuous.

CHOR. Alas! alas! The calamity of new evils is consummated, nor is there refuge from fate and from what must be.

THES. Through hate of the man, who has thus suffered, I was pleased with this account; but now, having respect unto the Gods, and to him, because he is of me, I am neither pleased, nor yet troubled at these ills.

MESS. How then? Must we bring him hither, or what must we do to the unhappy man to gratify thy wishes! Think; but if thou take my advice, thou wilt not be harsh toward thy son in his misfortunes.

THES. Bear him hither, that seeing him before my eyes that denied he had defiled my bed, I may confute him with words, and with what has happened from the Gods.

CHOR. Thou, Venus, bendest the stubborn mind of the Gods, and of mortals, and with thee he of varied plume, that darts about on swiftest wing; and flies over the earth and over the loud-resounding briny ocean; and Love charms to subjection, on whose maddened heart the winged urchin come gleaming with gold, the race of the mountain whelps, and of those that inhabit the sea, and as many things as the earth nourisheth, which the sun doth behold scorched [with its rays,] and men: but over all these things thou, Venus, alone holdest sovereign rule.

DIANA, THESEUS, CHORUS.

DI. Thee, the noble son of Ægeus, I command to listen; but it is I, Diana, daughter of Latona, who am addressing thee: Theseus, wherefore dost thou, wretched man, take delight in these things, seeing that thou hast slain in no just way thy son, being persuaded by the lying words of thy wife in things not seen? But the guilt that has seized on thee is manifest. How canst thou, shamed as thou art, refrain from hiding thy body beneath the dark recesses of the earth? or from withdrawing thy foot from this suffering, by changing thy nature, and becoming a winged creature above? Since among good men at least thou hast not a part in life to possess. Hear, O Theseus, the state of thy ills. Even though I gain no advantage from it, yet will I torment thee; but for this purpose came I to show thee the upright mind of thy son, that he may die with a good reputation, and thy wife's passion, or, in some sort, nobleness; for, gnawed by the stings of that deity most hateful to us, as many as delight in virginity, she became enamored of thy son. But while she endeavored by right feeling to conquer Venus, she was destroyed not willingly by the means employed by the nurse, who having first bound him by oaths, told thy son her malady. But he, as was right, obeyed not her words; nor, again, though evil-entreated by thee, did he violate the sanctity of his oaths, being a pious man. But she, fearing lest her conduct should be scrutinized, wrote a false letter, and by deceit destroyed thy son, but nevertheless persuaded thee.

THES. Ah me!

DI. My tale torments thee, Theseus, but be still, that having heard what follows thou mayest groan the more—Knowest thou then that thou receivedst from thy father three wishes with a certainty of their being granted? Whereof one thou hast expended, O most evil one, on thy son, when thou mightest have done it on some of thine enemies. Thy father then that dwelleth in the ocean, gave thee as much as he was bound to give, because he promised. But thou both in his eyes and in mine appearest evil, who neither didst await nor examine proof, nor the voice of the prophets, didst not leave the consideration to length of time, but, quicker than became thee, didst vent thy curses against thy son and slay him.

THES. Mistress, let me die!

DI. Thou hast committed dreadful deeds, but nevertheless, it is still possible even for thee to obtain pardon for these things. For Venus willed that these things should be in order to satiate her rage. But among the Gods the law is thus—None wishes to thwart the purpose of him that wills anything, but we always give way. Since, be well assured, were it not that I feared Jove, never should I have come to such disgrace, as to suffer to die a man of all mortals the most dear to me. But thine error, first of all thine ignorance frees from malice; and then thy wife by her dying put an end to the proof of words, so as to persuade thy mind. Chiefly then on thee these ills are burst, but sorrow is to me too; for Gods rejoice not when the pious die; the wicked however we destroy with their children and their houses.

CHOR. And lo! the unhappy man there is coming, all mangled his young flesh and auburn head. Oh the misery of the house! such double anguish coming down from heaven has been wrought in the palaces!

HIPPOLYTUS, DIANA, THESEUS, CHORUS.

HIPP. O! O! O! Unhappy I was thus foully mangled by the unjust prayers of an unjust father—I am destroyed miserably. Ah me! ah me! Pains rush through my head, and the spasm darts across my brain. Stop, I will rest my fainting body. Oh! oh! O those hateful horses of my chariot, things which I fed with my own hand, ye have destroyed me utterly and slain me. Oh! oh! by the Gods, gently, my servants, touch with your hands my torn flesh. Who stands by my side on the right? Lift me up properly, and take hold all equally on me, the unblessed of heaven, and cursed by my father's error—Jove, Jove, beholdest thou these things? Lo! I, the chaste, and the reverencer of the Gods, I who in modesty exceed all, have lost my life, and go to a manifest hell beneath the earth; but in vain have I labored in the task of piety toward men. O! O! O! O! and now the pain, the pain comes upon me, loose unhappy me, and let death come to be my physician. Destroy me, destroy the unhappy one—I long for a two-edged blade, wherewith to cut me in pieces, and to put my life to an eternal rest. Oh unhappy curse of my father! the evil too of my blood-polluted kinsmen, my old forefathers, bursts forth[50] upon me; nor is it at a distance; and it hath come on me, wherefore, I pray, who am nothing guilty of these ills? Alas me! me! what can I say? how can I free my life from this cruel calamity? Would that the black and nightly fate of Pluto would put me wretched to eternal sleep!

DI. Oh unhappy mortal, with what a calamity art thou enthralled! but the nobleness of thy mind hath destroyed thee.

HIPP. Let be. O divine breathing of perfume, for, even though being in ills, I perceived thee, and felt my body lightened of its pain.[51] The Goddess Dian is in this place.

DI. Oh unhappy one! she is, to thee the most dear of deities.

HIPP. Mistress, thou seest wretched me, in what state I am.

DI. I see; but it is not lawful for me to shed a tear down mine eyes.

HIPP. Thy hunter, and thy servant is no more.

DI. No in sooth; but beloved by me thou perishest.

HIPP. And he that managed they steeds, and guarded thy statutes.

DI. *Ay*, for the crafty Venus hath so wrought.

HIPP. Ah me! I perceive indeed the power that hath destroyed me.

DI. She thought her honor aggrieved, and hated thee for being chaste.

HIPP. One Venus hath destroyed us three.

DI. Thy father, and thee, and his wife the third.

HIPP. I mourn therefore also my father's misery.

DI. He was deceived by the devices of the Goddess.

HIPP. Oh! unhappy thou, because of this calamity, my father!

THES. I perish, my son, nor have I delight in life.

HIPP. I lament thee rather than myself on account of thy error.

THES. My son, would that I could die in thy stead!

HIPP. Oh! the bitter gifts of thy father Neptune!

THES. Would that the prayer had never come into my mouth.

HIPP. Wherefore this wish? thou wouldst have slain me, so enraged wert thou then.

THES. For I was deceived in my notions by the Gods.

HIPP. Alas! would that the race of mortals could curse the Gods!

DI. Let be; for not even when thou art under the darkness of the earth shall the rage arising from the bent of the Goddess Venus descend upon thy body unrevenged: by reason of thy piety and thy excellent mind. For with these inevitable weapons from mine own hand will I revenge me on another,[52] whoever to her be the dearest of mortals. But to thee, O unhappy one, in recompense for these evils, will I give the greatest honors in the land of Trœzene; for the unwedded virgins before their nuptials shall shear their locks to thee for many an age, owning the greatest sorrow tears can give; but ever among the virgins shall there be a remembrance of thee that shall awake the song, nor dying away without a name shall Phædra's love toward thee pass unrecorded:—But thou, O son of the aged Ægeus, take thy son in thine arms and clasp him to thee; for unwillingly thou didst destroy him, but that men should err, when the Gods dispose events, is but to be expected!—and thee, Hippolytus, I exhort not to remain at enmity with thy father; for thou perceivest the fate, whereby thou wert destroyed. And farewell! for it is not lawful for me to behold the dead, nor to pollute mine eye with the gasps of the dying; but I see that thou art now near this calamity.

HIPP. Go thou too, and farewell, blessed virgin! But thou easily quittest a long companionship. But I give up all enmity against my father at thy request, for before also I was wont to obey thy words. Ah! ah! darkness now covers me over mine eyes. Take hold on me, my father, and lift up my body.

THES. Ah me! my son, what dost thou, do to me unhappy?

HIPP. I perish, and do indeed see the gates of hell.

THES. What? leaving my mind uncleansed from thy blood?

HIPP. No in sooth, since I free thee from this murder.

THES. What sayest thou? dost thou remit me free from the guilt of blood?

HIPP. I call to witness Dian that slays with the bow.

THES. O most dear, how noble thou appearest to thy father!

HIPP. O farewell thou too, take my best farewell, my father!

THES. Oh me! for thy pious and brave soul!

HIPP. Pray to have legitimate sons like me.

THES. Do not, I prithee, leave me, my son, but be strong.

HIPP. My time of strength is past; for I perish, my father: but cover my face as quickly as possible with robes.

THES. O famous realms of Athens and of Pallas, of what a man will ye have been bereaved! Oh unhappy I! What abundant reason, Venus, shall I have to remember thy ills!

CHOR. This common grief to all the citizens hath come unexpectedly. There will be a fast falling of many tears; for the mournful stories of great men rather obtain.

NOTES ON HIPPOLYTUS

[1] The construction in the original furnishes a remarkable example of the "nominativus pendens."

[2] Or, *that posterity might know it.* TR. Dindorf would omit these words. B.

[3] Dindorf would omit these lines. I think the difficulty in the structure may be removed by reading ὅστις instead of ὅσοις. The enallage, ὅστις ... τούτοις, is by no means unusual. B.

[4] Cf. Soph. Œd. Col. 121, sqq. B.

[5] Which at present you do not appear to have.

[6] Monk would join ωκεανου with πετρα, as in the translation, but other commentators prefer, which is certainly more simple, to join it with ʽυδωρ. Then the difficulty occurs of sea-water being unfit for washing vests. This difficulty Beck obviates, by saying that ʽυδωρ ωκεανου may be applied to fresh water, Ocean being the parent of all streams, the word ωκεανου being here, in a manner, redundant. TR. Matthiæ is very wrath with the "all on a washing day" manner in which the Chorus learned Phædra's indisposition. The "Bothie of Toper na Fuosich" will furnish some similar simplicities, such as the meeting a lassie "digging potatoes." But we might as well object to the whole story of Nausicaa. It must be recollected that the duties of the laundry were considered more aristocratic by the ancients, than in modern times. B.

[7] Cf. Æsch. Pr. 23. Χροιας αμειψεις ανθος. B.

[8] Literally *a speech mounted on madness*. A similar expression occurs, Odyssey A. 297. Νηπιαας οχεειν.

[9] Plutarch in explanation of this line says, "καθαπερ ποδα νεως, επιδιδοντα και προσαγοντα ταις χρειαις την φιλιαν."

[10] I have followed the elegant interpretation of L. Dindorf, who observes that ου δηθ ʽεκουσα refers to Phædra's assertion, ου γαρ ες σʼ αμαρτανω, and that the meaning is, "non quidem consilio in me peccas, sed si tu peribis, ego quoque occidero." He compares Alcest. 389. B.

[11] See Matthiæ's note. I prefer, however, ολεις, with Musgrave. B.

[12] Matthiæ considers this as briefly expressed for τι τουτο, το εραν, ʽα λεγουσι ποιειν ανθρωπους. Still I can not help thinking ανθρωπων a better reading. B.

[13] Phædra struggles between shame and uncertainty, before she can pronounce the name. It should be read as if ʽοστις ποθʼ— ʽουτος—ʽο της Αμαζονος. B.

[14] Matthiæ takes παναμεριος as = εν τηιδε τηι ʽημεραι, i.e. up to this very time. I think the passage is corrupt. B.

[15] This passage, like many others in the play, is admirably burlesqued by Aristoph., Ran. 962. B.

[16] *Or, this is a second favor thou mayst grant me.*

[17] On the numberless references to this impious sophism, see the learned notes of Valckenaer and Monk. Compare more particularly Aristoph. Ran. 102, 1471. Thesmoph. 275. Arist. Rhet. iii. 15. B.

[18] Literally, "spurious coined race." B.

[19] The MSS. reading, φυτον, is preferable. B.

[20] The syntax appears to be δυσεκπερατον βιου, *such as my like can scarcely get over.* Musgrave has followed the other explanation of the Scholiast, which makes βιου depend on παθος. TR. I have followed the Scholiast and Dindorf. B.

[21] προτρεπουσα, αντι του ζητουσα και εξερευνωσα. Schol. Dindorf acknowledges the strangeness of the usage, and seems to prefer προσκοπουσ', with Monk. B.

[22] Cf. Soph. Ant. 751. 'ηδ' ουν θανειται, και θανουσ' ολει τινα. B.

[23] For the meaning and derivation of αλιβατοις, see Monk's note.

[24] 'αλικτυπον seems to be an awkward epithet of κυμα, unless it mean "*dashed [against the shore] by the waves.*" Perhaps αλικτυπον would be less forced. B.

[25] Ὑπεραντλος ουσα συμφοραι, a metaphor taken from a ship which can no longer keep out water.

[26] See the note on my Translation of Æsch. Agam., p. 121, note 1. ed. Bonn. B.

[27] Read ωμοι εγω πονων: επαθον ω ταλας with cod. Hav. See Dindorf. B.

[28] Cf. Matth. apud Dindorf. B.

[29] In the same manner the chorus in the Alcestis comforts Admetus. v.

Ου γαρ τι πρωτος, ουδε λοισθιος βροτων

γυναικος εσθλης ημπλακες.

[30] Ὑπερ is here to be understood. VALK.

[31] Σφενδονη, literally, the setting of the seal, which embraces the gem as a sling its stone.

[32] See a similar expression in Æsch. Eum. 254,

Οσμη βροτειων 'αιματων με προσγελαι.

[33] The construction is, ειη αν εμοι αβιωτος τυχα βιου, 'οστε τυχειν αυτης. MONK.

[34] η, *which land, together with the present earth.*

[35] On the Orphic abstinence from animal food, see Matth. apud Dind. Compare Porphyr. de Abst. ii. 3 sqq. B.

[36] Αθικτος appears here to have an active sense. So in Soph. Œd. c. 1521. αθικτος 'ηγητηρος. It is used in its more frequent sense (a passive) in v. 648, of this play. TR. Compare my note on Æsch. Prom. 110, p. 6, n. I. B.

[37] Cf. Med. 169. Ζηνα θ' 'ος ορκων θνατοις ταμιας νενομισται. B.

[38] There are various interpretations of this passage. The Scholiast puts this sense upon it, *Phædra was chaste (in your eyes), who had not the power of being chaste, I had the power, and is it likely that I did not exert it to good purpose?* Others translate the former part of the passage with the Scholiast, but make ου καλως εχρωμεθα refer to the present time, *had it to no good purpose,* i.e. am not now able to persuade you of my innocence. Some translate εσωφροησεν, *acted like a chaste woman.* TR. There is evidently a double meaning, which is almost lost by translation. Theseus is not intended to understand this. B.

[39] Cf. vs. 3. B.

[40] Κληροι were the notes the augurs took of their observations, and wrote down on tablets. See Phœn. 852.

[41] ξυνοικουρους appears to be metaphorically used, but I think the sense would be greatly improved by reading κακους, and taking ξυνοικουρους to mean "to dwell with him," referring it to 'οστις. B.

[42] But we must read γυμναδος 'ιππου with Reiske, Brunot, and Dindorf. See his notes. ποδι must be joined with γυμ. 'ιππου. B.

[43] ποτμον αποτμον. B.

[44] Αυταισιν αρβυλαισιν. Some have supposed αρβυλη to mean a part of the chariot, but this seems at variance with the best authorities (see Monk's note); perhaps the expression may mean what is implied in the translation; that Hippolytus did not wait to change any part of his dress. TR. But I agree with Dindorf, that αυταισιν is then utterly absurd and useless. The Scholiast seems

correct in saying, ταις τον 'αρματος περι την αντυγα, ενθα την οτασιν εχει 'ο 'ηνιοχος. B.

[45] "Adeo ut deficerent a visu, ne cernere possem, Scironis alta." B.

[46] Καχλαζω, a word formed from the noise of the sea—'ο γαρ ηχος του κυματος εν τοις κοιλωμασι των πετρων γινομενος, δοκει μιμεισθαι το καχλα, καχλα.—*Etym. Mag.*

[47] Τριχυμιαι. See Blomfield's *Glossary to the Prometheus*, 1051.

[48] Musgrave supposes that Hippolytus wound the reins round his body; but on this supposition, not to mention other objections, the comparison with the sailor does not hold so well. It is more natural to suppose that he leaned back in order to get a purchase: in this attitude he is made to describe himself in Ov. *Met.* xv. 519, *Et retro lentas tendo resupinus habenas.* If there be any doubt of εις τουμισθεν 'ιμασιν being Greek, this objection is obviated by putting a stop after 'ιμασιν, and making it depend on 'ελκει.

[49] i.e. in Crete. See Dindorf's note. B.

[50] Εξοριζεται, *valde prorumpit, liberat terminos, quibus hactenus septum fuit.* REISKE.

[51] Heath translates ανεκουφισθην *adtollebam corpus*, honoris scilicet gratia. Compare Iliad, O. 241. αταρ ασθμα και 'ιδρως παυετ', επει μιν εγειρε Διος νοος αιγιοχοιο, which Pope translates,

"Jove thinking of his pains, they pass'd away:"

in which the idea is much more sublime; for there the thought of a Deity effects what the presence of one does here.

[52] Probably meaning Adonis. See Monk. B.

ALCESTIS.

PERSONS REPRESENTED.

APOLLO.

DEATH.

CHORUS OF PHERŒANS.

ATTENDANTS.

ALCESTIS.

ADMETUS.

EUMELUS.

HERCULES.

PHERES.

THE ARGUMENT.

Apollo desired of the Fates that Admetus, who was about to die, might give a substitute to die for him, that so he might live for a term equal to his former life; and Alcestis, his wife, gave herself up, while neither of his parents were willing to die instead of their son. But not long after the time when this calamity happened, Hercules having arrived, and having learned from a servant what had befallen Alcestis, went to her tomb, and having made Death retire, covers the lady with a robe; and requested Admetus to receive her and keep her for him; and said he had borne her off as a prize in wrestling; but when he would not, he unveiled her, and discovered her whom he was lamenting.

ALCESTIS

APOLLO.

O mansions of Admetus, wherein I endured to acquiesce in the slave's table,[1] though a God; for Jove was the cause, by slaying my son Æsculapius, hurling the lightning against his breast: whereat enraged, I slay the Cyclops, forgers of Jove's fire; and me my father compelled to serve for hire with a mortal, as a punishment for these things. But having come to this land, I tended the herds of him who received me, and have preserved this house until this day: for being pious I met with a pious man,[2] the son of Pheres, whom I delivered from dying by deluding the Fates: but those Goddesses granted me that Admetus should escape the impending death, could he furnish in his place another dead for the powers below. But having tried and gone through all his friends, his father and his aged mother who bore him, he found not, save his wife, one who was willing to die for him, and view no more the light: who now within the house is borne in their hands, breathing her last; for on this day is it destined for her to die, and to depart from life. But I, lest the pollution[3] come upon me in the house, leave this palace's most dear abode. But already I behold Death near, priest of the dead, who is about to bear her down to the mansions of Pluto; but he comes at the right time, observing this day, in the which it was destined for her to die.

DEATH,[4] APOLLO.

DEA. Ah! Ah! Ah! Ah! What dost thou at the palace? why tamest here, Phœbus? Art thou again at thy deeds of injustice, taking away and putting an end to the honors of the powers beneath? Did it not suffice thee to stay the death of Admetus, when thou didst delude the Fates by fraudful artifice?[5] But now too dost thou keep guard for her, having armed thine hand with thy bow, who then promised, in order to redeem her husband, herself, the daughter of Pelias, to die for him?

AP. Fear not, I cleave to justice and honest arguments.

DEA. What business then has your bow, if you cleave to justice?

AP. It is my habit ever to bear it.

DEA. Yes, and without regard to justice to aid this house.

AP. *Ay*, for I am afflicted at the misfortunes of a man that is dear to me.

DEA. And wilt thou deprive me of this second dead?

AP. But neither took I him from thee by force.

DEA. How then is he upon earth, and not beneath the ground?

AP. Because he gave in his stead his wife, after whom thou art now come.

DEA. Yes, and will bear her off to the land beneath.

AP. Take her away, for I know not whether I can persuade thee.

DEA. What? to slay him, whom I ought? for this was I commanded.

AP. No: but to cast death upon those about to die.

DEA. Yes, I perceive thy speech, and what thou aim'st at.

AP. Is it possible then for Alcestis to arrive at old age?

DEA. It is not: consider that I too am delighted with my due honors.

AP. Thou canst not, however, take more than one life.

DEA. When the young die I earn the greater glory.

AP. And if she die old, she will be sumptuously entombed.[6]

DEA. Thou layest down the law, Phœbus, in favor of the rich.

AP. How sayest thou? what? hast thou been clever without my perceiving it?

DEA. Those who have means would purchase to die old.

AP. Doth it not then seem good to thee to grant me this favor?

DEA. No in truth; and thou knowest my ways.

AP. Yes, hostile to mortals, and detested by the Gods.

DEA. Thou canst not have all things, which thou oughtest not.

AP. Nevertheless, thou wilt stop, though thou art over-fierce; such a man will come to the house of Pheres, whom Eurystheus hath sent after the chariot and its horses,[7] *to bring them* from the wintry regions of Thrace, who in sooth, being welcomed in the mansions of Admetus, shall take away by force this woman from thee; and there will be no obligation to thee at my hands, but still thou wilt do this, and wilt be hated by me.

DEA. Much though thou talkest, thou wilt gain nothing. This woman then shall descend to the house of Pluto; and I am advancing upon her, that I may begin the rites on her with my sword; for sacred is he to the Gods beneath the earth, the hair of whose head this sword hath consecrated.[8]

CHORUS.

SEMICH. Wherefore in heaven's name is this stillness before the palace? why is the house of Admetus hushed in silence?

SEMICH. But there is not even one of our friends near, who can tell us whether we have to deplore the departed queen, or whether Alcestis, daughter of Pelias, yet living views this light, who has appeared to me and to all to have been the best wife toward her husband.

CHOR. Hears any one either a wailing, or the beating of hands within the house, or a lamentation, as though the thing had taken place?[9] There is not however any one of the servants standing before the gates. Oh would that thou wouldst appear, O Apollo, amidst the waves of this calamity!

SEMICH. They would not however be silent, were she dead.

SEMICH. For the corse is certainly not gone from the house.

SEMICH. Whence this conjecture? I do not presume this. What is it gives you confidence?

SEMICH. How could Admetus have made a private funeral of his so excellent wife?

CHOR. But before the gates I see not the bath of water from the fountain,[10] as is the custom at the gates of the dead: and in the vestibule is no shorn hair, which is wont to fall in grief for the dead; the youthful[11] hand of women for the youthful *wife* sound not.

SEMICH. And yet this is the appointed day,—

SEMICH. What is this thou sayest?

SEMICH. In the which she must go beneath the earth.

SEMICH. Thou hast touched my soul, hast touched my heart.

SEMICH. When the good are afflicted, he must mourn, who from the beginning has been accounted good.

CHOR. But there is not whither in the earth any one having sent naval equipment, or to Lycia, or to the thirsty site of Hammon's temple, can redeem the unhappy woman's life, for abrupt fate approaches, and I know not to whom of those that sacrifice at the hearths of the Gods I can go. But only if the son of Phœbus were viewing with his eyes this light, could she come, having left the darksome habitations and the gates of Pluto: for he raised up the dead, before that the stroke of the lightning's fire hurled by Jove destroyed him. But now what hope of life can I any longer entertain? For all things have already been done by the king, and at the altars of all the Gods abound the victims dropping with blood, and no cure is there of these evils.

CHORUS, FEMALE ATTENDANT.

CHOR. But here comes one of the female attendants from the house, in tears; what shall I hear has happened? To mourn indeed, if any thing happens to our lords, is pardonable: but whether the lady be still alive, or whether she be dead, we would wish to know.

ATT. You may call her both alive and dead.

CHOR. And how can the same woman be both alive and dead?

ATT. Already she is on the verge of death,[12] and breathing her life away.

CHOR. Oh wretched man, being what thyself of what a wife art thou bereft!

ATT. My master knows not this yet, until he suffer.

CHOR. Is there no longer hope that she may save her life?

ATT. No, for the destined day makes its attack upon her.

CHOR. Are not then suitable preparations made for these events?

ATT. Yes, the adornments[13] are ready, wherewith her husband will bury her.

CHOR. Let her know then that she will die glorious, and by far the best of women under the sun.

ATT. And how not the best? who will contest it? What must the woman be, who has surpassed her? and how can any give greater proof of esteeming her husband, than by being willing to die for him? And these things indeed the whole city knoweth. But what she did in the house you will marvel when you hear. For, when she perceived that the destined day was come, she washed her fair skin with water from the river; and having taken from her closets of cedar vesture and ornaments, she attired herself becomingly; and standing before the altar she prayed: "O mistress, since I go beneath the earth, adoring thee for the last time, I will beseech thee to protect my orphan children, and to the one join a loving wife, and to the other a noble husband: nor, as their mother perishes, let my children untimely die, but happy in their paternal country let them complete a joyous life."—But all the altars, which are in the house of Admetus, she went to, and crowned, and prayed, tearing the leaves from off the myrtle boughs, tearless, without a groan, nor did the approaching evil change the natural beauty of her skin. And then rushing to her chamber, and her bed, there indeed she wept and spoke thus: "O bridal bed, whereon I loosed my virgin zone with this man, for whom I die, farewell! for I hate thee not; but me alone hast thou lost; for dreading to betray thee, and my husband, I die; but thee some other woman will possess, more chaste there can not, but perchance more fortunate."[14]—And falling on it she kissed it; but all the bed was bathed with the flood that issued from her eyes. But when she had satiety of much weeping, she goes hastily forward,[15] rushing from the bed. And ofttimes having left her chamber, she oft returned, and threw herself upon the bed again. And her children, hanging to the garments of their mother, wept; but she, taking them in her arms, embraced them, first one and then the other, as about to die. But all the domestics wept throughout the house, bewailing their mistress, but she stretched out her right hand to each, and there was none so mean, whom she addressed not, and was answered in return. Such are the woes in the house of Admetus. And had he died indeed, he would have perished; but now that he has escaped death, he has grief to that degree which he will never forget.

CHOR. Surely Admetus groans at these evils, if he must be deprived of so excellent a wife.

ATT. Yes, he weeps, holding his dear wife in his hands, and prays her not to leave him, asking impossibilities; for she wastes away, and is consumed by sickness, but fainting a wretched burden in his arms, yet still though but feebly breathing, she fain would glance toward the rays of the sun; as though never again, but now for the last time she is to view the sun's beam and his orb. But I will go and announce your presence, for it is by no means all that are well-wishers to their lords, so as to come kindly to them in their misfortunes; but you of old are friendly to my master.

SEMICH. O Jove, what means of escape can there in any way be, and what method to rid us of the fortune which attends my master?

SEMICH. Will any appear? or must I cut my locks, and clothe me even now in black array of garments?

SEMICH. 'Tis plain, my friends, too plain; but still let us pray to the Gods, for the power of the Gods is mightiest.

SEMICH. O Apollo, king of healing, find out some remedy for the evils of Admetus, procure it, O! procure it. For before this also thou didst find *remedy*, and now become our deliverer from death, and stop the murderous Pluto.

SEMICH. Alas! alas! woe! woe! O son of Pheres, how didst thou fare when thou wert deprived of thy wife?

SEMICH. Alas! alas! these things would even justify self-slaughter, and there is more, than whereat one might thrust one's neck in the suspending noose.[16]

SEMICH. For not a dear, but a most dear wife, wilt thou see dead this day.

SEMICH. Behold, behold; lo! she doth come from the house, and her husband with her. Cry out, O groan, O land of Pheres, for the most excellent woman, wasting with sickness, *departing* beneath the earth to the infernal

Pluto. Never will I aver that marriage brings more joy than grief, forming my conjectures both from former things, and beholding this fortune of the king; who, when he has lost this most excellent wife, will thenceforward pass a life not worthy to be called life.[17]

ALCESTIS, ADMETUS, EUMELUS, CHORUS.

ALC. Thou Sun, and thou light of day, and ye heavenly eddies of the fleeting clouds—

ADM. He beholds[18] thee and me, two unhappy creatures, having done nothing to the Gods, for which thou shouldst die.

ALC. O earth, and ye roofs of the palace, and thou bridal bed of my native Iolcos.

ADM. Lift up thyself, unhappy one, desert me not; but entreat the powerful Gods to pity.

ALC. I see—I see the two-oared boat—and the ferryman of the dead, holding his hand on the pole—Charon even now calls me—"Why dost thou delay? haste, thou stoppest us here"—with such words vehement he hastens me.

ADM. Ah me! a bitter voyage this thou speakest of! Oh! unhappy one, how do we suffer!

ALC. He pulls me, some one pulls me—do you not see?—to the hall of the dead, the winged Pluto, staring from beneath his black eyebrows—What wilt thou do?—let me go—what a journey am I most wretched going!

ADM. Mournful to thy friends, and of these especially to me and to thy children, who have this grief in common.

ALC. Leave off[19] supporting me, leave off now, lay me down, I have no strength in my feet. Death is near, and darkling night creeps upon mine eyes—my children, my children, no more your mother is—no more.— Farewell, my children, long may you view this light!

ADM. Ah me! I hear this sad word, and more than any death to me. Do not by the Gods have the heart to leave me: do not by those children, whom thou wilt make orphans: but rise, be of good courage: for, thee dead, I should no longer be: for on thee we depend both to live, and not to live: for thy love we adore.

ALC. Admetus, thou seest both thy affairs and mine, in what state they are, I wish to tell thee, ere I die, what I would have done. I, honoring thee, and causing thee at the price of my life to view this light, die, it being in my power not to die, for thee: but though I might have married a husband from among the Thessalians whom I would, and have lived in a palace blessed with regal sway, was not willing to live, bereft of thee, with my children orphans; nor did I spare myself, though possessing the gifts of bloomy youth, wherein I delighted. And yet thy father and thy mother forsook thee, though they had well arrived at a point of life, in which they might have died, and nobly delivered their son, and died with glory: for thou wert their only one, and there was no hope, when thou wert dead, that they could have other children.[20] And I should have lived, and thou, the rest of our time. And thou wouldst not be groaning deprived of thy wife, and wouldst not have to bring up thy children orphans. But these things indeed, some one of the Gods hath brought to pass, that they should be thus. Be it so—but do thou remember to give me a return for this; for never shall I ask thee for an equal one, (for nothing is more precious than life,) but just, as thou wilt say: for thou lovest not these children less than I do, if thou art right-minded; them bring up lords over my house, and bring not in second marriage a step-mother over these children, who, being a worse woman than me, through envy will stretch out her hand against thine and my children. Do not this then, I beseech thee; for a step-mother that is in second marriage is enemy to the children of the former marriage, no milder than a viper. And my boy indeed has his father, a great tower of defense; but thou, O my child, how wilt thou be, brought up during thy virgin years? Having what consort of thy father's? *I fear*, lest casting some evil obloquy on thee, she destroys thy marriage in the bloom of youth.[21] For neither will thy mother ever preside over thy nuptials, nor strengthen thee being present, my daughter, at thy travails, where nothing is more kind than a mother. For I needs must die, and this evil comes upon me not to-morrow, nor on the third day of the month, but immediately shall I be numbered among those that are no more. Farewell, and may you be happy; and thou indeed, my husband, mayst boast, that thou hadst a most excellent wife, and you, my children, that you were born of a most excellent mother.

CHOR. Be of good cheer; for I fear not to answer for him: he will do this, if he be not bereft of his senses.

ADM. These things shall be so, they shall be, fear not: since I, when alive also, possessed thee *alone*, and when thou art dead, thou shalt be my only wife, and no Thessalian bride shall address me in the place of thee: there is not woman who shall, either of so noble a sire, nor otherwise most exquisite in beauty. But my children are enough; of these I pray the Gods that I may have the enjoyment; for thee we do not enjoy. But I shall not have this grief for thee for a year, but as long as my life endures, O lady, abhorring her indeed that brought me forth, and hating my father; for they were in word, not in deed, my friends. But thou, giving what was dearest to thee for my life, hast rescued me. Have I not then reason to groan deprived of such a wife?

But I will put an end to the feasts, and the meetings of those that drink together, and garland and song, which wont to dwell in my house. For neither can I any more touch the lyre, nor lift up my heart to sing to the Libyan flute; for thou hast taken away my joy of life. But by the cunning hand of artists imaged thy figure shall be lain on my bridal bed, on which I will fall, and clasping my hands around, calling on thy name, shall fancy that I hold my dear wife in mine arms, though holding her not:[22] a cold delight, I ween; but still I may draw off the weight that sits upon my soul: and in my dreams visiting me, thou mayst delight me, for a friend is sweet even to behold at night, for whatever time he may come. But if the tongue of Orpheus and his strain were mine, so that invoking with hymns the daughter of Ceres or her husband, I could receive thee from the shades below, I would descend, and neither the dog of Pluto, nor Charon at his oar, the ferryman of departed spirits, should stay me before I brought thy life to the light. But there expect me when I die and prepare a mansion for me, as about to dwell with me. For I will enjoin these[23] to place me in the same cedar with thee, and to lay my side near thy side: for not even when dead may I be separated from thee, the only faithful one to me!

CHOR. And I indeed with thee, as a friend with a friend, will bear this painful grief for her, for she is worthy.

ALC. My children, ye indeed hear your father saying that he will never marry another wife to be over you, nor dishonor me.

ADM. And now too, I say this, and will perform it

ALC. For this receive these children from my hand.

ADM. Yes, I receive a dear gift from a dear hand.

ALC. Be thou then a mother to these children in my stead.

ADM. There is much need that I should, when they are deprived of thee.

ALC. O my children, at a time when I ought to live I depart beneath.

ADM. Ah me; what shall I do of thee bereaved!

ALC. Time will soften thy grief: he that is dead is nothing.

ADM. Take me with thee, by the Gods take me beneath.

ALC. Enough are we *to go*, who die for thee.

ADM. O fate, of what a wife thou deprivest me!

ALC. And lo! my darkening eye is weighed down.

ADM. I am undone then, if thou wilt leave me, my wife.

ALC. As being no more, you may speak of me as nothing.

ADM. Lift up thy face; do not leave thy children.

ALC. Not willingly in sooth, but—farewell, my children.

ADM. Look on them, O! look.

ALC. I am no more.

ADM. What dost thou? dost thou leave us?

ALC. Farewell!

ADM. I am an undone wretch!

CHOR. She is gone, Admetus' wife is no more.

EUM. Alas me, for my state! my mother is gone indeed below; she is no longer, my father, under the sun; but unhappy leaving me has made my life an orphan's. For look, look at her eyelid, and her nerveless arms. Hear, hear, O mother. I beseech thee; I, I now call thee, mother, thy young one falling on thy mouth—

ADM. Who hears not, neither sees: so that I and you are struck with a heavy calamity.

EUM. Young and deserted, my father, am I left by my dear mother: O! I that have suffered indeed dreadful deeds!—and thou hast suffered with me, my sister. O father, in vain, in vain didst thou marry, nor with her didst thou arrive at the end of old age, for she perished before, but thou being gone, mother, the house is undone.

CHOR. Admetus, you must bear this calamity; for in no wise the first, nor the last of mortals hast thou lost thy dear wife: but learn, that to die is a debt we must all of us discharge.

ADM. I know it, and this evil hath not come suddenly on me; but knowing it long ago I was afflicted. But be present, for I will have the corse borne forth, and while ye stay, chant a hymn to the God below that accepteth not libations. And all the Thessalians, over whom I reign, I enjoin to share in the grief for this lady, by shearing *their locks* with steel, and by arraying themselves in sable garb. And harness[24] your teams of horses to your chariots, and cut from your single steeds the manes that fall upon their necks. And let there be no noise of pipes, nor of the lyre throughout the city for twelve completed moons. For none other corse more dear shall I inter, nor one more kind toward me. But she deserves to receive honor from me, seeing that she alone hath died for me.

CHORUS.

O daughter of Pelias, farewell where thou dwellest in sunless dwelling within the mansions of Pluto. And let Pluto know, the God with ebon locks, and the old man, the ferryman of the dead, who sits intent upon his oar and his rudder, that he is conducting by far the most excellent of women in his two-oared boat over the lake of Acheron. Oft shall the servants of the Muses sing of thee, celebrating thee both on the seven-stringed lute on the mountains, and in hymns unaccompanied by the lyre: in Sparta, when returns the annual circle in the season of the Carnean month,[25] when the moon is up the whole night long; and in splendid[26] and happy Athens. Such a song hast thou left by thy death to the minstrels of melodies. Would that it rested with me, and that I could waft thee to the light from the mansions of Pluto, and from Cocytus' streams, by the oar of that infernal river. For thou, O unexampled, O dear among women, thou didst dare to receive thy husband from the realms below in exchange for thine own life. Light may the earth from above fall upon thee, lady! and if thy husband chooses any other alliance, surely he will be much detested by me and by thy children. When his mother was not willing for him to hide her body in the ground, nor his aged father, but these two wretches, having hoary locks, dared not to rescue him they brought forth, yet thou in the vigor of youth didst depart, having died for thy husband. May it be mine to meet with another[27] such a dear wife; for rare in life is such a portion, for surely she would live with me forever without once causing pain.

HERCULES, CHORUS.

HER. Strangers, inhabitants of the land of Pheres, can I find Admetus within the palace?

CHOR. The son of Pheres is within the palace, O Hercules. But tell me, what purpose sends thee to the land of the Thessalians, so that thou comest to this city of Pheres?

HER. I am performing a certain labor for the Tirynthian Eurystheus.

CHOR. And whither goest thou? on what wandering expedition art bound?

HER. After the four chariot-steeds of Diomed the Thracian.

CHOR. How wilt thou be able? Art thou ignorant of this host?

HER. I am ignorant; I have not yet been to the land of the Bistonians.

CHOR. Thou canst not be lord of these steeds without battle.

HER. But neither is it possible for me to renounce the labors *set me.*

CHOR. Thou wilt come then having slain, or being slain wilt remain there.

HER. Not the first contest this that I shall run.

CHOR. But what advance will you have made, when you have overcome their master?

HER. I will drive away the horses to king Eurystheus.

CHOR. 'Tis no easy matter to put the bit in their jaws.

HER. 'Tis, except they breathe fire from their nostrils.

CHOR. But they tear men piecemeal with their devouring jaws.

HER. The provender of mountain beasts, not horses, you are speaking of.

CHOR. Their stalls thou mayst behold with blood bestained.

HER. Son of what sire does their owner boast to be?

CHOR. Of Mars, prince[28] of the Thracian target, rich with gold.

HER. And this labor, thou talkest of, is one my fate compels me to (for it is ever hard and tends to steeps); if I must join in battle with the children whom Mars begat, first indeed with Lycaon, and again with Cycnus, and I come to this third combat, about to engage with the horses and their master. But none there is, who shall ever see the son of Alcmena fearing the hand of his enemies.

CHOR. And lo! hither comes the very man Admetus, lord of this land, from out of the palace.

ADMETUS, HERCULES, CHORUS.

ADM. Hail! O son of Jove, and of the blood of Perseus.

HER. Admetus, hail thou too, king of the Thessalians!

ADM. I would I could *receive this salutation;* but I know that thou art well disposed toward me.

HER. Wherefore art thou conspicuous with thy locks shorn for grief?

ADM. I am about to bury a certain corse this day.

HER. May the God avert calamity from thy children!

ADM. My children whom I begat, live in the house.

HER. Thy father however is of full age, if he is gone.

ADM. Both he lives, and she who bore me, Hercules.

HER. Surely your wife Alcestis is not dead?

ADM. There are two accounts which I may tell of her.

HER. Speakest thou of her as dead or as alive?

ADM. She both is, and is no more, and she grieves me.

HER. I know nothing more; for thou speakest things obscure.

ADM. Knowest thou not the fate which it was doomed for her to meet with?

HER. I know that she took upon herself to die for thee.

ADM. How then is she any more, if that she promised this?

HER. Ah! do not weep for thy wife before the time; wait till this happens.

ADM. He that is about to die is dead, and he that is dead is no more.

HER. The being and the not being is considered a different thing.

ADM. You judge in this way, Hercules, but I in that.

HER. Why then dost weep? Who is he of thy friends that is dead?

ADM. A woman, a woman we were lately mentioning.

HER. A stranger by blood, or any by birth allied to thee?

ADM. A stranger; but on other account dear to this house.

HER. How then died she in thine house?

ADM. Her father dead, she lived an orphan here.

HER. Alas! Would that I had found thee, Admetus, not mourning!

ADM. As about to do what then, dost thou make use of these words?

HER. I will go to some other hearth of those who will receive a guest.

ADM. It must not be, O king: let not so great an evil happen!

HER. Troublesome is a guest if he come to mourners.

ADM. The dead are dead—but go into the house.

HER. 'Tis base however to feast with weeping friends.

ADM. The guest-chamber, whither we will lead thee, is apart.

HER. Let me go, and I will owe you ten thousand thanks.

ADM. It must not be that thou go to the hearth of another man. Lead on thou, having thrown open the guest-chamber that is separate from the house: and tell them that have the management, that there be plenty of meats; and shut the gates in the middle of hall: it is not meet that feasting guests should hear groans, nor should they be made sad.

CHOR. What are you doing? when so great a calamity is before you, Admetus, hast thou the heart to receive guests? wherefore art thou foolish?

ADM. But if I had driven him who came my guest from my house, and from the city, would you have praised me rather? No in sooth, since my calamity had been no whit the less, but I the more inhospitable: and in addition to my evils, there had been this other evil, that mine should be called the stranger-hating house. But I myself find this man a most excellent host, whenever I go to the thirsty land of Argos.

CHOR. How then didst thou hide thy present fate, when a friend, as thou thyself sayest, came?

ADM. He never would have been willing to enter the house if he had known aught of my sufferings. And to him[29] indeed, I ween, acting thus, I appear not to be wise, nor will he praise me; but my house knows not to drive away, nor to dishonor guests.

CHORUS.

O greatly hospitable and ever liberal house of this man, thee even the Pythian Apollo, master of the lyre, deigned to inhabit, and endured to become a shepherd in thine abodes, through the sloping hills piping to thy flocks his pastoral nuptial hymns. And there were wont to feed with them, through delight of his lays, both the spotted lynxes, and the bloody troop of lions[30] came having left the forest of Othrys; disported too around thy cithern, Phœbus, the dappled fawn, advancing with light pastern beyond the lofty-feathered pines, joying in the gladdening strain. Wherefore he dwelleth in a home most rich in flocks by the fair-flowing lake of Bœbe; and to the tillage of his fields, and the extent of his plains, toward that dusky *part of the heavens*, where the sun stays his horses, makes the clime of the Molossians the limit, and holds dominion as far as the portless shore of the Ægean Sea at Pelion. And now having thrown open his house he hath received his guest with moistened eyelid, weeping over the corse of his dear wife, who but now died in the palace: for a noble disposition is prone to reverence [of the guest]. But in the good there is all manner of wisdom. And confidence is seated on my soul that the man who reveres the Gods will fare prosperously.

ADMETUS, CHORUS.

ADM. Ye men of Pheræ that are kindly present, my servants indeed bear aloft[31] the corse, having every thing fit for the tomb, and for the pyre. But do you, as is the custom, salute[32] the dead going forth on her last journey.

CHOR. And lo! I see thy father advancing with his aged foot, and attendants bearing in their hands adornment for thy wife, due honors of those beneath.

PHERES, ADMETUS, CHORUS.

PHE. I am at present sympathizing in thy misfortunes, my son: for thou hast lost (no one will deny) a good and a chaste wife; but these things indeed thou must bear, though hard to be borne. But receive this adornment, and let it go with her beneath the earth: Her body 'tis right to honor, who in sooth died to save thy life, my son, and made me to be not childless, nor suffered me to waste away deprived of thee in an old age of misery. But she has made most illustrious the life of all women, having dared this noble action. O thou that hast preserved my son here, and hast raised us up who were falling, farewell,[33] and may it be well with thee even in the mansions of Pluto! I affirm that such marriages are profitable to men, or that it is not meet to marry.

ADM. Neither hast thou come bidden of me to this funeral, nor do I count thy presence among things acceptable. But she here never shall put on thy decorations; for in no wise shall she be buried indebted to what thou hast. Then oughtest thou to have grieved with me, when I was in danger of perishing.[34] But dost thou, who stoodest aloof, and permittedst another, a young person, thyself being old, to die, weep over this dead body? Thou wert not then really the father of me, nor did she, who says she bore me, and is called my mother, bear me; but born of slavish blood I was secretly put under the breast of thy wife. Thou showedst when thou camest to the test, who thou art; and I deem that I am not thy son. Or else surely thou exceedest all in nothingness of soul, who being of the age thou art, and having come to the goal of life, neither hadst the will nor the courage to die for thy son; but sufferedst this stranger lady, whom alone I might justly have considered both mother and father. And yet thou mightst have run this race for glory, hadst thou died for thy son. But at any rate the remainder of the time thou hadst to live was short: and I should have lived and she the rest of our days, and I should not, bereft of her, be groaning at my miseries. And in sooth thou didst receive as many things as a happy man should receive; thou passedst the vigor of thine age indeed in sovereign sway, but I was thy son to succeed thee in this palace, so that thou wert not about to die childless and leave a desolate house for others to plunder. Thou canst not however say of me, that I gave thee up to die, dishonoring thine old age, whereas I was particularly respectful toward thee; and for this behavior both thou, and she that bare me, have made me such return. Wherefore you have no more time to lose[35] in getting children, who will succor thee in thine old age, and deck thee when dead, and lay out thy corse; for I will not bury thee with this mine hand; for I in sooth died, as far as in thee lay; but if, having met with, another deliverer, I view the light, I say that I am both his child, and the friendly comforter of his old age. In vain then do old men pray to be dead, complaining of age, and the long time of life: but if death come near, not one is willing to die, and old age is no longer burdensome to them.[36]

CHOR. Desist, for the present calamity is sufficient; and do not, O son, provoke thy father's mind.

PHE. O son, whom dost thou presume thou art gibing with thy reproaches, a Lydian or a Phrygian bought with thy money?[37] Knowest thou not that I am a Thessalian, and born from a Thessalian father, truly free? Thou art too insolent, and casting the impetuous words of youth against us, shalt not having cast them thus depart. But I begat thee the lord of my house, and brought thee up, but I am not thy debtor to die for thee; for I received no paternal law like this, nor Grecian law, that fathers should die for their children; for for thyself thou wert born, whether unfortunate or fortunate, but what from us thou oughtest to have, thou hast. Thou rulest indeed over many, and I will leave thee a large demesne of lands, for these I received from my father. In what then have I injured thee? Of what do I deprive thee? Thou joyest to see the light, and dost think thy father does not joy?[38] Surely I count the time we must spend beneath long, and life is short, but still sweet. Thou too didst shamelessly fight off from dying, and livest, having passed over thy destined fate, by slaying her; then dost thou talk of my nothingness of soul, O most vile one, when thou art surpassed by a woman who died for thee, the handsome youth? But thou hast made a clever discovery, so that thou mayst never die, if thou wilt persuade the wife that is thine from time to time to die for thee: and then reproachest thou thy friends who are not willing to do this, thyself being a coward? Hold thy peace, and consider, if thou lovest thy life, that all love theirs; but if thou shalt speak evil against us, thou shalt hear many reproaches and not false ones.

CHOR. Too many evil things have been spoken both now and before, but cease, old man, from reviling thy son.

ADM. Speak, for I have spoken; but if thou art grieved at hearing the truth, thou shouldst not err against me.

PHE. But had I died for thee, I had erred more.

ADM. What? is it the same thing for a man in his prime, and for an old man to die?

PHE. We ought to live with one life, not with two.

ADM. Mayst thou then live a longer time than Jove!

PHE. Dost curse thy parents, having met with no injustice?

ADM. *I said it*, for I perceived thou lovedst a long life.

PHE. But art not thou bearing forth this corse instead of thyself?

ADM. A proof this, O most vile one, of thy nothingness of soul.

PHE. She died not by us at least; thou wilt not say this.

ADM. Alas! Oh that you may ever come to need my aid!

PHE. Wed many wives, that more may die.

ADM. This is a reproach to thyself, for thou wert not willing to die.

PHE. Sweet is this light of the God, sweet is it.

ADM. Base is thy spirit and not that of men.

PHE. Thou dost not laugh as carrying an aged corse.

ADM. Thou wilt surely however die inglorious, when thou diest.

PHE. To bear an evil report is no matter to me when dead.

ADM. Alas! alas! how full of shamelessness is old age!

PHE. She was not shameless: her you found mad.

ADM. Begone, and suffer me to bury this dead.

PHE. I will depart; but you will bury her, yourself being her murderer. But you will render satisfaction to your wife's relatives yet: or surely Acastus no longer ranks among men, if he shall not revenge the blood of his sister.

ADM. Get thee gone, then, thou and thy wife; childless, thy child yet living, as ye deserve, grow old; for ye no more come into the same house with me: and if it were necessary for me to renounce by heralds thy paternal hearth, I would renounce it. But let us (for the evil before us must be borne) proceed, that we may place the corse upon the funeral pyre.

CHOR. O! O! unhappy because of thy bold deed, O noble, and by far most excellent, farewell! may both Mercury[39] that dwells beneath, and Pluto, kindly receive thee; but if there too any distinction is shown to the good, partaking of this mayst thou sit by the bride of Pluto.

SERVANT.

I have now known many guests, and from all parts of the earth that have come to the house of Admetus, to whom I have spread the feast, but never yet did I receive into this house a worse one than this stranger. Who, in the first place, indeed, though he saw my master in affliction, came in, and prevailed upon himself to pass the gates. And then not at all in a modest manner received he the entertainment that there happened to be, when he heard of the calamity: but if we did not bring any thing, he hurried us to bring it. And having taken in his hands the cup wreathed with ivy,[40] he quaffs the neat wine of the purple mother, until the fumes of the liquor coming upon him inflamed him; and he crowns his head with branches of myrtles howling discordantly; and there were two strains to hear; for he was singing, not caring at all for the afflictions of Admetus, but we the domestics, were bewailing our mistress, and we showed not that we were weeping to the guest, for thus Admetus commanded. And now indeed I am performing the offices of hospitality to the stranger in the house, some deceitful thief and robber. But she is gone from the house, nor did I follow, nor stretched out my hand in lamentation for my mistress, who was a mother to me, and to all the domestics, for she saved us from ten thousand ills, softening the anger of her husband. Do I not then justly hate this stranger, who is come in our miseries?

HERCULES, SERVANT.

HER. Ho there! why dost thou look so grave and thoughtful? The servant ought not to be of woeful countenance before guests, but should receive them with an affable mind. But thou, though thou seest a companion of thy lord present, receivest him with a morose and clouded countenance, fixing thy attention on a calamity that thou hast nothing to do with. Come hither, that thou mayst become more wise. Knowest thou mortal affairs, of what nature they are? I think not; from whence should you? but hear me. Death is a debt that all mortals must pay: and there is not of them one, who knows whether he shall live the coming morrow: for what depends on fortune is uncertain how it will turn out, and is not to be learned, neither is it detected by art. Having heard these things then, and learned them from me, make thyself merry, drink, and think the life allowed from day to day thine own, but the rest Fortune's. And honor also Venus, the most sweet of deities to mortals, for she is a kind deity. But let go these other things, and obey my words, if I appear to speak rightly: I think so indeed. Wilt thou not then leave off thy excessive grief, and drink with me, crowned with garlands, having thrown open these gates? And well know I that the trickling of the cup falling down *thy throat* will change thee from thy present cloudy and pent state of mind. But we who are mortals should think as mortals. Since to all the morose, indeed, and to those of sad countenance, if they take me as judge at least, life is not truly life, but misery.

SERV. I know this; but now we are in circumstances not such as are fit for revel and mirth.

HER. The lady that is dead is a stranger; grieve not too much, for the lords of this house live.

SERV. What live! knowest thou not the misery within the house?

HER. Unless thy lord hath told me any thing falsely.

SERV. He is too, too hospitable.

HER. Is it unmeet that I should be well treated, because a stranger is dead?

SERV. Surely however she was very near.

HER. Has he forborne to tell me any calamity that there is?

SERV. Depart and farewell; we have a care for the evils of our lords.

HER. This speech is the beginning of no foreign loss.

SERV. For I should not, *had it been foreign*, have been grieved at seeing thee reveling.

HER. What! have I received so great an injury from mine host?

SERV. Thou camest not in a fit time for the house to receive thee, for there is grief to us, and thou seest that we are shorn, and our black garments.

HER. But who is it that is dead? Has either any of his children died, or his aged father?

SERV. The wife indeed of Admetus is dead, O stranger.

HER. What sayst thou? and yet did ye receive me?

SERV. *Yes*, for he had too much respect to turn thee from his house.

HER. O unhappy man, what a wife hast thou lost!

SERV. We all are lost, not she alone.

HER. But I did perceive it indeed, when I saw his eye streaming with tears, and his shorn hair, and his countenance; but he persuaded me, saying, that he was conducting the funeral of a stranger to the tomb: but spite of my inclination having passed over these gates, I drank in the house of the hospitable man, while he was in this case, and reveled, crowned as to my head with garlands. But 'twas thine to tell me not *to do it*, when such an evil was upon the house. Where is he burying her? whither going can I find her?

SERV. By the straight road that leads to Larissa, thou wilt see the polished tomb beyond the suburbs.

HERCULES.

O my much-daring heart and my soul, now show what manner of son the Tirynthian Alcmena, daughter of Electryon, bare thee to Jove. For I must rescue the woman lately dead, Alcestis, and place her again in this house, and perform this service for Admetus. And going I will lay wait for the sable-vested king of the departed, Death, and I think that I shall find him drinking of the libations near the tomb. And if having taken him by lying in wait, rushing from my ambush, I shall seize hold of him, and make a circle around him with mine arms, there is not who shall take him away panting as to his sides, until he release me the woman. But if however I fail of this capture, and he come not to the clottered mass of blood, I will go a journey beneath to the sunless mansions of Cora and her king, and will prefer my request; and I trust that I shall bring up Alcestis, so as to place her in the hands of that host, who received me into his house, nor drove me away, although struck with a heavy calamity, but concealed it, noble as he was, having respect unto me. Who of the Thessalians is more hospitable than he? Who that dwelleth in Greece? Wherefore he shall not say, that he did a service to a worthless man, himself being noble.

ADMETUS, CHORUS.

ADM. Alas! alas! O hateful approach, and hateful prospect of this widowed house. Oh me! Alas! alas! whither can I go! where rest! what can I say! and what not! would that I could perish! Surely my mother brought me forth to heavy fortune. I count the dead happy, them I long for! those houses I desire to dwell in: for neither delight I in viewing the sunbeams, nor treading with my foot upon the earth; of such a hostage has death robbed me, and delivered up to Pluto.

CHOR. Advance, advance; go into the recesses of the house.

(ADM. Oh! Oh!)

Thou hast suffered things that demand groans.

(ADM. Alas! alas!)

Thou hast gone through grief, I well know.

(ADM. Woe! Woe!)

Thou nothing aidest her that is beneath.

(ADM. Ah me! me!)

Never to see thy dear wife's face again before thee, is severe.

ADM. Thou hast made mention of that which ulcerated my soul; for what can be greater ill to man than to lose his faithful wife? Would that I never had married and dwelt with her in the palace. But I judge happy those, who are unmarried and childless; for theirs is one only life, for this to grieve is a moderate burden: but to behold the diseases of children, and the bridal bed wasted by death, is not supportable, when it were in one's power to be without children and unmarried the whole of life.

CHOR. Fate, fate hard to be struggled with hath come.

(ADM. Oh! Oh!)

But puttest thou no bound to thy sorrows?

(ADM. Alas! alas!)

Heavy are they to bear, but still

(ADM. Woe! woe!)

endure, thou art not the first man that hast lost

(ADM. Ah me! me!)

thy wife; but calamity appearing afflicts different men in different shapes.

ADM. O lasting griefs, and sorrows for our friends beneath the earth!—Why did you hinder me from throwing myself[41] into her hallowed grave, and from lying dead with her, by far the most excellent woman? And Pluto would have retained instead of one, two most faithful souls having together passed over the infernal lake.

CHOR. I had a certain kinsman, whose son worthy to be lamented, an only child, died in his house; but nevertheless he bore his calamity with moderation, being bereft of child, though now hastening to gray hairs, and advanced in life.

ADM. O house, how can I enter in? and how dwell in thee now my fortune has undergone this change? Ah me! for there is great difference between: then indeed with Pelian torches, and with bridal songs I entered in, bearing the hand of my dear wife, and there followed a loud-shouting revelry hailing happy both her that is dead and me, inasmuch as being noble, and born of illustrious parents both, we were united together: but now the groan instead of hymeneals, and black array instead of white robes, usher me in to my deserted couch.

CHOR. This grief came quick on happy fortune to thee unschooled in evil: but thou hast saved thy life. Thy wife is dead, she left her love behind: what new thing this? Death has ere this destroyed many wives.

ADM. My friends, I deem the fortune of my wife more happy than mine own, even although these things appear not so. For her indeed no grief shall ever touch, and she hath with glory ceased from many toils. But I, who ought not to have lived, though I have scaped destiny, shall pass a bitter life; I but now perceive. For how can I bear the entering into this house? Whom speaking to, or by whom addressed,[42] can I have joy in entering? Whither shall I turn me? For the solitude within will drive me forth, when I see the place where my wife used to lie, empty, and the seat whereon she used to sit, and the floor throughout the house all dirty, and when my children falling about my knees weep their mother, and they lament their mistress, *thinking* what a lady they have lost from out of the house. Such things within the house; but abroad the nuptials of the Thessalians and the assemblies full of women will torture me: for I shall not be able to look on the companions of my wife. But whoever is mine enemy will say thus of me: "See that man, who basely lives, who dared not to die, but giving in his stead her, whom he married, escaped Hades, (and then does he seem to be a man?) and hates his parents, himself not willing to die."—Such report shall I have in addition to my woes; why then is it the more honorable course for me to live, my friends, having an evil character and an evil fortune?

CHOR. I too have both been borne aloft through song, and having very much handled arguments have found nothing more powerful than Necessity: nor is there any cure in the Thracian tablets which Orpheus[43] wrote, nor among those medicines, which Phœbus gave the sons of Æsculapius, dispensing[44] them to wretched mortals. But neither to the altars nor to the image of this Goddess alone, is it lawful to approach, she hears not victims. Do not, O revered one, come on me more severe, than hitherto in my life. For Jove, whatever he have assented to, with thee brings this to pass. Thou too perforce subduest the iron among the Chalybi; nor has thy rugged spirit any remorse.

And thee, *Admetus*, the Goddess hath seized in the inevitable grasp of her hand; but bear it, for thou wilt never by weeping bring back on earth the dead from beneath. Even the sons of the Gods by stealth begotten perish in death. Dear she was while she was with us, and dear even now when dead. But thou didst join to thy bed[45] the noblest wife of all women. Nor let the tomb of thy wife be accounted as the mound over the dead that perish, but let it be honored equally with the Gods, a thing for travelers to adore:[46] and some one, going out of his direct road, shall say thus: "She in olden time died for her husband, but now she is a blest divinity: Hail, O adored one, and be propitious!" Such words will be addressed to her.—And lo! here comes, as it seems, the son of Alcmena to thy house, Admetus.

HERCULES, ADMETUS, CHORUS.

HER. One should speak freely to a friend, Admetus, and, not in silence keep within our bosoms what we blame. Now I thought myself worthy as a friend to stand near thy calamities, and to search them out;[47] but thou didst not tell me that it was thy wife's corse that demanded thy attention; but didst receive me in thy house, as though occupied in grief for one not thine. And I crowned my head and poured out to the Gods libations in thy house which had suffered this calamity. And I *do* blame thee, I blame thee, having met with this treatment! not that I wish to grieve thee in thy miseries. But wherefore I am come, having turned back again, I will tell thee. Receive and take care of this woman for me, until I come hither driving the Thracian mares, having slain the king of the Bistonians. But if I meet with what I pray I may not meet with, (for may I return!) I give thee her as an attendant of thy palace. But with much toil came she into my hands; for I find some who had proposed a public contest for wrestlers, worthy of my labors, from whence I bear off her, having received her as the prize of my victory; for those who conquered in the lighter exercises had to receive horses, but those again who conquered in the greater, the boxing and the wrestling, cattle, and a woman was added to these; but in me, who happened to be there, it had been base to neglect this glorious gain. But, as I said, the woman ought to be a care to you, for I am come not having obtained her by stealth, but with labor; but at some time or other thou too wilt perhaps commend me for it.

ADM. By no means slighting thee, nor considering thee among mine enemies, did I conceal from thee the unhappy fate of my wife; but this had been a grief added to grief, if thou hadst gone to the house of another host: but it was sufficient for me to weep my own calamity. But the woman, if it is in any way possible, I beseech thee, O king, bid some one of the Thessalians, who has not suffered what I have, to take care of (but thou hast many friends among the Pheræans) lest thou remind me of my misfortunes. I can not, beholding her in the house, refrain from weeping; add not a sickness to me already sick; for I am enough weighed down with misery. Where besides in the house can a youthful woman be maintained? for she is youthful, as she evinces by her garb and her attire; shall she then live in the men's apartment? And how will she be undefiled, living among young men? A man in his vigor, Hercules, it is no easy thing to restrain; but I have a care for thee. Or can I maintain her, having made her enter the chamber of her that is dead? And how can I introduce her into her bed? I fear a double accusation, both from the citizens, lest any should convict me of having betrayed my benefactress, and lying in the bed of another girl; and I ought to have much regard toward the dead (and she deserves my respect). But thou, O lady, whoever thou art, know that thou hast the same size of person with Alcestis, and art like her in figure. Ah me! take by the Gods this woman from mine eyes, lest you destroy me already destroyed. For I think, when I look upon her, that I behold my wife; and it agitates my heart, and from mine eyes the streams break forth; O unhappy I, how lately did I begin to taste this bitter grief!

CHOR. I can not indeed speak well of thy fortune; but it behooves thee, whatever thou art, to bear with firmness the dispensation of the Gods.

HER. Oh would that I had such power as to bring thy wife to the light from the infernal mansions, and to do this service for thee!

ADM. Well know I that thou hast the will: but how can this be? It is not possible for the dead to come into the light.

HER. Do not, I pray, go beyond all bound, but bear it decently,

ADM. Tis easier to exhort, than suffering to endure.

HER. But what advantage can you gain if you wish to groan forever?

ADM. I know that too myself; but a certain love impels me.

HER. For to love one that is dead draws the tear.

ADM. She hath destroyed me, and yet more than my words express.

HER. Thou hast lost an excellent wife; who will deny it?

ADM. *Ay,* so that I am no longer delighted with life.

HER. Time will soften the evil, but now it is yet in its vigor[48] on thee.

ADM. Time thou mayst say, if to die be time.

HER. A wife will bid it cease, and the desire of a new marriage.

ADM. Hold thy peace—What saidst thou? I could not have supposed it.

HER. But why? what, wilt not marry, but pass a widowed life alone?

ADM. There is no woman that shall lie with me.

HER. Dost thou think that thou art in aught benefiting her that is dead?

ADM. Her, wherever she is, I am bound to honor.

HER. I praise you indeed, I praise you; but you incur the charge of folly.

ADM. *Praise me, or praise me not;* for you shall never call me bridegroom.

HER. I do praise thee, because thou art a faithful friend to thy wife.

ADM. May I die, when I forsake her, although she is not!

HER. Receive then this noble woman into thine house.

ADM. Do not, I beseech thee by thy father Jove.

HER. And yet you will be acting wrong, if you do not this.

ADM. Yes, and if I do it, I shall have my heart gnawed with sorrow.

HER. Be prevailed upon: perhaps this favor may be proved a duty.

ADM. Ah! would that you had never borne her off from the contest!

HER. Yet with me conquering thou'rt victorious too.

ADM. Thou hast well spoken; but let the woman depart.

HER. She shall depart, if it is needful; but first see whether it be needful.

ADM. It is needful, if thou at least dost not mean to make me angry.

HER. I too have this desire, for I know somewhat.

ADM. Conquer then. Thou dost not however do things pleasing to me.

HER. But some time or other thou wilt praise me; only be persuaded.

ADM. Lead her in, if I must receive her in my house.

HER. I will not deliver up the woman into the charge of the servants.

ADM. But do thou thyself lead her into the house if it seems fit.

HER. I then will give her into thine hands.

ADM. I will not touch her; but she is at liberty to enter the house.

HER. I trust her to thy right hand alone.

ADM. O king, thou compellest me to do this against my will.

HER. Dare to stretch out thy hand and touch the stranger.

ADM. And in truth I stretch it out, as I would to the Gorgon with her severed head.[49]

HER. Have you her?

ADM. I have.

HER. Then keep her fast; and some time or other thou wilt say that the son of Jove is a generous guest. But look on her, whether she seems aught to resemble thy wife; and being blest leave off from thy grief.

ADM. O Gods, what shall I say? An unexpected wonder this! Do I truly see here my wife, or does the mocking joy of the Deity strike me from my senses?

HER. It is not so; but thou beholdest here thy wife.

ADM. Yet see, whether this be not a phantom from the realms beneath.

HER. Thou hast not made thine host an invoker of spirits.

ADM. But do I behold my wife, whom I buried?

HER. Be well assured *thou dost;* but I wonder not at thy disbelief of thy fortune.

ADM. May I touch her, may I speak to her as my living wife?[50]

HER. Speak to her; for thou hast all that thou desirest.

ADM. O face and person of my dearest wife, have I thee beyond my hopes, when I thought never to see thee more?

HER. Thou hast: but *take care* there be no envy of the Gods.

ADM. O noble son of the most powerful Jove, mayst thou be blest, and may thy father, who begot thee, protect thee, for thou alone hast restored me! How didst thou bring her from beneath into this light!

HER. Having fought a battle with the prince of those beneath.

ADM. Where dost thou say thou didst have this conflict with Death!

HER. At the tomb itself, having seized him from ambush with my hands.

ADM. But why, I pray, does this woman stand here speechless?

HER. It is not yet allowed thee to hear her address thee, before she is unbound from her consecrations[51] to the Gods beneath, and the third day come. But lead her in, and as thou oughtest, henceforward, Admetus, continue in thy piety with respect to strangers. And farewell! But I will go and perform the task that is before me for the imperial son of Sthenelus.

ADM. Stay with us, and be a companion of our hearth.

HER. This shall be some time hence, but now I must haste.

ADM. But mayst thou be prosperous, and return on thy journey back. But to the citizens, and to all the tetrarchy I issue my commands, that they institute dances in honor of these happy events, and make the altars odorous with their sacrifices of oxen that accompany their vows. For now are we placed in a better state of life than the former one: for I will not deny that I am happy.

CHOR. Many are the shapes of the things the deities direct, and many things the Gods perform contrary to our expectations. And those things which we looked for are not accomplished; but the God hath brought to pass things not looked for. Such hath been the event of this affair.

NOTES ON ALCESTIS

[1] Lactant. i. 10. "Quid Apollo? Nonne ... turpissime gregem pavit alienum?" B.

[2] Hygin. Fab. li. "Apollo ab eo in servitutem liberaliter acceptus." B.

[3] Cf. Hippol. 1437. B.

[4] No one will, I believe, object to this translation of ΘΑΝΑΤΟΣ; it seems rather a matter of surprise that Potter has kept the Latin ORCUS, a name clearly substituted as the nearest to ΘΑΝΑΤΟΣ of the masculine gender.

[5] Cf. Æsch. Eum. 723 sqq. B.

[6] It was customary to bury those, who died advanced in years, with greater magnificence than young persons.

[7] The horses of Diomed, king of Thrace. The construction is, Ευρυσθεως πεμψαντος [αυτον] μετα 'ιππειον οχημα [αξοντα] εκ τοπων δυσχει μερων Θρηικης. MONK.

[8] On this custom, see Monk, and Lomeier de Lustrationibus § xxviii. B.

[9] Perhaps, "as though all were over," B.

[10] Casaubon on Theophr. § 16, observes that it was customary to place a large vessel filled with lustral water before the doors of a house during the time the corpse was lying out, with which every one who came out sprinkled himself. See also Monk's note, Kirchmann de Funeribus, iii. 9. The same custom was observed on returning from the funeral. See Pollux, viii. 7. p. 391, ed. Seber. B.

[11] See Dindorf. B.

[12] Potterus, Arch. Gr. *mortuos* a *Græcis* προνωπεις vocari tradit, quod solebant ex penitiore ædium parte produci, ac in *vestibulo*, i.e. προνωπιωι collocari: atque hunc locum adducit, sed frustra, ut opinor. Non enim *mortua* jam erat, nec *producta*, sed, ut recte hanc vocem interpretatur schol. εις θανατον προνενευκυια, i.e. *morti propinqua*. Proprie προνωπης is dicitur, qui *corpore prono ad terram fertur*, ut Æschyl. Agam. 242. Inde, quia moribundi virium defectu terram petere solent, ad hos designandos translatum est. KUINOEL.

[13] The old word "dizening" is perhaps the most literal translation of κοσμος, which, however, here means the whole preparations for the funeral. Something like it is implied in Hamlet, v. 1.

... her virgin rites,

Her maiden strewments, and the bringing home

Of bell and burial.   B.

[14] Aristophanes is almost too bad in his burlesque, Equit. 1251. σε δ' αλλος τις λαβων κεκτησεται, κλεπτης μεν ουκ αν μαλλον, ευτυχης δ' 'ισως. B.

[15] Some would translate προνωπης in the same manner as in verse 144.

[16] Conf. Ter.: Phorm. iv. 4, 5. Opera tua ad *restim* mihi quidem res rediit planissume.

[17] Perhaps it is unnecessary to remark, that αβιωτον agrees with βιον implied in βιοτευσει.

[18] 'ωραι scilicet 'ηλιος. MONK.

[19] Cf. Hippol. 1372. B.

[20] It must be remembered that to survive one's children was considered the greatest of misfortunes. Cf. Plaut. Mil. Glor. l. 1. "Ita ut tuum vis unicum gnatum tuæ Superesse vitæ, sospitem et superstitem." B.

[21] Kuinoel carries on the interrogation to γαμους, and Buchanan has translated it according to this punctuation. Monk compares Iliad, p. 95; μηπως με περιστελωσ' 'ενα πολλοι.

[22] Compare my note on Æsch. Ag. 414 sqq. B.

[23] *These*, my children.

[24] Reiske proposes to read τεθριππα δε ζευγη τε και—*And both from your chariot teams, and from your single horses cut the manes.*

[25] This festival was celebrated in honor of Apollo at Sparta, from the seventh to the sixteenth day of the month Carneus. See Monk. B.

[26] On λιπαραις Αθαναις, see Monk. B.

[27] Literally, *the duplicate* of such a wife.

[28] αναξ πελτης, so αναξ κωπης in Æsch. Pers. 384, *of a rower.* Wakefield compares Ovid's *Clypei dominus septemplicis Ajax.* MONK.

[29] Heath and Markland take τωι for τινι.

[30] Cf. Theocrit. Id. i. 71 sqq. of Daphnis, τηνον μεν θωες, τηνον λυκοι ωρυσαντο, Τηνον χοι 'κ δρυμοιο λεων ανεκλαυσε θανοντα ... πολλαι μεν παρ ποσσι βοες, πολλοι δε τε ταυροι, πολλαι δ' αυ δαμαλαι και πορτιες ωδυραντο. Virg. Ecl. v. 27 sqq. Calpurnius, Ecl. ii. 18. Nemesianus, Ecl. i. 74 sqq.; ii. 32. B.

[31] αρδην γινεται απο του αιρειν. δηλοι δε το φοραδην. Schol.

[32] Cf. Suppl. 773. "Αιδου τε μολπας εκχεω δακρυρροους, φιλους προσαυδων, 'ων λελειμμενος ταλας ερημα κλαιω. See Gorius Monum. sive Columbar. Libert. Florent. mdccxxvii. p.186, who observes, "χαιρε was the accustomed salutation addressed to the dead. Catullus, Carm. xcvii. *Accipe fraterno multum manantia fletu, atque in perpetuum frater HAVE, atque VALE.*" The same scholar compares a monument, apud Fabretti, cap. v. p. 392, n. 265,

D. M
AVE SALVINIA
OMNIUM. AMAN
TISSIMA. ET.
VALE,

which is very apposite to the present occasion. B.

[33] Wakefield reads χαιρε καιν Αιδου δομοις; having in his mind probably Hom. Il. Ψ. 19. Χαιρε μοι 'ω Πατροκλε, και ειν Αϊδαο δομοισι.

[34] I should scarcely have observed that this is the proper sense of the imperfect, had not the former translator mistaken it. B.

[35] Cf. Iph. Taur. 244. χερνιβας δε και καταργματα ουκ αν φθανοις αν ευτρεπη ποιουμενη. B.

[36] An apparent allusion to the fable of Death and the Old Man. B

[37] Aristophanes' version of this line is, ω παι, τιν αυχεις, ποτερα Λυδον η Φρυγα Μορμολυττεσθαι δοκεις. B.

[38] Turned by Aristophanes into an apology for beating one's father, Nub. 1415. κλαουσι παιδες, πατερα δ' ου κλαειν δοκεις. See Thesmoph. 194. B.

[39] Cf. Æsch. Choeph. sub init. and Gorius, Monum. Libert. p. 24. ad Tab. x. lit. A.

[40] Theocrit. i. 27. Και βαθυ κισσυβιον κεκλυσμενον 'αδει καρωι, Τω περι μεν χειλη μαρευεται 'υψοθι κισσος. B.

[41] Hamlet, v. 1.

—Hold off the earth awhile,

Till I have caught her once more in mine arms:

[*leaps into the grave.*]

Now pile your dust upon the quick and dead.   B.

[42] Cf. vs. 195. ῾ον ου προσειπε και προσερρηθη παλιν. B.

[43] Ορφεια γαρυς, a paraphrasis for Ορφευς.

[44] αντιτεμων, μεταφορικως απο των τας ῾ριζας τεμνοντων και ῾ευρισκοντων. SCHOL. TR. Cf. on Æsch. Agam. 17. B.

[45] In Phavorinus, among the senses of κλισια is κλινη και κλινητηριον.

[46] It will be remembered that the tombs were built near the highways, with great magnificence, and sometimes very lofty, especially when near the sea-coast (cf. Æsch. Choeph. 351. D'Orville on Charit. lib. i. sub fin. Eurip. Hecub. 1273). They are often used as landmarks or milestones, as in Theocr. vi. 10, and as oratories or chapels, Apul. Florid, i. p.340, ed. Elm. B.

[47] This appears the most obvious sense, as connected with what follows. All the interpreters, however, translate it, *I thought myself worthy, standing, as I did, near thy calamities,*(i.e. near thee in thy calamities,) *to be proved thy friend.*

[48] In the same manner ῾ηβαι is used in Orestes, 687, ῾οταν γαρ ῾ηβαι δημος εις οργην πεσων.

[49] i.e. *the severed head of the Gorgon.* Valckenaer observes, that this is an expression meaning *facie aversa,* and compares l. 465 of the Phœnissæ.

[50] Winter's Tale, v. 3.

Start not: her actions shall be holy, as,

You hear, my spell is lawful: do not shun her,

Until you see her die again; for then

You kill her double: Nay, present your hand:

When she was young you woo'd her; now, in age,

Is she become the suitor?

Compare also Much Ado about Nothing, v. 4. B.

[51] ʽαφαγνιζειν h. l. non *purificare* sed *desecrare*. Orcus enim, quando gladio totondisset Alcestidis capillos, eam diis manibus sacram dicaverat, quod diserte ʽηγνισαι appellat noster, vide 75—77. Contraria igitur aliqua ceremonia desecranda erat, antequam Admeto ejus consuetudine et colloquio frui liceret. HEATH.

THE BACCHÆ.

PERSONS REPRESENTED,

BACCHUS.

CHORUS.

TIRESIAS.

CADMUS.

PENTHEUS.

SERVANT.

MESSENGER.

ANOTHER MESSENGER.

AGAVE.

THE ARGUMENT.

Bacchus, the son of Jove by Semele, had made Thebes, his mother's birth-place, his favorite place of abode and worship. Pentheus, the then reigning king, who, as others say, preferred the worship of Minerva, slighted the new God, and persecuted those who celebrated his revels. Upon this, Bacchus excited his mother Agave, together with the sisters of Semele, Autonoe and Ino, to madness, and visiting Pentheus in disguise of a Bacchanal, was at first imprisoned, but, easily escaping from his bonds, he persuaded Pentheus to intrude upon the rites of the Bacchants. While surveying them from a lofty tree, the voice of Bacchus was heard inciting the Bacchants to avenge themselves upon the intruder, and they tore the miserable Pentheus piecemeal. The grief and banishment of Agave for her unwitting offense conclude the play.

THE BACCHÆ.[1]

BACCHUS.

I, Bacchus, the son of Jove, am come to this land of the Thebans, whom formerly Semele, the daughter of Cadmus, brought forth, delivered by the lightning-bearing flame. And having taken a mortal form instead of a God's, I am present at the fountains of Dirce and the water of Ismenus. And I see the tomb of my thunder-stricken mother here near the palace, and the remnants of the house smoking, and the still living name of Jove's fire, the everlasting insult of Juno against my mother. But I praise Cadmus, who has made this place hallowed, the shrine of his daughter; and I have covered it around with the cluster-bearing leaf of the vine. And having left the wealthy lands of the Lydians and Phrygians, and the sun-parched plains of the Persians, and the Bactrian walls; and having come over the stormy land of the Medes, and the happy Arabia, and all Asia which lies along the coast of the salt sea, having fair-towered cities full of Greeks and barbarians mingled together; and there having danced and established my mysteries, that I might be a God manifest among men, I have come to this city first of the Grecian [cities,] and I have raised my shout first in Thebes of this land of Greece, fitting a deer-skin on my body, and taking a thyrsus in my hand, an ivy-clad[2] weapon, because the sisters of my mother, whom, it least of all became, said that I, Bacchus, was not born of Jove; but that Semele, having conceived by some mortal, charged the sin of her bed upon Jove, a trick of Cadmus; on which account they said that Jove had slain her, because she told a false tale about her marriage. Therefore I have now driven them from the house with frenzy, and they dwell on the mountain, insane of mind; and I have compelled them to wear the dress of my mysteries. And all the female seed of the Cadmeans, as many as are women, have I driven maddened from the house. And they, mingled with the sons of Cadmus, sit on the roofless rocks beneath the green pines. For this city must know, even though it be unwilling, that it is not initiated into my Bacchanalian rites, and that I plead the cause of my mother, Semele, in appearing manifest to mortals as a God whom she bore to Jove. Cadmus then gave his honor and power to Pentheus, born from his daughter, who fights against the Gods as far as I am concerned, and drives me from sacrifices, and in his prayers makes no mention of me; on which account I will show him and all the Thebans that I am a God. And having set matters here aright, manifesting myself, I will move to another land. But if the city of the Thebans should in anger seek by arms to bring down the Bacchæ from the mountain, I, general of the Mænads, will join battle.[3] On which account I have changed my form to a mortal one, and transformed my shape into the nature of a man. But, O ye who have left Tmolus, the

- 232 -

bulwark of Lydia; ye women, my assembly, whom I have brought from among the barbarians as assistants and companions to me; take your drums, your native instruments in the Phrygian cities, the invention of the mother Rhea[4] and myself, and coming beat them around this royal palace of Pentheus, that the city of Cadmus may see it. And I, with the Bacchæ, going to the dells of Cithæron, where they are, will share their dances.

CHOR. Coming from the land of Asia, having left the sacred Tmolus, I dance in honor of Bromius, a sweet labor and a toil easily borne, celebrating the god Bacchus. Who is in the way? who is in the way? who is in the halls? Let him depart. And let every one be pure as to his mouth speaking propitious things; for now I will with hymns celebrate Bacchus according to custom:—Blessed is he,[5] whoever being favored, knowing the mysteries of the gods, keeps his life pure, and has his soul initiated into the Bacchic revels, dancing o'er the mountains with holy purifications, and reverencing the mysteries of the mighty mother Cybele, and brandishing the thyrsus, and being crowned with ivy, serves Bacchus! Go, ye Bacchæ; go, ye Bacchæ, escorting Bromius, a God, the son of a God, from the Phrygian mountains to the broad streets of Greece! Bromius! whom formerly, being in the pains of travail, the thunder of Jove flying upon her, his mother cast from her womb, leaving life by the stroke of the thunder-bolt. And immediately Jupiter, the son of Saturn, received him in a chamber fitted for birth; and covering him in his thigh, shuts him with golden clasps hidden from Juno. And he brought him forth, when the Fates had perfected the horned God, and crowned him with crowns of snakes, whence the thyrsus-bearing Mænads are wont to cover their prey with their locks. O Thebes, thou nurse of Semele, crown thyself with ivy, flourish, flourish with the verdant yew bearing sweet fruit, and be ye crowned in honor of Bacchus with branches of oak or pine, and adorn your garments of spotted deer-skin with fleeces of white-haired sheep,[6] and sport in holy games with the insulting wands, straightway shall all the earth dance, when Bromius leads the bands to the mountain, to the mountain, where the female crowd abides, away from the distaff and the shuttle,[7] driven frantic by Bacchus. O dwelling of the Curetes, and ye divine Cretan caves,[8] parents to Jupiter, where the Corybantes with the triple helmet invented for me in their caves this circle o'erstretched with hide; and with the constant sweet-voiced breath of Phrygian pipes they mingled a sound of Bacchus, and put the instrument in the hand of Rhea, resounding with the sweet songs of the Bacchæ. And hard by the raving satyrs went through the sacred rites of the mother Goddess. And they added the dances of the Trieterides;[9] in which Bacchus rejoices; pleased on the mountains, when after the running dance he falls upon the plain, having a sacred garment of deer-skin, seeking a sacrifice of goats, a raw-eaten delight,[10] on his way to the Phrygian, the Lydian mountains; and the leader is Bromius, Evoe![11] but the plain flows with milk, and flows with wine, and flows with the nectar of bees; and the smoke is as of Syrian frankincense. But Bacchus bearing a flaming torch of pine on his thyrsus, rushes about arousing in his course the wandering Choruses, and agitating them with shouts, casting his rich locks loose in the air,—and with his songs he shouts out such words as this: O go forth, ye Bacchæ; O go forth, ye Bacchæ, delight of gold-flowing Tmolus. Sing Bacchus 'neath the loud drums, Evoe, celebrating the God Evius in Phrygian cries and shouts. When the sweet-sounding sacred pipe sounds a sacred playful sound suited to the frantic wanderers, to the mountain, to the mountain—and the Bacchant rejoicing like a foal with its mother at pasture, stirs its swift foot in the dance.

TIRESIAS. Who at the doors will call out Cadmus from the house, the son of Agenor, who, leaving the city of Sidon, erected this city of the Thebans? Let some one go, tell him that Tiresias seeks him; but he himself knows on what account I come, and what agreement I, an old man, have made with him, yet older; to twine the thyrsi, and to put on the skins of deer, and to crown the head with ivy branches.

CADMUS. O dearest friend! how I, being in the house, was delighted, hearing your voice, the wise voice of a wise man; and I am come prepared, having this equipment of the God; for we needs must extol him, who is the son sprung from my daughter, Bacchus, who has appeared as a God to men, as much as is in our power. Whither shall I dance, whither direct the foot, and wave the hoary head? Do you lead me, you, an old man! O Tiresias, direct me, an old man; for you are wise. Since I shall never tire, neither night nor day, striking the earth with the thyrsus. Gladly we forget that we are old.

TI. You have the same feelings indeed as I; for I too feel young, and will attempt the dance.

CA. Then we will go to the mountain in chariots.[12]

TI. But thus the God would not have equal honor.

CA. I, an old man, will lead you, an old man.[13]

TI. The God will without trouble guide us thither.

CA. But shall we alone of the city dance in honor of Bacchus?

TI. [Ay,] for we alone think rightly, but the rest ill.

CA. We are long in delaying;[14] but take hold of my hand.

TI. See, take hold, and join your hand to mine.

CA. I do not despise the Gods, being a mortal.

TI. We do not show too much wiseness about the Gods. Our ancestral traditions, and those which we have kept throughout our life, no argument will overturn them; not if any one were to find out wisdom with the highest genius. Some one will say that I do not respect old age, being about to dance, having crowned my head with ivy; for the God has made no distinction as to whether it becomes the young man to dance, or the elder; but wishes to have common honors from all; but does not at all wish to be extolled by a few.

CA. Since you, O Tiresias, do not see this light, I will be to you an interpreter of things. Hither is Pentheus coming to the house in haste, the son of Echion, to whom I give power over the land. How fluttered he is! what strange thing will he say?

PENTHEUS. I happened to be at a distance from this land, and I hear of strange evils in this city, that the women have left our palace in mad-wandering Bacchic rites; and that they are rushing about in the shady mountains, honoring with dances this new God Bacchus, whoever he is; and that full goblets stand in the middle of their assemblies, and that flying each different ways into secrecy, they yield to the embraces of men, on pretence, indeed, as [being] worshiping Mænads; but that they consider Venus before Bacchus. As many then as I have taken, the servants keep them bound as to their hands in the public strong-holds, and as many as are absent I will hunt from the mountain, Ino, and Agave who bore me to Echion, and the mother of Actæon, I mean Autonoe; and having bound them in iron fetters, I will soon stop them from this ill-working revelry. And they say that some stranger has come hither, a juggler, a charmer, from the Lydian land, fragrant in hair with golden curls, florid, having in his eyes the graces of Venus, who days and nights is with them, alluring the young maidens with Bacchic mysteries—but if I catch him under this roof, I will stop him from making a noise with the thyrsus, and waving his hair, by cutting off his neck from his body. He says he is the God Bacchus, [He was once on a time sown in the thigh of Jove,[15]] who was burned in the flame of lightning, together with his mother, because she falsely claimed nuptials with Jove. Are not these things deserving of a terrible halter, for a stranger to insult us with these insults, whoever he be? But here is another marvel—I see Tiresias the soothsayer, in dappled deer-skins, and the father of my mother, most great absurdity, raging about with a thyrsus—I deprecate it, O father, seeing your old age destitute of sense; will you not dash away the ivy?[16] will you not, O father of my mother, put down your hand empty of the thyrsus? Have you persuaded him to this, O Tiresias? do you wish, introducing this new God among men, to examine birds and to receive rewards for fiery omens? If your hoary old age did not defend you, you should sit as a prisoner in the midst of the Bacchæ, for introducing these wicked rites; for where the joy of the grape-cluster is present at a feast of women, I no longer say any thing good of their mysteries.

CHOR. Alas for his impiety! O host, do you not reverence the Gods! and being son of Echion, do you disgrace your race and Cadmus, who sowed the earth-born crop?

TI. When any wise man takes a good occasion for his speech, it is not a great task to speak well; but you have a rapid tongue, as if wise, but in your words there is no wisdom; but a powerful man, when bold, and able to speak, is a bad citizen if he has not sense. And this new God, whom you ridicule, I am unable to express how great he will be in Greece. For, O young man, two things are first among men; Ceres, the goddess, and she is the earth, call her whichever name you will.[17] She nourishes mortals with dry food; but he who is come as a match to her, the son of Semele, has invented the liquid drink of the grape, and introduced it among mortals, which delivers miserable mortals from grief,[18] when they are filled with the stream of the vine; and gives sleep an oblivion of daily evils: nor is there any other medicine for troubles. He who is a God is poured out in libations to the Gods, that by his means men may have good things—and you laugh at him, as to how he was sewn up in the thigh of Jove; I will teach you that this is well—when Jove snatched him out of the lightning flame, and bore him, a young infant, up to Olympus, Juno wished to cast him down from heaven; but Jove had a counter contrivance, as being a God. Having broken a part of the air which surrounds the earth, he placed in it, giving him as a pledge, Bacchus, safe from Juno's enmity; and in time, mortals say, that he was nourished in the thigh of Jove; changing his name, because a God gave him formerly as a pledge to a Goddess, they having made agreement.[19] But this God is a prophet—for Bacchanal excitement and frenzy have much divination in them.[20] For when the God comes violent[21] into the body, he makes the frantic to foretell the future; and he also possesses some quality of Mars; for terror flutters sometimes an army under arms and in its ranks, before they touch the spear; and this also is a frenzy from Bacchus. Then you shall see him also on the Delphic rocks, bounding with torches along the double-pointed district, tossing about, and shaking the Bacchic branch, mighty through Greece. But be persuaded by me, O Pentheus; do not boast that sovereignty has power among men, nor, even if you think so, and your mind is disordered, believe that you are at all wise. But receive the God into the land, and sacrifice to him, and play the Bacchanal, and crown your head. Bacchus will not compel women to be modest[22] with regard to Venus, but in his nature modesty in all things is ever innate. This you must needs consider, for she who is modest will not be corrupted by being at Bacchanalian revels. Dost see? Thou rejoicest when many stand at thy gates, and the city extols the name of Pentheus; and he, I ween, is pleased, when honored. I, then, and Cadmus whom you laugh to scorn, will crown ourselves with ivy, and dance, a hoary pair; but still we must dance; and I will not contend against the Gods, persuaded by your words—for you rave most grievously; nor can you procure any cure from medicine, nor are you now afflicted beyond their power.[23]

CHOR. O old man, thou dost not shame Apollo by thy words, and honoring Bromius, the mighty God, thou art wise.

CAD. My son, well has Tiresias advised you; dwell with us, not away from the laws. For now you flit about, and though wise are wise in naught; for although this may not be a God, as you say, let it be said by you that he is; and tell a glorious falsehood, that Semele may seem to have borne a God, and that honor may redound to all our race. You see the hapless fate of Actæon,[24] whom his blood-thirsty hounds, whom he had reared up, tore to pieces in the meadows, having boasted that he was superior in the chase to Diana. This may you not suffer; come, that I may crown thy head with ivy, with us give honor to the God—

PEN. Do not bring your hand toward me; but departing, play the Bacchanal, and wipe not off your folly on me; but I will follow up with punishment this teacher of your madness; let some one go as quickly as possible, and going to his seat where he watches the birds, upset and overthrow it with levers, turning every thing upside down; and commit his crowns to the winds and storms; for doing this, I shall gnaw him most. And some of you going along the city, track out this effeminate stranger, who brings this new disease upon women, and pollutes our beds. And if you catch him, convey him hither bound; that meeting with a judgment of stoning he may die, having seen a bitter revelry of Bacchus in Thebes.

TI. O wretched man! how little knowest thou what thou sayest! You are mad now, and before you was out of your mind. Let us go, O Cadmus, and entreat the God, on behalf of him, savage though he be, and on behalf of the city, to do him no ill: but follow me with the ivy-clad staff, and try to support my body, and I will yours; for it would be shameful for two old men to fall down: but let that pass, for we must serve Bacchus, the son of Jove; but beware lest Pentheus bring grief into thy house, O Cadmus. I do not speak in prophecy, but judging from the state of things, for a foolish man says foolish things.

CHOR. O holy venerable Goddess! holy, who bearest thy golden pinions along the earth, hearest thou these words of Pentheus? Hearest thou his unholy insolence against Bromius, the son of Semele, the first deity of the Gods, at the banquets where the guests wear beautiful chaplets! who has this office, to join in dances, and to laugh with the flute, and to put an end to cares, when the juice of the grape comes at the feast of the Gods, and in the ivy-bearing banquets the goblet sheds sleep over man? Of unbridled mouths and lawless folly misery is the end, but the life of quiet and wisdom remains unshaken, and supports a house; for the heavenly powers are afar indeed, but still inhabiting the air, they behold the deeds of mortals. But cleverness[25] is not wisdom, nor is the thinking on things unfit for mortals. Life is short; and in it who, pursuing great things, would not enjoy the present? These are the manners of maniacs; and of ill-disposed men, in my opinion. Would that I could go to Cyprus, the island of Venus, where the Loves dwell, soothing the minds of mortals, and to Paphos, which the waters of a foreign river flowing with an hundred[26] mouths, fertilize without rain—and to the land of Pieria, where is the beautiful seat of the Muses, the holy hill of Olympus. Lead me thither, O Bromius, Bromius, O master thou of Bacchanals! There are the Graces, and there is Love, and there is it lawful for the Bacchæ to celebrate their orgies; the God, the son of Jove, delights in banquets, and loves Peace, giver of riches, the Goddess the nourisher of youths. And both to the rich and the poor[27] has she granted to enjoy an equal delight from wine, banishing grief; and he who does not care for these things, hates to lead a happy life by day and by friendly night—but it is wise[28] to keep away the mind and intellect proceeding from over-curious men; what the baser multitude thinks and adopts, that will I say.

SERVANT. Pentheus, we are here; having caught this prey, for which you sent us: nor have we gone in vain; but the beast was docile in our hands, nor did he withdraw his foot in flight, but yielded not unwillingly; nor did he [turn] pale nor change his wine-complexioned cheek, but laughing, allowed us to bind and lead him away; and remained still, making my work easy; and I for shame said, O stranger, I do not take you of my own will, but by order of Pentheus who sent me. And the Bacchæ whom you shut up, whom you carried off and bound in the chains of the public prison, they being set loose are escaped, and are dancing in the meadows, invoking Bromius as their God, and of their own accord the fetters were loosed from their feet, and the keys opened the doors without mortal hand, and full of many wonders is this man come to Thebes; but the rest must be thy care.

PEN. Take hold of him by the hands; for being in the toils, he is not so swift as to escape me: but in your body you are not ill-formed, O stranger, for women's purposes, on which account you have come to Thebes. For your hair is long, not through wrestling, scattered over your cheeks, full of desire, and you have a white skin from careful preparation; hunting after Venus by your beauty not exposed to strokes of the sun, but [kept] beneath the shade. First then tell me who thou art in family.

BAC. There is no boast; but this is easy to say; thou knowest by hearsay of the flowery Tmolus?

PEN. I know, [the hill] which surrounds the city of Sardis.

BAC. Thence am I; and Lydia is my country.

PEN. And whence do you bring these rites into Greece?

BAC. Bacchus persuaded us, the son of Jove.

PEN. Is Jove then one who begets new Gods?

BAC. No, but having married Semele here,—

PEN. Did he compel you by night, or in your sight [by day]?

BAC. Seeing me who saw him; and he gave me orgies.

PEN. And what appearance have these orgies?

BAC. It is unlawful for the uninitiated among mortals to know.

PEN. And have they any profit to those who sacrifice?

BAC. It is not lawful for you to hear, but they are worth knowing.

PEN. You have well coined this story, that I may wish to hear.

BAC. The orgies of the God hate him who works impiety.

PEN. For you say, forsooth, that you saw the God clearly what he was like?

BAC. As he chose; I did not order this.

PEN. This too you have well contrived, saying mere nonsense.

BAC. One may seem, speaking wisely to one ignorant, not to be wise.

PEN. And did you come hither first, bringing the God?

BAC. Every one of the barbarians celebrates these orgies.

PEN. [Ay,] for they are much less wise than Greeks.

BAC. In these things they are wiser, but their laws are different.

PEN. Do you practice these rites at night, or by day?

BAG. Most of them at night;[29] darkness conveys awe.

PEN. This is treacherous toward women, and unsound.

BAC. Even by day some may devise base things.

PEN. You must pay the penalty of your evil devices.

BAC. And you of your ignorance, being impious to the God.

PEN. How bold is Bacchus, and not unpracticed in speech.

BAC. Say what I must suffer, what ill wilt thou do me?

PEN. First I will cut off your delicate hair.

BAC. The hair is sacred, I cherish it for the God.[30]

PEN. Next yield up this thyrsus out of your hands.

BAC. Take it from me yourself, I bear it as the ensign of Bacchus.

PEN. And we will guard your body within in prison.

BAC. The God himself will release me when I wish.[31]

PEN. Ay, when you call him, standing among the Bacchæ.

BAC. Even now, being near, he sees what I suffer.

PEN. And where is he? for at least he is not apparent to my eyes.

BAC. Near me, but you being impious, see him not.

PEN. Seize him, he insults me and Thebes!

BAC. I warn you not to bind me: I in my senses command you not in your senses.

PEN. And I bid them to bind you, as being mightier than you.

BAC. You know not why you live, nor what you do, nor who you are.

PEN. Pentheus, son of Agave, and of my father Echion.

BAC. You are suited to be miserable according to your name.[32]

PEN. Begone! confine him near the stable of horses that he may behold dim darkness! There dance; and as for these women whom you bring with you, the accomplices in your wickedness, we will either sell them away, or stopping their hand from this noise and beating of skins, I will keep them as slaves at the loom.

BAC. I will go—for what is not right it is not right to suffer; but as a punishment for these insults Bacchus shall pursue you, who you say exists not; for, injuring us, you put him in bonds.

CHOR. O daughter of Achelous, venerable Dirce, happy virgin, for thou didst receive the infant of Jove in thy fountains when Jove who begat him saved him in his thigh from the immortal fire; uttering this shout: Go, O Dithyrambus, enter this my male womb, I will make you illustrious, O Bacchus, in Thebes, so that they shall call you by this name. But you, O happy Dirce, reject me having a garland-bearing company about you. Why dost thou reject me? Why dost thou avoid me? Yet, I swear by the clustering delights of the vine of Bacchus, yet shall you have a care for Bacchus. What rage, what rage does the earth-born race show, and Pentheus once descended from the dragon, whom the earth-born Echion begat, a fierce-faced monster, not a mortal man, but like a bloody giant, an enemy to the Gods, who will soon bind me, the handmaid of Bacchus, in halters, he already has within the

- 240 -

house my fellow-reveler, hidden in a dark prison. Dost thou behold this, O son of Jove, Bacchus, thy prophets in the dangers of restraint? Come, O thou of golden face, brandishing your thyrsus along Olympus, and restrain the insolence of the blood-thirsty man. Where art thou assembling thy bands of thyrsus-bearers, O Bacchus, is it near Nysa which nourishes wild beasts, or in the summits of Corycus?[33] or perhaps in the deep-wooded lairs of Olympus, where formerly Orpheus playing the lyre drew together the trees by his songs, collected the beasts of the fields; O happy Pieria, Evius respects you, and will come to lead the dance with revelings having crossed the swiftly-flowing Axius, he will bring the dancing Mænads, and [leaving] Lydia[34] the giver of wealth to mortals, and the father whom I have heard fertilizes the country renowned for horses with the fairest streams.

BAC. Io! hear ye, hear ye my song, Io Bacchæ! O Bacchæ!

CHOR. Who is here, who? from what quarter did the shout of Evius summon me?

BAC. Io, Io, I say again! I, the son of Semele, the son of Jove!

CHOR. Io! Io! Master, master! come now to our company. O Bromius! Bromius! Shake this place, O holy Earth![35] O! O! quickly will the palace of Pentheus be shaken in ruin—Bacchus is in the halls. Worship him. We worship him. Behold these stone buttresses shaken with their pillars. Bacchus will shout in the palace.

BAC. Light the burning fiery lamp; burn, burn the house of Pentheus.

SEM. Alas! Dost thou not behold the fire, nor perceive around the sacred tomb of Semele the flame which formerly the bolt-bearing thunder of Jupiter left?

SEM. Cast on the ground your trembling bodies, cast them down, O Mænads, for the king turning things upside down is coming to this palace, [Bacchus,] the son of Jupiter.

BAC. O barbarian women! have ye fallen to the ground thus stricken with fear? Ye have felt, it seems, Bacchus shaking the house of Pentheus; but lift up your bodies, and take courage, casting off fear from your flesh.

CHOR. O thou most mighty light to us of Evian Bacchic rites, how gladly do I see thee, being before alone and desolate!

BAC. Ye came to despair, when I was sent in, as about to fall into the dark prison of Pentheus.

CHOR. How not?—who was my guardian if you met with misfortune? but how were you liberated, having met with an impious man?

BAC. I delivered myself easily without trouble.

CHOR. And did he not bind your hands in links of chains?

BAC. In this too I mocked him; for, thinking to bind me, he neither touched nor handled me, but fed on hope; and finding a bull in the stable, where having taken me, he confined me, he cast halters round the knees of that, and the hoofs of its feet;[36] breathing out fury, stilling sweat from his body, gnashing his teeth in his lips. But I, being near, sitting quietly, looked on; and, in the mean time, Bacchus coming, shook the house, and kindled flame on the tomb of his mother; and he, when he saw it, thinking the house was burning, rushed to and fro, calling to the servants to bring water,[37] and every servant was at work toiling in vain; and letting go this labor, I having escaped, seizing a dark sword he rushes into the house, and then Bromius, as it seems to me, I speak my opinion, made an appearance in the palace, and he rushing toward it, rushed on and stabbed at the bright air,[38] as if slaying me; and besides this, Bacchus afflicts him with these other things; and threw down his house to the ground, and every thing was shivered in pieces, while he beheld my bitter chains; and from fatigue dropping his sword, he falls exhausted—for he being a man, dared to join battle with a God: and I quietly getting out of the house am come to you, not regarding Pentheus. But, as it seems to me, a shoe sounds in the house; he will soon come out in front of the house. What will he say after this? I shall easily bear him, even if he comes vaunting greatly, for it is the part of a wise man to practice prudent moderation.

PEN. I have suffered terrible things, the stranger has escaped me, who was lately coerced in bonds. Hollo! here is the man; what is this? how do you appear near my house, having come out?

BAC. Stay your foot; and substitute calm steps for anger.

PEN. How come you out, having escaped your chains?

BAC. Did I not say, or did you not hear, that some one would deliver me?

PEN. Who? for you are always introducing strange things.

BAC. He who produces the rich-clustering vine for mortals.

PEN. This is a fine reproach you charge on Bacchus; I order ye to close every tower all round.

BAC. Why? do not Gods pass over walls too?

PEN. You are wise, wise at least in all save what you should be wise in.

BAC. In what I most ought, in that I was born wise; but first learn, hearing his words who is come from the mountain to bring a message to you; but we will await you, we will not fly.

MESSENGER. Pentheus, ruler o'er this Theban land, I come, having left Cithæron, where never have the brilliant flakes of white snow fallen.[39]

PEN. But bringing what important news are you come?

MESS. Having seen the holy Bacchæ, who driven by madness have darted their fair feet from this land, have I come, wishing to tell you and the city, O king, what awful things they do, things beyond marvel; and I wish to hear whether in freedom of speech I shall tell you the matters there, or whether I shall repress my report, for I fear, O king, the hastiness of thy mind, and your keen temper, and too imperious disposition.[40]

PEN. Speak, as you shall be in all things blameless as far as I am concerned; for it is not meet to be wrath with the just; and in proportion as you speak worse things of the Bacchæ, so much the more will we punish this man who has taught these tricks to the women.

MESS. I was just now driving up to the heights the herd of calves, when the sun sends forth his rays warming the land, and I see three companies of dances of women, of one of which Autonoe was chief; of a second, thy mother, Agave; and Ino led the third dance; and they were all sleeping, relaxed in their bodies, some resting their locks against the leaves of pine, and some laying their heads at random on the leaves of oak in the ground, modestly, not, as you say, that, drunk with the goblet and the noise of the flute, they solitary hunt Venus through the wood. But thy mother standing in the midst of the Bacchæ, raised a shout, to wake their bodies from sleep, when she heard the lowing of the horned oxen; but they, casting off refreshing sleep from their eyes, started upright, a marvel to behold for their elegance, young, old, and virgins yet unyoked, And first they let loose their hair over their shoulders; and arranged their deer-skins, as many as had had the fastenings of their knots unloosed, and they girded the dappled hides with serpents licking their jaws—and some having in their arms a kid, or the wild whelps of wolves, gave them white milk, all those who, having lately had children, had breasts still full, having left their infants, and they put on their ivy chaplets, and garlands of oak and blossoming yew; and one having taken a thyrsus, struck it against a rock, whence a dewy stream of water springs out; another placed her wand on the ground, and then the God sent up a spring of wine. And as many as had craving for the white drink, scratching the earth with the tips of their fingers, obtained abundance of milk; and from the ivy thyrsus sweet streams of honey dropped, so that, had you been present, beholding these things, you would have approached with prayers that God whom you now blame. And we came together, herdsmen and shepherds, to reason with one another concerning this strange matter, what terrible things and worthy of marvel they do; and some one, a wanderer about the city, and practiced in speaking, said to us all, O ye who inhabit the holy downs of the mountains, will ye that we hunt out Agave, the mother of Pentheus, back from the revels, and do the king a pleasure? And he seemed to us to speak well, and hiding ourselves, we lay in ambush in the foliage of the thickets; and they, at the appointed hour, waved the thyrsus in their solemnities, calling on Bacchus with united voice, the son of Jove, Bromius; and the whole mountain and the beasts were in a revel; and nothing was unmoved by their running; and Agave was bounding near to me, and I sprang forth, as wishing to seize her, leaving my ambush where I was hidden. But she cried out, O my fleet hounds, we are hunted by these men; but follow me, follow, armed with thyrsi in your hands. We then flying, avoided the tearing of the Bacchæ, but they sprang on the heifers browsing the grass with unarmed hand, and you might see one rending asunder a fatted lowing calf, and others rent open cows, and you might see either ribs, or a cloven-footed hoof, tossed here and there, and hanging beneath the pine-trees the fragments were dripping, dabbled in gore; and the fierce bulls before showing their fury with their horns, were thrown to the ground, overpowered by myriads of maiden hands; and quicker were the coverings of flesh torn asunder by the royal maids than you could shut your eyes; and like birds raised in their course, they proceed along the level plain, which by the streams of the Asopus produce the fertile crop of the Thebans, and falling on Hysiæ and Erythræ,[41] which, are below Cithæron, they turned every thing upside down; they dragged children from the houses; and whatever they put on their shoulders stuck there without chains, and fell not on the dark plain, neither brass nor iron; and they bore fire on their tresses, and it burned not; but some from rage betook themselves to arms, being plundered by the Bacchæ, the sight of which was fearful to behold, O king! For their pointed spear was not made bloody, but the women hurling the thyrsi from their hands, wounded them, and turned their backs to flight, women [defeating] men; not without the aid of some God. And they went back again to whence they had departed, to the same fountains which the God had caused to spring up for them, and they washed off the blood; and the snakes with their tongues cleaned off the drops from their cheeks. Receive then, O master, this deity, whoever he be, in this city, since he is mighty in other respects, and they say this too of him, as I hear, that he has given mortals the vine which puts an end to grief,—for where wine exists not there is no longer Venus, nor any thing pleasant to men.[42]

CHOR. I fear to speak unshackled words to the king, but still they shall be spoken; Bacchus is inferior to none of the Gods.

PEN. Already like fire does this insolence of the Bacchæ extend thus near, a great reproach to the Greeks. But I must not hesitate; go to the Electra gates, bid all the shield-bearers and riders of swift-footed horses to assemble, and all who brandish the light shield, and twang with their hand the string of the bow, as we will make an attack upon the Bacchæ; but it is too much, if we are to suffer what we are suffering at the hands of women.

BAC. O Pentheus, you obey not at all hearing my words; but although suffering ill at your hands, still I say that you ought not to take up arms against a God, but to rest quiet; Bromius will not endure your moving the Bacchæ from their Evian mountains.

PEN. You shall not teach me; but be content,[43] having escaped from prison, or else I will again bring punishment upon you.

BAC. I would rather sacrifice to him than, being wrath, kick against the pricks; a mortal against a God.

PEN. I will sacrifice, making a great slaughter of the women, as they deserve, in the glens of Cithæron.

BAC. You will all fly, (and that will be shameful,) so as to yield your brazen shields to the thyrsi of the Bacchæ.

PEN. We are troubled with this impracticable stranger, who neither suffering nor doing will be silent.

BAC. My friend, there is still opportunity to arrange these things well.

PEN. By doing what? being a slave to my slaves?

BAC. I will bring the women here without arms.

PEN. Alas! you are contriving some trick against me.

BAC. Of what sort, if I wish to save you by my contrivances?

PEN. You have devised this together, that ye may have your revelings forever.

BAC. And indeed, know this, I agreed on it with the God.

PEN. Bring hither the arms! and do you cease to speak.

BAC. Hah! Do you wish to see them sitting on the mountains?

PEN. Very much, if I gave countless weight of gold for it.

BAC. But why? have you fallen into a great wish for this?

PEN. I should like to see them drunk grievously [for them].

BAC. Would you then gladly see what is grievous to you?

PEN. To be sure, sitting quietly under the pines.

BAC. But they will track you out, even though you come secretly.

PEN. But [I will come] openly, for you have said this well.

BAC. Shall I then guide you? and will you attempt the way?

PEN. Lead me as quickly as possible; for I do not grudge you the time.

BAC. Put on then linen garments on your body.

PEN. What then, shall I be reckoned among women, being a man?

BAC. Lest they slay you if you be seen there, being a man.

PEN. You say this well, and you have been long wise.

BAC. Bacchus taught me this wisdom.

PEN. How then can these things which you advise me be well done?

BAC. I will attire you, going into the house.

PEN. With what dress—a woman's? but shame possesses me.

BAC. Do you no longer wish to be a spectator of the Mænads?

PEN. But what attire do you bid me put on my body?

BAC. I will spread out your hair at length on your head.

PEN. And what is the next point of my equipment?

BAC. A garment down to your feet; and you shall have a turban on your head.

PEN. Shall you put any thing else on me besides this?

BAC. A thyrsus in your hand, and the dappled hide of a deer.

PEN. I can not wear a woman's dress.

BAC. But you will shed blood if you join battle with the Bacchæ.

PEN. True; we must first go and see.

BAC. That is wiser at least than to hunt evils with evils.

PEN. And how shall I go through the city escaping the notice of the Cadmeans?

BAC. We will go by deserted roads, and I will guide you.

PEN. Every thing is better than for the Bacchæ to mock me.

BAC. We will go into the house and consider what seems best.

PEN. We can do what we like; my part is completely prepared. Let us go; for either I will go bearing arms, or I will be guided by your counsels.

BAC. O women! the man is in the toils,[44] and he will come to the Bacchæ, where, dying, he will pay the penalty. Now, Bacchus, 'tis thine office, for you are not far off. Let us punish him; but first drive him out of his wits, inspiring vain frenzy, since, being in his right mind, he will not be willing to put on a female dress, but driving him out of his senses he will put it on; and I wish him to furnish laughter to the Thebans, being led in woman's guise through the city, after[45] his former threats, with which he was terrible. But I will go to fit on Pentheus the dress, which, having taken, he shall die, slain by his mother's hand. And he shall know Bacchus, the son of Jupiter, who is in fact to men at once the most terrible, and the mildest of deities.[46]

CHOR. Shall I move my white foot in the night-long dance, honoring Bacchus, exposing my neck to the dewy air, sporting like a fawn in the verdant delights of the mead, when it has escaped a fearful chase beyond the watch of the well-woven nets, (and the huntsman cheering hastens on the course of his hounds,) and with toil like the swift storm[47] rushes along the plain that skirts the river, exulting in the solitude apart from men, and in the thickets of the shady-foliaged wood? What is wisdom, what is a more glorious gift from the Gods among mortals than to hold one's hand on the heads of one's enemies? What is good is always pleasant; divine strength is roused with difficulty, but still is sure, and it chastises those mortals who honor folly, and do not extol the Gods in their insane mind. But the Gods cunningly conceal the long foot[48] of time, and hunt the impious man; for it is not right to determine or plan any thing beyond the laws: for it is a light expense to deem that that has power whatever is divine, and that what has been law for a long time has its origin in nature. What is wisdom, what is a more noble gift from the Gods among men, than to hold one's hand on the heads of one's enemies? what is honorable is always pleasant. Happy is he who has escaped from the wave of the sea, and arrived in harbor.[49] Happy, too, is he who has overcome his labors; and one surpasses another in different ways, in wealth and power. Still are there innumerable hopes to innumerable men, some result in wealth to mortals, and some fail, but I call him happy whose life is happy day by day.

BAC. You, who are eager to see what you ought not, and hasty to do a deed not of haste, I mean Pentheus, come forth before the house, be seen by me, having the costume of a woman, of a frantic Bacchant, as a spy upon your mother and her company! In appearance, you are like one of the daughters of Cadmus.

PEN. And indeed I think I see two suns,[50] and twin Thebes, and seven-gated city; and you seem to guide me, being like a bull, and horns seem to grow on your head. But were you ever a beast? for you look like a bull.

BAC. The God accompanies us, not propitious formerly, but now at truce with us. You see what you should see.

PEN. How do I look? Does not my standing seem like that of Ino, or of Agave, my mother?

BAC. I seem to see them as I behold you; but this lock of hair of yours is out of its place, not as I dressed it beneath the turban.

PEN. Moving it within doors backward and forward, and practicing Bacchic revelry, I disarranged it.

BAC. But we who ought to wait upon you will again rearrange it. But hold up your head.

PEN. Look, do you arrange it, for we depend on you.

BAC. And your girdle is loosened, and the fringes of your garments do not extend regularly round your legs.

PEN. They seem so to me, too, about the right foot at least; but on this side the robe sits well along the leg.

BAC. Will you not think me the first of your friends when, contrary to your expectation, you see the Bacchæ acting modestly?

PEN. But shall I be more like a Bacchant holding the thyrsus in my right hand, or in this?

BAC. You should [hold it in] your right hand, and raise it at the same time with your right foot; and I praise you for having changed your mind.

PEN. Could I bear on my shoulders the glens of Cithæron, Bacchæ and all?

BAC. You could if you were willing; but you had your mind unsound before; but now you have such as you ought.

PEN. Shall we bring levers, or shall I tear them up with my hands, putting my shoulder or arm under the summits?

BAC. No, lest you ruin the habitations of the Nymphs, and the seats of Pan where he plays his pipes.

PEN. You speak well,—it is not with strength we should conquer women; but I will hide my body among the pines.

BAC. Hide you the hiding in which you should be hidden, coming as a crafty spy on the Mænads.

PEN. And, indeed, I think to catch them in the thickets, like birds in the sweet nets of beds.

BAC. You go then as a watch for this very thing; and perhaps you will catch them, if you be not caught first.

PEN. Conduct me through the middle of the Theban land, for I am the only man of them who would dare these things.

BAC. You alone labor for this city, you alone; therefore the labors, which are meet,[51] await you. But follow me, I am your saving guide, some one else will guide you away from thence.

PEN. Yes, my mother.

BAC. Being remarkable among all.

PEN. For this purpose do I come.

BAC. You will depart being borne.[52]

PEN. You allude to my delicacy.

BAC. In the hands of your mother.

PEN. And wilt thou compel me to be effeminate?

BAC. Ay, with such effeminacy.

PEN. I lay mine hands to worthy things.

BAC. You are terrible, terrible: and you go to terrible sufferings; so that you shall find a renown reaching to heaven. Spread out, O Agave, your hands, and ye, her sister, daughters of Cadmus! I lead this young man to a mighty contest; and the conqueror shall be I and Bacchus! The rest the matter itself will show.

CHOR. Go, ye fleet hounds of madness, go to the mountain where the daughters of Cadmus hold their company; drive them raving against the frantic spy on the Mænads,—him in woman's attire. First shall his mother from some smooth rock or paling, behold him in ambush; and she will cry out to the Mænads: Who is this of the Cadmeans who has come to the mountain, the mountain, as a spy on us, who are on the mountain? Io Bacchæ! Who brought him forth? for he was not born of the blood of women: but, as to his race, he is either born of some lion, or of the Libyan Gorgons. Let manifest justice go forth, let it go with sword in hand, slaying the godless, lawless, unjust, earth-born offspring of Echion through the throat; who, with wicked mind and unjust rage about your orgies, O Bacchus, and those of thy mother,[53] with raving heart and mad disposition proceeds as about to overcome an invincible deity by force. To possess without pretext a wise understanding in respect to the Gods, and [a disposition] befitting mortals, is a life ever free from grief. I joyfully hunt after wisdom, if apart from envy, but the other conduct is evidently ever great throughout life, directing one rightly the livelong day, to reverence things honorable.[54] Appear as a bull, or a many-headed dragon, or a fiery lion, to be seen. Go, O Bacchus! cast a snare around the hunter of the Bacchæ, with a smiling face falling upon the deadly crowd of the Mænads.

MESS. O house, which wast formerly prosperous in Greece! house of the Sidonian old man, who sowed in the land the earth-born harvest of the dragon; how I lament for you, though a slave. But still the [calamities] of their masters are a grief to good servants.

CHOR. But what is the matter? Tellest thou any news from the Bacchæ?

MESS. Pentheus is dead, the son of his father Echion.

CHOR. O, king Bacchus! truly you appear a great God!

MESS. How sayest thou? Why do you say this? Do you, O woman, delight at my master being unfortunate?

CHOR. I, a foreigner, celebrate it in foreign strains; for no longer do I crouch in fear under my fetters.

MESS. But do you think Thebes thus void of men?

CHOR. Bacchus, Bacchus, not Thebes, has my allegiance.

MESS. You, indeed may be pardoned; still, O woman, it is not right to rejoice at the misfortunes which have been brought to pass.

CHOR. Tell me, say, by what fate is the wicked man doing wicked things dead, O man?

MESS. When having left Therapnæ of this Theban land, we crossed the streams of Asopus, we entered on the height of Cithæron, Pentheus and I, for I was following my master, and the stranger who was our guide in this search, for the sight: first, then, we sat down in a grassy vale, keeping our steps and tongues in silence, that we might see, not being seen; and there was a valley surrounded by precipices, irrigated with streams, shaded around with pines, where the Mænads were sitting employing their hands in pleasant labors, for some of them were again crowning the worn-out thyrsus, so as to make it leafy with ivy; and some, like horses quitting the painted yoke, shouted in reply to another a Bacchic melody. And the miserable Pentheus, not seeing the crowd of women, spake thus: O stranger, where we are standing, I can not come at the place where is the dance of the Mænads; but climbing a mound, or pine with lofty neck, I could well discern the shameful deeds of the Mænads. And on this I now see a strange deed of the stranger;

for seizing hold of the extreme lofty branch of a pine, he pulled it down, pulled it, pulled it to the dark earth, and it was bent like a bow, or as a curved wheel worked by a lathe describes a circle as it revolves, thus the stranger, pulling a mountain bough with his hands, bent it to the earth; doing no mortal's deed; and having placed Pentheus on the pine branches, he let it go upright through his hands steadily, taking care that it should not shake him off; and the pine stood firm upright to the sky, bearing on its back my master, sitting on it; and he was seen rather than saw the Mænads, for sitting on high he was apparent, as not before.[55] And one could no longer see the stranger, but there was a certain voice from the sky; Bacchus, as one might conjecture, shouted out: O youthful women, I bring you him who made you and me and my orgies a laughing-stock: but punish ye him. And at the same time he cried out, and sent forth to heaven and earth a light of holy fire;[56] and the air was silent, and the fair meadowed grove kept its leaves in silence, and you could not hear the voice of the beasts; but they not distinctly receiving the voice, stood upright, and cast their eyes around. And again he proclaimed his bidding. And when the daughters of Cadmus' recognized the distinct command of Bacchus, they rushed forth, having in the eager running of their feet a speed not less than that of a dove; his mother, Agave, and her kindred sisters, and all the Bacchæ: and frantic with the inspiration of the God, they bounded through the torrent-streaming valley, and the clefts. But when they saw my master sitting on the pine, first they threw at him handfuls of stones, striking his head, mounting on an opposite piled rock; and with pine branches some aimed, and some hurled their thyrsi through the air at Pentheus, wretched mark;[57] but they failed of their purpose; for he having a height too great for their eagerness, sat, wretched, destitute through perplexity. But at last thundering together[58] some oaken branches, they tore up the roots with levers not of iron; and when they could not accomplish the end of their labors, Agave said, Come, standing round in a circle, seize each a branch, O Mænads, that we may take the beast[59] who has climbed aloft, that he may not tell abroad the secret dances of the God. And they applied their innumerable hands to the pine, and tore it up from the ground; and sitting on high, Pentheus falls to the ground from on high, with numberless lamentations; for he knew that he was near to ill. And first his mother, as the priestess, began his slaughter, and falls upon him; but he threw the turban from his hair, that the wretched Agave, recognizing him, might not slay him; and touching her cheek, he says, I, indeed, O mother, am thy child,[60] Pentheus, whom you bore in the house of Echion; but pity me, O mother! and do not slay me, thy child, for my sins. But she, foaming and rolling her eyes every way, not thinking as she ought to think, was possessed by Bacchus, and he did not persuade her; and seizing his left hand with her hand, treading on the side of the unhappy man, she tore off his shoulder, not by [her own] strength, but the God gave facility to her hands; and Ino completed the work on the other side, tearing his flesh. And Autonoe and the whole crowd of the Bacchæ pressed on; and there was a noise of all together; he, indeed, groaning as much as he had life in him, and they shouted; and one bore his arm, another his foot, shoe and all; and his sides were bared by their tearings, and the whole band, with gory hands, tore to pieces the flesh of Pentheus: and his body lies in different places, part under the rugged rocks, part in the deep shade of the wood, not easy to be sought; and as to his miserable head, which his mother has taken in her hands, having fixed it on the top of a thyrsus, she is bearing it, like that of a savage lion, through the middle of Cithæron, leaving her sisters in the dances of the Mænads; and she goes along rejoicing in her unhappy prey, within these walls, calling upon Bacchus, her fellow-huntsman, her fellow-workman in the chase, of glorious victory, by which she wins a victory of tears. I, therefore, will depart out of the way of this calamity before Agave comes to the palace; but to be wise, and to reverence the Gods, this, I think, is the most honorable and wisest thing for mortals who adopt it.

CHOR. Let us dance in honor of Bacchus; let us raise a shout for what has befallen Pentheus, the descendant of the dragon, who assumed female attire and the wand with the beautiful thyrsus,—a certain death, having a bull[61] as his leader to calamity. Ye Cadmean Bacchants, ye have accomplished a glorious victory, illustrious, yet for woe and tears. It is a glorious contest to plunge one's dripping hand in the blood of one's son. But—for I see Agave, the mother of Pentheus, coining to the house with starting eyes; receive the revel of the Evian God.

AGAVE. O Asiatic Bacchæ!

CHOR. To what dost thou excite me? O!

AG. We bring from the mountains a fresh-culled wreathing[62] to the house, a blessed prey.

CHOR. I see it, and hail you as a fellow-reveler, O!

AG. I have caught him without a noose, a young lion, as you may see.

CHOR. From what desert?

AG. Cithæron.

CHOR. What did Cithæron?

AG. Slew him.

CHOR. Who was it who first smote him?

AG. The honor is mine. Happy Agave! We are renowned in our revels.

CHOR. Who else?

AG. Cadmus's.

CHOR. What of Cadmus?

AG. Descendants after me, after me laid hands on this beast.

CHOR. You are fortunate in this capture.

AG. Partake then of our feast.

CHOR. What shall I, unhappy, partake of?

AG. The whelp is young about the chin; he has just lost his soft-haired head-gear.[63]

AG. For it is beautiful as the mane of a wild beast.

CHOR. Bacchus, a wise huntsman, wisely hurried the Mænads against this beast.

CHOR. For the king is a huntsman.

AG. Do you praise?

CHOR. What? I do praise.

AG. But soon the Cadmeans.

CHOR. And thy son Pentheus his mother—

AG. —will praise, as having caught this lion-born prey.

CHOR. An excellent prey.

AG. Excellently.

CHOR. You rejoice.

AG. I rejoice greatly, having accomplished great and illustrious deeds for this land.

CHOR. Show now, O wretched woman, thy victorious booty to the citizens, which you have come bringing with you.

AG. O, ye who dwell in the fair-towered city of the Theban land, come ye, that ye may behold this prey, O daughters of Cadmus, of the wild beast which we have taken; not by the thonged javelins of the Thessalians, not by nets, but by the fingers, our white arms; then may we boast that we should in vain possess the instruments of the spear-makers; but we, with this hand, slew this beast, and tore its limbs asunder. Where is my aged father? let him come near; and where is my son Pentheus? let him take and raise the ascent of a wattled ladder against the house, that he may fasten to the triglyphs this head of the lion which I am present having caught.

CAD. Follow me, bearing the miserable burden of Pentheus; follow me, O servants, before the house; whose body here, laboring with immeasurable search, I bear, having found it in the defiles of Cithæron, torn to pieces, and finding nothing in the same place, lying in a thicket, difficult to be searched. For I heard from some one of the daring deeds of my daughters just as I came to the city within the walls, with the old Tiresias, concerning the Bacchæ; and having returned again to the mountain, I bring back my child, slain by the Mænads. And I saw Autonoe, who formerly bore Actæon to Aristæus, and Ino together, still mad in the thicket, unhappy creatures; but some one told me that Agave was coming hither with frantic foot; nor did I hear a false tale, for I behold her, an unhappy sight.

AG. O father! you may boast a great boast, that you of mortals have begotten by far the best daughters; I mean all, but particularly myself, who, leaving my shuttle at the loom, have come to greater things, to catch wild beasts with my hands. And having taken him, I bear in my arms, as you see, these spoils of my valor, that they may be suspended against your house. And do you, O father, receive them in your hands; and rejoicing over my successful capture, invite your friends to a feast; for you are blessed, blessed since I have done such deeds.

CAD. O, woe! and not to be seen, of those who have accomplished a slaughter not to be measured by wretched hands; having stricken down a glorious victim for the Gods, you invite Thebes and me to a banquet. Alas me, first for thy ills, then for mine own; how justly, but how severely, has king Bromius destroyed us, being one of our own family!

AG. How morose is old age in men! and sullen to the eye; would that my son may be fond of hunting, resembling the disposition of his mother, when with the Theban youths he would strive after the beasts—but he is only fit to contend with Gods. He is to be admonished, O father, by you and me, not to rejoice in clever evil. Where is he? Who will summon him hither to my sight, that he may see me, that happy woman?

CAD. Alas, alas! knowing what ye have done, ye will grieve a sad grief; but if forever ye remain in the condition in which ye are, not fortunate, you will seem not to be unfortunate.

AG. But what of these matters is not well, or what is grievous?

CAD. First cast your eyes up to this sky.

AG. Well; why do you bid me look at it?

CAD. Is it still the same, or think you it is changed?

AG. It is brighter than formerly, and more divine.

CAD. Is then this fluttering still present to your soul?

AG. I understand not your word; but I become somehow sobered, changing from my former mind.

CAD. Can you then hear any thing, and answer clearly?

AG. How I forget what we said before, O father!

CAD. To what house did you come in marriage?

AG. You gave me, as they say, to the sown Echion.

CAD. What son then was born in your house to your husband?

AG. Pentheus, by the association of myself and his father.

CAD. Whose head then have you in your arms?

AG. That of a lion, as those who hunted him said.

CAD. Look now rightly; short is the toil to see.

AG. Ah! what do I see? what is this I bear in my hands?

CAD. Look at it, and learn more clearly.

AG. I see the greatest grief, wretch that I am!

CAD. Does it seem to you to be like a lion?

AG. No: but I, wretched, hold the head of Pentheus.

CAD. Ay, much lamented before you recognized him.

AG. Who slew him, how came he into my hands?

CAD. O wretched truth, how unseasonably art thou come!

AG. Tell me, since delay causes a quivering at my heart.

CAD. You and your sisters slew him.

AG. And where did he die, in the house, or in what place?

CAD. Where formerly the dogs tore Actæon to pieces.

AG. But why did he, unhappy, go to Cithæron?

CAD. He went deriding the God and your Bacchic revels.

AG. But on what account did we go thither?

CAD. Ye were mad, and the whole city was frantic with Bacchus.[64]

AG. Bacchus undid us—now I perceive.

CAD. Being insulted with insolence—for ye thought him not a God.

AG. But the dear body of my child, O father!

CAD. I having with difficulty traced it, bring it all.

AG. What! rightly united in its joints? * * * *

AG. But what part had Pentheus in my folly?[65]

CAD. He was like you, not reverencing the God, therefore he joined all in one ruin, both ye and this one, so as to ruin the house, and me, who being childless of male children, see this branch of thy womb, O unhappy woman! most miserably and shamefully slain—whom the house respected; you, O child, who supported my house, born of my daughter, and was an object of fear to the city; and no one wished to insult the old man, seeing you; for he would have received a worthy punishment. But now I shall be cast out of my house dishonored, I, the mighty Cadmus, who sowed the Theban race, and reaped a most glorious crop; O dearest of men, for although no longer in being, still thou shalt be counted by me as dearest of my children; no longer touching this, my chin, with thy hand, addressing me, your mother's father, wilt thou embrace me, my son, saying, Who injures, who insults you, O father, who harasses your heart, being troublesome I say, that I may punish him who does you wrong, O father. But now I am miserable, and thou art wretched, and thy mother is pitiable, and thy relations are wretched. But if there is any one who despises the Gods, looking on this man's death, let him acknowledge the Gods.

CHOR. I grieve for thy state, O Cadmus; but your child has the punishment of your daughter, deserved indeed, but grievous to you.

AG. O father, for you see how I am changed ...

BAC ... changing, you shall become a dragon, and your wife becoming a beast, shall receive in exchange the form of a serpent, Harmonia, the daughter of Mars, whom you had, being a mortal. And as the oracle of Jove says, you shall drive with your wife a chariot of heifers, ruling over barbarians; and with an innumerable army you shall sack many cities; and when they plunder the temple of Apollo, they shall have a miserable return, but Mars shall defend you and Harmonia, and shall settle your life in the islands of the blessed. I say this, I, Bacchus, not born of a mortal father, but of Jove; and if ye had known how to be wise when ye would not, ye would have been happy, having the son of Jupiter for your ally.

CAD. Bacchus, we beseech thee, we have erred.

BAC. Ye have learned it too late; but when it behooved you, you knew it not.

CAD. I knew it, but you press on us too severely.

BAC. [Ay,] for I, being a God, was insulted by you.

CAD. It is not right for Gods to resemble mortals in anger.[66]

BAC. My father, Jove, long ago decreed this.

AG. Alas! a miserable banishment is the decree[67] [for us,] old man.

BAC. Why do ye then delay what must needs be?

CAD. O child, into what terrible evil have we come; both you wretched and your * * * * sisters,[68] and I miserable, shall go, an aged sojourner, to foreigners. Still it is foretold that I shall bring into Greece a motley barbarian army, and leading their spears, I, a dragon, shall lead the daughter of Mars, Harmonia, my wife, having the fierce nature of a dragon, to the altars and tombs of the Greeks. Nor shall I, wretched, rest from ills, nor even sailing over the Acheron below shall I be at rest.

AG. O, my father! and I being deprived of you shall be banished.

CAD. Why do you embrace me with your hands, O unhappy child, as a white swan does its exhausted[69] parent?

AG. For whither can I turn, cast out from my country?

CAD. I know not, my child; your father is a poor ally.

AG. Farewell, O house! farewell, O ancestral city! I leave you in misfortune a fugitive from my chamber.

CAD. Go then, my child, to the land of Aristæus * * * *.

AG. I bemoan thee, O father!

CAD. And I thee, my child; and I lament your sisters.

AG. Terribly indeed has king Bacchus brought this misery upon thy house.

BAC. [Ay,] for I have suffered terrible things from ye, having a name unhonored in Thebes.

AG. Farewell, my father.

CAD. And you farewell, O miserable daughter; yet you can not easily arrive at this.

AG. Lead me, O guides, where I may take my miserable sisters as the companions of my flight; and may I go where neither accursed Cithæron may see me, nor I may see Cithæron with my eyes, and where there is no memory of the thyrsus hallowed, but they may be a care to other Bacchæ.

CHOR. There are many forms of divine things; and the Gods bring to pass many in an unexpected manner: both what has been expected has not been accomplished, and God has found out a means for doing things unthought of. So, too, has this event turned out.[70]

NOTES ON THE BACCHÆ

[1] For illustrations of the fable of this play, compare Hyginus, Fab. clxxxiv., who evidently has a view to Euripides. Ovid, Metam. iii. fab. v. Oppian, Cyneg. iv. 241 sqq. Nonnus, 45, p. 765 sq. and 46, p. 783 sqq., some of whose imitations I shall mention in my notes. With the opening speech of this play compare the similar one of Venus in the Hippolytus.

[2] Cf. vs. 176; and for the musical instruments employed in the Bacchanalian rites, vs. 125 sqq. Oppian, Cyn. iv. 243. νεβρισι δ' αμφεβαλοντο, και εστεψαντο κορυμβοις, Εν σπεϊ, και περι παιδα το μυστικον ωρχησαντο. Τυμπανα δ' εκτυπεον, και κυμβαλα χερσι κροταινον. Compare Gorius, Monum. Libert. et Serv. ad Tab. vii. p. 15 sq.

[3] Such is the sense of συναψομαι, μαχην being understood. See Matthiæ.

[4] Drums and cymbals were invented by the Goddess in order to drown the cries of the infant Jupiter. Minutius Felix, xxi. "Avido patri subtrahitur infans ne voretur, et Corybantum cymbalis, ne pater audiat, vagitus initus eliditur" (read *audiat vagitus, tinnitus illi editur,* from the *vestigia* of Cod. Reg.). Cf. Lactant. i. 13.

[5] Cf. Homer, Hymn. in Cerer. 485. ολβιος, 'ος ταδ' οπωπεν επιχθονιων ανθρωπων: 'Ος δ' ατελης, 'ιερων 'οστ' αμμορος, ουποθ' 'ομοιων Αισαν εχει, φθιμενος περ, 'υπο ζοφωι ευρωεντι. See Ruhnken's note, and Valck. on Eur. Hippol.

[6] This passage is extremely difficult. Πλοκαμων seems decidedly corrupt. Reiske would read ποκαδων, Musgrave λευκοτριχων πλοκαμοις μαλλων. Elmsley would substitute προβατων, "si προβατον apud Euripidem exstaret." This seems the most probable view as yet expressed. The εριοστεπτοι κλαδοι are learnedly explained by Lobeck on Ag. p. 375 sq., quoted by Dindorf. The μαλλωσις or insertion of spots of party-colored fur upon the plain skin of animals, was a favorite ornament of the wealthy. The spots of ermine similarly used now are the clearest

illustration to which I can point. Lobeck also observes, "κατα βακχιουσθαι non bacchari significat, sed coronari."

[7] These ladies seem to have been rather undomestic in character, as Agave makes this very fact a boast, vs. 1236.

[8] Cf. Apollodor. l. i., § 3, interpp. ad Virg. G. iv. 152. Compare Porphyr. de Nymph. Antr. p. 262, ad. Holst. σπηλαια τοινυν και αντρα των παλαιοτατων πριν και ναους επινοησαι θεοις αφοσιουντων. και εν Κρητηι μεν κουρητων, Διϊ εν Αρκαδιαι δε, σεληνηι και Πανι Λυκειωι: και εν Ναξωι Διονυσωι. πανταχου δ' 'οπου τον Μιθραν εγνωσαν, δια σπηλαιου τον θεον 'ιλεουμενων. Cf. Moll. ad Longi Past. i. 2. p. 22 sq. ed. Boden.

[9] Cf. Virg. Æn. iv. 301, and Ritterh. on Oppian, Cyn. i, 24.

[10] Compare the epithet of Bacchus Ωμαδιος, Orph. Hymn. xxx. 5; l. 7, which has been wrongly explained by Gesner and Hermann. The true interpretation is given by Porphyr. de Abst. ii. 55, who states that human sacrifices were offered ωμαδιωι Διονυσωι the man being torn to pieces (διααπωντες).

[11] Persius i. 92. "et lynceus Mænas flexura corymbis Evion ingeminat, reparabilis assonat Echo." Euseb. Pr. Ev. ii. 3, derives the cry from Eve!

[12] I should read this line interrogatively, with Elmsley.

[13] Quoted by Gellius, xiii. 18.

[14] Elmsley would read μακρον το μελλον. Perhaps the true reading is μελλειν ακαιρον = *it is no season for delay*.

[15] The construction is so completely akward, that I almost feel inclined to consider this verse as an interpolation, with Dindorf.

[16] Compare Nonnus, 45. p. 765 4. Τειρεσιαν και Καδμον ατασθαλον ιαχε Πενθευς. Καδμε, τι μαργαινεις, τινι δαιμονι κωμον εγειρεις; Καδμε, μιαινομενης αποκατθεο κισσον εθειρης, Κατθεο και ναρθεκα νοοπλανεος Διονυσου.... Νηπιε Τειρεσια στεφανηφορε 'ριφον αηταις Σων πλοκαμων ταδε φυλλα νοθον στεφος, κ.τ.λ.

[17] Compare the opinion of Perseus in Cicero de N.D. i. 15, with Minutius Felix, xxi.

[18] Pseud-Orpheus Hymn. l. 6. παυσιπονον θνητοισι φανεις ακος.

[19] Dindorf truly says that this passage smacks rather of Proclus, than of Euripides, and I agree with him that its spuriousness is more than probable. Had Euripides designed an etymological

quibble, he would probably have made some allusion to Merus, a mountain of India, where Bacchus is said to have been brought up. See Curtius, viii. 10. "Sita est sub radicibus montis, quem Meron incolæ appellant. Inde Græci mentiendi traxere licentiam, Jovis femine liberum patrem esse celatum." Cf. Eustath. on Dionys. Perieg. 1159. Lucian. Dial. Deor. ix. and Hermann on Orph. Hymn. lii. 3.

[20] The gift of μαντικη was supposed to follow initiation, and is often joined with the rites of this deity. Philostratus, Heroic. p. 22, ed. Boiss. 'οτε δη και μαντικης σοφιας εμφορουνται, και το χρησμωδες αυταις προσβακχευει.

[21] Cf. Hippol. 443. Κυπρις γαρ ου φορητον ην πολλη 'ρυηι.

[22] I have followed Matthiæ's interpretation of this passage.

[23] See Hermann's note.

[24] The fate of Actæon is often joined with that of Pentheus.

[25] i.e. over-cunning in regard to religious matters. Cf. 200. ουδεν σοφιζομεσθα τοισι δαιμοσιν.

[26] Probably a mere hyperbole to denote great fruitfulness. See Elmsley.

[27] Cf. Hor. Od. iii. 21, 20.

[28] I follow Dindorf in reading σοφα δ', but am scarcely satisfied.

[29] Hence his epithet of Bacchus Νυκτελιος. See Herm. on Orph. Hymn. xlix. 3.

[30] See my note on Æsch. Choeph. 7.

[31] Cf Person Advers. p. 265. Hor. Ep. i. 16. 73 "Vir bonus et sapiens audebit dicere Pentheu, Rector Thebarum, quid me perferre patique Indignum coges? Adima bona, nempe pecus, rem, Lectos, argentum: tollas licet. In manicis et Compedibus sævo te sub custode tenebo. Ipse deus, simul atque volam, me solvet. Opinor, Hoc sentit: moriar. Mors ultima linea rerum est."

[32] Punning on πενθος, *grief.* Cf. Arist. Rhet. ii. 23, 29.

[33] i.e. of Parnassus. Elmsley (after Stanl. on Æsch. Eum. 22.) remarks that Κωρυκις πετρα means the Corycian cave in Parnassus, Κωρυκιαι κορυφαι, the heights of Parnassus.

[34] Hermann and Dindorf correct Λοιδιαν from Herodot. vii. 127.

[35] The earth and buildings were supposed to shake at the presence of a deity. Cf. Callimach. Hymn. Apol. sub init. Virg. Æn. iii. 90; vi. 255. For the present instance Nonnus, 45. p. 751.

ηδη δ' αυτοελικτος εσειετο Πενθεος αυλη,

ακλινεων σφαιρηδον αναϊσσουσα θεμεθλων,

και πολεων δεδονητο θορων ενοσιχθονι παλμωι

πηματος εσσομενοιο προαγγελος.

[36] The madness of Ajax led to a similar delusion. Cf. Soph. Aj. 56 sqq.

[37] Compare a fragment of Didymus apud Macrob. Sat. v. 18, who states Αχελωον παν ὑδωρ Ευριπιδης φησιν εν Ὑψιπυληι. See also comm. on Virg. Georg. i. 9.

[38] The reader of Scott will call to mind the fine description of Ireton lunging at the air, in a paroxysm of fanatic raving. See "Woodstock." So also Orestes in Iph. Taur. 296 sqq.

[39] ανεισαν, *solvuntur, liquescunt.* BRODEUS.

[40] Cf. Soph Ant. 243 sqq.

[41] These two cities were in ruins in the time of Pausanias. See ix. 3. p. 714, ed. Kuhn.

[42] Cf. Athenæus, p. 40. B. Terent. Eun. iv. 5. "Sine Cerere et Libero friget Venus." Apul Met. ii. p. 119, ed. Elm. "Ecce, inquam, Veneris hortator et armiger Liber advenit ultro," where see Pricæus.

[43] More literally, perhaps, "keep it and be thankful."

[44] Theocrit. i. 40. μεγα δικτυον ες βολον ῾ελκει.

[45] But εκ των απειλων conveys a notion of change = *instead of.*

[46] Elmsley remarks that ανθρωποισι belongs to both members of the sentence. I have therefore supplied. The sense may be illustrated from Hippol. 5 sq.

[47] See Matthiæ.

[48] i.e. step. This is ridiculed by Aristoph. Ran. 100, where the Scholiast quotes a similar example from our author's Alexandra.

[49] Compare Havercamp on Lucret. ii. sub init.

[50] Compare Virgil, Æn. iv. 469. "Et solem geminum, et duplices se ostendere Thebas." In the second passage of Clemens Alexandrinus quoted by Elmsley, γερων is probably a mistaken reference to Tiresias.

[51] An obscure hint at the impending fate of Pentheus. Nonnus has led the way to the catastrophe by a graphic description of Agave's dream. Dionys. 45. p. 751.

[52] φερομενος may mean either "carried in a litter," or "carried to burial." There is a somewhat similar play in the epigram of Ausonius, xxiii. "Mater Lacæna clypeo obarmans filium, cum hoc, inquit, aut in hoc, redi."

[53] Burges more rightly reads ματρος τε Γας. See Elmsley's note.

[54] As one must make some translation, I have done my best with this passage, which is, however, utterly unintelligible in Dindorf's text. A reference to his selection of notes will furnish some new readings, but, as a whole, quite unsatisfactory.

[55] Compare the parallel account in Nonnus, 46. p. 784.

[56] Alluded to by Oppian, Cyn. iv. 300. απτε σελας φλογερον πατρωιον, αν δ' ελεληξον Δαιαν, αταρτηρον δ' οπασον τισιν ωκα τυραννου. He then relates that Pentheus was transformed into a bull, the Mænads into panthers, who tore him to pieces.

[57] στοχος is either the aim itself, or the mark aimed at, as in this passage, and Xenoph. Ages. 1. 25.

[58] I have done my best with this extraordinary expression, of which Elmsley quotes another example from Archilochus Fragm. 36. Perhaps the notion of excessive rapidity is intended to be expressed.

[59] θηρ seems metaphorically said, as in Æsch. Eum. 47. Nonnus, 45. p. 784, 23. above, 922.

[60] Compare Nonnus, 46. p. 784.

Και τοτε μιν λιπε λυσσα νοοσφαλεος Διονυσου,

και προτερας φρενας εσχε το δευτερον: αμφι δε γαιηι

γειτονα ποτμον εχων κενυρην εφθεγξατο φωνην.

* * * * * *

μητερ εμη δυσμητερ απηνεος ιοχεο λυσσης,

θηρα ποθεν καλεεις με τον 'υιεα.

The whole passage is very elegant, and even pathetic.

[61] Alluding to the horns of Bacchus. Cf. Sidon. Apoll. Burg. Pontii Leontii, vs. 26, "Caput ardua rumpunt Cornua, et indigenam jaculantur fulminis ignem." See some whimsical reasons for this in Isidor. Origg viii. 2. Albricus de Deor. Nu. xix. But compare above, vs. 920. Και ταυρος 'ημιν προσθεν 'ηγεισθαι δοκεις, και σωι κερατε κρατι προσπεφυκεναι.

[62] Elmsley has rightly shown that 'ελικα could not of itself mean "a bull" or "heifer," although Homer has ειλιποδας 'ελικας βους. I have therefore followed Hermann, who remarks, "'ελιξ seems properly to be meant for the clusters of ivy with which the thyrsus was entwined. Hence Agave says that she adorns the thyrsus with a new-fashioned wreath, viz. the head of her son." Such language is, however, more like the proverbial boldness of Æschylus, than the even style of our poet.

[63] "κορυθα, ornamentum capitis, vix potest dubitari quin pro ipso capite posuerit." HERMANN. There is considerable variation in the manner in which the following lines are disposed.

[64] Or, "Bacchus-mad."

[65] I have marked a lacuna with Dindorf.

[66] See the commentators on Virg. Æn. i. 11. "Tantæne animis cœlestibus iræ?"

[67] After τλημονες φυγαι supply μενουσιν. ELMSLEY.

[68] A word is wanting to complete the verse.

[69] See Musgrave. Cranes are chiefly celebrated for parental affection.

[70] These verses are found at the ends of no less than four others of our author's plays, viz. Andromacha, Helen, Medea, and Alcestis.

THE HERACLIDÆ.

PERSONS REPRESENTED.

IOLAUS.

COPREUS.*

CHORUS.

DEMOPHOON.

APOLLO.

MACARIA.*

SERVANT.

ALCMENA.

MESSENGER.

EURYSTHEUS.

Note.—The names of Copreus and Macaria were wanting in the MSS., but have been supplied from the mythologists. See Elmsley on vss. 49 and 474.

THE ARGUMENT.

Iolaus, son of Iphiclus, and nephew of Hercules, whom he had joined in his expeditions during his youth, in his old age protected his sons. For the sons of Hercules having been driven out of every part of Greece by Eurystheus, he came with them to Athens; and, embracing the altars of the Gods, was safe, Demophoon being king of the city; and when Copreus, the herald of Eurystheus, wished to remove the suppliants, he prevented him. Upon this he departed, threatening war. Demophoon despised him; but hearing the oracles promise him victory if he sacrificed the most noble Athenian virgin to Ceres, he was grieved; not wishing to slay either his own daughter, or that of any citizen, for the sake of the suppliants. But Macaria, one of the daughters of Hercules, hearing of the prediction, willingly devoted herself. They honored her for her noble death, and, knowing that their enemies were at hand, went forth to battle. The play ends with their victory, and the capture of Eurystheus.

THE HERACLIDÆ.

IOLAUS.

This has long since been my established opinion, the just man is born for his neighbors; but he who has a mind bent upon gain is both useless to the city and disagreeable to deal with, but best for himself. And I know this, not having learned it by word of mouth; for I, through shame, and reverencing the ties of kindred, when it was in my power to dwell quietly in Argos, partook of more of Hercules' labors, while he was with us, than any one man besides:[1] and now that he dwells in heaven, keeping these his children under my wings, I preserve them, I myself being in want of safety. For since their father was removed from the earth, first Eurystheus wished to kill me, but I escaped; and my country indeed is no more, but my life is saved, and I wander in exile, migrating from one city to another. For, in addition to my other ills, Eurystheus has chosen to insult me with this insult; sending heralds whenever on earth he learns we are settled, he demands us, and drives us out of the land; alleging the city of Argos, one not paltry either to be friends with or to make an enemy, and himself too prospering as he is; but they seeing my weak state, and that these too are little, and bereaved of their sire, respecting the more powerful, drive us from the land. And I am banished, together with the banished children, and fare ill together with those who fare ill, loathing to desert them, lest some may say thus, Behold, now that the children have no father, Iolaus, their kinsman born, defends them not. But being bereft of all Greece, coming to Marathon and the country under the same rule, we sit suppliants at the altars of the Gods, that they may assist us; for it is said that the two sons of Theseus inhabit the territory of this land, of the race of Pandion, having received it by lot, being near akin to these children; on which account we have come this way to the frontiers of illustrious Athens. And by two aged people is this flight led, I, indeed, being alarmed about these children; and the female race of her son Alcmena preserves within this temple, clasping it in her arms; for we are ashamed that virgins should mingle with the mob, and stand at the altars. But Hyllus and his brothers, who are older, are seeking where there is a strong-hold that we may inhabit, if we be thrust forth from this land by force. O children, children! hither; take hold of my garments; I see the herald of Eurystheus coming hither toward us, by whom we are pursued as wanderers, deprived of every land.[2] O detested one, may you perish, and the man who sent you: how many evils indeed have you announced to the noble father of these children from that same mouth!

COPREUS. I suppose you think that this is a fine seat you are sitting in, and have come to a city which is an ally, thinking foolishly; for there is no one who will choose your useless power in preference to Eurystheus. Depart; why toilest thou thus? You must rise up and go to Argos, where punishment by stoning awaits you.

IOL. Not so, since the altar of the God will aid me, and the free land in which we tread.

COP. Do you wish to cause me trouble with this band?

IOL. Surely you will not drag me away, nor these children, seizing by force?

COP. You shall know; but you are not a good prophet in this.

IOL. This shall never happen, while I am alive.

COP. Depart; but I will lead these away, even though you be unwilling, considering them, wherever they may be, to belong to Eurystheus.

IOL. O ye who have dwelt in Athens a long time, defend us; for, being suppliants of Jove, the Presider over the Forum,[3] we are treated with violence, and our garlands are profaned, both a reproach to the city, and an insult to the Gods.

CHORUS. Hollo! hollo! what is this noise near the altar? what calamity will it straightway portend?

IOL. Behold me, a weak old man, thrown down on the plain; miserable that I am.

CHOR. By whose hand do you fall this unhappy fall?

* * * *

IOL. This man, O strangers, dishonoring your Gods, drags me violently from the altar of Jupiter.

CHOR. From what land, O old man, have you come hither to this people dwelling together in four cities?[4] or, have you come hither from across [the sea] with marine oar, having quitted the Eubœan shore?

IOL. O strangers, I am not accustomed to an islander's life, but we are come to your land from Mycenæ.

CHOR. What name, O old man, did the Mycenæan people call you?

IOL. Know that I am Iolaus, once the companion of Hercules; for this body is not unrenowned.

CHOR. I know, having heard of it before; but say whose youthful children you are leading in your hand.

IOL. These, O strangers, are the sons of Hercules, who are come as suppliants of you and the city.

CHOR. What do ye seek? or, tell me, is it wanting to have speech of the city?

IOL. Not to be given up, and not to go to Argos, being dragged from your Gods by force.

COP. But this will not be sufficient for your masters, who, having power over you, find you here.

CHOR. It is right, O stranger, to reverence the suppliants of the Gods, and not for you to leave by violent hands the habitations of the deities, for venerable Justice will not suffer this.

COP. Send now Eurystheus's subjects out of this land, and I will not use this hand violently.

CHOR. It is impious for a state to reject the suppliant prayer of strangers.

COP. But it is good to have one's foot out of trouble, being possessed of the better counsel.

CHOR. You should then have dared this, having spoken to the king of this land, but you should not drag strangers away from the Gods by force, if you respect a free land.

COP. But who is king of this country and city?

CHOR. Demophoon, the son of Theseus, of a noble father.

COP. With him, then, the contest of this argument had best be; all else is spoken in vain.

CHOR. And indeed hither he comes in haste, and Acamas, his brother, to hear these words.

DEMOPHOON. Since you, being an old man, have anticipated us, who are younger, in running to this hearth of Jove, say what hap collects this multitude here.

CHOR. These sons of Hercules sit here as suppliants, having crowned the altar, as you see. O king, and Iolaus, the faithful companion of their father.

DE. Why then did this chance occasion clamors?

CHOR. This man caused the noise, seeking to lead him by force from this hearth; and he tripped up the legs of the old man, so that I shed the tear for pity.

- 267 -

DE. And indeed he has a Grecian robe and style of dress; but these are the doings of a barbarian hand; it is for you then to tell me, and not to delay, leaving the confines of what land you are come hither.

COP. I am an Argive; for this you wish to learn: and I am willing to say why, and from whom, I am come. Eurystheus, the king of Mycenæ, sends me hither to lead away these men; and I have come, O stranger, having many just things at once to do and to say; for I being an Argive myself, lead away Argives, having them as fugitives from my country condemned to die by the laws there; and we have the right, managing our city ourselves by ourselves, to fix our own punishments: but they having come to the hearths of many others also, there also we have taken our stand on these same arguments, and no one has dared to bring evils upon himself. But either perceiving some folly in you, they have come hither, or in perplexity running the risk, whether it shall be or not. For surely they do not think that you alone are mad, in so great a portion of Greece as they have been over, so as to commiserate their foolish distresses. Come, compare the two; admitting them into your land, and suffering us to lead them away, what will you gain? Such things as these you may gain from us; you may add to this city the whole power of Argos, and all the might of Eurystheus; but if looking to the words and pitiable condition of these men, you are softened by them, the matter comes to the contest of the spear; for think not that we will give up this contest without steel. What then will you say? deprived of what lands, making war with the Tirynthians and Argives, and repelling them, with what allies, and on whose behalf will you bury the dead that fall? Surely you will obtain an evil report among the citizens, if, for the sake of an old man, a mere tomb,[5] one who is nothing, as one may say, and of these children, you will put your foot into a mess;[6] you will say, at best, that you shall find, at least, hope; and this too is at present much wanting; for these who are armed would fight but ill with Argives if they were grown up, if this encourages your mind, and there is much time in the mean while in which ye may be destroyed; but be persuaded by me, giving nothing, but permitting me to lead away my own, gain Mycenæ. And do not (as you are wont to do) suffer this, when it is in your power to choose the better friends, choose the worse.

CHOR. Who can decide what is right, or understand an argument, till he has clearly heard the statement of both?

IOL. O king, this exists in thy city; I am permitted in turn to speak and to hear, and no one will reject me before that, as in other places; but with this man we have nothing to do; for since nothing of Argos is any longer ours, (it having been decreed by a vote,) but we are exiled our country, how can this man justly lead us away as Mycenæans, whom they have driven from the land? for we are strangers; or else you decide that whoever is banished Argos is banished the boundaries of the Greeks. Surely not from Athens; they will not, for fear of the Argives, drive out the children of Hercules from their land; for it is not Trachis, nor the Achæan city, from whence you, not by justice, but bragging about Argos; just as you now speak, drove these men, sitting at the altars as suppliants; for if this shall be, and they ratify your words, I no longer know this Athens as free. But I know their disposition and nature; they will rather die; for among virtuous men, disgrace is considered before life. Enough of the city; for indeed it is an invidious thing to praise it too much; and often I know myself I have been oppressed at being overpraised: but I wish to say to you that it is necessary for you to save these men, since you are ruler over this land. Pittheus was son of Pelops and Æthra, daughter of Pittheus, and your father Theseus was born of her. And again I trace for you their descent: Hercules was son of Jupiter and Alcmena, and she was the child of the daughter of Pelops; so your father and theirs must be fellow-cousins. Thus you, O Demophoon, are related to them by birth; and, besides this connection, I will tell you for what you are bound to requite the children. For I say, I formerly, when shield-bearer to their father, sailed with Theseus after the belt,[7] the cause of much slaughter, and from the murky recesses of hell did he bring forth your father. All Greece bears witness to this; for which things they beseech you to return a kindness, and that they may not be yielded up, nor be driven from this land, torn from your Gods by violence; for this would be disgraceful to you by yourself, and an evil to the city,[8] that suppliant relations, wanderers—alas for the misery! look on them, look—should be dragged away by force. But I beseech you, and offer you suppliant garlands, by your hands and your chin, do not dishonor the children of Hercules, having received them in your power; but be thou a relation to them, be a friend, father, brother, master; for all these things are better than [for them] to fall into the power of the Argives.

CHOR. Hearing of these men's misfortunes, I pitied them, O king! and now particularly I have witnessed nobleness overcome by fortune; for these men, being sons of a noble father, are undeservedly unhappy.

DE. Three ways of misfortune urge me, O Iolaus, not to reject these suppliants. The greatest, Jupiter, at whose altars you sit, having this procession of youths with you; and my relationship to them, and because I am bound of old that they should fare well at my hands, in gratitude to their father; and the disgrace,[9] which one ought exceedingly to regard. For if I permitted this altar to be violated by force by a strange man, I shall not seem to inhabit a free country. But I fear to betray my suppliants to the Argives; and this is nearly as bad as the noose. But I wish you had come with better fortune; but still, even now, fear not that any one shall drag you and these children by force from this altar. And do thou, going to Argos, both tell this to Eurystheus; and besides that, if he has any charge against these strangers, he shall meet with justice; but you shall never drag away these men.

COP. Not if it be just, and I prevail in argument?

DE. And how can it be just to drag away a suppliant by force?

COP. This, then, is not disgraceful to me, but an injury to you.

DE. To me indeed, if I allow you to drag them away.

COP. But do you depart, and then will I drag them thence.

DE. You are stupid, thinking yourself wiser than a God.

COP. Hither it seems the wicked should fly.

DE. The seat of the Gods is a common defense to all.

COP. Perhaps this will not seem good to the Mycenæans.

DE. Am not I then master over those here?

COP. [Ay,] but not to injure them, if you are wise.

DE. Are ye hurt, if I do not defile the Gods?

COP. I do not wish you to have war with the Argives.

DE. I, too, am the same; but I will not let go of these men.

COP. At all events, taking possession of my own, I shall lead them away.

DE. Then you will not easily depart back to Argos.

COP. I shall soon see that by experience.

DE. You will touch them to your own injury, and that without delay.

CHOR. For God's sake, venture not to strike a herald!

DE. I will not, if the herald at least will learn to be wise.

CHOR. Depart thou; and do not you touch him, O king!

COP. I go; for the struggle of a single hand is powerless. But I will come, bringing hither many a brazen spear of Argive war; and ten thousand shield-bearers await me, and Eurystheus, the king himself, as general. And he waits, expecting news from hence, on the extreme confines of Alcathus; and, having heard of your insolence, he will make himself too well known to you, and to the citizens, and to this land, and to the trees; for in vain should we have so much youth in Argos, if we did not chastise you.

DE. Destruction on you! for I do not fear your Argos. But you are not likely, insulting me, to drag these men away from hence by force; for I possess this land, not being subject to that of Argos, but free.

CHOR. It is time to provide, before the army of the Argives approaches the borders. And very impetuous is the Mars of the Mycenæans, and on this account more than before; for it is the habit of all heralds to tower up what is twice as much. What do you not think he will say to his princes about what terrible things he has suffered, and how within a little he was losing his life.

IOL. There is not, to this man's children, a more glorious honor than to be sprung from a good and valiant father, and to marry from a good family; but I will not praise him who, overcome by desire, has mingled with the vulgar, to leave his children a reproach instead of pleasure; for noble birth wards off misfortune better than low descent; for we, having fallen into the extremity of evils, find these men friends and relations, who alone, in so large a country as Greece, have stood forward [on our behalf.] Give, O children, give them your right hand; and do ye give yours to the children, and draw near to them. O children, we have come to experience of our friends; and if you ever have a return to your country, and [again] possess the homes and honors of your father, always consider them your saviors and friends, and never lift the hostile spear against the land, remembering these things; but consider it the dearest city of all. And they are worthy that you should revere them, who have chosen to have so great a country and the Pelasgic people as enemies instead of us, though seeing us to be beggared wanderers; but still they have not given us up, nor driven us from their land. But I, living and dying, when I do die, with much praise, my friend, will extol you when I am in company with Theseus; and telling this, I will delight him, saying how well you received and aided the children of Hercules; and, being noble, you preserve through Greece your ancestral glory; and being born of noble parents, you are nowise inferior to your father, with but few others; for among many you may find perhaps but one who is not inferior to his father.[10]

CHOR. This land is ever willing to aid in a just cause those in difficulty; therefore it has borne numberless toils for its friends, and now I see this contest at hand.

DE. Thou hast spoken well; and I boast, old man, that their disposition is such that the kindness will be remembered. And I will make an assembly of the citizens, and draw them up so as to receive the army of the Mycenæans with a large force. First, I will send spies toward it, that it may not fall upon me by surprise: for in Argos every warrior is eager to run to assistance. And having collected the soothsayers, I will sacrifice. And do you go to my palace with the children, leaving the hearth of Jove, for there are those who, even if I be from home, will take care of you; go then, old man, to my palace.

IOL. I will not leave the altar; but we will sit here, as suppliants, waiting till the city is successful; and when you are well freed from this contest, we will go to thy palace. But we have Gods as allies not inferior to those of the

Argives, O king; for Juno, the wife of Jove, is their champion, but Minerva ours; and I say that this also tends to success, to have the best Gods, for Pallas will not endure to be conquered.

CHOR. If thou boastest greatly, others do not therefore care for thee the more, O stranger, coming from Argos; but with thy big words thou wilt not terrify my mind: may it not be so to the mighty Athens, with the beauteous dances. But both thou art foolish, the son of Sthenelus, king in Argos, who, coming to another city not less than Argos, being a stranger, seek by violence to lead away wanderers, suppliants of the Gods, and claiming the protection of my land, not yielding to our kings, nor saying any thing else that is just. How can this be thought well among the wise? Peace indeed pleases me; but, O foolish king, I tell thee, if thou comest to this city, thou wilt not thus obtain what thou thinkest for. You are not the only one who has a spear and a brazen shield; but, O lover of war, mayest thou not with the spear disturb my city dear to the Graces; but restrain thyself.

IOL. O my son, why comest thou, bringing solicitude to my eyes? Hast thou any news of the enemy? Do they delay, or are they at hand I or what do you hear? for I fear the word of the herald will in no wise be false, for their leader will come, having been fortunate in previous affairs, I clearly know, and with no moderate pride, against Athens; but Jove is the chastiser of over-arrogant thoughts.[11]

DE. The army of the Argives is coming, and Eurystheus the king. I have seen it myself;[12] for it behooves a man who says he knows well the duty of a general not to reconnoitre the enemy by means of messengers. He has not then, as yet, let loose his army on these plains, but, sitting on a lofty crag, he reconnoitres (I should tell thee this as a conjecture) to see by which way he shall now lead his expedition, and place it in a safe station in this land; and my preparations are already well arranged, and the city is in arms, and the victims stand ready for those Gods to whom they ought to be slain offered; and the city, by means of soothsayers, is preparing by sacrifices flight for the enemy and safety for the city.[13] And having collected together all the bards who proclaim oracles, I have tested the ancient oracles, both public and concealed, which might save this land; and in their other counsels many things are different; but one opinion of all is conspicuously the same, they command me to sacrifice to the daughter of Ceres a damsel who is of a noble father.[14] And I have indeed, as you see, such great good-will toward you, but I will neither slay my own child[15] nor compel any other of my citizens to do so unwillingly; and who is so mad of his own accord, as to give out of his hands his dearest children? And now you may see bitter meetings; some saying that it is right to aid foreign suppliants, and some blaming my folly; and if I do this, a civil war is at once prepared. This, then, do you consider, and devise how both you yourselves may be saved and this land, and I be not brought into ill odor with the citizens; for I have not absolute sovereignty, as over barbarians; but if I do just things, I shall receive just things.

CHOR. But does not the Goddess allow this city, although eager, to aid strangers?

IOL. O children, we are like sailors, who, fleeing from the fierce rage of the storm, have come close to land, and then, again, by gales from the land, have been driven again out to sea; thus also shall we be driven from this land, being already on shore, as if saved. Alas! why, O wretched hope, did you then delight me, not being about to perfect my joy? For his thoughts, in truth, are to be pardoned if he is not willing to slay the children of his citizens; and I acquiesce in their conduct here, if the Gods decree that I shall fare thus. My gratitude to you shall never perish. O children, I know not what to do with you: whither shall we turn? for who of the Gods has been uncrowned by us? and what bulwark of land have we not approached? We shall perish, my children, we shall be given up; and for myself I care nothing if it behooves me to die, except that, dying, I shall gratify my enemies; but I weep for and pity you, O children, and Alcmena, the aged mother of your father; O! unhappy art thou, because of thy long life; and miserable am I, having labored much in vain. It was our fate then, our fate, falling into the hands of an enemy, to leave life disgracefully and miserably. But do you know in what you may aid me? for all hope of their safety has not deserted me. Give me up to the Argives instead of them, O king, and so neither run any risk yourself, and let the children be saved for me; I must not love my own life, let it go; and above all, Eurystheus would like taking me, the ally of Hercules, to insult me; for he is a froward man; and the wise should pray to have enmity with a wise man, not with an ignorant disposition, for in that case one, even if unfortunate, may meet with much respect.

CHOR. O old man, do not now blame the city, perhaps it might be a gain to us; but still it would be an evil reproach that we betrayed strangers,

DE. You have spoken things noble indeed, but impossible; the king does not lead his army hither wanting you; for what profit were it to Eurystheus for an old man to die? but he wishes to slay these children; for noble youths, who remember their fathers' injuries, springing up, are terrible to enemies; all which he must needs foresee; but if you know any other more seasonable counsel, prepare it, since I am perplexed and full of fear, having heard the oracle.

MACARIA. O strangers, do not impute boldness to me because of my advances,[16] this I will beg first; for silence and modesty are best for a woman, and to remain quietly in-doors; but, having heard your lamentations, O Iolaus, I have come forth, not being commissioned to act as embassador for my race, but I am in some wise fit to do so; but chiefly do I care for these, my brothers: concerning myself I wish to ask whether, besides our former evils, any additional distress gnaws your mind?

IOL. O daughter, it is not a new thing that I justly have to praise you most of the children of Hercules; but our house having appeared to us to progress well, has again changed to perplexity, for this man says, that the deliverers of oracles order us to sacrifice not a bull or a heifer, but a virgin, who is of a noble father, if we and this city would exist. About this then we are perplexed, for this man says he will neither slay his own children nor those of any one else; and to me he says, not plainly indeed, but somehow or other, unless I can devise any remedy for this, that we must find some other land, but he himself wishes to preserve this country.

MAC. On this condition can we then be saved?

IOL. On this, being fortunate in other respects.

MAC. Fear not then any longer the hostile spear of the Argives; for I myself, old man, before I am commanded, am prepared to die, and to stand for slaughter; for what shall we say if the city thinks fit for our sakes to encounter a great danger, but we putting toils on others, avoid death when we can be saved? Not so, since this would be ridiculous for suppliants sitting at the shrines of the Gods to mourn, but being of such a sire as we are, to be seen to be cowards; how can this seem good! it were more noble, I think, (which may it never happen!) to fall into the hands of the enemy, this city being taken, and afterward, being born of a noble father, having suffered dreadful things, to see Hades none the less; but shall I wander about, driven from this land, and shall I not indeed be ashamed if any one says, "Why have ye come hither with your suppliant branches, yourselves being too fond of life! Depart from the land, for we will not aid cowards." But neither, indeed, if these die, and I myself am saved, have I any hope to fare well; for before now many have in this way betrayed their friends. For who would choose to have me, a solitary damsel, for his wife, or to raise children from me? therefore it is better to die than to have such an unworthy fate as this; and this may even be more seemly for some other, who is not illustrious as I. Lead me then where this body must needs die, and crown me and begin the rites, if you think fit, and conquer your enemies; for this life is ready for you, willing, and not unwilling; and I promise to die for these my brethren, and for myself; for not caring for life, I have found this most glorious thing to find, namely, to leave life gloriously.

CHOR. Alas! alas! what shall I say, hearing this noble speech of the maiden who is willing to die on behalf of her brothers? Who can utter more noble words than these I who of men can do [a greater deed?][17]

IOL. My child, your head comes from no other source, but thou, the seed of a divine mind, art sprung from Hercules.[18] I am not ashamed at your words, but I am grieved for your fortune; but how it may be more justly done, I will say: we must call hither all her sisters, and then let her who draws the lot die for her family; but it is not right for thee to die without casting lots.

MAC. I will not die, obtaining the lot by chance, for then there are no thanks [to me;]—speak it not, old man; but if you accept me, and are willing to use me willing, I readily give up my life to them, but not, being compelled.

IOL. Alas! this word of thine is again nobler than the former, and that other was most excellent; but you surpass daring by daring, and [good] words by good words. I do not bid you, nor do I forbid you, to die, my child; but you will benefit your brothers by dying.

MAC. Thou biddest wisely; fear not to partake of my pollution, but I shall die freely. But follow me, O old man; for I wish to die by your hand; and do you, being present, wrap my body in my garments, since I am going to the terror of sacrifice, because I am born of the father of whom I boast to be.

IOL. I could not be present at your death.

MAC. At least, then, entreat of him that I may die, not by the hands of men, but of women.

CHOR. It shall be so, O hapless virgin; since it were disgraceful to me too not to deck thee honorably on many accounts; both for your valiant spirit, and for justice' sake: but you are the most unhappy of all women that I have beheld with mine eyes; but, if thou wilt, depart, bespeaking a last address to these and to the old man.

MAC. Farewell, old man, farewell; and train up for me these children to be such as thyself, wise in all respects, nothing more, for they will suffice; and endeavor to save them, not being over-willing to die. We are your children; by your hands we were brought up, and behold see me yielding up my nuptial hour, dying for them. And ye, my company of brothers now present, may ye be happy, and may every thing be yours, for the sake of which my soul is sacrificed; and honor the old man, and the old woman in the house, Alcmena, the mother of my father, and these strangers. And if a release from troubles, and a return should ever be found for you through the Gods, remember to bury her who saves you, as is fitting; most honorably were just, for I was not wanting to you, but died for my race. This is my heir-loom instead of children and virginity, if indeed there be aught under the earth. May there indeed be nothing; for if we, mortals who die, are to have cares even there, I know not where one can turn, for to die is considered the greatest remedy for evils.

IOL. But, O you, who mightily surpass all women in courage, know that, both living and dying, you shall be most honored by us: and farewell; for I abhor to speak words of ill omen about the Goddess to whom your body is given as the first-fruits, the daughter of Ceres. O children, we are undone; my limbs are relaxed by grief; take me, and place me in my seat, veiling me there with these garments, O children; since neither am I pleased at these things which are done, and if the oracle were not fulfilled, life would be unbearable, for the ruin would be greater; but even this is a calamity.

CHOR. I say that no man is either happy or miserable but through the Gods, and that the same family does not always walk in good fortune, but different fates pursue it different ways; it is wont to make one from a lofty station insignificant, and makes the wanderer wealthy: but it is impossible to avoid what is fated; no one can repel it by wisdom, but he who is hasty without purpose will always have trouble; but do not thus bear the fortune sent by the Gods, falling down [in prayer,] and do not over-pain your mind with grief, for she hapless possesses a glorious portion of death on behalf of her brethren and her country; nor will an inglorious reputation among men await her: but virtue proceeds through toils. These things are worthy of her father, and worthy of her noble descent; and if you respect the deaths of the good, I share your feelings.

SERVANT. O children, hail! But at what distance from this place is the aged Iolaus and your father's mother?

IOL. We are here, such a presence as mine is.

SERV. On what account dost thou lie thus, and have an eye so downcast?

IOL. A domestic care has come upon me, by which I am constrained.

SERV. Raise now thyself, erect thy head.

IOL. I am an old man, and by no means strong.

SERV. But I am come, bearing to you a great joy.

IOL. And who art thou, where having met you, do I forget you?

SERV. I am a poor servant of Hyllus; do you not recognize me, seeing me?

IOL. O dearest one, dost thou then come as a savior to us from injury?

SERV. Surely; and moreover you are prosperous as to the present state of affairs.

IOL. O mother of a doughty son, I mean Alcmena, come forth, hear these most welcome words; for you have been long wasting away as to your soul in anxiety concerning those who have come hither, where they would ever arrive.[19]

ALCMENA. Wherefore has a mighty shout filled all this house? O Iolaus, does any herald, coming from Argos, again do you violence? my strength indeed is weak, but thus much you must know, O stranger, you shall never drag these away while I am living, else may I no longer be thought to be his mother; but if you touch them with your hand, you will have no honorable contest with two old people.

IOL. Be of good cheer, old woman; fear not, the herald is not come from Argos bearing hostile words.

ALC. Why then did you raise a shout, a messenger of fear?

IOL. To you, that you should approach near before this temple.

ALC. I do not understand this; for who is this man?

IOL. He announces that your son's son is come.

ALC. O! hail thou also for this news; but why and where[20] is he now absent putting his foot in this country? what calamity prevents him from appearing hither with you, and delighting my mind?

SERV. He is stationing and marshaling the army which he has come bringing.

ALC. I no longer understand this speech.

IOL. I do; but it is my business to inquire about this.

SERV. What then of what has been done do you wish to learn?

IOL. With how great a multitude of allies is he come?

SERV. With many; but I can say no other number.

IOL. The chiefs of the Athenians know, I suppose.

SERV. They do; and they occupy the left wing.[21]

IOL. Is then the army already armed as for the work?

SERV. Ay; and already the victims are led away from the ranks.

IOL. And how far distant is the Argive army?

SERV. So that the general can be distinctly seen.

IOL. Doing what? arraying the ranks of the enemies?

SERV. We conjectured this, for we did not hear him; but I will go; I should not like my masters to join battle with the enemy, deserted as far as my part is concerned.

IOL. And I will go with you; for we think the same things, being present to aid our friends as much as we can.

SERV. It is not your part to say a foolish word.

IOL. And not to share the sturdy battle with my friends!

SERV. One can not see a wound from an inactive hand.

IOL. But what, can not I too strike through a shield?

SERV. You might strike, but you yourself would fall first.

IOL. No one of the enemy will dare to behold me.

SERV. You have not, my good friend, the strength which once you had.

IOL. But I will fight with them who will not be the fewer in numbers.

SERV. You add but a slight weight to your friends.

IOL. Do not detain me who am prepared to act.

SERV. You are not able to do any thing, but you may perhaps be to advise.

IOL. You may say the rest, as I not staying to hear.

SERV. How then will you appear to the soldiers without arms?

IOL. There are within this palace arms taken in war, which I will use and restore if alive; but the God will not demand them back of me, if I fall; but go in, and taking them down from the pegs, bring me as quickly as possible the panoply of a warrior; for this is a disgraceful house-keeping, for some to fight, and some to remain behind through fear.

CHOR. Time does not depress your spirit, but it grows young again, but your body is weak: why dost thou toil in vain? which will harm you indeed, but profit our city but little; you should consider your age, and leave alone impossibilities, it can not be that you again should acquire youth.

ALC. Why are you, not being in your senses, about to leave me alone with my children?

IOL. For valor is the part of men; but it is your duty to take care of them.

ALC. But what if you die? how shall I be saved?

IOL. Your sons who are left will take care of your son.

ALC. But if they, which Heaven forbid, should meet with fate!

IOL. These strangers will not betray you, do not fear.

ALC. Such confidence indeed I have, nothing else.

IOL. And Jove, I well know, cares for your toils.

ALC. Alas! Jupiter shall never be reproached by me, but he himself knows whether he is just toward me.

SERV. You see now this panoply of arms; but you can not make too much haste[22] in arraying your body in them, as the contest is at hand, and, above all things, Mars hates those who delay; but if you fear the weight of arms, now then go forth unarmed,[23] and in the ranks be clad with this equipment, and I will carry it so far.

IOL. Thou hast said well; but bring the arms, having them close at hand, and put a spear in my hand, and support my left arm guiding my foot.

SERV. Is it right to lead a warrior like a child?

IOL. One must go safely for the sake of the omen.

SERV. Would you were able to do as much as you are willing.

IOL. Make haste, I shall suffer sadly if too late for the battle.

SERV. It is you who delay, and not I, seeming to do something.

IOL. Do you not see how my foot presses on?

SERV. I see you rather seeming to hasten than hastening.

IOL. You will not say so, when you behold me there.

SERV. Doing what? I wish I may see you successful.

IOL. Striking some of the enemy through the shield.

SERV. If indeed we get there; for that I have fears of.

IOL. Alas! O arm, would thou wert such an ally to me as I recollect you in your youth, when you ravaged Sparta with Hercules, how would I put Eurystheus to flight; since he is but a coward in abiding a spear. But in prosperity then is this too which is not right, a reputation for courage; for we think that he who is prosperous knows all things well.

CHOR. O earth, and moon that shinest through the night, and most brilliant rays of the God, that gave light to mortals, bring me news, and shout in heaven and at the queenly throne of the blue-eyed Minerva. I am about, on behalf of my country, on behalf of my house, having received suppliants I am about to cut through danger with the white steel. It is terrible that a city, prosperous as Mycenæ, and much praised for valor in war, should nourish secret[24] anger against my land; but it is evil too, O city, if we are to give up strangers at the bidding of Argos.[25] Jupiter is my ally, I fear not; Jupiter rightly has favor toward me. Never shall the Gods seem inferior to men in my opinion.[26] But, O venerable Goddess, for the soil of this land is thine, and the city of which you are mother, mistress, and guardian, lead away by some other way him who unjustly leads on this spear-brandishing host from Argos; for as far as my virtue is concerned, I do not deserve to be banished from these halls. For honor, with much sacrifice, is ever offered to you; nor does the waning[27] day of the month forget you, nor the songs of youths, nor the measures of dances; but on the lofty hill shouts resound in accordance with the beatings of the feet of virgins the livelong night.

SERV. O mistress, I bring news most concise for you to hear, and to myself most glorious; we have conquered our enemies, and trophies are set up bearing the panoply of your enemies.

ALC. O best beloved, this day has caused thee to be made free for this thy news; but from one disaster you do not yet free me, for I fear whether they be living to me whom I wish to be.

SERV. They live, the most glorious in the army.

ALC. Does not the aged Iolaus survive?

SERV. Surely, and having done most glorious deeds by help of the Gods.

ALC. But what? has he done any doughty act in the fight?

SERV. He has changed from an old into a young man again.

ALC. Thou tellest marvelous things, but first I wish you to relate the prosperous contest of your friends in battle.

SERV. One speech of mine shall tell you all this; for when stretching out [our ranks] face to face, we arrayed our armies against one another, Hyllus putting his foot out of his four-horse chariot, stood in the mid-space of the field;[28] and then said, O general, you are come from Argos, why leave we not this land alone? and you will do Mycenæ no harm, depriving it of one man; but you fighting alone with me alone, either killing me, lead away the children of Hercules, or dying, allow me to possess my ancestral prerogative and palaces. And the army gave praise; that the speech was well spoken for a termination of their toils, and in respect of courage. But he neither regarding those who had heard the speech, nor, although he was general, his [own character for] cowardice, ventured not to come near the warlike spear, but was most cowardly; and being such, he came to enslave the descendants of Hercules. Hyllus then returned again back to his ranks; but the soothsayers, when they saw that the affair could not be arranged by single combat of one shield, sacrificed, and delayed not, but let fall forth immediately the propitious slaughter of mortal throats; and some mounted chariots, and some concealed their sides under the sides of their shields; but the king of the Athenians gave to his army such orders as become a high-born man. "O fellow-citizens, now it behooves one to defend the land that has produced and cherished us."[29] And the other also besought his allies not to disgrace Argos and Mycenæ. But when the signal was sounded on a Tyrrhenian trumpet, and they joined battle with one another, what a clash of spears dost thou think sounded, how great a groaning and lamentation at the same time! And first the dashing on of the Argive spear broke us; then they again retreated; and next foot being interchanged with foot, and man standing against man, the battle waged fierce; and many fell; and there were two cries, O ye who [dwell in] Athens, O ye who sow the land of the Argives, will ye not avert disgrace from the city? And with difficulty doing every thing, not without toils did we put the Argive force to flight; and then the old man, seeing Hyllus rushing on, Iolaus, stretching forth his right hand, besought him to place him on the horse-chariot; and seizing the reins in his hands, he pressed hard upon the horses of Eurystheus. And what happened after this I must tell by having heard from others, I myself hitherto having seen all; for passing by the venerable hill of the divine Minerva of Pellene, seeing the chariot of Eurystheus, he prayed to Juno and Jupiter to be young for one day, and to work vengeance on his enemies. But you have a marvel to hear; for two stars standing on the horse-chariot, concealed the chariot in a dim cloud, the wiser men say it was thy son and Hebe; but he from the obscure darkness showed forth a youthful image of youthful arms. And the glorious Iolaus takes the four-horse chariot of Eurystheus at the Scironian rocks— and having bound his hands in fetters, he comes bringing as glorious first-fruits of victory, the general, him who before was prosperous; but by his present fortune he proclaims clearly to all mortals to learn not to envy him who seems prosperous, till one sees him dead, as fortune is but for the day.

CHOR. O Jupiter, thou turner to flight, now is it mine to behold a day free from dreadful fear.

ALC. O Jupiter, at length you have looked upon my miseries, but still I thank you for what has been done: and I, who formerly did not think that my son dwelt with the Gods, now clearly know it. O children, now indeed you shall be free from toils, and free from Eurystheus, who shall perish miserably; and ye shall see the city of your sire, and you shall tread on your inheritance of land; and ye shall sacrifice to your ancestral gods, debarred from whom ye have had, as strangers, a wandering miserable life. But devising what clever thing has Iolaus spared Eurystheus, so as not to slay him, tell me; for in my opinion this is not wise, having taken our enemies, not to exact punishment of them.

SERV. Having respect for you, that with your own eyes you may see him[30] defeated and subjected to your hand; not, indeed, of his own will, but he has bound him by force in constraint, for he was not willing to come alive into your sight and to be punished. But, O old woman, farewell, and remember for me what you first said when I began my tale. Make me free; and in such noble people as you the mouth ought to be free from falsehood.

- 281 -

CHOR. To me the dance is sweet, if there be the thrilling delight of the pipe at the feast; and may Venus be kind. And sweet it is to see the good fortune of friends who did not expect it before; for the fate which accomplishes gifts gives birth to many things; and Time, the son of Saturn. You have, O city, a just path, you should never be deprived of it, to honor the Gods; and he who bids you not do so, is near madness, such proofs as these being shown. God, in truth, evidently exhorts us, taking away the arrogance of the unjust forever. Your son, O old woman, is gone to heaven; he shuns the report of having descended to the realm of Pluto, being consumed as to his body in the terrible flame of fire; and he embraces the lovely bed of Hebe in the golden hall. O Hymen, you have honored two children of Jupiter. Many things agree with many; for in truth they say that Minerva was an ally of their father, and the city and people of that Goddess has saved them, and has restrained the insolence of a man to whom passion was before justice, through violence. May my mind and soul, never be insatiable.

MESS. O mistress, you see, but still it shall be said, we are come, bringing to you Eurystheus here, an unhoped-for sight, and one no less so for him to meet with, for he never expected to come into your hands when he went forth from Mycenæ with a much-toiling band of spearmen, proudly planning things much greater than his fortune, that he should destroy Athens; but the God changed his fortune, and made it contrary. Hyllus, therefore, and the good Iolaus, have set up a statue, in honor of their victory, of Jove, the putter to flight; and they send me to bring this man to you, wishing to delight your mind; for it is most delightful to see an enemy unfortunate, after having been fortunate.

ALC. O hateful thing, art thou come? has justice taken you at last? first then indeed turn hither your head toward me, and dare to look your enemies in the face; for now you are ruled, and you rule no more. Art thou he, for I wish to know, who chose, O wretch, much to insult my son, though no longer existing? For in what respect didst thou not dare to insult him? who led him, while alive, down to hell, and sent him forth, bidding him destroy hydras and lions? And I am silent concerning the other evils you contrived, for it would be a long story; and it did not satisfy you that he alone should endure these things, but you drove me also, and my children, out of all Greece, sitting as suppliants of the Gods, some old, and some still infants; but you found men and a city free, who feared you not. Thou needs must die miserably, and you shall gain every thing, for you ought to die not once only, having wrought many evil deeds.

MESS. It is not practicable for you to put him to death.[31]

ALC. In vain then have we taken him prisoner. But what law hinders him from dying?

MESS. It seems not so to the chiefs of this land.

ALC. What is this? not good to them to slay one's enemies?

MESS. Not any one whom they have taken alive in battle.

ALC. And did Hyllus endure this decision?

MESS. He could, I suppose, disobey this land![32]

ALC. He ought no longer to live, nor behold the light.

MESS. Then first he did wrong in not dying.

ALC. Then it is no longer right for him to be punished?[33]

MESS. There is no one who may put him to death.

ALC. I will. And yet I say that I am some one.

MESS. You will indeed have much blame if you do this.

ALC. I love this city. It can not be denied. But as for this man, since he has come into my power, there is no mortal who shall take him from me. For this, whoever will may call me bold, and thinking things too much for a woman; but this deed shall be done by me.

CHOR. It is a serious and excusable thing, O lady, for you to have hatred against this man, I well know it.

EURYSTHEUS. O woman, know plainly that I will not flatter you, nor say any thing else for my life, whence I may incur any imputation of cowardice. But not of my own accord did I undertake this strife—I knew that I was your cousin by birth, and a relation to your son Hercules; but whether I wished it or not, Juno, for it was a Goddess, forced me to toil through this ill. But when I took up enmity against him, and determined to contest this contest, I became a contriver of many evils, and sitting continually in council with myself, I brought forth many plans by night, how dispersing and slaying my enemies, I might dwell for the future not with fear, knowing that your son was not one of the many, but truly a man; for though he be mine enemy, yet shall he be well spoken of, as he was a doughty man. And when he was released [from life], did it not behoove me, being hated by these children, and knowing their father's hatred to me, to move every stone, slaying and banishing them, and contriving, that, doing such things, my own affairs would have been safe? You, therefore, had you obtained my fortunes, would not have oppressed with evils the hostile offspring of a hated lion, but would wisely have permitted them to live in Argos; you will persuade no one of this. Now then, since they did not destroy me then, when I was willing, by the laws of the Greeks I shall, if slain, bear pollution to my slayer; and the city, being wise, has let me go, having greater honor for God than for its enmity toward me. And to what you said you have heard a reply: and now you may call me at once suppliant and brave.[34] Thus is the case with me, I do not wish to die, but I should not be grieved at leaving life.

CHOR. I wish, O Alcmena, to advise you a little, to let go this man, since it seems so to the city.

ALC. But how, if he both die, and still we obey the city?

CHOR. That would be best; but how can that be?

ALC. I will teach you, easily; for having slain him, then I will give his corpse to those of his friends who come after him; for I will not deny his body to the earth, but he dying, shall satisfy my revenge.

EU. Slay me, I do not deprecate thy wrath. But this city indeed, since it has released me, and feared to slay me, I will present with an ancient oracle of Apollo, which, in time, will be of greater profit than you would expect; for ye will bury me when I am dead, where it is fated, before the temple of the divine virgin of Pallene; and being well disposed to you, and a protector to the city, I shall ever lie as a sojourner under the ground, but most hostile to their descendants when they come hither with much force, betraying this kindness: such strangers do ye now defend. How then did I, knowing this, come hither, and not respect the oracle of the God? Thinking Juno far more powerful than oracles, and that she would not betray me, [I did so.] But suffer neither libations nor blood to be poured on my tomb, for I will give them an evil return as a requital for these things; and ye shall have a double gain from me, I will both profit you and injure them by dying.

ALC. Why then do ye delay, if you are fated to accomplish safety to the city and to your descendants, to slay this man, hearing these things? for they show us the safest path. The man is an enemy, but he will profit us dying. Take him away, O servants; then having slain him, ye must give him to the dogs; for hope not thou, that living, thou shalt again banish me from my native land.

CHOR. These things seem good to me, proceed, O attendants, for every thing on our part shall be done completely for our sovereigns.

NOTES ON THE HERACLYDÆ

[1] Such seems to be the force of εις ανηρ.

[2] But the construction is probably αληται γης, (compare my note on Æsch. Eum. 63,) and απεστερημενοι is *bereaved, destitute.*

[3] Cf. Æsch. Eum. 973.

[4] i.e. Œnoe, Marathon, Probalinthus, and Tricorythus.

[5] Elmsley compares Med. 1209. τις τον γεροντα τυμβον ορθανον σεθεν τιθησι; so the Latins used "Silicernium." Cf. Fulgent. Expos. Serm. Ant. p. 171, ed. Munck.

[6] αντλος, sentina, bilge-water. See Elmsley.

[7] See Elmsley's note.

[8] See Dindorf, who repents of the reading in the text, and restores σοι γαρ τοδ' αισχρον χωρις εν πολει κακον. He, however, condemns this and the two next lines as spurious.

[9] i.e. if I neglect them.

[10] Cf. Hor. Od. iii. 6, 48. "Ætas parentum, pejor avis, tulit Nos nequiores, mox daturos Progeniem vitiosiorem."

[11] Cf. Soph. Ant. 127. Ζευς γαρ μεγαλης γλωσσης κομπους Ὑπερεχθαιρει.

[12] Cf. Æsch. Sept. c. Th. 40 sq., also Soph. Œd. T. 6 sqq.

[13] i.e. μαντεις κατ' αστυ θυηφολουσι. ELMSLEY.

[14] Pausanias, i. 32, states that the oracle expressly required that one of the descendants of Hercules should be devoted, and that upon this Macaria, his daughter by Deianira, voluntarily offered herself. Her name was afterward given to a fountain. Enripides probably omitted this fact, in order to place the noble-mindedness of Macaria in a stronger light. The curious reader may compare the similar sacrifices of Codrus, (Pausan. vii. 25. Vell. Patere. i. 4,) Menœceus, (Eur. Phœn. 1009, Statius Theb. x. 751 sqq.,) Chaon (Serv. on Virg. Æn. iii. 335). See also Lomeier de Lustrationibus, § xxii., where the whole subject is learnedly treated.

[15] Cf. Æsch. Ag. 206 sqq.

[16] I prefer understanding ʽενεκα εξοδων εμων with Elmsley, to Matthiæ's forced interpretation. Compare Med. 214 sqq.

[17] The cognate accusative to δρασειεν must be supplied from the context.

[18] There is some awkwardness in the construction. Perhaps if we read σπερμα, της θειας φρενος! πεφ. the sense will be improved.

[19] The construction is thus laid down by Elmsley: παλαι γαρ ωδινουσα [περι] των αφιγ. ψ. ετ. ει. ν. [αυτων] γενησεται. He remarks that νοστος often means "arrival," in the tragedians.

[20] See Matthiæ. I should, however, prefer παις for που, with Elmsley.

[21] κατα is understood, as in Thucyd. v. 67. ELMSLEY.

[22] See Alcest. 662, Iph. Taur. 245, and Elmsley's note on this passage.

[23] γυμνος, *expeditus*. As in agriculture it is applied to the husbandman who casts off his upper garment, so also in war it simply denotes being without armor.

[24] κευθειν.

[25] I have corrected κελευσμασιν Αργους, with Reiske and Dindorf.

[26] I have adopted Dindorf's correction, 'ησσονες παρ' εμοι θεοι φανουνται.

[27] i.e. the last, says Brodæus. But Elmsley prefers taking it for the νουμηνια or Kalends, with Musgrave.

[28] δορος, which is often used to signify *the fight*, is here somewhat boldly put for the arrangement of the battle.

[29] Cf. Æsch. Soph. c. Th. 14 sqq. Elmsley's notes on the whole of this spirited passage deserve to be consulted.

[30] κρατουντα can not be used passively. κλαιοντα is the conjecture of Orelli, approved by Dindorf. I have expressed the sense, not the text.

[31] See Musgrave's note (apud Dindorf). Tyrwhitt considers all the dramatis personæ wrongly assigned.

[32] Ironically spoken.

[33] There seems to be something wrong here.

[34] See Matthiæ, who explains it: "*me et supplicem*, qui mortem deprecetur, *et fortem*, qui mortem contemnat, *dicere licet.*"

IPHIGENIA IN AULIS.

PERSONS REPRESENTED.

AGAMEMNON.

OLD MAN.

MENELAUS.

ACHILLES.

MESSENGER.

ANOTHER MESSENGER.

IPHIGENIA.

CLYTÆMNESTRA.

CHORUS.

THE ARGUMENT.

When the Greeks were detained at Aulis by stress of weather, Calchas declared that they would never reach Troy unless the daughter of Agamemnon, Iphigenia, was sacrificed to Diana. Agamemnon sent for his daughter with this view, but repenting, he dispatched a messenger to prevent Clytæmnestra sending her. The messenger being intercepted by Menelaus, an altercation between the brother chieftains arose, during which Iphigenia, who had been tempted with the expectation of being wedded to Achilles, arrived with her mother. The latter, meeting with Achilles, discovered the deception, and Achilles swore to protect her. But Iphigenia, having determined to die nobly on behalf of the Greeks, was snatched away by the Goddess, and a stag substituted in her place. The Greeks were then enabled to set sail.

IPHIGENIA IN AULIS.

AGAMEMNON. Come before this dwelling, O aged man.

OLD MAN. I come. But what new thing dost thou meditate, king Agamemnon?

AG. You shall learn.[1]

OLD M. I hasten. My old age is very sleepless, and sits wakeful upon mine eyes.

AG. What star can this be that traverses this way?

OLD M. Sirius, flitting yet midway (between the heavens and the ocean,)[2] close to the seven Pleiads.

AG. No longer therefore is there the sound either of birds or of the sea, but silence of the winds reigns about this Euripus.

OLD M. But why art thou hastening without the tent, king Agamemnon? But still there is silence here by Aulis, and the guards of the fortifications are undisturbed. Let us go within.

AG. I envy thee, old man, and I envy that man who has passed through a life without danger, unknown, unglorious; but I less envy those in honor.

OLD M. And yet 'tis in this that the glory of life is.

AG. But this very glory is uncertain, for the love of popularity is pleasant indeed, but hurts when present. Sometimes the worship of the Gods not rightly conducted upturns one's life, and sometimes the many and dissatisfied opinions of men harass.

OLD M. I praise not these remarks in a chieftain. O Agamemnon, Atreus did not beget thee upon a condition of complete good fortune.[3] But thou needs must rejoice and grieve; [in turn,] for thou art a mortal born, and even though you wish it not, the will of the Gods will be thus. But thou, opening the light of a lamp, art both writing this letter, which thou still art carrying in thy hands, and again you blot out the same characters, and seal, and loose again, and cast the tablet to the ground, pouring abundant tears, and thou lackest naught of the unwonted things that tend to madness. Why art thou troubled, why art thou troubled? What new thing, what new thing [has happened] concerning thee, O king? Come, communicate discourse with me. But thou wilt speak to a good and faithful man, for to thy wife Tyndarus sent me once on a time, as a dower-gift, and disinterested companion.[4]

AG. To Leda, daughter of Thestias, were born three virgins, Phœbe, and Clytæmnestra my spouse, and Helen. Of this latter, the youths of Greece that were in the first state of prosperity came as suitors. But terrible threats of bloodshed[5] arose against one another, from whoever should not obtain the virgin. But the matter was difficult for her father Tyndarus, whether to give, or not to give [her in marriage,] and how he might best deal with the circumstances, when this occurred to him; that the suitors should join oaths and plight right hands with one another, and over burnt-offerings should enter into treaty, and bind themselves by this oath, "Of whomsoever the daughter of Tyndarus shall become wife, that they will join to assist him, if any one should depart from his house taking [her] with him, and excluding the possessor from his bed, and that they will make an expedition in arms, and sack the city [of the ravisher,] Greek or barbarian alike." But after they had pledged themselves, the old man Tyndarus somehow cleverly overreached them by a cunning plan. He permits his daughter to choose one of the suitors, toward whom the friendly gales of Venus might impel her. But she chose (whom would she had never taken!) Menelaus. And he who, according to the story told by men, once judged the Goddesses, coming from Phrygia to Lacedæmon, flowered in the vesture of his garments, and glittering with gold, barbarian finery, loving Helen who loved him, he stole and bore her away to the bull-stalls of Ida, having found Menelaus abroad. But he, goaded hastily[6] through Greece, calls to witness the old oath given to Tyndarus, that it behooves to assist the aggrieved. Henceforth the Greeks hastening with the spear, having taken their arms, come to this Aulis with its narrow straits, with ships and shields together, and accoutred with many horses and chariots. And they chose me general of the host, out of regard for Menelaus, being his brother forsooth. And would that some other than I had obtained the dignity. But when the army was assembled and levied, we sat, having no power of sailing, at Aulis. But Calchas the seer proclaimed to us, being at a loss, that we should sacrifice Iphigenia, whom I begat, to Diana, who inhabits this place, and that if we sacrificed her, we should have both our voyage, and the sacking of Troy, but that this should not befall us if we did not sacrifice her. But I hearing this in rousing proclamation, bade Talthybius dismiss the whole army, as I should never have the heart to slay my daughter. Upon this, indeed, my brother, alleging every kind of reasoning, persuaded me to dare the dreadful deed, and having written in the folds of a letter, I sent word to my wife to send her daughter as if to be married to Achilles, both enlarging on the dignity of the man, and asserting that he would not sail with the Greeks, unless a wife for him from among us should come to Phthia. For I had this means of persuading my wife, having made up a pretended match for the virgin. But we alone of the Greeks know how these matters are, Calchas, Ulysses, and Nestor. But the things which I then determined not well, I am now differently writing so as to be well, in this letter, which by the shadow of night thou beheldest me opening and closing, old man. But come, go thou, taking these letters, to Argos. But as to what the letter conceals in its folds, I will tell thee in words all that is written therein; for thou art faithful to my wife and house.

OLD M. Speak, and tell me, that with my tongue I may also say what agrees with your letter.

AG. (reading) "I send to thee, O germ of Leda, besides[7] my former dispatches, not to send thy daughter to the bay-like wing of Eubœa,[8] waveless Aulis. For we will delay the bridals of our daughter till another season."

OLD M. And how will not Achilles raise up his temper against thee and thy wife, showing great wrath at failing of his spouse? This also is terrible. Show what thou meanest.

AG. Achilles, furnishing the pretext, not the reality, knows not these nuptials, nor what we are doing; nor that I have professed to give my daughter into the nuptial chain of his arms by marriage.[9]

OLD M. Thou venturest terrible things, king Agamemnon, who, having promised thy daughter as wife to the son of the Goddess, dost lead her as a sacrifice on behalf of the Greeks.

AG. Ah me! I was out of my senses. Alas! And I am falling into calamity. But go, plying thy foot, yielding naught to old age.

OLD M. I hasten, O king.

AG. Do not thou either sit down by the woody fountains, nor repose in sleep.

OLD M. Speak good words.

AG. But every where as you pass the double track, look about, watching lest there escape thee a chariot passing with swift wheels, bearing my daughter hither to the ships of the Greeks.

OLD M. This shall be.

AG. And go out of the gates[10] quickly,† for if you meet with the procession,† again go forth, shake the reins, going to the temples reared by the Cyclops.

OLD M. But tell me, how, saying this, I shall obtain belief from thy daughter and wife.

AG. Preserve the seal, this which thou bearest on this letter. Go: morn, already dawning forth this light, grows white, and the fire of the sun's four steeds. Aid me in my toils. But no one of mortals is prosperous or blest to the last, for none hath yet been born free from pain.

CHORUS. I came to the sands of the shore of marine Aulis, having sailed through the waves of Euripus, quitting Chalcis with its narrow strait, my city, the nurse of the sea-neighboring waters[11] of renowned Arethusa, in order that I might behold the army of the Greeks, and the ship-conveying oars of the Grecian youths, whom against Troy in a thousand ships of fir, our husbands say that yellow-haired Menelaus and Agamemnon of noble birth, are leading in quest of Helen,[12] whom the herdsman Paris bore from reed-nourishing Eurotas, a gift of Venus, when at the fountain dews Venus held contest, contest respecting beauty with Juno and Pallas. But I came swiftly through the wood of Diana with its many sacrifices, making my cheek red with youthful modesty, wishing to behold the defense of the shield, and the arm-bearing tents[13] of the Greeks, and the crowd of steeds. But I saw the two Ajaces companions, the son of Oileus, and the son of Telamon, the glory of Salamis, and Protesilaus and Palamedes, whom the daughter of Neptune bore, diverting themselves[14] with the complicated figures of draughts, and Diomede rejoicing in the pleasures of the disk, and by them Merione, the blossom of Mars, a marvel to mortals, and the son of Laertes from the mountains of the isle, and with them Nireus, fairest of the Greeks, and Achilles, tempest-like in the course, fleet as the winds, whom Thetis bore, and Chiron trained up, I beheld him on the shore, coursing in arms along the shingles. And he toiled through a contest of feet, running against a chariot of four steeds for victory. But the charioteer cried out, Eumelus, the grandson of Pheres,[15] whose most beauteous steeds I beheld, decked out with gold-tricked bits, hurried on by the lash, the middle ones in yoke dappled with white-spotted hair, but those outside, in loose harness, running contrariwise in the bendings of the course, bays, with dappled skins under their legs with solid hoofs. Close by which Pelides was running in arms, by the orb and wheels of the chariot.[16] And I came to the multitude of ships, a sight not to be described, that I might satiate the sight of my woman's eyes, a sweet delight. And at the right horn [of the fleet] was the Phthiotic army of the Myrmidons, with fifty valiant ships. And in golden effigies the Nereid Goddesses stood on the summit of the poops, the standard of the host of Achilles. And next to these there stood the Argive ships, with equal number of oars, of which [Euryalus] the grandson of Mecisteus was general, whom his father Talaus trains up, and Sthenelus son of Capaneus. But [Acamas] son of Theseus, leading sixty ships from Athens, kept station, having the Goddess Pallas placed[17] in her equestrian winged chariot, a prosperous sign to sailors. But I beheld the armament of the Bœotians, fifty sea-bound ships, with signs at the figure-heads, and their sign was Cadmus, holding a golden dragon, at the beaks of the ships, and Leitus the earth-born was leader of the naval armament, and [I beheld] those from the Phocian land. But the son of

Oileus, leading an equal number of Locrian ships, came, having left the Thronian city. But from Cyclopian Mycenæ the son of Atreus sent the assembled mariners of a hundred ships. And with him was Adrastus, as friend with friend, in order that Greece might wreak vengeance on those who fled their homes, for the sake of barbarian nuptials. But from Pylos we beheld on the poops of Gerenian Nestor, a sign bull-footed to view, his neighbor Alpheus. But there were twelve beaks of Ænian ships, which king Gyneus led, and near these again the chieftains of Elis, whom all the people named Epeians, and o'er these Eurytus had power. But the white-oared Taphian host * * * * led,[18] which Meges ruled, the offspring of Phyleus, leaving the island Echinades, inaccessible to sailors. And Ajax, the foster-child of Salamis, joined the right horn to the left, to which he was stationed nearest, joining them with his furthermost ships, with twelve most swift vessels, as I heard, and beheld the naval people. To which if any one add the barbarian barks, * * * * it will not obtain a return. * * * * Where I beheld the naval expedition, but hearing other things at home I preserve remembrance of the assembled army.

OLD M. Menelaus, thou art daring dreadful deeds thou shouldst not dare.

MENELAUS. Away with thee! thou art too faithful to thy masters.

OLD M. An honorable rebuke thou hast rebuked me with!

MEN. To thy cost shall it be, if thou dost that thou shouldst not do.

OLD M. You have no right to open the letter which I was carrying.

MEN. Nor shouldst thou bear ills to all the Greeks.

OLD M. Contest this point with others, but give up this [letter] to me.

MEN. I will not let it go.

OLD M. Nor will I let it go.

MEN. Then quickly with my sceptre will I make thine head bloody.

OLD M. But glorious it is to die for one's masters.

MEN. Let go. Being a slave, thou speakest too many words.

OLD M. O master, I am wronged, and this man, having snatched thy letter out of my hands, O Agamemnon, is unwilling to act rightly.

MEN. Ah! what is this tumult and disorder of words?

OLD M. My words, not his, are fittest to speak.[19]

AG. But wherefore, Menelaus, dost thou come to strife with this man and art dragging him by force?

MEN. Look at me, that I may take this commencement of my speech.

AG. What, shall I through fear not open mine eyelids, being born of Atreus?

MEN. Seest thou this letter, the minister of writings most vile?

AG. I see it, and do thou first let it go from thy hands.

MEN. Not, at least, before I show to the Greeks what is written therein.

AG. What, knowest thou what 'tis unseasonable thou shouldst know, having broken the seal?

MEN. Ay, so as to pain thee, having unfolded the ills thou hast wrought privily.

AG. But where didst thou obtain it? O Gods, for thy shameless heart!

MEN. Expecting thy daughter from Argos, whether she will come to the army.

AG. What behooves thee to keep watch upon my affairs? Is not this the act of a shameless man?

MEN. Because the will [to do so] teased me, and I am not born thy slave.

AG. Is it not dreadful? Shall I not be suffered to be master of my own family?

MEN. For thou thinkest inconsistently, now one thing, before another, another thing presently.

AG. Well hast thou talked evil. Hateful is a too clever tongue.[20]

MEN. But an unstable mind is an unjust thing to possess, and not clear[21] for friends. I wish to expostulate with thee, but do not thou in wrath turn away from the truth, nor will I speak overlong. Thou knowest when thou wast making interest to be leader of the Greeks against Troy—in seeming indeed not wishing it, but wishing it in will—how humble thou wast, taking hold of every right hand, and keeping open doors to any of the people that wished, and giving audience to all in turn even if one wished it not, seeking by manners to purchase popularity among the multitude. But when you obtained the power, changing to different manners, you were no longer the same friend as before to your old friends, difficult of access,[22] and rarely within doors. But it behooves not a man who has met with great fortune to change his manners, but then chiefly to be firm toward his friends, when he is best able to benefit them, being prosperous. I have first gone over these charges against thee, in which I first found thee base. But when thou afterward camest into Aulis and to the army of all the Greeks, thou wast naught, but wast in stupefaction at the fortune which then befell us from the Gods, lacking a favorable breeze for the journey. But the Greeks demanded that you should dismiss the ships, and not toil vainly at Aulis. But how cheerless and distressed a countenance you wore, because you were not able to land your army at Priam's land, having a thousand ships under command.[23] And thou besoughtest me, "What shall I do?" "But what resource shall I find from whence?" so that thou mightest not lose an ill renown, being deprived of the command. And then, when Calchas o'er the victims said that thou must sacrifice thy daughter to Diana, and that there would [then] be means of sailing for the Greeks, delighted in heart, you gladly promised to sacrifice your child, and of your own accord, not by compulsion—do not say so—you send to your wife to convoy your daughter hither, on a pretext of being wedded to Achilles. And then changing [your mind] you are caught altering to other writings, to the effect that you will not now be the slayer of your daughter. Very pretty, forsooth! This is the same air which heard these very protestations from thee. But innumerable men experience this in their affairs; they persevere in labor when in power,[24] and then make a bad result, sometimes through the foolish mind of the citizens, but sometimes with reason, themselves becoming incapable of preserving the state, I indeed chiefly groan for hapless Greece, who, wishing to work some doughty deed against these good-for-nothing barbarians, will let them, laughing at us, slip through her hands, on account of thee and thy daughter. I would not make any one ruler of the land for the sake of necessity,[25] nor chieftain of armed men. It behooves the general of the state to possess sense, for every man is a ruler who possesses sense.

CHOR. 'Tis dreadful for words and strife to happen between brothers, when they fall into dispute.

AG. I wish to address thee in evil terms, but mildly,[26] in brief, not uplifting mine eyelids too much aloft through insolence, but moderately, as being my brother. For a good man is wont to show respect [to others.] Tell me, why dost thou burst forth thus violently, having thy face suffused with rage? Who wrongs thee? What lackest thou? Wouldst fain gain a good wife! I can not supply thee, for thou didst ill rule over the one you possessed. Must I therefore pay the penalty of your mismanagement, who have made no mistake? Or does my ambition annoy thee? But wouldst thou fain hold in thine arms a fair woman, forgetting discretion and honor? Evil pleasures belong to an evil man. But if I, having before resolved ill, have changed to good counsel, am I mad? Rather art thou [mad,] who, having lost a bad wife, desirest to recover her, when God has well prospered thy fortune. The nuptial-craving suitors in their folly swore the oath to Tyndarus, but hope, I ween, was their God, and wrought this more than thyself and thy strength. Whom taking[27] make thou the expedition, but I think thou wilt know [that it is] through the folly of their hearts, for the divinity is not ignorant, but is capable of discerning oaths ill plighted and perforce. But I will not slay my children, so that thy state will in justice be well, revenge upon the worst of wives, but nights and days will waste me away in tears, having wrought lawless, unjust deeds against the children whom I begat. These words are briefly spoken to thee, both plain and easy, but if thou art unwilling to be wise, I will arrange my own affairs well.

CHOR. These words are different from those before spoken, but they are to a good effect, that the children be spared.

MEN. Alas! alas! have I then wretched no friends?

AG. [Yes, you have,] at least, if you do not wish to ruin your friends.

MEN. But how will you show that you are born of the same sire with me?

AG. I am born to be wise with you, not foolish.[28]

MEN. It behooves friends to grieve in common with friends.

AG. Admonish me by well doing, not by paining me.

MEN. Dost thou not then think fit to toil through this with Greece?

AG. But Greece, with thee, is sickening through some deity.

MEN. Vaunt then on thy sceptre, having betrayed thy brother. But I will seek some other schemes, and other friends.

[Enter a Messenger.[29]]

MESSENGER. O Agamemnon, king of all the Greeks, I am come, bringing thy daughter to thee, whom thou didst name Iphigenia in thy palace. But her mother follows, the person of thy [wife] Clytæmnestra, and the boy Orestes, that thou mayest be pleased at the sight, being away from thine home a long season. But as they have come a long way, they and their mares are refreshing their female feet by the fair-flowing fountain, and we let loose the mares in a grassy meadow, that they might taste fodder. But I am come before them to prepare you [for their reception,] for a swift report passed through the army, that thy daughter had arrived. And all the multitude comes out hastily to the spectacle, that they may behold thy child. For prosperous men are renowned and conspicuous among all mortals. And they say, "Is there a marriage on foot? or what is going on?" Or, "Has king Agamemnon, having a yearning after his daughter, brought his child hither?" But from some you would have heard this: "They are initiating[30] the damsel in honor of Artemis, queen of Aulis, who will marry her." But come, get ready the baskets,[31] which come next, crown thine head. And do thou, king Menelaus, prepare a nuptial lay, and through the house let the pipe sound and let there be noise of feet, for this day comes blessed upon the virgin.

AG. I commend [your words,] but go thou within the house, and it shall be well, as fortune takes its course. Alas! what shall I wretched say? Whence shall I begin? Into what fetters of necessity have I fallen! Fortune has upturned me, so as to become far too clever for my cleverness. But lowness of birth has some advantage thus. For such persons are at liberty to weep, and speak unhappy words, but to him that is of noble birth, all these things belong. We have our dignity as ruler of our life, and are slaves to the multitude. For I am ashamed indeed to let fall the tear, yet again wretched am I ashamed not to weep, having come into the greatest calamities. Well! what shall I say to my wife? How shall I receive her? What manner of countenance shall I present? And truly she hath undone me, coming uncalled amidst the ills which before possessed me. And with reason did she follow her daughter, being about to deck her as a bride,[32] and to perform the dearest offices, where she will find us base. But for this hapless virgin—why [call her] virgin? Hades, as it seems, will speedily attend on her nuptials,—how do I pity her! For I think that she will beseech me thus: O father, wilt thou slay me? Such a wedding mayest thou thyself wed, and whosoever is a friend to thee. But Orestes being present will cry out knowingly words not knowing, for he is yet an infant. Alas! how has Priam's son, Paris, undone me by wedding the nuptials of Paris, who has wrought this!

CHOR. And I also pity her, as it becomes a stranger woman to moan for the misfortune of her lords.

MEN. Brother, give me thy right hand to touch.

AG. I give it, for thine is the power, but I am wretched.

MEN. I swear by Pelops, who was called the sire of my father and thine, and my father Atreus, that I indeed will tell thee plainly from my heart, and not any thing out of contrivance, but only what I think. I, beholding thee letting fall the tear from thine eyes, pitied thee, and myself let fall [a tear] for thee in return. And I have changed[33] my old determinations, not being wrath against you, but I will place myself in your present situation, and I recommend you neither to slay your child, nor to take my part; for it is not just that thou shouldst groan, but my affairs be in a pleasant state, and that thine should die, but mine behold the light. For what do I wish? Might I not obtain another choice alliance, if I crave nuptials? But, having undone my brother, whom it least behooved me, shall I receive Helen, an evil in place of a good? I was foolish and young, before that, viewing the matter closely, I saw what it is to beget children. Besides, pity came over me, considering our connection, for the hapless girl, who is about to be sacrificed because of my marriage. But what has thy virgin [daughter] to do with Helen? Let the army go, being disbanded from Aulis. But cease thou bedewing thine eyes with tears, my brother, and exciting me to tears. But if I have any concern in the oracle respecting thy daughter, let me have none: to thee I yield my part. But I have come to a change[34] from terrible resolutions. I have experienced[35] what was meet. I have changed to regard him who is sprung from a common source. Such changes belong not to a bad man, [viz.] to follow the best always.

CHOR. Thou hast spoken generous words, and becoming Tantalus the son of Jove. Thou disgracest not thine ancestors.

AG. I commend thee, Menelaus, in that, contrary to my expectation, you have subjoined these words, rightly, and worthily of thee.

MEN. A certain disturbance[36] between brothers arises on account of love, and avarice in their houses. I abhor such a relationship, mutually sore.

AG. But [consider,] for we are come into circumstances that render it necessary to accomplish the bloody slaughter of my daughter.

MEN. How? Who will compel thee to slay thy child?

AG. The whole assembly of the armament of the Greeks.

MEN. Not so, if at least thou dismiss it back to Argos.

AG. In this matter I might escape discovery, but in that I can not.[37]

MEN. What? One should not too much fear the multitude.

AG. Calchas will proclaim his prophecy to the army of the Greeks.

MEN. Not if he die first—and this is easy.

AG. The whole race of seers is an ambitious ill.

MEN. And in naught good or profitable, when at hand.[38]

AG. But dost thou not fear that which occurs to me?

MEN. How can I understand the word you say not?

AG. The son of Sisyphus knows all these matters.

MEN. It can not be that Orestes can pain thee and me.

AG. He is ever changeable, and with the multitude.

MEN. He is indeed possessed with the passion for popularity, a dreadful evil.

AG. Do you not then think that he, standing in the midst of the Greeks, will tell the oracles which Calchas pronounced, and of me, that I promised to offer a sacrifice to Diana, and then break my word. With which [words] having carried away the army, he will bid the Greeks slay thee and me, and sacrifice the damsel. And if I flee to Argos, they will come and ravage and raze the land, Cyclopean walls and all. Such are my troubles. O unhappy me! How, by the Gods, am I at a loss in these present matters! Take care of one thing for me, Menelaus, going through the army, that Clytæmnestra may not learn these matters, before I take and offer my daughter to Hades, that I may fare ill with as few tears as possible. But do ye, O stranger women, preserve silence.

CHORUS. Blest are they who share the nuptial bed of the Goddess Aphrodite,[39] when she is moderate, and with modesty, obtaining a calm from the maddening stings, when Love with his golden locks stretches his twin bow of graces, the one for a prosperous fate, the other for the upturning of life. I deprecate this [bow,] O fairest Venus, from our beds, but may mine be a moderate grace, and holy endearments, and may I share Aphrodite, but reject her when excessive. But the natures of mortals are different, and their manners are different,[40] but that which is clearly good is ever plain. And the education which trains[41] [men] up, conduces greatly to virtue, for to have reverence is wisdom, and it possesses an equivalent advantage, viz. to perceive what is fitting by one's mind, where report bears unwasting glory to life.[42] 'Tis a great thing to hunt for [the praise of] virtue, among women indeed, by a secret affection,[43] but among men, on the other hand, honor being inherent,[44] [bears that praise, honor,] which increases a state to an incalculable extent.[45]

Thou earnest, O Paris, †where thou wast trained up a shepherd with the white heifers of Ida, trilling a barbarian lay, breathing an imitation of the Phrygian pipes of Olympus on a reed. And the cows with their well-filled udders browsed, when the judgment of the Goddesses drove thee mad, which sends thee into Greece,† before the ivory-decked palaces, thou who didst strike love into the eyes of Helen which were upon thee, and thyself wast fluttered with love. Whence strife, strife brings Greece against the bulwarks of Troy with spears and ships.† Alas! alas! great are the fortunes of the great.[46] Behold the king's daughter, Iphigenia, my queen, and Clytæmnestra, daughter of Tyndarus, how are they sprung from the great, and to what suitable fortune they are come. The powerful, in sooth, and the wealthy, are Gods to those of mortals who are unblest. [Let us stand still, ye children of Chalcis, let us receive the queen from her chariot to the earth, not unsteadily, but gently with the soft attention of our hands, lest the renowned daughter of Agamemnon, newly coming to me, be alarmed, nor let us, as strangers to strangers, cause disturbance or fear to the Argive ladies.[47]]

[*Enter* Clytæmnestra, IPHIGENIA, *and probably* ORESTES *in a chariot. They descend from it, while the Chorus make obeisance.*]

CLY. I regard both your kindness and your favorable words as a good omen, and I have some hope that I am here as escort [of my daughter] to honorable nuptials. But take out of my chariot the dower-gifts which I bear for my girl, and send them carefully into the house. And do thou, my child, quit the horse-chariot, setting [carefully] thy foot delicate and at the same time tender. But you,[48] maidens, receive her in your arms, and lift her from the chariot. And let some one give me the firm support of his hand, that I may beseemingly leave the chariot-seat. But do some[49] of you stand in front of the horses' yoke, for the uncontrolled eye of horses is timorous, and take this boy, the son of Agamemnon, Orestes, for he is still an infant. Child! dost sleep, overcome by the ride? Wake up happily for thy sisters' nuptials. For thou thyself being noble shalt obtain relationship with a good man, the God-like son of the daughter of Nereus. [[50]Next come thou close to my foot, O daughter, to thy mother, Iphigenia, and standing near, show these strangers how happy I am, and come hither indeed, and address thy dear father.] O thou most great glory to me, king Agamemnon, we are come, not disobeying thy bidding.

IPH. O mother, running indeed, (but be thou not angry,) I will apply my breast to my father's breast. [[51]But I wish, rushing to embrace thy breast, O father, after a long season. For I long for thy face. But do not be angry.]

CLY. But, O my child, enjoy [thine embraces,] but thou wert ever most fond of thy father, of all the children I bore.

IPH. O father, joyous do I behold thee after a long season.

AG. And I, thy father, [joyously behold] thee. Thou speakest thus equally in respect to both.

IPH. Hail! But well hast thou done in bringing me to thee, O father.

AG. I know not how I shall say, yet not say so, my child.

IPH. Ah! how uneasily dost thou regard me, joyfully beholding me [before.]

AG. A king and general has many cares.

IPH. Give thyself up to me now, and turn not thyself to cares.

AG. But I am altogether concerned with thee, and on no other subject.

IPH. Relax thy brow, and open thy eyes in joy.

AG. See, I rejoice as I rejoice, at seeing thee, child.[52]

IPH. And then dost let fall a tear from thine eyes?

AG. For long to us is the coming absence.

IPH. I know not what you mean, I know not, dearest father mine.

AG. Speaking sensibly, thou movest me the more to pity.

IPH. I will speak foolishly, if I so may rejoice you.

AG. Alas! I can not keep silence, but I commend thee.

IPH. Remain, O father, in the house with thy children,

AG. I fain would, but not having what I would, I am pained.

IPH. Perish war and the ills of Menelaus![53]

AG. What has undone me will first undo others.

IPH. How long a time wast thou absent in the recesses of Aulis!

AG. And now also there is something hinders me from sending on the army.

IPH. Where say they that the Phrygians dwell, father?

AG. Where would that Paris, Priam's son, had never dwelt.

IPH. And dost thou go a long distance, O father, when thou leavest me?

AG. Thou art come, my daughter, to the same state with thy father.[54]

IPH. Alas! would that it were fitting me and thee to take me with thee as thy fellow-sailor.

AG. But there is yet a sailing for thee, where thou wilt remember thy father.

IPH. Shall I go, sailing with my mother, or alone?

AG. Alone, apart from thy father and mother.

IPH. What, art thou going to make me dwell in other houses, father?

AG. Cease. It is not proper for girls to know these matters.

IPH. Hasten back from Phrygia, do, my father, having settled matters well there.

AG. It first behooves me to offer a certain sacrifice here.

IPH. But it is with the priests that thou shouldst consider sacred matters.

AG. [Yet] shalt thou know it, for thou wilt stand round the altar.

IPH. What, shall we stand in chorus round the altar, my father?[55]

AG. I deem thee happier than myself, for that thou know-est nothing. But go within the house, that the girls may behold thee,[56] having given me a sad kiss and thy right hand, being about to dwell a long time away from thy sire. O bosom and cheeks, O yellow tresses, how has the city of the Phrygians proved a burden to us, and Helen! I cease my words, for swift does the drop trickle from mine eyes when I touch thee. Go into the house. But I, I crave thy pardon, (*to Clytæmnestra,*) daughter of Leda, if I showed too much feeling, being about to bestow my daughter on Achilles. For the departure [of a girl] is a happy one, but nevertheless it pains the parents, when a father, who has toiled much, delivers up his children to another home.

CLY. I am not so insensible—but think thou that I shall experience the same feelings, (so that I should not chide thee,) when I lead forth my girl with nuptial rejoicings, but custom wears away these thoughts in course of time. I know, however, the name of him to whom thou hast promised thy daughter, but I would fain know of what race, and whence [he is.]

AG. Ægina was the daughter of her father Asopus.

CLY. And who of mortals or of Gods wedded her?

AG. Jove, and she gave birth to Æacus, prince of Œnone.

CLY. But what son obtained the house of Æacus?

AG. Peleus, and Peleus obtained the daughter of Nereus.

CLY. By the gift of the God, or taking her in spite of the Gods?

AG. Jove acted as a sponsor, and bestowed her, having the power.[57]

CLY. And where does he wed her? In the wave of the sea?

AG. Where Chiron dwells at the sacred foot of Pelion.

CLY. Where they say that the race of Centaurs dwells?

AG. Here the Gods celebrated the nuptial feast of Peleus.

CLY. But did Thetis, or his father, train up Achilles?

AG. Chiron, that he might not learn the manners of evil mortals.

CLY. Hah! wise was the instructor, and wiser he who intrusted him.

AG. Such a man will be the husband of thy child.

CLY. Not to be found fault with. But what city in Greece does he inhabit?

AG. Near the river Apidanus in the confines of Phthia.

CLY. Thither will he lead thy virgin [daughter] and mine.

AG. This shall be the care of him, her possessor.

CLY. And may the pair be happy; but on what day will he wed her?

AG. When the prospering orb of the moon comes round.

CLY. But hast thou already sacrificed the first offerings for thy daughter to the Goddess?

AG. I am about to do so. In this matter we are now engaged.

CLY. And wilt thou then celebrate a wedding-feast afterward?

AG. [Ay,] having sacrificed such offerings as it behooves me to sacrifice to the Gods.

CLY. But where shall we set out a banquet for the women?

AG. Here, by the fair-pooped ships of the Greeks.

CLY. Well, and poorly,[58] forsooth! but may it nevertheless turn out well.

AG. Do then thou knowest what, O lady, and obey me.

CLY. In what? for I am accustomed to obey thee.

AG. We indeed in this place, where the bridegroom is—

CLY. Will do what without the mother, [of those things] which it behooves me to do?

AG. —will bestow your daughter among the Greeks.

CLY. But where must I be in the mean time?

AG. Go to Argos, and take care of your virgins.

CLY. Leaving my child? And who will bear the [nuptial] torch?

AG. I will furnish the light that becomes the nuptials.

CLY. The custom is not thus, but you think these matters trifles.

AG. It is not proper that thou shouldst mingle in the crowd of the army.

CLY. It is proper that I, the mother, should bestow at least my own daughter.

AG. And it [is proper] that the damsels at home should not be alone.

CLY. They are well guarded in their close chambers.

AG. Obey me.

CLY. [No,] by the Argive Goddess queen. But go you, and attend to matters abroad, but I [will mind] the affairs at home, as to the things which should be present to virgins at their wedding.[59]

AG. Alas! In vain have I toiled,[60] and have been frustrated in my hope, wishing to send my wife out of my sight. But I am using stratagems, and finding contrivances against those I best love, overcome at all points. But nevertheless with the prophet Calchas I will go and ask the pleasure of the Goddess, not fortunate for me, the trouble of Greece.[61] But it behooves a wise man either to support a useful and good wife in his house or not to marry at all.[62]

CHORUS. The assembly of the Grecian army will come to Simois, and to the silver eddies, both with ships and with arms, to Ilium, and to the Phœbeian plain of Troy, where I hear that Cassandra, adorned with a green-blossoming crown of laurel, lets loose her yellow locks, when the prophetic influence of the Gods breathes upon her. And the Trojans will stand upon the towers of Troy and around its walls, when brazen-shielded Mars, borne over the sea in fair-prowed ships, approaches the beds of Simois by rowing, seeking to bear away Helen, [the sister] of the twain sons of Jove in heaven, into the land of Greece, by the war-toiling shields and spears of the Greeks. But having surrounded Pergamus,[63] the city of the Phrygians, around its towers of stone, with bloody Mars, having torn off the heads [of the citizens] cut from their necks, having completely ravaged the city of Troy, he will make the daughters and wife of Priam shed many tears. But Helen, the daughter of Jove, will sit† in sad lamentation, having left her husband. Never upon me or upon my children's children may this expectation come, such as the wealthy Lydian and Phrygian wives possess while at their spinning, conversing thus with each other. Who,[64] dragging out my fair-haired tresses, will choose me as his spoil despite my tears, while my country is perishing? Through thee [forsooth,] the offspring of the long-necked swan, if indeed the report is true, that Leda † met with[65] a winged bird, when the body of Jove was transformed, and then in the tablets of the muses fables spread these reports among men, inopportunely, and in vain.

[*Enter* ACHILLES.]

ACHILLES. Where about here is the general of the Greeks? Who of the servants will tell him that Achilles, the son of Peleus, is seeking him at the gates? For we do not remain by the Euripus in equal condition; for some of us being unyoked in nuptials, having left our solitary homes, sit here upon the shore, but others, having wives and children:[66] so violent a passion for this expedition has fallen upon Greece, not without the will of the Gods. It is therefore right that I should speak of what concerns me, and whoever else wishes will himself speak for himself. For leaving the Pharsalian land, and Peleus, I am waiting for these light gales of Euripus,[67] restraining the Myrmidons, who are continually pressing me, and saying, "Achilles, why tarry we? what manner of time must the armament against Troy yet measure out? At any rate act, if you are going to do any thing, or lead the army home, not abiding the delays of the Atrides."

CLY. O son of the Goddess, daughter of Nereus, hearing from within thy words, I have come out before the house.

ACH. O hallowed modesty, who can this woman be whom I behold here, possessing a fair-seeming form?

CLY. It is no wonder that you know me not, whom you have never seen before, but I commend you because you respect modesty.

ACH. But who art thou? And wherefore hast thou come to the assembly of the Greeks, a woman to men guarded with shields?

CLY. I am the daughter of Leda, and Clytæmnestra is my name, and my husband is king Agamemnon.

ACH. Well hast thou in few words spoken what is seasonable. But it is unbecoming for me to converse with women. (*Is going.*)

CLY. Remain, (why dost thou fly?) at least join thy right hand with mine, as a happy commencement of betrothal.

ACH. What sayest thou? I [give] thee my right hand? I should be ashamed of Agamemnon, if I touched what is not lawful for me.

CLY. It is particularly lawful, since you are going to wed my daughter, O son of the sea Goddess, daughter of Nereus.

ACH. What marriage dost thou say? Surprise possesses me, lady, unless, being beside yourself, you speak this new thing.

CLY. This is the nature of all people, to be ashamed when they behold new friends, and are put in mind of nuptials.

ACH. I never wooed thy daughter, lady, nor has any thing been said to me on the subject of marriage by the Atrides.

CLY. What can it be? Do you in turn marvel at my words, for thine are a marvel to me.

ACH. Conjecture; these matters are a common subject for conjecture, for both of us perhaps are deceived in our words.[68]

CLY. But surely I have suffered terrible things! I am acting as match-maker in regard to a marriage that has no existence. I am ashamed of this.

ACH. Perhaps some one has trifled with both me and thee. But pay no attention to it, and bear it with indifference.

CLY. Farewell, for I can no longer behold thee with uplifted eyes, having appeared as a liar, and suffered unworthy things.

ACH. And this same [farewell] is thine from me. But I will go seek thy husband within this house.

[*The* OLD MAN *appears at the door of the house.*]

OLD M. O stranger, grandson of Æacus, remain. Ho! thee, I say, the son of the Goddess, and thee, the daughter of Leda.

ACM. Who is it that calls, partially opening the doors? With what terror he calls!

OLD M. A slave. I will not be nice about the title, for fortune allows it not.

ACH. Of whom? for thou art not mine. My property and Agamemnon's are different.

OLD M. Of this lady who is before the house, the gift of her father Tyndarus.

ACH. We are still. Say if thou wantest any thing, for which thou hast stopped me.

OLD M. Are ye sure that ye alone stand before these gates?

CLY. Ay, so that you may speak to us only. But come out from the royal dwelling.

OLD M. (Coming forward) O fortune, and foresight mine, preserve whom I wish.

ACH. These words will do for[69] a future occasion, for they have some weight.

CLY. By thy right hand [I beseech thee,] delay not, if thou hast aught to say to me.

OLD M. Thou knowest then, being what manner of man, I have been by nature well disposed to thee and thy children.

CLY. I know thee as being a faithful servant to my house.

OLD M. And that king Agamemnon received me among thy dowry.

CLY. Thou camest into Argos with us, and thou wast always mine.

OLD M. So it is, and I am well disposed to thee, but less so to thy husband.

CLY. Unfold now at least to me what words you are saying.

OLD M. The father who begat her is about to slay thy daughter with his own hand.

CLY. How? I deprecate thy words, old man, for thou thinkest not well.

OLD M. Cutting the fair neck of the hapless girl with the sword.

CLY. O wretched me! Is my husband mad?

OLD M. He is in his right mind, save with respect to thee and thy daughter, but in this he is not wise.

CLY. Upon what grounds? What maddening fiend impels him?

OLD M. The oracles, as at least Calchas says, in order that the army may be able to proceed.

CLY. Whither? Wretched me, and wretched she whom her father is about to slay?

OLD M. To the house of Dardanus, that Menelaus may recover Helen.

CLY. To the destruction, then, of Iphigenia, was the return of Helen foredoomed?

OLD M. Thou hast the whole story. Her father is going to offer thy daughter to Diana.

CLY. What! what pretext had the marriage, that brought me from home?

OLD M. That thou rejoicing mightest bring thy child, as if about to wed her to Achilles.

CLY. O daughter, both thou and thy mother are come to meet with destruction.

OLD M. Ye twain are suffering sad things, and dreadful things hath Agamemnon dared.

CLY. I wretched am undone, and my eyes no longer restrain the tear.

OLD M. For bitter 'tis to mourn, deprived of one's children.

CLY. But whence, old man, sayest thou that thou hast learned and knowest these things?

OLD M. I went to bear a letter to thee, in reference to what was before written.

CLY. Not allowing, or bidding me to bring my child, that she might die?

OLD M. [It was] that you should not bring her, for your husband then thought well.

CLY. And how was it then, that, bearing the letter, thou gavest it not to me?

OLD M. Menelaus, who is the cause of these evils, took it from me.

CLY. O child of Nereus' daughter, O son of Peleus, dost hear these things?

ACH. I hear that thou art wretched, and I do not bear my part indifferently.

CLY. They will slay my child, having deceived her with thy nuptials.

ACH. I also blame thy husband, nor do I bear it lightly.

CLY. I will not be ashamed to fall down at thy knee, mortal, to one born of a Goddess. For wherefore should I make a show of pride? Or what should I study more than my children? But, O son of the Goddess, aid me in my unhappiness, and her who is called thy wife, vainly indeed, but nevertheless, having decked her out, I led her as if to be married, but now I lead her to sacrifice, and reproach will come upon thee, who gavest no aid. For though thou wast not yoked in nuptials, at least thou wast called the beloved husband of the hapless virgin. By thy beard, by thy right hand, by thy mother [I beseech] thee, for thy name hath undone me, to whom thou shouldst needs give assistance. I have no other altar to fly to, but thy knee, nor is any friend near me,[70] but thou hearest the cruel and all-daring conduct of Agamemnon. But I a woman, as thou seest, have come to a naval host, uncontrolled, and bold for mischief, but useful, when they are willing. But if thou wilt venture to stretch thine hand in my behalf, we are saved, but if not, we are not saved.

CHOR. A terrible thing it is to be a mother, and it bears a great endearment, and one common to all, so as to toil on behalf of their children.

ACH. My mind is high-lifted in its thoughts,[71] and knows both how to grieve [moderately] in troubles, and to rejoice moderately in high prosperity. For the discreet among mortals are such as pass through life correctly with wisdom. Now there are certain cases where it is pleasant not to be too wise, and also where it is useful to possess wisdom. But I, being nurtured [in the dwelling] of a most pious man, Chiron, have learned to possess a candid disposition. And I will obey the Atrides, if indeed they order well, but when not well, I obey not. But here in Troy showing a free nature I will glorify Mars with the spear, as far as I can. But, O thou who hast suffered wretchedly at the hands of those dearest, in whatever can be done by a youth, I, showing so much pity, will set thee right, and thy daughter, having been called my bride, shall never be sacrificed by her father, for I will not furnish thy husband with my person to weave stratagems upon. For my name, even if he lift not up the sword, will slay thy daughter, but thy husband is the cause. But my body is no longer pure, if on my account, and because of my marriage, there perish a virgin who has gone through sad and unbearable troubles, and has been marvelously and undeservedly ill treated. I were the worst man among the Greeks, I were of naught (but Menelaus would be among men), not as born from Peleus, but from some fiend, if my name acts the murderer for thy husband.[72] By Nereus, nurtured in the damp waves, the father of Thetis, who begat me, king Agamemnon shall not lay hands on thy daughter, not so much as with a little finger, so as to touch her garments. I' faith, Sipylus, a fortress of barbarians, whence the [royal] generals trace their descent, shall be deemed a city, but the name of Phthia shall nowhere be named. And the seer Calchas will to his cost consecrate the sacrificial cakes and lustral waters. (But what man is a prophet?) who tells[73] a few things true, (but many falsely,) when he has made a hit, but when he fails, is undone. These words are not spoken for the sake of my wedding, (ten thousand girls are hunting after alliance with me,) but [because] king Agamemnon has been guilty of insult toward me. But it behooved him to ask [the use of] my name from me, as an enticement for his daughter, and Clytæmnestra would have been most readily persuaded to give her daughter to me as a husband. And I would have given her up to the Greeks, if on this account their passage to Troy had been impeded: I would not have refused to augment the common interest of those with whom I set out on the expedition. But now I am held as of no account by the generals, and it is a matter of indifference whether I benefit them or not. Soon shall my sword witness, which, before death came against the Phrygians,[74] I stained with spots of blood, whether any one shall take thy daughter from me. But keep quiet, I have appeared to thee as a most mighty God, though not [a God,] but nevertheless I will be such.

CHOR. O son of Peleus, thou hast spoken both worthily of thyself, and of the marine deity, hallowed Goddess.

CLY. Alas! how can I praise thee neither too much in words, nor, being deficient in this respect, [not] lose thy favor? For in a certain wise the praised dislike their praisers, if they praise too much. But I am ashamed at alleging pitiable words, being troubled in myself, while thou art not diseased with my ills. But in fact the good man has some reason, even though he be unconnected with them, for assisting the unfortunate. But pity us, for we have suffered pitiably; I, who, in the first place, thinking to have thee for a kinsman, cherished a vain hope.—Moreover, my child, by dying, might perchance become an omen to thy future bridals,[75] which thou must needs avoid. But well didst thou speak both first and last, for, if thou art willing, my child will be saved. Dost wish that she embrace thy knee as a suppliant? Such conduct is not virgin-like, but if thou wilt, she shall come, with her noble face suffused with modesty. Or shall I obtain these things from thee, without her presence?

ACH. Let her remain within doors, for with dignity she preserves her dignity.

CLY. Yet one must needs have modesty [only] as far as circumstances allow.

ACH. Do thou neither bring forth thy daughter into my sight, lady, not let us fall into reproach for inconsiderate conduct, for our assembled army, being idle from home occupations, loves evil and slanderous talk. But at all events you will accomplish the same, whether you come to me as a suppliant, or do not supplicate, for a mighty contest awaits me, to release you from these evils. Wherefore, having heard one thing, be persuaded that I will not speak falsely. But if I speak falsely, and vainly amuse you, may I perish; but may I not perish, if I preserve the virgin.

CLY. Mayest thou be blest, ever assisting the unhappy.

ACH. Hear me then, that the matter may be well.

CLY. What is this thou sayest? for one must listen to thee.

ACH. Let us again persuade her father to be wiser.

CLY. He is a coward, and fears the army too much.

ACH. But words can conquer words.

CLY. Chilly is the hope, but tell me what I must do.

ACH. Beseech him first not to slay his child, but if he oppose this, you must come to me. For if he will be persuaded what you wish, there is no occasion for my efforts, for this very [consent] contains her safety. And I also shall appear in a better light with my friend, and the army will not blame me, if I transact matters by discretion rather than force. And if this turn out well, these things, even without my help, may turn out satisfactorily to thy friends and thyself.[76]

CLY. How wisely hast thou spoken! But what thou sayest must be done. But if I do not obtain what I seek, where shall I again see thee? Where must I wretched woman, coming, find thee an assistant in my troubles?

ACH. We guards will watch thee when there is occasion, lest any one behold thee going in agitation through the host of the Greeks. But do not shame thy ancestral home, for Tyndarus is not worthy of an evil reputation, seeing he is great among the Greeks.

CLY. These things shall be. Command; it is meet that I obey thee. But if there are Gods, you, being a just man, will receive a good reward; but if not, why should one toil?

CHOR. What was that nuptial song that raised[77] its strains on the Libyan reed, and with the dance-loving lyre, and the reedy syrinx, when o'er Pelion at the feast of the Gods the fair-haired muses, striking their feet with golden sandals against the ground, came to the wedding of Peleus, celebrating with melodious sounds Thetis, and the son of Æacus, on the mountains of the Centaurs, through the Palian wood.

But the Dardan,[78] [Phrygian Ganymede,] dear delight of Jove's bed, poured out the nectar in the golden depths of the goblets, and along the white sands the fifty daughters of Nereus, entwining in circles, adorned the nuptials of Nereus with the dance. But with darts of fir, and crowns of grass, the horse-mounted troop of the Centaurs came to the banquet of the Gods and the cup of Bacchus. And the Thessalian girls shouted loud,[79] "O daughter of Nereus," and the prophet Phœbus, and Chiron, skilled in letters, declared,

"Thou shalt bring forth a mighty light, who shall come to the [Trojan] land with Myrmidons armed with spear and shield, to burn the renowned city of Priam, around his body armed with a covering of golden arms wrought by Vulcan, having them as a gift from his Goddess Thetis, who begat him blessed." Then the deities celebrated the nuptials of the noble daughter of Nereus first,[80] and of Peleus. But thee, [O Iphigenia,] they will crown on the head with flowery garlands, like as a pure spotted heifer from a rocky cave, making bloody the mortal throat [of one] not trained up with the pipe, nor amidst the songs of herdsmen, but as a bride[81] prepared by thy mother for some one of the Argives. Where has the face of shame, or virtue any power to prevail? Since impiety indeed has influence, but virtue is left behind and disregarded by mortals, and lawlessness governs law, and it is a common struggle for mortals, lest any envy of the Gods befall.

CLY. I have come out of the house to seek for my husband, who has been absent, and has quitted the house a long time. But my hapless daughter is in tears, casting forth many a change of complaint, having heard the death her father devises for her. But I was mindful of Agamemnon who is now coming hither,[82] who will quickly be detected doing evil deeds against his own children.

AG. Daughter of Leda, opportunely have I found you without the house, that I may tell thee, apart from the virgin, words which it is not meet for those to hear who are about to marry.

CLY. And what is it, on which your convenience lays hold?

AG. Send forth thy daughter from the house with her father, since the lustral waters are ready prepared, and the salt-cakes to scatter with the hands upon the purifying flame, and heifers, which needs must be slain in honor of the Goddess Diana before the marriage solemnities, a shedding of black gore.

CLY. In words, indeed, thou speakest well, but for thy deeds, I know not how I may say thou speakest well. But come without, O daughter, for thou knowest all that thy father meditates, and beneath thy robes bring the child Orestes, thy brother. See, she is here present to obey thee. But the rest I will speak on her behalf and mine.

AG. Child, why weepest thou, and no longer beholdest me cheerfully, but fixing thy face upon the ground, keepest thy vest before it?

CLY. Alas! What commencement of my sorrows shall I take? For I may use them all as first, [both last, and middle throughout.[83]]

AG. But what is it? How all of you are come to one point with me, bearing disturbed and alarmed countenances.

CLY. Wilt thou answer candidly, husband, if I ask thee?

AG. There needs no admonition: I would fain be questioned.

CLY. Art thou going to slay thy child and mine?

AG. Ah! wretched things dost thou say, and thinkest what thou shouldst not.

CLY. Keep quiet, and first in turn answer me that.

AG. But if thou askest likely things, thou wilt hear likely.

CLY. I ask no other things, nor do thou answer me others.

AG. O revered destiny, and fate, and fortune mine!

CLY. Ay, and mine too, and this child's, one of three unfortunates!

AG. But in what art thou wronged?

CLY. Dost thou ask me this? This thy wit hath no wit.[84]

AG. I am undone. My secret plans are betrayed.

CLY. I know and have learned all that you are about to do to me, and the very fact of thy silence, and of thy groaning much, is a proof that you confess it. Do not take the trouble to say any thing.

AG. Behold, I am silent: for what need is there that, falsely speaking, I add shamelessness to misfortune?

CLY. Listen, then, for I will unfold my story, and will no longer make use of riddles away from the purpose. In the first place, that I may first reproach thee with this—thou didst wed me unwilling, and obtain me by force, having slain Tantalus, my former husband, and having dashed[85] my infant living to the ground, having torn him by force from my breast. And the twin sons of Jove, my brothers, glorying in their steeds, made war [against thee] but my old father Tyndarus saved you, when you had become a suppliant, and thou again didst possess me as a wife. When I, being reconciled to thee in respect to thy person and home, thou wilt bear witness how blameless a wife I was, both modest in respect to affection, and enriching thy house, so that thou both going within and without thy doors wast blessed. And 'tis a rare prize for a man to obtain such a wife, but there is no lack of getting a bad spouse. And I bear thee this son, besides three virgins, of one of whom thou art cruelly going to deprive me. And if any one ask thee on what account thou wilt slay her, say, what will you answer? or must I needs make your plea, "that Menelaus may obtain Helen?" A pretty custom, forsooth, that children must pay the price of a bad woman. We gain the most hateful things at the hand of those dearest. Come, if thou wilt set out, leaving me at home, and then wilt be a long time absent, what sort of feelings dost think I shall experience, when I behold every seat empty of this child's presence, and every virgin chamber empty, but myself sit in tears alone, ever mourning her [in such strains as these:] "My child, thy father, who begat thee, hath destroyed thee, himself, no other, the slayer, by no other hand, leaving such a reward for [my care of] the house."[86] Since there wants but a little reason for me and my remaining daughters to give thee such a reception as you deserve to receive. Do not, by the Gods, either compel me to act evilly toward thee, nor do thou thyself be so. Ah well! thou wilt sacrifice thy daughter—what prayers wilt thou then utter? What good thing wilt thou crave for thyself, slaying thy child? An evil return, seeing, forsooth, thou hast disgracefully set out from home. But is it right that I should pray for thee any good thing? Verily we must believe the Gods are senseless, if we feel well disposed to murderers. But wilt thou, returning to Argos, embrace thy children? But 'tis not lawful for thee. Will any of your children look upon you, if thou offerest one of them for slaughter? Thus far have I proceeded in my argument. What! does it only behoove thee to carry about thy sceptre and marshal the army?— whose duty it were to speak a just speech among the Greeks: "Do ye desire, O Greeks, to sail against the land of the Phrygians? Cast lots, whose daughter needs must die"—for this would be on equal terms, but not that you should give thy daughter to the Greeks as a chosen victim. Or Menelaus, whose affair it was, ought to slay Hermione for her mother's sake. But now I, having cherished thy married life, shall be bereaved of my child, but she who has sinned, bearing her daughter under her care to Sparta, will be blest. As to these things, answer me if I say aught not rightly, but if I have spoken well, do not then slay thy child and mine, and thou wilt be wise.

CHOR. Be persuaded, Agamemnon, for 'tis right to join in saving one's children. No one of mortals will gainsay this.

IPH. If, O father, I possessed the eloquence of Orpheus, that I might charm by persuasion, so that rocks should follow me, and that I might soften whom I would by my words, to this would I have resorted. But now I will offer tears as all my skill, for these I can. And, as a suppliant bough, I press against thy knees my body, which this [my mother] bore thee, [beseeching] that thou slay me not before my time, for sweet it is to behold the light, nor do thou compel me to visit the places beneath the earth. And I first[87] hailed thee sire, and thou [didst first call] me daughter, and first drawing nigh to thy knees, I gave and in turn received sweet tokens of affection. And such, were thy words: "My daughter, shall I some time behold thee prospering in a husband's home, living and flourishing worthily of me?" And mine in turn ran thus, as I hung about thy beard, which now with my hand I embrace: "But how shall I [treat] thee? Shall I receive thee when an old man, O father, with the hearty reception of my house, repaying thee the careful nurture of my youth?" Of such words have remembrance, but thou hast forgotten them, and fain wouldst slay me. Do not, [I beseech you] by Pelops and by thy father Atreus, and this my mother, who having before brought me forth with throes, now suffers this second throe. What have I to do with the marriage of Paris and Helen? Whence came he, father, for my destruction? Look upon me; give me one look, one kiss, that this memorial of thee at least I, dying, may possess, if thou wilt not be persuaded by my words. Brother, thou art but a little helpmate to those dear, yet weep with me, beseech thy sire that thy sister die not. Even in babes there is wont to be some sense of evil. Behold, O father, he silently implores thee. But respect my prayer, and have pity on my years. Yea, by thy beard we, two dear ones, implore thee; the one is yet a nursling, but the other grown up. In one brief saying I will overcome all arguments. This light of heaven is sweetest of things for men to behold, but that below is naught; and mad is he who seeks to die. To live dishonorably is better than to die gloriously.

CHOR. O wretched Helen, through thee and thy nuptials there is come a contest for the Atrides and their children.

AG. I can understand what merits pity, and what not; and I love my children, for [otherwise] I were mad. And dreadful 'tis for me[88] to dare these things, O woman, and dreadful not to do so—for so I must needs act. Thou seest how great is this naval host, and how many are the chieftains of brazen arms among the Greeks, to whom there is not a power of arriving at the towers of Troy, unless I sacrifice you, as the seer Calchas says, nor can we take the renowned plain of Troy. But a certain passion has maddened the army of the Greeks, to sail as quickly as possible upon the land of the barbarians, and to put a stop to the rapes of Grecian wives. And they will slay my daughters at Argos, and you, and me, if I break through the commands of the Goddess. It is not Menelaus who has enslaved me, O daughter, nor have I followed his device, but Greece, for whom I, will or nill, must needs offer thee. And I am inferior on this head. For it behooves her, [Helen,] as far as thou, O daughter, art concerned, to be free, nor for us, being Greeks, to be plundered perforce of our wives by barbarians.

CLY. O child! O ye stranger women! O wretched me for thy death! Thy father flees from thee, giving thee up to Hades.

IPH. Alas for me! mother, mother. The same song suits both of us on account of our fortunes, and no more to me is the light, nor this bright beam of the sun. Alas! alas! thou snow-smitten wood of Troy, and mountains of Ida, where once on a time Priam exposed a tender infant, having separated him from his mother, that he might meet with deadly fate, Paris, who was styled Idæan, Idæan [Paris] in the city of the Phrygians. Would that the herdsman Paris, who was nurtured in care of steers, had ne'er dwelt near the white stream, where are the fountains of the Nymphs, and the meadow flourishing with blooming flowers, and roseate flowers and hyacinths for Goddesses to cull. Where once on a time came Pallas, and artful Venus, and

Juno, and Hermes, the messenger of Jove; Venus indeed, vaunting herself in charms, and Pallas in the spear, and Juno in the royal nuptials of king Jove, [these came] to a hateful judgment and strife concerning beauty; but my death, my death, O virgins, bearing glory indeed to the Greeks, Diana hath received as first-fruits [of the expedition] against Troy.[89] But he that begot me wretched, O mother, O mother, has departed, leaving me deserted. O hapless me! having †beheld† bitter, bitter, ill-omened Helen, I am slain, I perish, by the impious slaughter of an impious sire. Would[90] for me that Aulis had never received the poops of the brazen-beaked ships into these ports, the fleet destined for Troy, nor that Jove had breathed an adverse wind over Euripus, softening one breeze so that some mortals might rejoice in their [expanded] sails, but to others a pain, to others difficulty, to some to set sail, to others to furl their sails, but to others to tarry. In truth the race of mortals is full of troubles, is full of troubles, and it necessarily befalls men to find some misfortune. Alas! alas! thou daughter of Tyndarus, who hast brought many sufferings, and many griefs upon the Greeks.

CHOR. I indeed pity you having met with an evil calamity, such as thou never shouldst have met with.

IPH. O mother, to whom I owe my birth, I behold a crowd of men near.

CLY. Ay, the son of the Goddess, my child, for whom thou camest hither.

IPH. Open the house, ye servants, that I may hide myself.

CLY. But why dost thou fly hence, my child?

IPH. I am ashamed to behold this Achilles.

CLY. On what account?

IPH. The unfortunate turn-out of my nuptials shames me.

CLY. Thou art not in a state to give way to delicacy in the present circumstances. But do thou remain, there is no use for punctilio, if we can [but save your life.]

ACH. O hapless lady, daughter of Leda.

CLY. Thou sayest not falsely.

ACH. Terrible things are cried out among the Greeks.

CLY. What cry? tell me.

ACH. Concerning thy child.

CLY. Thou speakest a word of ill omen.

ACH. That it is necessary to slay her.

CLY. Does no one speak the contrary to this?

ACH. Ay, I myself have got into trouble.

CLY. Into what [trouble,] O friend?

ACH. Of having my body stoned with stones.

CLY. What, in trying to save my daughter!

ACH. This very thing.

CLY. And who would have dared to touch thy person?

ACH. All the Greeks.

CLY. And was not the host of the Myrmidons at hand for thee?

ACH. That was the first that showed enmity.

CLY. Then are we utterly undone, my daughter.

ACH. For they railed at me as overcome by a betrothed—

CLY. And what didst thou reply?

ACH. That they should not slay my intended bride.

CLY. For so 'twas right.

ACH. [She] whom her father had promised me.

CLY. Ay, and had sent for from Argos.

ACH. But I was worsted by the outcry.

CLY. For the multitude is a terrible evil.

ACH. But nevertheless I will aid thee.

CLY. And wilt thou, being one, fight with many?

ACH. Dost see these men bearing [my] arms?

CLY. Mayest thou gain by thy good intentions.

ACH. But I will gain.

CLY. Then my child will not be slain?

ACH. Not, at least, with my consent.

CLY. And will any one come to lay hands on the girl?

ACH. Ay, a host of them, but Ulysses will conduct her.

CLY. Will it be the descendant of Sisyphus?

ACH. The very man.

CLY. Doing it of his own accord, or appointed by the army?

ACH. Chosen willingly.

CLY. A wicked choice forsooth, to commit slaughter!

ACH. But I will restrain him.

CLY. But will he lead her unwillingly, having seized her?

ACH. Ay, by her auburn locks.

CLY. But what must I then do?

ACH. Keep hold of your daughter.

CLY. As far as this goes she shall not be slain.

ACH. But it will come to this at all events.[91]

IPH. Mother, do thou hear my words, for I perceive that thou art vainly wrathful with thy husband, but it is not easy for us to struggle with things [almost] impossible. It is meet therefore to praise our friend for his willingness, but it behooves thee also to see that you be not an object of reproach to the army, and we profit nothing more, and he meet with calamity. But hear me, mother, thinking upon what has entered my mind. I have determined to die, and this I would fain do gloriously, I mean, by dismissing all ignoble thoughts. Come hither, mother, consider with me how well I speak. Greece, the greatest of cities, is now all looking upon me, and there rests in me both the passage of the ships and the destruction of Troy, and, for the women hereafter, if the barbarians do them aught of harm, to allow them no longer to carry them off from prosperous Greece, having avenged the destruction of Helen, whom Paris bore away.[92] All these things I dying shall redeem, and my renown, for that I have freed Greece, will be blessed. Moreover, it is not right that I should be too fond of life; for thou hast brought me forth for the common good of Greece, not for thyself only. But shall ten thousand men armed with bucklers, and ten thousand, oars in hand, their country being injured, dare to do some deed against the foes, and perish on behalf of Greece, while my life, being but one, shall hinder all these things? What manner of justice is this? Have we a word to answer? And let me come to this point: it is not meet that this man should come to strife with all the Greeks for the sake of a woman, nor lose his life. And one man, forsooth, is better than ten thousand women, that he should behold the light. But if Diana hath wished to receive my body, shall I, being mortal, become an opponent to the Goddess! But it can not be. I give my body for Greece. Sacrifice it, and sack Troy. For this for a long time will be my memorial, and this my children, my wedding, and my glory. But it is meet that Greeks should

- 316 -

rule over barbarians, O mother, but not barbarians over Greeks, for the one is slavish, but the others are free.

CHOR. Thy part, indeed, O virgin, is glorious; but the work of fortune and of the Gods sickens.

ACH. Daughter of Agamemnon, some one of the Gods destined me to happiness, if I obtained thee as a wife, and I envy Greece on thy account, and thee on account of Greece. For well hast thou spoken this, and worthily of the country, for, ceasing to strive with the deity, who is more powerful than thou art, thou hast considered what is good and useful. But still more does a desire of thy union enter my mind, when I look to thy nature, for thou art noble. But consider, for I wish to benefit you, and to receive you to my home, and, Thetis be my witness, I am grieved if I shall not save you, coming to conflict with the Greeks. Consider: death is a terrible ill.

IPH. I speak these words, no others, with due foresight. Enough is the daughter of Tyndarus to have caused contests and slaughter of men through her person: but do not thou, O stranger, die in my behalf, nor slay any one. But let me preserve Greece, if I am able.

ACH. O best of spirits, I have naught further to answer thee, since it seems thus to thee, for thou hast noble thoughts; for wherefore should not one tell the truth? But nevertheless thou mayest perchance repent these things. In order, therefore, that thou mayest all that lies in my power, I will go and place these my arms near the altar, as I will not allow you to die, but hinder it. And thou too wilt perhaps be of my opinion, when thou seest the sword nigh to thy neck. I will not allow thee to die through thy wild determination, but going with these mine arms to the temple of the Goddess, I will await thy presence there.

IPH. Mother, why dost thou silently bedew thine eyes with tears?

CLY. I wretched have a reason, so as to be pained at heart.

IPH. Cease; do not daunt me, but obey me in this.

CLY. Speak, for thou shalt not be wronged at my hands, my child.

IPH. Neither then do thou cut off the locks of thine hair, [nor put on black garments around thy body.]

CLY. Wherefore sayest thou this, my child? Having lost thee—

IPH. Not you indeed—I am saved, and thou wilt be glorious as far as I am concerned.

CLY. How sayest thou? Must I not bemoan thy life?

IPH. Not in the least, since no tomb will be upraised for me.

CLY. Why, what then is death? Is not a tomb customary?[93]

IPH. The altar of the Goddess, daughter of Jove, will be my memorial.

CLY. But, O child, I will obey thee, for thou speakest well.

IPH. Ay, as prospering like the benefactress of Greece.

CLY. What then shall I tell thy sisters?

IPH. Neither do thou clothe them in black garments.

CLY. But shall I speak any kind message from thee to the virgins?

IPH. Ay, [bid them] fare well, and do thou, for my sake, train up this [boy] Orestes to be a man.

CLY. Embrace him, beholding him for the last time.

IPH. O dearest one, thou hast assisted thy friends to the utmost in thy power.

CLY. Can I, by doing any thing in Argos, do thee a pleasure?

IPH. Hate not my father, yes, thy husband.

CLY. He needs shall go through terrible trials on thy account.

IPH. Unwillingly he hath undone me on behalf of the land of Greece.

CLY. But ungenerously, by craft, and not in a manner worthy of Atreus.

IPH. Who will come and lead me, before I am torn away by the hair?[94]

CLY. I will go with thee.

IPH. Not you indeed, thou sayest not well.

CLY. Ay [but I will,] clinging to thy garments.

IPH. Be persuaded by me, mother. Remain, for this is more fitting both for me and thee. But let some one of these my father's followers conduct me to the meadow of Diana, where I may be sacrificed.

CLY. O child, thou art going.

IPH. Ay, and I shall ne'er return.

CLY. Leaving thy mother—

IPH. As thou seest, though, not worthily.

CLY. Hold! Do not leave me.

IPH. I do not suffer thee to shed tears. But, ye maidens, raise aloft the pæan for my sad hap, [celebrate] Diana, the daughter of Jove,[95] and let the joyful strain go forth to the Greeks. And let some one make ready the baskets, and let flame burn with the purifying cakes, and let my father serve the altar with his right hand, seeing I am going to bestow upon the Greeks safety that produces victory.[96]

Conduct me, the conqueror of the cities of Troy and of the Phrygians. Surround[97] me with crowns, bring them hither. Here is my hair to crown. And [bear hither] the lustral fountains.[98] Encircle [with dances] around the temple and the altar, Diana, queen Diana, the blessed, since by my blood and offering I will wash out her oracles, if it needs must be so. O revered, revered mother, thus † indeed † will we [now] afford thee our tears, for it is not fitting during the sacred rites. O damsels, join in singing Diana, who dwells opposite Chalcis, where the warlike ships have been eager [to set out,] being detained in the narrow harbors of Aulis here through my name.[99] Alas! O my mother-land of Pelasgia, and my Mycenian handmaids.

CHOR. Dost thou call upon the city of Perseus, the work of the Cyclopean hands?

IPH. Thou hast nurtured me for a glory to Greece, and I will not refuse to die.

CHOR. For renown will not fail thee.

IPH. Alas! alas! lamp-bearing day, and thou too, beam of Jove, another, another life and state shall we dwell in. Farewell for me, beloved light!

CHOR. Alas! alas! Behold[100] the destroyer of the cities of Troy and of the Phrygians, wending her way, decked as to her head with garlands and with lustral streams, to the altar of the sanguinary Goddess, about to stream with drops of gore, being stricken on her fair neck. Fair dewy streams, and lustral waters from ancestral sources[101] await thee, and the host of the Greeks eager to reach Troy. But let us celebrate Diana, the daughter of Jove, queen of the Gods, as upon a prosperous occasion. O hallowed one, that rejoicest in human sacrifices, send the army of the Greeks into the land of the Phrygians, and the territory of deceitful Troy, and grant that by Grecian spears Agamemnon may place a most glorious crown upon his head, a glory ever to be remembered.

[*Enter a* MESSENGER.[102]]

MESS. O daughter of Tyndarus, Clytæmnestra, come without the house, that thou mayest hear my words.

CLY. Hearing thy voice, I wretched came hither, terrified and astounded with fear, lest thou shouldst be come, bearing some new calamity to me in addition to the present one.

MESS. Concerning thy daughter, then, I wish to tell thee marvelous and fearful things.

CLY. Then delay not, but speak as quickly as possible.

MESS. But, my dear mistress, thou shalt learn every thing clearly, and I will speak from the very commencement, unless my memory, in something failing, deceive my tongue. For when we came to the inclosure and flowery meads of Diana, the daughter of Jove, where there was an assembly of the army of the Greeks, leading thy daughter, the host of the Greeks was straightway convened. But when king Agamemnon beheld the girl wending her way to the grove for slaughter, he groaned aloud, and turning back his head, he shed tears, placing his garments[103] before his eyes. But she, standing near him that begot her, spake thus: "O father, I am here for thee, and I willing give my body on behalf of my country, and of the whole land of Greece, that, leading it to the altar of the Goddess, they may sacrifice it, since this is ordained. And, as far as I am concerned, may ye be fortunate, and obtain the gift of victory, and reach your native land. Furthermore, let no one of the Greeks lay hands on me, for with a stout heart I will present my neck in silence." Thus much she spoke, and every one marveled on hearing the courage and valor of the virgin. But Talthybius, whose office this was, standing in the midst, proclaimed good-omened silence to the people. And the seer Calchas placed in a golden canister a sharp knife,[104] which he had drawn out,† within its case,† and crowned the head of the girl. But the son of Peleus ran around the altar of the Goddess, taking the canister and lustral waters at the same time. And he said: "O Diana, beast-slaying daughter of Jove, that revolvest thy brilliant light by night, receive this offering which we bestow on thee, [we] the army of the Greeks, and king Agamemnon, the pure blood from a fair virgin's neck; and grant that the sail may be without injury to our ships, and that we may take the towers of Troy by the spear." But the Atrides and all the army stood looking on the ground, and the priest, taking the knife, prayed, and viewed her neck, that he might find a place to strike. And no little pity entered my mind, and I stood with eyes cast down, but suddenly there was a marvel to behold. For every one could clearly perceive the sound of the blow, but beheld not the virgin, where on earth she had vanished. But the priest exclaimed, and the whole army shouted, beholding an unexpected prodigy from some one of the Gods, of which, though seen, they had scarcely belief. For a stag lay panting on the ground, of mighty size to see and beautiful in appearance, with whose blood the altar of the Goddess was abundantly wetted. And upon this Calchas (think with what joy!) thus spake: "O leaders of this common host of the Greeks, behold this victim which the Goddess hath brought to her altar, a mountain-roaming stag. This she prefers greatly to the virgin, lest her altar should be denied with generous blood. And she hath willingly received this, and grants us a prosperous sail, and attack upon Troy. Upon this do every sailor take good courage, and go to his ships, since on this day it behooves us, quitting the hollow recesses of Aulis, to pass over the Ægean wave." But when the whole victim was reduced to ashes, he prayed what was meet, that the army might obtain a passage. And Agamemnon sends me to tell thee this, and to say what a fortune he hath met with from the Gods, and hath obtained unwaning glory through Greece. But I speak, having been present, and witnessing the matter. Thy child has evidently flown to the Gods; away then with grief, and cease wrath against your husband. But the will of the Gods is unforeseen by mortals, and them they love, they save. For this day hath beheld thy daughter dying and living [in turn.]

CHOR. How delighted am I at hearing this from the messenger; but he says that thy daughter living abides among the Gods.

CLY. O daughter, of whom of the Gods art thou the theft? How shall I address thee? What shall I say that these words do not offer me a vain comfort, that I may cease from my mournful grief on thy account?

CHOR. And truly king Agamemnon draws hither, having this same story to tell thee.

[*Enter* AGAMEMNON.]

AG. Lady, as far as thy daughter is concerned, we may be happy, for she really possesses a companionship with the Gods. But it behooves thee, taking this young child [Orestes,] to go home, for the army is looking toward setting sail. And fare thee well, long hence will be my addresses to thee from Troy, and may it be well with thee.

CHOR. Atrides, rejoicing go thou to the land of the Phrygians, and rejoicing return, having obtained for me most glorious spoils from Troy.

NOTES ON IPHIGENIA IN AULIS

[1] From the answer of the old man, Porson's conjecture, σπευδε, seems very probable.

[2] See Hermann's note. The passage has been thus rendered by Ennius:

AG. "Quid nocti" videtur in altisono

Cœli clupeo?

SEN. Temo superat stellas, cogens

Sublime etiam atque etiam noctis

Itiner.

See Scaliger on Varr. de L.L. vi. p.143, and on Festus s.v. Septemtriones. All the editors have overlooked the following passage of Apuleius de Deo Socr. p. 42, ed. Elm. "Suspicientes in hoc perfectissimo mundi, ut ait Ennius, clypeo," whence, as I have already observed in my notes on the passage, there is little doubt that Ennius wrote "in altisono mundi clypeo," of which *cæli* was a gloss, naturally introduced by those who were ignorant of the use of *mundus* in the same sense. The same error has taken place in some of the MSS. of Virg. Georg. i. 5, 6. Compare the commentators on Pompon. Mela. i. 1, ed. Gronov.

[3] Such seems the force of επι πασιν αγαθοις. The Cambridge editor aptly compares Hipp. 461. χρην σ' επι ῾ρητοις αρα Πατερα φυτευειν.

[4] The συννυμφοκομος was probably a kind of gentleman usher, but we have no correlative either to the custom or the word.

[5] Hermann rightly regards this as a hendiadys.

[6] δρομωι for μορωι is Markland's, and, doubtless, the correct, reading. μονος is merely a correction of the Aldine edition.

[7] But read τας—δελτους with the Cambridge editor, = "in relation to my former dispatches."

[8] ταν should probably be erased before κολπωδη, with the Cambridge editor. He remarks, "the sea-port, although separated from the island by the narrow strait of Euripus, is styled its *wing*." On the metrical difficulties and corruptions throughout this chorus, I must refer the reader to the same critic.

[9] But λεκτρον, *uxorem*, is better, with ed. Camb.

[10] It is impossible to get a satisfactory sense as these lines now stand. I have translated εξορμα. There seems to be a lacuna. The following are the readings of the Camb. ed. εν γαρ π. αντησης, παλιν εξ. ς. χαλινους, επι κυκλωπων νιν ῾ιεις θυμ.

[11] But αγχιαλον is better, with ed. Camb. from the Homeric χαλκιδα τ' αγχιαλον. He remarks that this word, in tragedy, is always the epithet of a place.

[12] i.e. to exact satisfaction for her abduction.

[13] i.e. the tents containing the armed soldiers.

[14] ἡδομενους refers both to Πρωτεσιλαον and Παλαμηδεα, divided by the schema Alcmanicum. See Markland.

[15] Cf. Homer, Il. B. 763 sqq.

[16] Cf. Monk on Hippol. 1229. I have translated συριγγας according to the figure of a part for the whole. The whole of the remainder of this chorus has been condemned as spurious by the Cambridge editor. See his remarks, p. 219 sqq.

[17] Can θετον refer to αγαλμα understood?

[18] This part of the chorus is hopeless, as it is evidently imperfect. See Herm.

[19] The Cambridge editor would assign this line to Menelaus.

[20] I read ευ κεκομψευσαι, with Ruhnken. The Cambridge editor also reads πονηρα, which is better suited to the style of Euripides.

[21] The same scholar has anticipated my conjecture, σαφης for σαφες.

[22] Compare the similar conduct of Pausanias in Thucyd. i. 130, Dejoces in Herodot. i., with Livy, iii. 36, and Apul. de Deo Socr. p. 44, ed. Elm.

[23] I read το Πριαμου with Elmsley. See the Camb. ed.

[24] With the Cambridge editor I have restored the old reading εχοντες.

[25] But see ed. Camb.

[26] αυ is a better reading. See Markland and ed. Camb.

[27] There is little hope of this passage, unless we adopt the readings of the Cambridge editor, ʽους λαβων στρατευμʼ. ʽετοιμοι δʼ εισι. The next line was lost, but has been restored from Theophilus ad Autol. p. 258, and Stob. xxviii. p. 128, Grot.

[28] Cf. Soph. Antig. 523. ουτοι συνεχθειν, αλλα συμφιλειν εφυν.

[29] Dindorf condemns the whole of this speech of the messenger, as well as the two following lines. Few will perhaps be disposed to follow him, although the awkwardness of the passage may be admitted. Hermann considers that the hasty entrance of the messenger is signified by his commencing with half a line.

[30] There seems an intended allusion to the double sense of προτελεια, both as a marriage and sacrificial rite. See the Cambridge editor, and my note on Æsch. Agam. p. 102, n. 2, ed. Bohn.

[31] "Auspicare canistra, id quod proximum est." MUSGR.

[32] I think this is the meaning implied by νυμφευσουσα, as in vs. 885. 'ιν' αγαγοις χαιρουσ' Αχιλλει παιδα νυμφευσουσα σην. Alcest. 317. ου γαρ σε μητηρ ουτε νυμφευσει ποτε. The word seems to refer to the whole business of a mamma on this important occasion.

[33] The Cambridge editor on vs. 439, p. 109, well observes, "the actual arrival of Iphigenia having convinced Menelaus that her sacrifice could not any longer be avoided, he bethinks him of removing from his brother's mind the impression produced by their recent altercation; and knowing his open and unsuspicious temper, he feels that he may safely adopt a false position, and deprecate that of which he was at the same time most earnestly desirous."

[34] So Markland, but Hermann and the Cambridge editor prefer the old reading μετεστι σοι.

[35] This and the two following lines are condemned by Dindorf.

[36] Bœckh, Dindorf, and the Cambridge editor rightly explode these three lines, which are not even correct Greek.

[37] λησομεν, *latebo faciens*.

[38] παρα for παρον, ed. Camb.

[39] i.e. by the gift of Venus. For the sense, compare Hippol. 443.

[40] Read διαφοροι δε τροποι with Monk, and ορθως with Musgrave.

[41] But παιδευομενων is better, with ed. Camb.

[42] I have partly followed Markland, partly Matthiæ, in rendering this awkward passage. But there is much awkwardness of expression, and the notes of the Cambridge editor well deserve the attention of the student. εξαλλασσουσαν χαριν seems to refer to μετρια χαρις in vs. 555, and probably signifies that the grace of a reasonable affection leads to the equal grace of a clear perception, the mind being unblinded by vehement impulses of passion.

[43] i.e. quiet, domestic.

[44] ενων is only Markland's conjecture. The whole passage is desperate.

[45] I read μυριοπληθη with ed. Camb. The pronoun 'ο I can not make out, but by supplying an impossible ellipse.

[46] The Cambridge editor rightly reads ιου, ιου, as an exclamation of pleasure, not of pain, is required.

[47] Dindorf condemns this whole paragraph.

[48] The Cambridge editor thinks these two lines a childish interpolation. They certainly are childish enough, but the same objection applies to the whole passage.

[49] But read 'οι δ' with Dobree. The grooms are meant.

[50] Porson condemns these four lines, which are utterly destitute of sense or connection.

[51] These "precious" lines are even worse than the preceding, and rightly condemned by all.

[52] See Elmsl. on Soph. Œd. C. 273. The student must carefully observe the hidden train of thought pervading Agamemnon's replies.

[53] τα Μενελεω κακα must mean the ills resulting from Menelaus, the mischiefs and toils to which his wife led, as in Soph. Antig. 2. των απ Οιδιπου κακων, "the ills brought about by the misfortunes or the curse of Œdipus." But I should almost prefer reading λεχη for κακα, which would naturally refer to Helen.

[54] This line is metrically corrupt, but its emendation is very uncertain.

[55] I have endeavored to convey the play upon the words as closely as I could. Elmsley well suggests that the proper reading is 'εστηξεις in vs. 675.

[56] οφθηναι κοραις, "non, ut hic, a viris et exercitu." BRODÆUS.

[57] Porson on Orest. 1090, remarks on that 'ο κυριος was the term applied to the father or guardian of the bride. We might therefore render, "Jove gave her away," etc.

[58] If this be the correct reading, we must take καλως ironically. But I think with Dindorf, that κακως, αναγκαιως δε.

[59] This verse is condemned by the Cambridge editor.

[60] Barnes rightly remarked that ηιξα is the aorist of αισσω, *conor, aggredior.*

[61] These three lines are expunged by the Cambridge editor.

[62] I have expressed the sense of η μη τρεφειν (= μη εχειν γυναικα), rather than the literal meaning of the words.

[63] I must inform the reader that the latter portion of this chorus is extremely unsatisfactory in its present state. The Cambridge editor, who has well discussed its difficulties, thinks that Περγαμον is wrong, and that ερυμα should be introduced from vs. 792, where it appears to be quite useless.

[64] I have ventured to read δακρυοεν τανυσας with MSS. Pariss., omitting ερυμα with the Cambridge editor, by which the difficulty is removed. The same scholar remarks that δακρυοεν is used adverbially.

[65] There is obviously a defect in the structure, but I am scarcely pleased with the attempts made to supply it.

[66] Read και παιδας with Musgrave.

[67] But see ed. Camb.

[68] But see ed. Camb.

[69] But the Cambridge editor admirably amends, εις μελλοντα σωσει χρονον, i.e. "it will be a long time before it preserves them," a hit at the self-importance of the old gentleman.

[70] I have little hesitation in reading πελας μοι with Markland, in place of γελαι μοι.

[71] There is much difficulty in this passage, and Markland appears to give it up in despair. Matthiæ simply takes the first part as equivalent to 'υψηλοφρον εστι, referring μετριως to both verbs. The Cambridge editor takes διαζην as an infinitive disjoined from the construction. Vss. 922 sq. are indebted to Mr. G. Burges for their present situation, having before been assigned to the chorus.

[72] I have closely followed the Cambridge editor.

[73] See the notes of the same scholar.

[74] Dindorf has rightly received Porson's successful emendation. See Tracts, p. 224, and the Cambridge editor.

[75] Read σοις τε μελλουσιν with Markland.

[76] The Cambridge editor would omit vs. 1022. There is certainly a strange redundancy of meaning.

[77] Read εστασεν with Mark. Dind.

[78] So called, either because he was carried off by Jove while hunting in the promontory of Dardanus, or from his Trojan descent.

[79] I have adopted Tyrwhitt's view, considering the words inclosed in inverted commas as the actual words of the epithalamium. See Musgr. and ed. Camb. Hermann is strangely out of his reckoning.

[80] Read, however, Νηρηιδων with Heath, "first of the Nereids."

[81] The Cambridge editor would read νυμφοκομοι, Reiske νυμφοκομον. There is much difficulty in the whole of this last part of the chorus.

[82] Such is Hermann's explanation, but βεβηκοτος can not bear the sense. The Cambridge editor suspects that these five lines are a forgery.

[83] The Cambridge editor rightly, I think, condemns this line as the addition of some one "who thought that something more was wanting to comprise all the complaints of the speaker." I do not think the sense or construction is benefited by their existence.

[84] "Verum astus hic astu vacat." ERASMUS.

[85] Dindorf has apparently done wrong in admitting προσουδισας, but I have some doubt about every other reading yet proposed.

[86] See Camb. ed., who suspects interpolation.

[87] Cf. Lucret. i. 94. "Nec miseræ prodesse in tali tempore quibat, Quod patrio princeps donarat nomine regum." Æsch. Ag. 242 sqq.

[88] The Cambridge editor clearly shows that μοι is the true reading, as in vs. 54, το πραγμα δ' απορως ειχε Τυνδαρεωι πατρι, and 370.

[89] There is much doubt about the reading of this part of the chorus. See Dind. and ed. Camb.

[90] I have partly followed Abresch in translating these lines, but I do not advise the reader to rest satisfied with my translation. A reference to the notes of the elegant scholar, to whom we owe the Cambridge edition of this play, will, I trust, show that I have done as much as can well be done with such corrupted lines.

[91] Achilles is supposed to lay his hand on his sword. See however ed. Camb.

[92] Obviously a spurious line.

[93] I have punctuated with ed. Camb.

[94] See ed. Camb.

[95] ευφημησατε here governs two distinct accusatives.

[96] The Cambridge editor here takes notice of Aristotle's charge of inconsistency, 'οτι ουδεν εοικεν 'η 'ικετευουσα [Iphigenia] τηι 'υστεραι. He well remarks, that Iphigenia at first naturally gives way before the suddenness of the announcement of her fate, but that when she collects her feelings, her natural nobleness prevails.

[97] Cf. Lucret. i. 88. "Cui simul *infula* virgineos *circumdata* comtus, Ex utraque pari malarum parte profusa est."

[98] Read παγας with Reiske, Dind. ed. Camb. There is much corruption and awkwardness in the following verses of this ode.

[99] On the sense of μεμονε see ed. Camb., who would exclude δι' εμον ονομα.

[100] Cf. Soph. Ant. 806 sqq. The whole of this passage has been admirably illustrated by the Cambridge editor.

[101] There is much awkwardness about this epithet πατρωιαι. One would expect a clearer reference to Agamemnon. I scarcely can suppose it correct, although I do not quite see my way in the Cambridge editor's readings.

[102] Porson, Præf. ad Hec. p. xxi., and the Cambridge editor (p. 228 sqq.) have concurred in fully condemning the whole of this last scene. It is certain that in the time of Ælian something different must have been in existence, and equally certain that the whole abounds in repetitions and inconsistencies, that seem to point either to spuriousness, or, at least, to the existence of interpolations of a serious character. In this latter opinion Matthiæ and Dindorf agree.

[103] An allusion to the celebrated picture of Timanthes. See Barnes.

[104] I have done my best with this passage, following Matthiæ's explanation, which, however, I do not perfectly understand. If vs. 1567 were away, we should be less at a loss, but the same may be said of the whole scene.

IPHIGENIA IN TAURIS.

PERSONS REPRESENTED.

IPHIGENIA.

ORESTES.

PYLADES.

HERDSMAN.

THOAS.

MESSENGER.

MINERVA.

CHORUS OF GRECIAN CAPTIVE WOMEN.

THE ARGUMENT.

Orestes, coming into Tauri in Scythia, in company with Pylades, had been commanded to bear away the image of Diana, after which he was to meet with a respite from the avenging Erinnyes of his mother. His sister Iphigenia, who had been carried away by Diana from Aulis, when on the point of being sacrificed by her father, chances to be expiating a dream that led her to suppose Orestes dead, when a herdsman announces to her the arrival and detection of two strangers, whom she is bound by her office to sacrifice to Diana. On meeting, a mutual discovery takes place, and they plot their escape. Iphigenia imposes on the superstitious fears of Thoas, and, removing them to the sea-coast, they are on the point of making their escape together, when they are surprised, and subsequently detained and driven back by stress of weather. Thoas is about to pursue them, when Minerva appears, and restrains him from doing so, at the same time procuring liberty of return for the Grecian captives who form the chorus.

IPHIGENIA IN TAURIS.

IPHIGENIA.

Pelops,[1] the son of Tantalus, setting out to Pisa with his swift steeds, weds the daughter of Œnomaus, from whom sprang Atreus; and from Atreus his sons, Menelaus and Agamemnon, from which [latter] I was born, Iphigenia, child of [Clytæmnestra,] daughter of Tyndarus, whom my father, as he imagined, sacrificed to Diana on account of Helen, near the eddies, which Euripus continually whirls to and fro, upturning the dark blue sea with frequent blasts, in the famed[2] recesses of Aulis. For here indeed king Agamemnon drew together a Grecian armament of a thousand ships, desiring that the Greeks might take the glorious prize of victory over Troy,[3] and avenge the outraged nuptials of Helen, for the gratification of Menelaus. But, there being great difficulty of sailing,[4] and meeting with no winds, he came to [the consideration of] the omens of burnt sacrifices, and Calchas speaks thus. O thou who rulest over this Grecian expedition, Agamemnon, thou wilt not lead forth thy ships from the ports of this land, before Diana shall receive thy daughter Iphigenia as a victim; for thou didst vow to sacrifice to the light-bearing Goddess whatsoever the year should bring forth most beautiful. Now your wife Clytæmnestra has brought forth a daughter in your house, referring to me the title of the most beautiful, whom thou must needs sacrifice. And so, by the arts of Ulysses,[5] they drew me from my mother under pretense of being wedded to Achilles. But I wretched coming to Aulis, being seized and raised aloft above[6] the pyre, would have been slain by the sword; but Diana, giving to the Greeks a stag in my stead, stole me away, and, sending me through the clear ether,[7] she settled me in this land of the Tauri, where barbarian Thoas rules[8] the land, o'er barbarians, [Thoas,] who guiding his foot swift as the pinion, has arrived at this epithet [of Thoas, i.e. *the swift*] on account of his fleetness of foot. And she places me in this house as priestess, since which time the Goddess Diana is wont to be pleased with such rites as these,[9] the name of which alone is fair. But, for the rest, I am silent, fearing the Goddess. For I sacrifice even as before was the custom in the city, whatever Grecian man comes to this land. I crop the hair, indeed, but the slaying that may not be told is the care of others within these shrines.[10] But the new visions which the [past] night hath brought with it, I will tell to the sky,[11] if indeed this be any remedy. I seemed in my sleep, removed from this land, to be dwelling in Argos, and to slumber in my virgin chamber, but the surface of the earth [appeared] to be shaken with a movement, and I fled, and standing without beheld the coping[12] of the house giving way, and all the roof falling stricken to the ground from the high supports. And one pillar alone, as it seemed to me, was left of my ancestral house, and from its capital it seemed to stream down yellow locks, and to receive a human voice, and I, cherishing this man-slaying office which I hold, weeping [began] to besprinkle it, as though about to be slain. But I thus interpret my dream. Orestes is dead, whose rites I was beginning. For male children are the pillars of the house, and those whom my lustral waters[13] sprinkle die. Nor yet can I connect the dream with my friends, for Strophius had no son, when I was to have died. Now, therefore, I being present, will to my absent brother offer the rites of the dead—for this I can do—in company with the attendants whom the king gave to me, Grecian women. But from some cause they are not yet present. I will go[14] within the home wherein I dwell, these shrines of the Goddess.

ORESTES. Look out! Watch, lest there be any mortal in the way.

PYLADES. I am looking out, and keeping watch, turning my eyes every where.

OR. Pylades, does it seem to you that this is the temple of the Goddess, whither we have directed our ship through the seas from Argos?[15]

PYL. It does, Orestes, and must seem the same to thee.

OR. And the altar where Grecian blood is shed?

PYL. At least it has its pinnacles tawny with blood.

OR. And under the pinnacles themselves do you behold the spoils?

PYL. The spoils, forsooth, of slain strangers.

OR. But it behooves one, turning one's eye around, to keep a careful watch. O Phœbus, wherefore hast thou again led me into this snare by your prophecies, when I had avenged the blood of my father by slaying my mother? But by successive[16] attacks of the Furies was I driven an exile, an outcast from the land, and fulfilled many diverse bending courses. But coming [to thy oracle] I required of thee how I might arrive at an end of the madness that drove me on, and of my toils [which I had labored through, wandering over Greece.[17]] But thou didst answer that I must come to the confines of the Tauric territory, where thy sister Diana possesses altars, and must take the image of the Goddess, which they here say fell from heaven[18] into these shrines; and that taking it either by stratagem or by some stroke of fortune, having gone through the risk, I should give it to the land of the Athenians—but no further directions were given—and that having done this, I should have a respite from my toils.[19] But I am come hither, persuaded by thy words, to an unknown and inhospitable land. I ask you, then, Pylades, for you are a sharer with me in this toil, what shall we do? For thou beholdest the lofty battlements of the walls. Shall we proceed to the scaling of the walls? How then should we escape notice[20] [if we did so?] Or shall we open the brass-wrought fastenings of the bolts? of which things we know nothing.[21] But if we are caught opening the gates and contriving an entrance, we shall die. But before we die, let us flee to the temple, whither we lately sailed.

PYL. To fly is unendurable, nor are we accustomed [to do so,] and we must not make light of the oracle of the God. But quitting the temple, let us hide our bodies in the caves, which the dark sea splashes with its waters, far away from the city, lest any one beholding the bark, inform the rulers, and we be straightway seized by force. But when the eye of dim night shall come, we must venture, bring all devices to bear, to seize the sculptured image from the temple. But observe the eaves [of the roof,[22]] where there is an empty space between the triglyphs in which you may let yourself down. For good men dare encounter toils, but the cowardly are of no account any where. We have not indeed come a long distance with our oars, so as to return again from the goal.[23]

OR. But one must follow your advice, for you speak well. We must go whithersoever in this land we can conceal our bodies, and lie hid. For the [will] of the God will not be the cause of his oracle falling useless. We must venture; for no toil has an excuse for young men.[24]

[ORESTES *and* PYLADES *retire aside.*]

CHORUS. Keep silence,[25] O ye that inhabit the twain rocks of the Euxine that face each other. O Dictynna, mountain daughter of Latona, to thy court, the gold-decked pinnacles of temples with fine columns, I, servant to the hallowed guardian of the key, conduct my pious virgin foot, changing [for my present habitation] the towers and walls of Greece with its noble steeds, and Europe with its fields abounding in trees, the dwelling of my ancestral home. I am come. What new matter? What anxious care hast thou? Wherefore hast thou led me, led me to the shrines, O daughter of him who came to the walls of Troy with the glorious fleet, with thousand sail, ten thousand spears of the renowned Atrides?[26]

IPHIGENIA. O attendants mine,[27] in what moans of bitter lamentation do I dwell, in the songs of a songless strain unfit for the lyre, alas! alas! in funereal griefs for the ills which befall me, bemoaning my brother, what a vision have I seen in the night whose darkness has passed away![28] I am undone, undone. No more is my father's house, ah me! no more is our race. Alas! alas! for the toils in Argos! Alas! thou deity, who hast now robbed me of my only brother, sending him to Hades, to whom I am about to pour forth on the earth's surface these libations and this bowl for the departed, and streams from the mountain heifer, and the wine draughts of Bacchus, and the work of the swarthy bees,[29] which are the wonted peace-offerings to the departed. O germ of Agamemnon beneath the earth, to thee as dead do I send these offerings. And do thou receive them, for not before [thine own] tomb do I offer my auburn locks,[30] my tears. For far away am I journeyed from thy country and mine, where, as opinion goes, I wretched lie slaughtered.

CHOR. A respondent strain and an Asiatic hymn of barbarian wailing will I peal forth to thee, my mistress, the song of mourning which, delighting the dead, Hades hymns in measure apart from Pæans.[31] Alas! the light of the sceptre in the Atrides' house is faded away. Alas! alas for my ancestral home! And what government of prosperous kings will there be in Argos?[32] * * * * And labor upon labor comes on * * * * [33] with his winged mares driven around. But the sun, changing from its proper place, [laid aside] its eye of light.[34] And upon other houses woe has come, because of the golden lamb, murder upon murder, and pang upon pang, whence the avenging Fury[35] of those sons slain of old comes upon the houses of the sons of Tantalus, and some deity hastens unkindly things against thee.

IPH. From the beginning the demon of my mother's zone[36] was hostile to me, and from that night in which the Fates hastened the pangs of childbirth[37] * * * * whom, the first-born germ the wretched daughter of Leda, (Clytæmnestra,) wooed from among the Greeks brought forth, and trained up as a victim to a father's sin, a joyless sacrifice, a votive offering. But in a horse-chariot they brought[38] me to the sands of Aulis, a bride, alas! unhappy bride to the son of Nereus' daughter, alas! And now a stranger I dwell in an unpleasant home on the inhospitable sea, unwedded, childless, without city, without a friend, not chanting Juno in Argos, nor in the sweetly humming loom adorning with the shuttle the image of Athenian Pallas[39] and of the Titans, but imbruing altars with the shed blood of strangers, a pest unsuited to the harp, [of strangers] sighing forth[40] a piteous cry, and shedding a piteous tear. And now indeed forgetfulness of these matters [comes upon] me, but now I mourn my brother dead in Argos, whom I left yet an infant at the breast, yet young, yet a germ in his mother's arms and on her bosom, Orestes [the future] holder of the sceptre in Argos.

CHOR. But hither comes a herdsman, leaving the sea-coast, about to tell thee some new thing.

HERDSMAN. Daughter of Agamemnon and child of Clytæmnestra, hear thou from me a new announcement.

IPH. And what is there astonishing in the present report?

HERDS. Two youths are come into this land, to the dark-blue Symplegades, fleeing into a ship, a grateful sacrifice and offering to Diana. But you can not use too much haste[41] in making ready the lustral waters and the consecrations.

IPH. Of what country? of what land do the strangers bear the name?

HERDS. Greeks, this one thing I know, and nothing further.

IPH. Hast thou not heard the name of the strangers, so as to tell it?

HERDS. One of them was styled Pylades by the other.

IPH. But what was the name of the yoke-fellow of this stranger?

HERDS. No one knows this. For we heard it not.

IPH. But how saw ye them, and chanced to take them?

HERDS. Upon the furthest breakers of the inhospitable sea.

IPH. And what had herdsmen to do with the sea?

HERDS. We came to lave our steers in the dew of the sea.

IPH. Go back again to this point—how did ye catch them, and by what means, for I would fain know this? For they are come after a long season, nor has the altar of the Goddess yet been crimsoned with Grecian blood.[42]

HERDS. After we woodland herdsmen had brought our cattle down to the sea that flows between the Symplegades, there is a certain hollow cave,[43] broken by the frequent lashing of the waves, a retreat for those who hunt for the purple fish. Here some herdsman among us beheld two youths, and he retired back, piloting his step on tiptoe, and said: See ye not? these who sit here are some divine powers. And one of us, being religiously given, uplifted his hand, and addressed them, as he beheld: O son of Leucothea, guardian of ships, Palæmon our lord, be propitious to us, whether indeed ye be the twin sons of Jove (Castor and Pollux) who sit upon our shores, or the image of Nereus, who begot the noble chorus of the fifty Nereids. But another vain one, bold in his lawlessness, scoffed at these prayers, and said that they were shipwrecked[44] seamen who sat upon the cleft through fear of the law, hearing that we here sacrifice strangers. And to most of us he seemed to speak well, and [we resolved] to hunt for the accustomed victims for the Goddess. But meanwhile one of the strangers leaving the rock, stood still, and shook his head up and down, and groaned, with his very fingers quaking, wandering with ravings, and shouts with voice like that of hunter, "Pylades, dost thou behold this? Dost not behold this snake of Hades, how she would fain slay me, armed against me with horrid vipers?[45] And she breathing from beneath her garments[46] fire and slaughter, rows with her wings, bearing my mother in her arms, that she may cast upon me this rocky mass. Alas! she will slay me. Whither shall I fly?" And one beheld not the same form of countenance, but he uttered in turn the bellowings of calves and howls of dogs, which imitations [of wild beasts] they say the Furies utter. But we flinching, as though about to die, sat mute; and he drawing a sword with his hand, rushing among the calves, lion-like, strikes them on the flank with the steel, driving it into their sides, fancying that he was thus avenging himself on the Fury Goddesses, till that a gory foam was dashed up from the sea. Meanwhile, each one of us, as he beheld the herds being slain and ravaged, armed himself, and inflating the conch[47] shells and assembling the inhabitants—for we thought that herdsmen were weak to fight against well-trained and youthful strangers. And a large number of us was assembled in a short time. But the stranger, released from the attack of madness, drops down, with his beard befouled with foam. But when we saw him fallen opportunely [for us,] each man did his part, with stones, with blows. But the other of the strangers wiped away the foam, and tended his mouth, and spread over him the well-woven texture of his garments, guarding well the coming wounds, and aiding his friend with tender offices. But when the stranger returning to his senses leaped up, he perceived that a hostile tempest and present calamity was close upon them, and he groaned aloud. But we ceased not hurling rocks, each standing in a different place. But then indeed we heard a dread exhortation, "Pylades, we shall die, but that we die most gloriously! Follow me, drawing thy sword in hand." But when we saw the twain swords of the enemy[48] brandished, in flight we filled the woods about the crag. But if one fled, others pressing on pelted them; and if they drove these away, again the party who had just yielded aimed at them with rocks. But it was incredible, for out of innumerable hands no one succeeded in hitting these victims to the Goddess. And we with difficulty, I will not say overcome them by force, but taking them in a circle, beat[49] their swords out of their hands with stones, and they dropped their knees to earth [overcome] with toil. And we brought them to the king of this land, but he, when he beheld them, sent them as quickly as possible to thee for lustral waters and sacrifice. But do thou, O virgin, wish that such strangers may be here as victims, and if thou slayest these strangers, Hellas will atone for thy [intended] murder, paying the penalty of the sacrifice at Aulis.[50]

CHOR. Thou hast told wondrous things concerning him who has appeared, whosoever he be that has come to the inhospitable sea from the Grecian earth.[51]

IPH. Be it so. Do thou go and bring the strangers, but I will take care respecting the matters[52] here. O hapless heart, that once wast mild and full of pity toward strangers, awarding the tear to those of thine own land, when thou didst receive Grecian men into thine hands.[53] But now, because of the dreams by which I am driven wild, thinking that Orestes no longer beholds the sun, ye will find me ill disposed, whoever ye be that come. For this is true, I perceive it, my friends,[54] for the unhappy who themselves fare ill have no good feelings toward those more fortunate. But neither has any wind sent by Jove ever come [hither,] nor ship, which could have brought hither Helen, who destroyed me, and Menelaus, in order that I might be avenged on them, placing an Aulis here to the account[55] of the one there, where the sons of Danaus seized, and would have slain me like as a calf, and the father who begat me was the priest. Ah me! for I can not forget the ills of that time, how oft I stretched out my hands to his beard, and hanging on the knees of him who gave me life, spake words like these: "O father, basely am I, basely am I wedded at thine hands. But my mother, while thou art slaying me, and her Argive ladies are hymning my wedding[56] with their nuptial songs, and all the house resounds with the flute, while I perish by thy hands. Hades in truth was Achilles, not the son of Peleus, whom thou didst name as my husband, and in the chariot didst pilot me by craft unto a bloody wedding." But I, casting mine eye through my slender woven veil, neither took up with mine hands my brother who is now dead, nor joined my lips to my sister's,[57] through modesty, as departing to the home of Peleus; and many a salutation I deferred, as though about to come again to Argos. Oh wretched one, if thou hast died! from what glorious state, Orestes, and from how envied a sire's fortune art thou fallen! But I reproach the devices of the Goddess, who, if any one work the death of a man, or touch with hands a woman newly delivered, or a corpse, restrains him from her altars, as deeming him impure, but yet herself takes pleasure in man-slaying sacrifices. It can not be that the consort of Jove, Latona, hath brought forth so much ignorance. I even disbelieve the banquets of Tantalus set before the Gods, [as that they] should be pleased with feeding on a boy. But I deem that those in this land, being themselves man-slayers, charge the Goddess with their own baseness, for I think not that any one of the Gods is bad.

CHOR. Ye dark blue, dark blue meetings of the sea, which Io, hurried along by the brize, once passed through to the Euxine wave, having changed the territory of Asia for Europe,—who were they who left fair-watered Eurotas, flourishing in reeds, or the sacred founts of Dirce, and came, and came to the inhospitable land, where the daughter of Jove bedews her altars and column-girt temples with human blood? Of a truth by the surge-dashing oars of fir, worked on both sides, they sailed in a nautical carriage o'er the ocean waves, striving in the emulation after loved wealth in their houses. For darling hope is in dangers insatiate among men, who bear off the weight of riches, wandering in vain speculation on the wave and o'er barbarian cities. But to some[58] there is a mind immoderate after riches, to others they come unsought. How did they pass through the rocks that run together, the ne'er resting beaches of Phineus, [and] the marine shore, running o'er the surge of Amphitrite,[59]—where the choruses of the fifty daughters of Nereus entwine in the dance,—[although] with breezes that fill the sails, the creaking rudders resting at the poop, with southern gales or the breezes of Zephyr, to the bird-haunted land, the white beach, the glorious race-course of Achilles, near the Euxine Sea. Would that, according to my mistress' prayers, Helen, the dear daughter of Leda, might sometime chance to come, quitting the city of Troy, that, having been drenched about the head with the blood-stained lustral dews, she might die by my mistress' hand, paying in turn an equal penalty [for her death.] Most joyfully then would we receive this news, if any one came sailing from the Grecian land, to make the toils of my hapless slavery to cease. And would that in my dreams I might tread[60] in mine home and ancestral city, enjoying the hymns of delight, a joy shared with the prosperous. But hither they come, bound as to their two[61] hands with chains, a new sacrifice for the Goddess. Be silent, my friends, for these first-fruits of the Greeks approach the temples, nor has the herdsman told a false tale. O reverend Goddess, if the city performs these things agreeably to thee, receive the sacrifice which, not hallowed among the Greeks, the custom of this place presents as a public offering.[62]

IPH. Be it so. I must first take care that the rites of the Goddess are as they should be. Let go the hands of the strangers, that being consecrated they may no longer be in bonds. And, going within the temple, make ready the things which are necessary and usual on these occasions. Alas! Who is the mother who once bore you? And who your father, and your sister, if there be any born? Of what a pair of youths deprived will she be brotherless! For all the dispensations of the Gods creep into obscurity, and no one [absent] knows misfortune,[63] for fortune leads astray to what is hardly known. Whence come ye, O unhappy strangers? After how long a time have ye sailed to this land, and ye will be a long time from your home, ever among the shades![64]

OR. Why mournest thou thus, and teasest us[65] concerning our future ills, whoever thou art, O lady? In naught do I deem him wise, who, when about to die, with bewailings seeks to overcome the fear of death, nor him who deplores death now near at hand,[66] when he has no hope of safety, in that he joins two ills instead of one, both incurs the charge of folly, and dies none the less. But one must needs let fortune take its course. But mourn us not, for we know and are acquainted with the sacrificial rites of this place.

IPH. Which of ye twain here is named Pylades? This I would fain know first.

OR. This man, if indeed 'tis any pleasure for thee to know this.

IPH. Born citizen of what Grecian state?

OR. And what wouldst thou gain by knowing this, lady?

IPH. Are ye brothers from one mother?

OR. In friendship we are, but we are not related, lady.

IPH. But what name did the father who begot thee give to thee?

OR. In truth we might be styled the unhappy.

IPH. I ask not this. Leave this to fortune.

OR. Dying nameless, I should not be mocked.

IPH. Wherefore dost grudge this, and art thus proud?

OR. My body thou shalt sacrifice, not my name.

IPH. Nor wilt thou tell me which is thy city?

OR. No. For thou seekest a thing of no profit, seeing I am to die.

IPH. But what hinders thee from granting me this favor?

OR. I boast renowned Argos for my country.

IPH. In truth, by the Gods I ask thee, stranger, art thou thence born?

OR. From Mycenæ,[67] that was once prosperous.

IPH. And hast thou set out a wanderer from thy country, or by what hap?

OR. I flee in a certain wise unwilling, willingly.

IPH. Wouldst thou tell me one thing that I wish?

OR. That something, forsooth,[68] may be added to my misfortune.

IPH. And truly thou hast come desired by me, in coming from Argos.

OR. Not by myself, at all events; but if by thee, do thou enjoy it.[69]

IPH. Perchance thou knowest Troy, the fame of which is every where.

OR. Ay, would that I never had, not even seeing it in a dream!

IPH. They say that it is now no more, and has fallen by the spear.

OR. And so it is, nor have you heard what is not the case.

IPH. And is Helen come back to the house of Menelaus?

OR. She is, ay, coming unluckily to one of mine.

IPH. And where is she? For she has incurred an old debt of evil with me also.

OR. She dwells in Sparta with her former consort.

IPH. O hateful pest among the Greeks, not to me only!

OR. I also have received some fruits of her nuptials.

IPH. And did the return of the Greeks take place, as is reported?

OR. How dost thou question me, embracing all matters at once!

IPH. For I wish to obtain this before that thou diest.

OR. Examine me, since thou hast this longing, and I will speak.

IPH. Has a certain seer named Calchas returned from Troy?

OR. He perished, as the story ran, at Mycenæ.

IPH. O revered Goddess, how well it is! And how fares the son of Laertes?

OR. He has not yet returned to his home, but he is alive, as report goes.

IPH. May he perish, never obtaining a return to his country!

OR. Invoke nothing—all his affairs are in a sickly state.

IPH. But is the son of Thetis, the daughter of Nereus, yet alive?

OR. He is not. In vain he held his wedding in Aulis.

IPH. A crafty [wedding] it was, as those who have suffered say.

OR. Who canst thou be? How well dost ken the affairs of Greece!

IPH. I am from thence. While yet a child I was undone.

OR. With reason thou desirest to know the affairs there, O lady.

IPH. But how [fares] the general, who they say is prosperous.

OR. Who? For he whom I know is not of the fortunate.

IPH. A certain king Agamemnon was called the son of Atreus.

OR. I know not—cease from these words, O lady.

IPH. Nay, by the Gods, but speak, that I may be rejoiced, O stranger.

OR. The wretched one is dead, and furthermore hath ruined one.[70]

IPH. Is dead? By what mishap? O wretched me!

OR. But why dost mourn this? Was he a relation of thine?

IPH. I bemoan his former prosperity.

OR. [Ay, well mayest thou,] for he has fallen, slain shamefully by a woman.

IPH. O all grievous she that slew and he that fell!

OR. Cease now at least, nor question further.

IPH. Thus much at least, does the wife of the unhappy man live?

OR. She is no more. The son she brought forth, he slew her.

IPH. O house all troubled! with what intent, then?[71]

OR. Taking satisfaction on her for the death of his father.

IPH. Alas! how well he executed an evil act of justice.[72]

OR. But, though just, he hath not good fortune from the Gods.

IPH. But does Agamemnon leave any other child in his house?

OR. He has left a single virgin [daughter,] Electra.

IPH. What! Is there no report of his sacrificed daughter?[73]

OR. None indeed, save that being dead she beholds not the light.

IPH. Hapless she, and the father who slew her!

OR. She perished, a thankless offering[74] because of a bad woman.

IPH. But is the son of the deceased father at Argos?

OR. He, wretched man, is nowhere and every where.

IPH. Away, vain dreams, ye were then of naught!

OR. Nor are the Gods who are called wise any less false than winged dreams. There is much inconsistency both among the Gods and among mortals. But one thing alone is left, when[75] a man not being foolish, persuaded by the words of seers, has perished, as he hath perished in man's knowledge.

CHOR. Alas! alas! But what of us and our fathers? Are they, or are they not in being, who can tell?

IPH. Hear me, for I am come to a certain discourse, meditating what is at once profitable for you and me. But that which is well is chiefly produced thus, when the same matter pleases all. Would ye be willing, if I were to save you, to go to Argos, and bear a message for me to my friends there, and carry a letter, which a certain captive wrote, pitying me, nor deeming my hand that of a murderess, but that he died through custom, as the Goddess sanctioned such things as just? For I had no one who would go and bear the news back to Argos, and who, being preserved, would send my letters to some one of my friends.[76] But do thou, for thou art, as thou seemest, of no ignoble birth, and knowest Mycenæ and the persons I wish, do thou, I say,[77] be saved, receiving no dishonorable reward, your safety for the sake of trifling letters. But let this man, since the city compels it, be a sacrifice to the Goddess, apart from thee.

OR. Well hast thou spoken the rest, save one thing, O stranger lady, for 'tis a heavy weight upon me that this man should be slain. For I was steersman of the vessel to these ills,[78] but he is a fellow-sailor because of mine own troubles. In no wise then is it right that I should do thee a favor to his destruction, and myself escape from ills. But let it be thus. Give him the letter, for he will send it to Argos, so as to be well for thee, but let him that will slay me. Base is the man, who, casting his friends into calamity, himself is saved. But this man is a friend, who I fain should see the light no less that myself.

IPH. O noblest spirit, how art thou sprung from some generous root, thou truly a friend to thy friends! Such might he be who is left of my brothers! For in good truth, strangers, I am not brotherless, save that I behold him not. But since thou willest thus, let us send this man bearing the letter, but thou wilt die, and some great desire of this chances to possess thee?[79]

OR. But who will sacrifice me, and dare this dreadful deed?

IPH. I; for I have this sacrificial duty[80] from the Goddess.

OR. Unenviable indeed. O damsel, and unblest.

IPH. But we lie under necessity, which one must beware.

OR. Thyself, a female, sacrificing males with the sword?

IPH. Not so; but I shall lave around thy head with the lustral stream.

OR. But who is the slayer, if I may ask this?

IPH. Within the house are they whose office is this.

OR. And what manner of tomb will receive me, when I die?

IPH. The holy flame within, and the dark chasm of the rock.[81]

OR. Alas! Would that a sister's hand might lay me out.[82]

IPH. A vain prayer hast thou uttered, whoever thou art, O stranger, for she dwells far from this barbarian land. Nevertheless, since thou art an Argive, I will not fail to do thee kindness in what is possible. For on thy tomb will I place much adornment, and with the tawny oil will I cause thy body to be soon consumed,[83] and on thy pyre will I pour the flower-sucked riches of the swarthy bee. But I will go and fetch the letter from the shrines of the Goddess. But do thou not bear ill will against me. Guard them, ye servants, [but] without fetters.[84] Perchance I shall send unexpected tidings to some one of my friends at Argos, whom I chiefly love, and the letter, telling to him that she lives whom he thinks dead, will announce a faithful pleasure.

CHOR. I deplore thee now destined to the gory streams of the lustral waters.[85]

OR. 'Tis piteous, truly;[86] but fare ye well, stranger ladies.

CHOR. But thee, (to Pylades) O youth, we honor for thy happy fortune, that at some time thou wilt return to thy country.

PYL. Not to be coveted[87] by friends, when friends are to die.

CHOR. O mournful journeying! Alas! alas! thou art undone. Woe! woe! which is the [victim] to be? For still my mind resolves[88] twain doubtful [ills,] whether with groans I shall bemoan thee (to Orestes) or thee (to Pylades) first.

OR. Pylades, hast thou, by the Gods, experienced the same feeling as myself?

PYL. I know not. Thou askest me unable to say.

OR. Who is this damsel? With what a Grecian spirit she asked us concerning the toils in Troy, and the return of the Greeks, and Calchas wise in augury, and about Achilles, and how she pitied wretched Agamemnon, and asked me of his wife and children. This stranger lady is[89] some Greek by race; for otherwise she never would have been sending a letter and making these inquiries, as sharing a common weal in the well-doing of Argos.

PYL. Thou hast outstripped me a little, but thou outstrippest me in saying the same things, save in one respect—for all, with whom there is any communication, know the fate of the king. But I was[90] considering another subject.

OR. What? laying it down in common, you will better understand.

PYL. 'Tis base that I should behold the light, while you perish; and, having sailed with you, with you I must needs die also. For I shall incur the imputation of both cowardice and baseness in Argos and the Phocian land with its many dells, and I shall seem to the many, for the many are evil, to have arrived alone in safety to mine home, having deserted thee, or even to have murdered thee, taking advantage of the sickly state of thine house, and to have devised thy fate for the sake of reigning, in order that, forsooth, I might wed thy sister as an heiress[91]. These things, then, I dread, and hold in shame, and it shall not be but I will breathe my last with thee, be slain, and have my body burned with thee, being a friend, and dreading reproach.

OR. Speak words of better omen. I must needs bear my troubles, but when I may [endure] one single trouble, I will not endure twain. For what thou callest bitter and reproachful, that is my portion, if I cause thee to be slain who hast shared my toils. For, as far as I am concerned, it stands not badly with me, faring as I fare at the hands of the Gods, to end my life. But thou art prosperous, and hast a home pure, not sickening, but I [have] one impious and unhappy. And living thou mayest raise children from my sister, whom I gave thee to have[92] as a wife, and my name might exist, nor would my ancestral house be ever blotted out. But go, live, and dwell in my father's house; and when thou comest to Greece and chivalrous Argos, by thy right hand, I commit to thee this charge. Heap up a tomb, and place upon it remembrances of me, and let my sister offer tears and her shorn locks upon my sepulchre. And tell how I died by an Argive woman's hand, sacrificed as an offering by the altar's side. And do thou never desert my sister, seeing my father's connections and home bereaved. And fare thee well! for I have found thee best among my friends. Oh thou who hast been my fellow-huntsman, my mate! Oh thou who hast borne the weight of many of my sorrows! But

Phœbus, prophet though he be, has deceived me. For, artfully devising, he has driven me as far as possible from Greece, in shame of his former prophecies. To whom I, yielding up mine all, and obeying his words, having slain my mother, myself perish in turn.

PYL. Thou shalt have a tomb, and never will I, hapless one, betray thy sister's bed, since I shall hold thee more a friend dead than living. But the oracle of the God has never yet wronged thee, although thou art indeed on the very verge of death. But excessive mischance is very wont, is very wont to present changes, when the matter so falls.

OR. Be silent—the words of Phœbus avail me naught, for the lady is coming hither without the temple.

IPH. Depart ye, and go and make ready the things within for those who superintend the sacrifice. These, O stranger, are the many-folded inclosures of the letter, but hear thou what I further wish. No man is the same in trouble, and when he changes from fear into confidence. But I fear, lest he having got away from this land, will deem my letter of no account, who is about to bear this letter to Argos.[93]

OR. What wouldst thou? Concerning what art thou disturbed?

IPH. Let him make me oath that he will ferry these writings to Argos, to those friends to whom I wish to send them.

OR. Wilt thou in turn make the same assertion to him?

IPH. That I will do, or will not do what thing? say.

OR. That you will release him from this barbarian land, not dying.

IPH. Thou sayest justly; for how could he bear the message?

OR. But will the ruler also grant this?

IPH. Yea. I will persuade him, and will myself embark him on the ship's hull.

OR. Swear, but do thou commence such oath as is holy.

IPH. Thou must say "I will give this [letter] to my friends."

PYL. I will give this letter to thy friends.

IPH. And I will send thee safe beyond the Cyanean rocks.

PYL. Whom of the Gods dost thou call to witness of thine oath in these words?

IPH. Diana, in whose temple I hold office.

PYL. But I [call upon] the king of heaven, hallowed Jove.

IPH. But if, deserting thine oath, thou shouldst wrong me—

PYL. May I not return? But thou, if thou savest me not—

IPH. May I never living set footprint in Argos.

PYL. Hear now then a matter which we have passed by.

IPH. There will be opportunity hereafter, if matters stand aright.

PYL. Grant me this one exception. If the vessel suffer any harm, and the letter be lost[94] in the storm, together with the goods, and I save my person only, that this mine oath be no longer valid.[95]

IPH. Knowest thou what I will do?[96] for the many things contained in the folds of the letter bear opportunity for many things.[97] I will tell you in words all that you are to convey to my friends, for this plan is safe. If indeed thou preservest the letter, it will itself silently tell the things written, but if these letters be lost at sea, saving thy body, thou wilt preserve my message.

PYL. Thou hast spoken well on behalf of the Gods[98] and of myself. But tell me to whom at Argos I must needs bear these epistles, and what hearing from thee, I must tell.

IPH. Bear word to Orestes, the son of Agamemnon, (*reading*) "she[99] that was sacrificed at Aulis gives this commission, Iphigenia alive, but no longer alive as far as those in Argos are concerned."

OR. But where is she? Does she come back again having died?

IPH. She, whom you see. Do not confuse me with speaking. (*Continues reading*) "Bear me to Argos, my brother, before I die, remove me from this barbarian land and the sacrifices of the Goddess, in which I have the office of slaying strangers."

OR. Pylades, what shall I say? where shall we be found to be?[100]

IPH. (*still reading*) "Or I will be a cause of curses upon thine house, Orestes," (*with great stress upon the name and turning to Pylades,*) "that thou, twice hearing the name, mayest know it."

PYL. O Gods!

IPH. Why callest thou upon the Gods in matters that are mine?

PYL. 'Tis nothing. Go on. I was wandering to another subject. Perchance, inquiring of thee, I shall arrive at things incredible.[101]

IPH. (*continues reading*) "Say that the Goddess Diana saved me, giving in exchange for me a hind, which my father sacrificed, thinking that it was upon me that he laid the sharp sword, and she placed me to dwell in this land." This is the burden of my message, these are the words written in my letter.

PYL. O thou who hast secured me in easy oaths, and hast sworn things fairest, I will not delay much time, but I will firmly accomplish the oath I have sworn. Behold, I bear and deliver to thee a letter, O Orestes, from this thy sister.

OR. I receive it. And letting go the opening of the letter, I will first seize a delight not in words (*attempts to embrace her*). O dearest sister mine, in amazement, yet nevertheless embracing thee with a doubting arm, I go to a source of delight, hearing things marvelous to me.[102]

CHOR. Stranger,[103] thou dost not rightly pollute the servant of the Goddess, casting thine arm around her garments that should ne'er be touched.

OR. O fellow-sister born of one sire, Agamemnon, turn not from me, possessing a brother whom you never thought to possess.

IPH. I [possess] thee my brother? Wilt not cease speaking? Both Argos and Nauplia are frequented by him.[104]

OR. Unhappy one! thy brother is not there.

IPH. But did the Lacedæmonian daughter of Tyndarus beget thee?

OR. Ay, to the grandson of Pelops, whence I am sprung.[105]

IPH. What sayest thou? Hast thou any proof of this for me?

OR. I have. Ask something relative to my ancestral home.

IPH. Thou must needs then speak, and I learn.

OR. I will first speak from hearsay from Electra, this.[106] Thou knowest the strife that took place between Atreus and Thyestes?

IPH. I have heard of it, when it was waged concerning the golden lamb.

OR. Dost thou then remember weaving [a representation of] this on the deftly-wrought web?

IPH. O dearest one. Thou art turning thy course near to my own thoughts.[107]

OR. And [dost thou remember] a picture on the loom, the turning away of the sun?

IPH. I wove this image also in the fine-threaded web.

OR. And didst thou receive[108] a bath from thy mother, sent to Aulis?

IPH. I know it: for the wedding, though good, did not take away my recollection.[109]

OR. But what? [Dost thou remember] to have given thine hair to be carried to thy mother?

IPH. Ay, as a memorial for the tomb[110] in place of my body.

OR. But the proofs which I have myself beheld, these will I tell, viz. the ancient spear of Pelops in my father's house, which brandishing in his hand, he [Pelops] won Hippodameia, having slain Ænomaus, which is hidden in thy virgin chamber.

IPH. O dearest one, no more, for thou art dearest. I hold thee, Orestes, one darling son[111] far away from his father-land, from Argos, O thou dear one!

OR. And I [hold] thee that wast dead, as was supposed. But tears, yet tearless,[112] and groans together mingled with joy, bedew thine eyelids, and mine in like manner.

IPH. This one, this, yet a babe I left, young in the arms of the nurse, ay, young in our house. O thou more fortunate than my words[113] can tell, what shall I say? This matter has turned out beyond marvel or calculation.

OR. [Say this.] May we for the future be happy with each other!

IPH. I have experienced an unaccountable delight, dear companions, but I fear lest it flit[114] from my hands, and escape toward the sky. O ye Cyclopean hearths, O Mycenæ, dear country mine. I am grateful to thee for my life, and grateful for my nurture, in that thou hast trained for me this brother light in my home.

OR. In our race we are fortunate, but as to calamities, O sister, our life is by nature unhappy.

IPH. But I wretched remember when my father with foolish spirit laid the sword upon my neck.

OR. Ah me! For I seem, not being present, to behold you there.[115]

IPH. Without Hymen, O my brother, when I was being led to the fictitious nuptial bed of Achilles. But near the altar were tears and lamentations. Alas! alas, for the lustral waters there!

OR. I mourn aloud for the deed my father dared.

IPH. I obtained a fatherless, a fatherless lot. But one calamity follows upon another.[116]

OR. [Ay,] if thou hadst lost thy brother, O hapless one, by the intervention of some demon.

IPH. O miserable for my dreadful daring! I have dared horrid, I have dared horrid things. Alas! my brother. But by a little hast thou escaped an unholy destruction, stricken by my hands. But what will be the end after this? What fortune will befall me? What retreat can I find for thee away from this city? can I send you out of the reach of slaughter to your country Argos, before that my sword enter on the contest concerning thy blood?[117] This is thy business, O hapless soul, to discover, whether over the land, not in a ship, but by the gust[118] of your feet thou wilt approach death, passing through[119] barbarian hordes, and through ways not to be traversed? Or[120] [wilt thou pass] through the Cyanean creek, a long journey in the flight of ships. Wretched, wretched one! Who then or God, or mortal, or [unexpected event,[121]] having accomplished a way out of inextricable difficulties, will show forth to the sole twain Atrides a release from ills?

CHOR. Among marvels and things passing even fable are these things which I shall tell as having myself beheld, and not from hearsay.

PYL. It is meet indeed that friends coming into the presence of friends, Orestes, should embrace one another with their hands, but, having ceased from mournful matters, it behooves you also to betake you to those measures by which we, obtaining the glorious name of safety, may depart from this barbarian earth. For it is the part of wise men, not wandering from their present chance, when they have obtained an opportunity, to acquire further delights.[122]

OR. Thou sayest well. But I think that fortune will take care of this with us. For if a man be zealous, it is likely that the divine power will have still greater power.

IPH. Do not restrain or hinder me from your words, not first to know what fortune of life Electra has obtained, for this were pleasant to me [to hear.][123]

OR. She is partner with this man, possessing a happy life.

IPH. And of what country is he, and son of what man born?

OR. Strophius the Phocian is styled his father.

IPH. And he is of the daughter of Atreus, a relative of mine?

OR. Ay, a cousin, my only certain friend.

IPH. Was he not in being, when my father sought to slay me?

OR. He was not, for Strophius was childless some time.

IPH. Hail! O thou spouse of my sister.

OR. Ay, and my preserver, not relation only.

IPH. But how didst thou dare the terrible deeds in respect to your mother?

OR. Let us be silent respecting my mother—'twas in avenging my father.

IPH. And what was the reason for her slaying her husband?

OR. Let go the subject of my mother. Nor is it pleasant for you to hear.

IPH. I am silent. But Argos now looks up to thee.

OR. Menelaus rules: I am an exile from my country.

IPH. What, did our uncle abuse our house unprospering?

OR. Not so, but the fear of the Erinnyes drives me from my land.

IPH. For this then wert thou spoken of as being frantic even here on the shore.

OR. We were beheld not now for the first time in a hapless state.

IPH. I perceive. The Goddesses goaded thee on because of thy mother.

OR. Ay, so as to cast a bloody bit[124] upon me.

IPH. For wherefore didst thou pilot thy foot to this land?

OR. I came, commanded by the oracles of Phœbus—

IPH. To do what thing? Is it one to be spoken of or kept in silence?

OR. I will tell you, but these are the beginning for me of many[125] woes. After these evil things concerning my mother, on which I keep silence, had been wrought, I was driven an exile by the pursuits of the Erinnyes, when Loxias sent my foot[126] to Athens, that I might render satisfaction to the deities that must not be named. For there is a holy council, that Jove once on a time instituted for Mars on account of some pollution of his hands.[127] And coming thither, at first indeed no one of the strangers received me willingly, as being abhorred by the Gods, but they who had respect to me, afforded me[128] a stranger's meal at a separate table, being under the same house roof, and silently devised in respect to me, unaddressed by them, how I might be separated from their banquet[129] and cup, and, having filled up a share of wine in a separate vessel, equal for all, they enjoyed themselves. And I did not think fit to rebuke my guests, but I grieved in silence, and did not seem to perceive [their conduct,] deeply groaning, because I was my mother's slayer.[130] But I hear that my misfortunes have been made a festival at Athens, and that this custom still remains, that the people of Pallas honor the Libation Vessel.[131] But when I came to the hill of Mars, and stood in judgment, I indeed occupying one seat, but the eldest of the Erinnyes the other, having spoken and heard respecting my mother's death, Phœbus saved me by bearing witness, but Pallas counted out for me[132] the equal votes with her hand, and I came off victor in the bloody trial.[133] As many then as sat [in judgment,] persuaded by the sentence, determined to hold their dwelling near the court itself.[134] But as many of the Erinnyes as did not yield obedience to the sentence passed, continually kept driving me with unsettled wanderings, until I again returned to the holy ground of Phœbus, and lying stretched before the adyts, hungering for food, I swore that I would break from life by dying on the spot, unless Phœbus, who had undone, should preserve me. Upon this Phœbus, uttering a voice from the golden tripod, sent me hither to seize the heaven-sent image, and place it in the land of Athens. But that safety which he marked out for me do thou aid in. For if we can lay hold on the image of the Goddess, I both shall cease from my madness, and embarking thee in the bark of many oars, I shall settle thee again in Mycenæ. But, O beloved one, O sister mine, preserve my ancestral home, and preserve me, since all my state and that of the Pelopids is undone, unless we seize on the heavenly image of the Goddess.

CHOR. Some dreadful wrath of the Gods hath burst forth, and leads the seed of Tantalus through troubles.[135]

IPH. I entertained the desire to reach Argos, and behold thee, my brother, even before thou camest. But I wish, as you do, both to save thee, and to restore again our sickening ancestral home from troubles, in no wise wrath with him who would have slain me. For I should both release my hand from thy slaughter, and preserve mine house. But I fear how I shall be able to escape the notice of the Goddess and the king, when he shall find the stone pedestal bared of the image. And how shall I escape death? What account can I give? But if indeed these matters can be effected at once, and thou wilt bear away the image, and lead me in the fair-pooped ship, the risk will be a glorious one. But separated from this I perish, but you, arranging your own affairs, would obtain a prosperous return. Yet in no wise will I fly, not even if I needs must perish, having preserved thee. In no wise, I say;[136] for a man who dies from among his household is regretted, but a woman is of little account.

OR. I would not be the murderer both of thee and of my mother. Her blood is enough, and being of the same mind with you, [with you] I should wish, living or dying, to obtain an equal lot. †But I will lead thee, even though I myself fall here, to my house, or, remaining with thee, will die.[137]† But hear my opinion. If this had been disagreeable to Diana, how would Loxias have answered, that I should remove the image of the Goddess to the city of Pallas, and behold thy face? For, putting all these matters together, I hope to obtain a return.

IPH. How then can it happen that neither you die, and that we obtain what we wish? For it is in this respect that our journey homeward is at fault, but the will is not wanting.

OR. Could we possibly destroy the tyrant?

IPH, Thou tellest a fearful thing, for strangers to slay their receivers.

OR. But if it will preserve thee and me, one must run the risk.

IPH. I could not—yet I approve your zeal.

OR. But what if you were secretly to hide me in this temple?

IPH. In order, forsooth, that, taking advantage of darkness, we might be saved?

OR. For night is the time for thieves, the light for truth.

IPH. But within are the sacred keepers,[138] whom we can not escape.

OR. Alas! we are undone. How can we then be saved?

IPH. I seem to have a certain new device.

OR. Of what kind? Make me a sharer in your opinion, that I also may learn.

IPH. I will make use of thy ravings as a contrivance.

OR. Ay, cunning are women to find out tricks.

IPH. I will say that thou, being slayer of thy mother, art come from Argos.

OR. Make use of my troubles, if you can turn them to account.

IPH. I will say that it is not lawful to sacrifice thee to the Goddess.

OR. Having what pretext? For I partly suspect.

IPH. As not being pure, but I will [say that I will][139] give what is holy to sacrifice.

OR. How then the more will the image of the Goddess be obtained?

IPH. I [will say that I] will purify thee in the fountains of the sea.

OR. The statue, in quest of which, we have sailed, is still in the temple.

IPH. And I will say that I must wash that too, as if you had laid hands on it.

OR. Where then is the damp breaker of the sea of which you speak?

IPH. Where thy ship rides at anchor with rope-bound chains.

OR. But wilt thou, or some one else, bear the image in their hands?

IPH. I, for it is lawful for me alone to touch it.

OR. But in what part of this contrivance will our friend Pylades[140] be placed?

IPH. He will be said to bear the same pollution of hands as thyself.

OR. And wilt thou do this unknown to, or with the knowledge of the king?

IPH. Having persuaded him by words, for I could not escape notice.

OR. And truly the well-rowed ship is ready for sailing.[141]

IPH. You must take care of the rest, that it be well.

OR. There lacks but one thing, namely, that these women who are present preserve our secret. But do thou beseech them, and find words that will persuade. A woman in truth has power to move pity. But all the rest will perchance fall out well.

IPH. O dearest women, I look to you, and my affairs rest in you, as to whether they turn out well, or be of naught, and I be deprived of my country, my dear brother, and dearest sister. And let this first be the commencement of my words. We are women, a race well inclined to one another, and most safe in keeping secret matters of common interest. Do ye keep silence for us, and labor out our escape. Honorable is it for the man who possesses a faithful tongue. But behold how one fortune holds the three most dear, either a return to our father-land, or to die. But, being preserved, that thou also mayest share my fortune, I will restore thee safe to Greece. But, by thy right hand, thee, and thee [addressing the women of the chorus in succession] I beseech, and thee by thy beloved cheek, and thy knees, and those most dear at home, mother, and father, and children, to whom there are such.[142] What say ye? Who of you will, or will not [speak!] these things.[143] For if ye assent not to my words, I am undone, and my wretched sister.

CHOR. Be of good cheer, dear mistress, and think only of being saved, since on my part all shall be kept secret, the mighty Jove be witness! in the things thou enjoinest.

IPH. May your words profit ye, and may ye be blest. 'Tis thy part now, and thine [to the different women] to enter the house, as the ruler of this land will straightway come, inquiring concerning the sacrifice of the strangers, whether it is over. O revered Goddess, who in the recesses of Aulis didst save me from the dire hand of a slaying father, now also save me and these, or the voice of Loxias will through thee be no longer truthful among mortals. But do thou with good will quit the barbarian land for Athens, for it becomes thee not to dwell here, when you can possess a blest city.

CHORUS. Thou bird, that by the rocky cliffs of the sea, halcyon,[144] dost chant thy mournful elegy, a sound well understood by the skilled, namely, that thou art ever bemoaning thine husband in song, I, a wingless bird, compare my dirge with thine, longing for the assemblies[145] of the Greeks, longing for Lucina, who dwells along the Cynthian height, and near the palm[146] with its luxuriant foliage, and the rich-springing laurel, and the holy shoot of the deep blue olive, the dear place of Latona's throes,[147] and the lake that rolls its waters in a circle,[148] where the melodious swan honors the muses. O ye many tricklings of tears which fell upon my cheeks, when, our towers being destroyed, I traveled in ships beneath the oars and the spears of the foes.[149] And through a bartering of great price I came a journey to a barbarian land,[150] where I serve the daughter of Agamemnon, the priestess of the Goddess, and the sheep-slaughtering[151] altars, envying her who has all her life been unfortunate;[152] for she bends not under necessity, who is familiar with it. Unhappiness is wont to change,[153] but to fare ill after prosperity is a heavy life for mortals. And thee indeed, O mistress, an Argive ship of fifty oars will conduct home, and the wax-bound reed of mountain Pan with Syrinx tune cheer on the oarsmen, and prophet Phœbus, plying the tones of his seven-stringed lyre, with song will lead thee prosperously to the rich land of Athens. But leaving me here thou wilt travel by the dashing oars. And the halyards by the prow,[154] will stretch forth the sails to the air, above the beak, the sheet lines of the swift-journeying ship. Would that I might pass through the glittering course, where the fair light of the sun wends its way, and over my own chamber might rest from rapidly moving the pinions on my shoulders.[155] And would that I might stand in the dance, where also [I was wont to stand,] a virgin sprung from honorable nuptials,[156] wreathing the dances of my companions at the foot of my dear mother,[157] bounding to the rivalry of the graces, to the wealthy strife respecting [beauteous] hair, pouring my variously-painted garb and tresses around, I shadowed my cheeks.[158]

[*Enter* THOAS.]

THOAS. Where is the Grecian woman who keeps the gate of this temple? Has she yet begun the sacrifice of the strangers, and are the bodies burning in the flame within the pure recesses?

CHOR. Here she is, O king, who will tell thee clearly all.

TH. Ah! Why art thou removing in your arms this image of the Goddess from its seat that may not be disturbed, O daughter of Agamemnon?

IPH. O king, rest there thy foot in the portico.

TH. But what new matter is in the house, Iphigenia?

IPH. I avert the ill—for holy[159] do I utter this word.

TH. What new thing art thou prefacing? speak clearly.

IPH. O king, no pure offerings hast thou hunted out for me.

TH. What hath taught you this? or dost thou speak it as matter of opinion?

IPH. The image of the Goddess hath again turned away from her seat.[160]

TH. Of its own accord, or did an earthquake turn it?

IPH. Of its own accord, and it closed its eyes.

TH. But what is the cause? is it pollution from the strangers?

IPH. That very thing, naught else, for they have done dreadful things.

TH. What, did they slay any of the barbarians upon the shore?

IPH. They came possessing the stain of domestic murder.

TH. What? for I am fallen into a longing to learn this.

IPH. They put an end to a mother's life by conspiring sword.

TH. Apollo! not even among barbarians would any one have dared this.

IPH. By persecutions they were driven out of all Greece.

TH. Is it then on their account that thou bearest the image without?

IPH. Ay, under the holy sky, that I may remove it from blood stains.

TH. But how didst thou discover the pollution of the strangers?

IPH. I examined them, when the image of the Goddess turned away.

TH. Greece hath trained thee up wise, in that thou well didst perceive this.

IPH. And now they have cast out a delightful bait for my mind.

TH. By telling thee any charming news of those at Argos?

IPH. That my only brother Orestes fares well.

TH. So that, forsooth, thou mightest preserve them because of their pleasant news!

IPH. And that my father lives and fares well.

TH. But thou hast with reason attended to the interest of the Goddess.

IPH. Ay, because hating all Greece that destroyed me.

TH. What then shall we do, say, concerning the two strangers?

IPH. We needs must respect the established law.

TH. Are not the lustral waters and thy sword already engaged?[161]

IPH. First I would fain lave them in pure cleansings.

TH. In the fountains of waters, or in the dew of the sea?

IPH. The sea washes out all the ills of men.

TH. They would certainly fall in a more holy manner before the Goddess.

IPH. And my matters would be in a more fitting state.[162]

TH. Does not the wave dash against the very temple?

IPH. There is need of solitude, for we have other things to do.

TH. Lead them whither thou wilt, I crave not to see things that may not be told.

IPH. The image of the Goddess also must be purified by me.

TH. If indeed the stain of the matricide hath fallen on it.

IPH. For otherwise I should not have removed it from its pedestal.

TH. Just piety and foresight! How reasonably doth all the city marvel at thee!

IPH. Knowest thou then what must be done for me?

TH. 'Tis thine to explain this.

IPH. Cast fetters upon the strangers.

TH. Whither could they escape from thee?

IPH. Greece knows nothing faithful.

TH. Go for the fetters, attendants.

IPH. Ay, and let them bring the strangers hither.

TH. This shall be.

IPH. Having enveloped their heads in robes.

TH. Against the scorching of the sun?

IPH. And send thou with me of thy followers—

TH. These shall accompany thee.

IPH. And send some one to signify to the city—

TH. What hap?

IPH. That all remain in their homes.

TH. Lest they encounter homicide?

IPH. For such things are unclean.

TH. Go thou, and order this.

IPH. That no one come into sight.

TH. Thou carest well for the city.

IPH. Ay, and more particularly friends must not be present.[163]

TH. This you say in reference to me.

IPH. But do thou, abiding here before the temple of the Goddess—

TH. Do what?

IPH. Purify the house with a torch.

TH. That it may be pure when thou comest back to it?

IPH. But when the strangers come out,

TH. What must I do?

IPH. Place your garment before your eyes.

TH. Lest I contract contagion?

IPH. But if I seem to tarry very long,

TH. What limit of this shall I have?

IPH. Wonder at nothing.

TH. Do thou rightly the business of the Goddess at thy leisure.

IPH. And may this purification turn out as I wish!

TH. I join in your prayer.

IPH. I now see these strangers coming out of the house, and the adornments of the Goddess, and the young lambs, in order that I may wash out foul slaughter by slaughter, and the shining light of lamps, and the other things, as many as I ordered as purifications for the strangers and the Goddess. But I proclaim to the strangers to get out of the way of this pollution, if any gate-keeper of the temples keeps pure hands for the Gods, or is about to join in nuptial alliance, or is pregnant, flee, get out of the way, lest this pollution fall on any. O thou queen, virgin daughter of Jove and Latona, if I wash away the blood-pollution from these men, and sacrifice where 'tis fitting, thou wilt occupy a pure house, and we shall be prosperous. But although I do not speak of the rest, I nevertheless signify my meaning to the Gods who know most things,[164] and to thee, O Goddess.

CHORUS.[165] Of noble birth is the offspring of Latona, whom once on a time in the fruitful valleys of Delos, Phœbus with his golden locks, skilled on the lyre, (and she who rejoices in skill of the bow,) his mother bore while yet an infant[166] from the sea-side rock, leaving the renowned place of her delivery, destitute of waters,[167] the Parnassian height haunted by Bacchus,

- 356 -

where the ruddy-visaged serpent, with spotted back, † brazen † beneath the shady laurel with its rich foliage, an enormous prodigy of the earth, guarded the subterranean oracle. Him thou, O Phœbus, while yet an infant, while yet leaping in thy dear mother's arms, didst slay, and entered upon thy divine oracles, and thou sittest on the golden tripod, on the throne that is ever true, distributing to mortals prophecies from the divine adyts beneath the Castalian streams, dwelling hard by, occupying a dwelling in the middle of the earth.[168] But when, having gone against Themis, daughter of earth, he expelled her from the divine oracles, earth begot dark phantoms of dreams, which to many mortals explain what first, what afterward, what in future will happen, during their sleep in the couches of the dusky earth.[169] But † the earth † deprived Phœbus of the honor of prophecies, through anger on her daughter's account, and the swift-footed king, hastening to Olympus, stretched forth his little hand to the throne of Jove.[170] [beseeching him] to take away the earth-born[171] wrath of the Goddess, † and the nightly responses. † But he laughed, because his son had come quickly to him, wishing to obtain the wealthy office, and he shook his hair, and put an end to the nightly dreams,[172] and took away nightly divination from mortals, and again conferred the honor on Loxias, and confidence to mortals from the songs of oracles [proclaimed] on this throne, thronged to by many strangers.[173]

[*Enter* A MESSENGER.]

MESS. O ye guardians of the temple and presidents of the altars, where in this land has king Thoas gone? Do ye, opening the well-fastened gates, call the ruler of this land outside the house.

CHOR. But what is it, if I may speak when I am not bidden?

MESS. The two youths have escaped, and are gone by the contrivances of Agamemnon's daughter, endeavoring to fly from this land, and taking the sacred image in the bosom of a Grecian ship.

CHOR. Thou tellest an incredible story, but the king of this country, whom you wish to see, is gone, having quitted the temple.

MESS. Whither? For he needs must know what has been done.

CHOR. We know not. But go thou and pursue him to wheresoever, having met with him, thou mayest recount this news.

MESS. See, how faithless is the female race! and ye are partners in what has been done.

CHOR. Art thou mad? What have we to do with the flight of the strangers? Will you not go as quickly as possible to the gates of the rulers?

MESS. Not at least before some distinct informer[174] tell me this, whether the ruler of the land is within or not within. Ho there! Open the fastenings, I speak to those within, and tell the master that I am at the gates, bearing a weight of evil news.

THOAS. (*coming out*) Who makes this noise near the temple of the Goddess, hammering at the door, and sending fear within?

MESS. These women told me falsely, (and tried to drive me from the house,) that you were away, while you really were in the house.

TH. Expecting or hunting after what gain?

MESS. I will afterward tell of what concerns them, but hear the present, immediate matter. The virgin, she that presided over the altars here, Iphigenia, has gone out of the land with the strangers, having the sacred image of the Goddess; but the expiations were pretended.

TH. How sayest thou? possessed by what breath of calamity?[175]

MESS. In order to preserve Orestes, for at this thou wilt marvel.

TH. What [Orestes]? Him, whom the daughter of Tyndarus bore?

MESS. Him whom she consecrated to the Goddess at these altars.

TH. Oh marvel! How can I rightly[176] call thee by a greater name?

MESS. Do not turn thine attention to this, but listen to me; and having perceived and heard, clearly consider what pursuit will catch the strangers.

TH. Speak, for thou sayest well, for they do not flee by the way of the neighboring sea, so as to be able to escape my fleet.

MESS. When we came to the sea-shore, where the vessel of Orestes was anchored in secret, to us indeed, whom thou didst send with her, bearing fetters for the strangers, the daughter of Agamemnon made signs that we should get far out of the way, as she was about to offer the secret[177] flame and expiation, for which she had come. But she, holding the fetters of the strangers in her hands, followed behind them. And these matters were suspicious, but they satisfied your attendants, O king. But at length, in order forsooth that she might seem to us to be doing something, she screamed aloud, and chanted barbarian songs like a sorceress, as if washing out the stain of murder. But after we had remained sitting a long time, it occurred to us whether the strangers set at liberty might not slay her, and take to flight. And through fear lest we might behold what was not fitting, we sat in silence, but at length the same words were in every body's mouth, that we should go to where they were, although not permitted. And upon this we behold the hull of the Grecian ship, [the rowing winged with well-fitted oars,[178]] and fifty sailors holding their oars in the tholes, and the youths, freed from their fetters, standing [on the shore] astern of the ship.[179] But some held in the prow with their oars, and others from the epotides let down the anchor, and others hastily applying the ladders, drew the stern-cables through their hands, and giving them to the sea, let them down to the strangers.[180] But we unsparing [of the toil,] when we beheld the crafty stratagem, laid hold of the female stranger and of the cables, and tried to drag the rudders from the fair-prowed ship from the steerage-place. But words ensued: "On what plea do ye take to the sea, stealing from this land the images and priestess? Whose son art thou, who thyself, who art carrying this woman from the land?" But he replied, "Orestes, her brother, that you may know, the son of Agamemnon, I, having taken this my sister, whom I had lost from my house, am bearing her off." But naught the less we clung to the female stranger, and compelled them by force to follow us to thee, upon which arose sad smitings of the cheeks. For they had not arms in their hands, nor had we; but fists were sounding against fists, and the arms of both the youths at once were aimed against our sides and to the liver, so that we at once were exhausted[181] and worn out in our limbs. But stamped with horrid marks we fled to a precipice, some having bloody wounds on the head, others in the eyes, and standing on the heights, we waged a safer warfare, and pelted stones. But archers, standing on the poop, hindered us with their darts, so that we returned back. And meanwhile—for a tremendous wave drove the ship against the land, and there was alarm [on board] lest she might dip her sheet-line[182]—Orestes, taking his sister on his left shoulder, walked into the sea, and leaping upon the ladder, placed her within the well-banked ship, and also the image of the daughter of Jove, that fell from heaven. And from the middle of the ship a voice spake thus, "O mariners of the Grecian ship, seize[183] on your oars, and make white the surge, for we have obtained the things on account of which we sailed o'er the Euxine within the Symplegades." But they shouting forth a pleasant cry, smote the brine. The ship, as long indeed as it was within the port, went on; but, passing the outlet, meeting with a strong tide, it was driven back. For a terrible gale coming suddenly, drives [the bark winged with well-fitted oars] poop-wise,[184] but they persevered, kicking against the wave, but an ebbing tide brought them again aground. But the daughter of Agamemnon stood up and prayed, "O daughter of Latona, bring me, thy priestess, safe into Greece from a barbarian land, and pardon the stealing away of me. Thou also, O Goddess, lovest thy brother, and think thou that I also love my kindred." But the sailors shouted a pæan in assent to the prayers of the girl, applying on a given signal the point of the shoulders,[185] bared from their hands, to the oars. But more and more the vessel kept nearing the rocks, and one indeed leaped into the sea with his feet, and another fastened woven nooses.[186] And I was immediately sent hither to thee, to tell thee, O king, what had happened there. But go, taking fetters and halters in your hands, for, unless the wave shall become tranquil, there is no hope of safety for the strangers. For the ruler of the sea, the revered Neptune, both favorably regards Troy, and is at enmity with the Pelopidæ. And he will now, as it seems, deliver up to thee and the citizens the son of Agamemnon, to take him into your hands, and his sister, who is detected ungratefully forgetting the Goddess in respect to the sacrifice at Aulis.[187]

CHOR. O hapless Iphigenia, with thy brother wilt thou die, again coming into the hands of thy masters.

TH. O all ye citizens of this barbarian land, will ye not, casting bridles on your horses, run to the shore, and receive the casting on of the Grecian ship? But hastening, by the favor of the Goddess, will ye not hunt down the impious men, and some of you haul the swift barks down to the sea, that by sea, and by horse-coursings on the land seizing them, we may either hurl them down the broken rock, or impale their bodies upon stakes. But you women, the accomplices in these plots, I will punish hereafter, when I have leisure, but now, having such a present duty, we will not remain idle.

[MINERVA *appears*.]

MIN. Whither, whither sendest thou this troop to follow [the fugitives,] king Thoas? List to the words of me, Minerva. Cease pursuing, and stirring on the onset of your host. For by the destined oracles of Loxias Orestes came hither, fleeing the wrath of the Erinnyes, and in order to conduct his sister's person to Argos, and to bear the sacred image into my land, by way of respite from his present troubles. Thus are our words for thee, but as to him, Orestes, whom you wish to slay, having caught him in a tempest at sea, Neptune has already, for my sake, rendered the surface of the sea waveless, piloting him along in the ship. But do thou, Orestes, learning my commands, (for thou hearest the voice of a Goddess, although not present,) go, taking the image and thy sister. And when thou art come to heaven-built Athens, there is a certain sacred district in the farthest bounds of Atthis, near the Carystian rock, which my people call Aloe—here, having built a temple, do thou enshrine the image named after the Tauric land and thy toils, which thou hast labored through, wandering over Greece, under the goad of the Erinnyes. But mortals hereafter shall celebrate her as the Tauric Goddess Diana. And do thou ordain this law, that, when the people celebrate a feast in grateful commemoration of thy release from slaughter,[188] let them apply the sword to the neck of a man, and let blood flow on account of the holy Goddess, that she may have honor. But, O Iphigenia, thou must needs be guardian of the temple of this Goddess at the hallowed ascent of Brauron;[189] where also thou shalt be buried at thy death, and they shall offer to you the honor of rich woven vestments, which women, dying in childbed, may leave in their houses. But I command thee to let these Grecian women depart from the land on account of their disinterested disposition,[190] I, having saved thee also on a former occasion, by determining the equal votes in the Field of Mars, Orestes, and that, according to the same law, he should conquer, whoever receive equal suffrages. But, O son of Agamemnon, do thou remove thy sister from this land, nor be thou angered, Thoas.

TH. Queen Minerva, whosoever, on hearing the words of the Gods, is disobedient, thinks not wisely. But I will not be angry with Orestes, if he has carried away the image of the Goddess with him, nor with his sister. For what credit is there in contending with the potent Gods? Let them depart to thy land with the image of the Goddess, and let them prosperously enshrine the effigy. But I will also send these women to blest Greece, as thy mandate bids. And I will stop the spear which I raised against the strangers, and the oars of the ships, as this seems fit to thee, O Goddess.

MIN. I commend your words, for fate commands both thee and the Gods [themselves.] Go, ye breezes, conduct the vessel of Agamemnon's son to Athens. And I will journey with you, to guard the hallowed image of my sister.

CHOR. Go ye, happy because of your preserved fortune. But, O Athenian Pallas, hallowed among both immortals and mortals, we will do even as thou biddest. For I have received a very delightful and unhoped-for voice in my hearing. O thou all hallowed Victory, mayest thou possess my life, and cease not to crown it.[191]

NOTES ON IPHIGENIA IN TAURIS

[1] This verse and part of the following are set down among the "oil cruet" verses by Aristophanes, Ran. 1232. Aristotle, Poet. § xvii. gives a sketch of the plot of the whole play, by way of illustrating the general form of tragedy. Hyginus, who constantly has Euripides in view, also gives a brief analysis of the plot, fab. cxx. For a description of the quadrigæ of Pelops, see Philostratus Imagg. i. 19. It must be observed, that Antoninus Liberalis, § 27, makes Iphigenia only the supposititious daughter of Agamemnon, but really the daughter of Theseus and Helen. See Meurs. on Lycophron, p. 145.

[2] I must confess that I can not find what should have so much displeased the critics in this word. Iphigenia, in using such an

epithet, evidently refers to her own intended sacrifice, which had rendered the recesses of Aulis a place of no small fame.

[3] But Lenting prefers Αχαιους, with the approbation of the Cambridge editor.

[4] See Reiske apud Dindorf. Compare my note on Æsch. Ag. 188, p. 101, ed. Bohn. So also Callimachus, Hymn. iii. μειλιον απλοϊης, 'οτε 'οι κατεδησας αητας.

[5] Sinon made the same complaint. Cf. Virg. Æn. ii. 90.

[6] Cf. Æsch. Ag. 235.

[7] This whole passage has been imitated by Ovid, de Ponto, iii. 2, 60. "Sceptra tenente illo, liquidas fecisse per auras, Nescio quam dicunt Iphigenian iter. Quam levibus ventis sub nube per aera vectam Creditur his Phœbe deposuisse locis." Cf. Lycophron, p. 16, vs. 3 sqq. Nonnus xiii. p. 332, 14 sqq.

[8] Observe the double construction of ανασσει. Orest. 1690. ναυταις μεδεουσα θαλασσης.

[9] The Cambridge editor would expunge this line, which certainly seems languid and awkward. Boissonade on Aristænet. Ep. xiii. p. 421, would simply read τα δ' αλλα ς. τ. θ. φοβουμενη: θυω γαρ. He also retains 'ιερειαν, referring to Gaisford on Hephæst. p. 216.

[10] The Cambridge editor would throw out vs. 41.

[11] The Cambridge editor refers to Med. 56, Androm. 91, Soph. El. 425. Add Plaut. Merc. i. 1, 3. "Non ego idem facio, ut alios in comœdiis vidi facere amatores, qui aut nocti, aut die, Aut Soli, aut Lunæ miserias narrant suas." Theognetus apud Athen. xv. p. 671. Casaub. πεφιλοσοφηκας γηι και ουρανωι λαλων. Cf. Davis, on Cicero, Tusc. Q. iii. 26, and Lomeier de Lustrat. § xxxvii.

[12] Θριγκον is properly the uppermost part of the walls of any building (Pollux, vii. 27) surrounding the roof, στεγος is the roof itself.

[13] Cf. Meurs. ad Lycophron, p. 148.

[14] I read ειμ' εισω with Hermann and the Cambridge editor.

[15] This line is condemned by the Cambridge editor. Burges has transposed it.

[16] But διαδρομαις, the correction of the Cambridge editor, seems preferable.

[17] An interpolation universally condemned.

[18] See Barnes, and Wetstein on Acts xix. 35.

[19] On the wanderings of Orestes see my note on Æsch. Eum. 238 sqq. p. 187, ed. Bohn.

[20] See the note of the Cambridge editor, with whom we must read εισβησομεσθα.

[21] 'ων ουδεν ισμεν ad interiora templi spectat. HERM.

[22] We must read γεισα τριγλυφων 'οποι, with Blomfield and the Cambridge editor. See Philander on Vitruv. ii. p. 35, and Pollux, vii. 27.

[23] The sense is ουτοι, μακραν ελθοντες, εκ τερματων (sc. a meta) νοστησομεν. ED. CAMB.

[24] The Cambridge editor appositely compares a fragment of our author's Cresphontes, iii. 2, αισχρον τε μοχθειν μη θελειν νεανιαν.

[25] On the whole of this chorus, which is corrupt in several places, the notes of the Cambridge editor should be consulted.

[26] This last lumbering line must be corrupt.

[27] Compare the similar scene in Soph. El. 86 sqq.

[28] Cf. Elect. 90. νυκτος δε τησδε προς ταφον μολων πατρος. Hecub. 76. Æsch. Pers. 179. Aristoph. Ran. 1331.

[29] Compare my note on Æsch. Pers. 610 sqq.

[30] See on Æsch. Choeph. 6.

[31] Markland's emendation has been unanimously adopted by the later editors.

[32] Schema Colophonium. The Cambridge editor compares vs. 244. Αργει σκηπτουχον. Phœn. 17. Θηβαισιν αναξ. Heracl. 361. Αργει τυραννος.

[33] I have marked lacunæ, as some mythological particulars have evidently been lost.

[34] An imperfect allusion to the Thyestean banquet. Cf. Seneca Thyest. 774. "O Phœbe patiens, fugeris retro licet, medioque ruptum merseris cœlo diem, sero occidisti—" vs. 787 sqq.

[35] Cf. Æsch. Ag. 1501 sqq. Seneca, Ag. 57 sqq.

[36] i.e. the demon allotted to me at my birth (cf. notes on Æsch. 1341, p. 135, ed. Bohn). Statius, Theb. i. 60, makes Œdipus invoke Tisiphone under the same character.—"Si me de matre cadentem Fovisti gremio."

[37] See the note of the Cambridge editor.

[38] εβησαν is active.

[39] The Cambridge editor aptly refers to Hecub. 464.

[40] These participles refer to the preceding αιμορραντων ξεινων.

[41] See on Heracl. 721.

[42] The Cambridge editor would omit these two lines.

[43] Cf. vs. 107. κατ' αντρ', 'α ποντιος νοτιδι διακλυζει μελας. On αγμος (Brodæus' happy correction for 'αρμος) the Cambridge editor quotes Nicander Ther. 146. κοιλη τε φαραγξ, και τρηχεες αγμοι, and other passages. The manner of hunting the purple fish is thus described by Pollux, i. 4, p. 24. They plat a long rope, to which they fasten, like bells, a number of hempen baskets, with an open entrance to admit the animal, but which does not allow of its egress. This they let down into the sea, the baskets being filled with such food as the murex delights in, and, having fastened the end of the rope to the rock, they leave it, and returning to the place, draw up the baskets full of the fish. Having broken the shells, they pound the flesh to form the dye.

[44] εφθαρμενους. Cf. Cycl. 300. Hel. 783. Ed. Camb.

[45] Compare Orest. 255 sqq.

[46] χιτωνων is probably corrupt.

[47] Cf. Lobeck on Aj. 17. Hesych. κοχλος τοις θαλαττιοις (i.e. κοχλοις) εχρωντο, προ της των σαλπιγγων ευρεσεως. Virg. Æn. vi. 171. "Sed tum forte cava dum personat æquora concha."

[48] "Moriamur, et in media arma ruamus." Virg. Æn. ii.

[49] Such seems to be the sense, but εξεκλεψαμεν is ridiculous, and Hermann's emendation more so. Bothe reads εξεκοψαμεν, which is better. The Cambridge editor thinks that the difficulty lies in πετροισι.

[50] I would omit this line as an evident gloss.

[51] See the Cambridge editor.

[52] Reiske's emendation, ʽοσια for ʽοια, seems deserving of admission.

[53] The Cambridge editor would omit these lines.

[54] This line also the Cambridge editor trusts "will never hereafter be reckoned among the verses of Euripides."

[55] Such is the proper sense of αντιθεισα.

[56] νιν is νυμφευματα.

[57] Read κασιγνητηι.

[58] I read τοις μεν and τοις δ' with the Cambridge editor. Hermann's emendation is unheard of.

[59] This clause interrupts the construction. δραμοντες must be understood with all the following sentence, as no finite verb is expressed except επερασαν.

[60] I have partly followed Hermann, reading επεβαιην ... απολαυων, but, as to reading ʽυπνων for ʽυμνων, the Cambridge editor well calls it "one of the wonders of his edition." I should prefer reading ολβου with the same elegant scholar.

[61] I follow the Cambridge editor in reading διδυμας, from Ovid, Ep. Pont. iii. 2, 71. "Protinus immitem Triviæ ducuntur ad aram, Evincti geminas ad sua terga manus."

[62] *"displays while she offers"* i.e. *"presents as a public offering"* ED. CAMB.

[63] I am but half satisfied with this passage.

[64] Read εσεσθε δη κατω with the Cambridge editor.

[65] We must read νω with Porson.

[66] Probably a spurious line.

[67] Read Μυκηνων γ', *ay, from Mycenæ,* with the Cambridge editor.

[68] Hermann seems rightly to read ʽος γ' εν.

[69] Dindorf rightly adopts Reiske's emendation συ τουδ' ερα.

[70] The Cambridge editor rightly reads τινά with an accent, as Orestes obviously means himself. Compare Soph. Ant. 751. ʽηδ' ουν θανειται, και θανουσ' ολει τινά.

[71] Such is the force of δη.

[72] I would read εξεπραξατο with Emsley, but I do not agree with him in substituting κακην. The oxymoron seems intentional, and by no means unlike Euripides.

[73] The Cambridge editor would read εστ' ουτις λογος.

[74] But χαριν, as Matthiæ remarks, is taken in two senses; as a preposition with γυναικος, *ob improbam mulierem*, and as a substantive, with αχαριν added. Cf. Æsch. Choeph. 44. Lucretius uses a similar oxymoron respecting the same subject, i. 99. "Sed *casta inceste* nubendi tempore in ipso Hostia concideret mactatu mæsta parentis."

[75] This passage is very corrupt. The Cambridge editor supposes something lost respecting the fortunes of Orestes. Hermann reads 'εν δε λυπεισθαι μονον, 'ο τ' ουκ αφρων ων. But I am very doubtful.

[76] These three lines are justly condemned as an absurd interpolation by Dindorf and the Cambridge editor.

[77] This seems the easiest way of expressing και συ after συ δ'.

[78] I am partly indebted to Potter's happy version. The Cambridge editor is as ingenious as usual, but he candidly allows that conjecture is scarcely requisite.

[79] i.e. thou seemest reckless of life.

[80] προστροπη, this mode of offering supplication, i.e. this duty of sacrifice.

[81] Diodorus, xx. 14. quotes this and the preceding line reading χθονος for πετρας. He supposes that Euripides derived the present account from the sacrifices offered to Saturn by the Carthaginians, who caused their children to fall from the hands of the statue εις τι χασμα πληρες πυρος. Compare Porphyr. de Abst. ii. 27. Justin, xviii. 6. For similar human sacrifices among the Gauls, Cæsar de B.G. vi. 16, with the note of Vossius. Compare also Saxo Grammaticus, Hist. Dan. iii. p. 42, and the passages of early historians quoted in Stephens' entertaining notes, p. 92.

[82] Cf. Tibull. i. 3, 5. "Abstineas, mors atra, precor, non hic mihi mater, Quæ legat in mæstos ossa perusta sinus; non soror, Assyrios cineri quæ dedat odores, et fleat effusis ante sepulchra comis."

[83] This must be what the poet *intends* by καταϭβεϭω, however awkwardly expressed. See Hermann's note.

[84] Compare vs. 468 sq.

[85] This line is hopelessly corrupt.

[86] I read μεν ουν with the Cambridge editor.

[87] αζηλα is in opposition to the whole preceding clause.

[88] See the note of the Cambridge editor on Iph. Aul. 1372.

[89] I should prefer εϭτι δη,"*she surely is.*"

[90] We must evidently read either διηλθον with Porson, or διελθε with Jan., Le Fevre, and Markland.

[91] I almost agree with Dindorf in considering this line spurious.

[92] For this construction compare Ritterhus. ad Oppian, Cyn. i. 11.

[93] I can not help thinking this line is spurious, and the preceding θηται corrupt. One would expect θηϭηι.

[94] Cf. Kuinoel on Cydon. de Mort. Contem. § 1, p. 6, n. 18.

[95] Literally, "no longer a hinderance," i.e. "that I be no longer responsible for its fulfillment."

[96] The Cambridge editor, however, seems to have settled the question in favor of οιϭθ' 'ουν 'ο δραϭον.

[97] I must candidly confess that none of the explanations of these words satisfy me. Perhaps it is best to regard them, with Seidler, as merely signifying the mutability of fortune.

[98] i.e. as far as the fulfilling of my oath is concerned.

[99] The letter evidently commences with the words 'η 'ν Αυλιδι ϭφαγειϭα. I can not imagine how Markland and others should have made it commence with the previous line.

[100] i.e. in what company.

[101] This line is either spurious or out of place. See the Cambridge editor.

[102] The Cambridge editor in a note exhibiting his usual chastened and elegant judgment, regards these three lines as an absurd and trifling interpolation. For the credit of Euripides, I would fain do the same.

[103] The same elegant scholar justly assigns these lines to Iphigenia.

[104] So Erfurdt.

[105] See the Cambridge editor.

[106] This line seems justly condemned by the Cambridge editor.

[107] With καμπτεις understand δρομον = thou art fast arriving at the goal of the truth.

[108] Read απεδεξω with ed. Camb.

[109] "I remember it: for the wedding did not, by its happy result, take away the recollection of that commencement of nuptial ceremonies." CAMB. ED.

[110] i.e. Iphigenia sent it with a view to a cenotaph at Mycenæ, as she was about to die at Aulis. See Seidler.

[111] "This Homeric epithet of an only son is used, I believe, nowhere else in Attic poetry. Its adoption here seems owing to Hom. Il. I. 142 and 284. τισω δε μιν 'ισον Ορεστηι 'Ος μοι τηλυγετος τρεφεται θαλιηι ενι πολληι." ED. CAMB.

[112] This is Musgrave's elegant emendation, which Hermann, unwilling to let well alone, has attempted to spoil. See, however, the Cambridge editor, who possesses taste and clear perception, unbiased by self-love.

[113] Read εμοις with the Cambridge editor.

[114] But φυγηις, and ω φιλος, the emendation of Burges, seems far better, and is followed by the Cambridge editor.

[115] i.e. I can imagine your sufferings at Aulis.

[116] The Cambridge editor compares Hec. 684. 'ετερα δ' αφ' 'ετερων κακα κακων κυρει.

[117] This is Reiske's interpretation, taking the construction πριν ξιφος παλ. επι 'αιματι. But Seidler would recall the old reading πελασαι, comparing Hel. 361. αυτοσιδαρον εσω πελασω δια σαρκος 'αμιλλαν. This is better, but we must also read ετι for επι with the Cambridge editor.

[118] 'ριπαι ποδων is a bold way of expressing rapid traveling.

[119] Read ανα with Markland, for αρα.

[120] I read η δια κυαν. with the Cambridge editor. The following words are rendered thus by Musgrave, "Per ... *est* longum iter."

[121] Unintelligible, and probably spurious.

[122] The Cambridge editor finds fault with the obvious clumsiness of the expression, and proposes εχειν for λαβειν. I have still greater doubts about εκβαντας τυχης. The sense ought to be, "'tis the part of wise men, *when fortune favors*, not to lose the opportunity, but to gain other advantages."

[123] See Dindorf's notes. But the Cambridge editor has shown so decided a superiority to the German critics, that I should unhesitatingly adopt his reading, as follows: ου μη μ' επισχηις, ουδ' αποστησεις λογου, το μη ου πυθεσθαι ... φιλα γαρ ταυτα, (with Markland,) although πρωτον may perhaps be defended.

[124] See the Cambridge editor. The same elegant scholar has also improved the arrangement of the lines.

[125] "Quanquam animus meminisse horret, luctuque refugit, Incipiam." Virg. Æn. i.

[126] I read ενθ' εμον ποδα with Herm. and Dind.

[127] Cf. Elect. 1258 sqq., and Meurs. Areop. § i. ψηφος seems here used to denote the place where the council was held. The pollution of Mars was the murder of Hallirothius. Cf. Pausan. i. 21.

[128] An instance of the nominativus pendens.

[129] So Valckenaer, Diatr. p. 246, who quotes some passages relative to the treatment of Orestes at Athens.

[130] See the Cambridge editor.

[131] See Barnes, who quotes the Schol. on Arist. Eq. 95. Χους was the name of the festival.

[132] εμοι is the dativus commodi.

[133] I am indebted to Maltby for this translation.

[134] Cf. Piers, on Mœr. p. 351, and the Cambridge editor.

[135] But see ed. Camb.

[136] Such is the force, of ου γαρ αλλ'.

[137] These lines are very corrupt, and perhaps, as Dindorf thinks, spurious.

[138] Markland rightly reads ἱεροφυλακες.

[139] "dicam me daturam." MARKLAND.

[140] 'οδ' is the correction of Brodæus.

[141] νεως πιτυλος seems not merely a periphrase, but implies that the oars are in the row-locks, as if ready for starting.

[142] But the Cambridge editor very elegantly reads ει τοι.

[143] Put φθεγξασθε in an inclosure, and join ταυτα with θελει. See ed. Camb.

[144] Schol. Theocr. Id. vii. 57. θρηνητικον το ζωιον, και παρα τοις αιγιαλοις νεοττευον. Cf. Aristoph. Ran. 1309, who perhaps had the passage in view.

[145] αγορος is a somewhat rare word for αγυρις.

[146] Cf. Hecub. 457 sqq.

[147] So Matthiæ, "locum ubi Latona partum edidit."

[148] Read κυκλιον with Seidler. On the λιμνη τροχοειδης at Delos, see Barnes.

[149] "I was conveyed by sailors and soldiers." ED. CAMB.

[150] The same scholar quotes Soph. Ph. 43. αλλ' η' πι φορβης νοστον εξεληλυθεν, vhere νοστος is used in the same manner as here, simply meaning "a journey."

[151] But see Camb. ed.

[152] I read ζηλουσα ταν with the same.

[153] The Cambridge critic again proposes μεταβολαι δ' ευδαιμονια, which he felicitously supports. Musgrave has however partly anticipated this emendation.

[154] Dindorf has shown so little care in editing this passage, that I have merely recalled the old reading, αερι δ' ιστια προτονοι κ. πρ. 'υπερ στολον εκπ., following the construction proposed by Heath, and approved, as it appears, by the Cambridge editor. Seidler's note is learned and instructive, but I have some doubts about his criticism.

[155] i.e. I wish I might become a bird and fly homeward.

[156] See ed. Camb.

[157] But see ibid. Dindorf's text is a hopeless display of bad readings and worse punctuation.

[158] Reading γεννας, I have done my best with this passage, but I can only refer to the Cambridge editor for a text and notes worthy of the play.

[159] I have recalled the old reading, ὁσια.

[160] On these sort of prodigies, see Musgrave, and Dansq. on Quintus Calaber, xii. 497 sqq.

[161] "in eo, ut" is the force of εν εργωι.

[162] Perhaps a sly allusion to their escape.

[163] See ed. Camb.

[164] But we must read τοις τε with the Cambridge editor = "who know more than men."

[165] I can not too early impress upon the reader the necessity of a careful attention to the criticisms of the Cambridge editor throughout this difficult chorus, especially to his masterly sketch of the whole, p. 146, 147.

[166] φερεν ινιν is Burges' elegant emendation, the credit of which has been unduly claimed by Seidler.

[167] i.e. the place afterward called Inopus. See Herm., whose construction I have followed.

[168] On the ομφαλος see my note on Æsch. Eum. p. 180, ed. Bohn. On the Delphic priesthood, compare ibid. p. 179.

[169] See, however, the Cambridge editor.

[170] Read ες θρονον with Barnes and Dind., or rather επι Ζηνος θρονον with Herm.

[171] But see Dindorf.

[172] See Dindorf's note, but still better the Cambridge editor.

[173] I follow Seidler.

[174] So ed. Camb.

[175] i.e. what evil inspiration of the Gods impelled her to this act? Thoas, who is represented as superstitious to the most barbarian extent, naturally regards the infidelity of Iphigenia as proceeding from the intervention of heaven.

[176] Cf. Monk. on Hippol. 828.

[177] Cf. vs. 1197. εϱημιας δει.

[178] Dindorf and the Cambridge editor follow Hermann, who would place this line after vs. 1394.

[179] So Musgrave.

[180] Seidler has deserved well of this passage, both by his correction τοιν ξενοιν for την ξενην, and by his learned and clear explanation of the nautical terms.

[181] Dindorf has adopted Markland's emendation, but I prefer 'ωστ' εξαναπνειν with the Cambridge editor.

[182] i.e. capsize.

[183] But see ed. Camb.

[184] I have introduced the line above mentioned, and have likewise adopted Hermann's introduction of παλιμπϱυμνηδον from Hesychius, in lieu of παλιν πϱυμνηϛι'.

[185] See ed. Camb.

[186] "The obvious intent of these measures was to fasten the vessel to some point of the rocks, and thus prevent her being wrecked." ED. CAMB.

[187] "Our passage is thus to be understood, 'η 'αλισϰεται πϱοδουσα το μνημονευειν θεαι φονον." ED. CAMB.

[188] So Hermann rightly explains the sense. I agree with the Cambridge editor, that if Euripides had intended to use 'οσιας substantively, he would hardly have joined it with θεας, thereby causing an ambiguity.

[189] There is another construction, taking ϰλιμ. θεας together. On the whole introduction of Minerva, see the clever note of the Cambridge editor, p. 158, 159.

[190] There is evidently a lacuna, as the transition to Orestes is worse than abrupt. The mythological allusions in the following lines are well explained in the notes of Barnes and Seidler.

[191] On these last verses see the end of the Orestes, with Dindorf's note.